Through
Middle Eastern Eyes

Through Middle Eastern Eyes

A Life of Kenneth E. Bailey

Michael Parker

WIPF & STOCK · Eugene, Oregon

THROUGH MIDDLE EASTERN EYES
A Life of Kenneth E. Bailey

Copyright © 2024 Michael Parker. All rights reserved. Except for brief quotations in critical publications or reviews, no part of this book may be reproduced in any manner without prior written permission from the publisher. Write: Permissions, Wipf and Stock Publishers, 199 W. 8th Ave., Suite 3, Eugene, OR 97401.

Wipf & Stock
An Imprint of Wipf and Stock Publishers
199 W. 8th Ave., Suite 3
Eugene, OR 97401

www.wipfandstock.com

PAPERBACK ISBN: 979-8-3852-0779-4
HARDCOVER ISBN: 979-8-3852-0780-0
EBOOK ISBN: 979-8-3852-0781-7

VERSION NUMBER 03/28/25

The cover photograph and all photographs in the book are courtesy of the Bailey family. Guillernmo A. Sollano of Greater Art Soulutions improved the cover photograph and figures 1, 2, 21, and 22, and he also provided the back cover photograph of the author.

For David and Joani Dawson
whose friendship and assistance along the way
helped to make this book a pleasure to write.

Contents

List of Illustrations | ix

Prologue | 1

1. The Bailey Family and the American Mission | 7
2. Childhood and Education, 1931–55 | 26
3. Learning the Heavenly Language, 1955–57 | 49
4. Mission in Minia, 1957–60 | 64
5. Master's Degree and Work with CEOSS in Minia, 1960–61 | 79
6. Immersion in Egyptian Culture and Ministry, 1962–64 | 92
7. Expulsion from Egypt and Furlough in Pittsburgh, 1964–67 | 109
8. At Home in the Paris of the Middle East, 1967–70 | 126
9. Doctorate from Concordia and *The Cross and the Prodigal*, 1970–73 | 143
10. A Fourth Arab-Israeli War, and Civil War Comes to Lebanon, 1973–76 | 156
11. Discerning the Poet in the Peasant, 1976–77 | 174
12. Seeing through the Eyes of Peasants, 1977–80 | 191
13. The Israeli Invasion of Lebanon, 1981–84 | 208
14. The Antiochian Missionary, 1984–86 | 225
15. O Jerusalem, Jerusalem, 1986–90 | 241
16. On the Island of Aphrodite, 1990–95 | 259
17. A Tale of Two Brothers, Redux, 1996–2003 | 277
18. Seeing Anew through Middle Eastern Eyes, 2004–8 | 292

Contents

19 Chiasms Everywhere, 2009–11 | 311
20 The Shepherd King's Thousand-Year Prologue, 2011–16 | 327

Author's Note and Acknowledgments | 343
Select Bibliography | 351
Index | 363

List of Illustrations

Figure 1.	Ewing Bailey in the US Navy during World War I, 1918 | 14
Figure 2.	Annette Meader, circa 1914 | 15
Figure 3.	Ewing, Annette, and Bruce Bailey, 1929 | 28
Figure 4.	Bailey family—Ken, Ewing, Annette, and Bruce—circa 1935, at work on their annual Christmas cards, Cairo, Egypt | 28
Figure 5.	Bailey family, mid-1930s | 29
Figure 6.	Presbyterian missionaries at the New Wilmington Missionary Conference, August 1942. Ken is in the first row, third from the left. Annette and Ewing are behind him. Bruce is in the back row, second from the right. | 34
Figure 7.	Bruce and Ken Bailey, Monmouth, IL, circa 1947 | 35
Figure 8.	Leslie Milligan, circa 1913 | 40
Figure 9.	Bertha Kilpatrick, high school graduation, 1916 | 41
Figure 10.	Ethel Jean "Mickey" Milligan, high school graduation, Des Moines, IA, 1947 | 42
Figure 11.	Ken Bailey as a student at Monmouth College, Monmouth, IL, circa 1950 | 42
Figure 12.	Mickey, in the wedding dress she made, and Ken Bailey, just married, June 12, 1952 | 43
Figure 13.	Leslie Milligan with Mickey on her wedding day, June 12, 1952 | 44

List of Illustrations

Figure 14. Mickey Bailey with Jonas Salk in the Virus Research Laboratory at the University of Pittsburgh's School of Medicine, circa 1952–55 | 46

Figure 15. Christmas in Cairo, Egypt, 1956: Ewing, Annette, Mickey, and Ken Bailey | 62

Figure 16. Ken Bailey in Asmara, Ethiopia, April 1959 | 63

Figure 17. Mickey, Ken, and Sara Bailey, Cairo, Egypt, summer 1962 | 91

Figure 18. Ken with pre-seminary students in Assuit, Egypt, 1963. Pastor Emile Zaki is standing on the right | 96

Figure 19. Mickey Bailey, Christmas, in Beirut, Lebanon, 1968 | 138

Figure 20. Mickey and Ken Bailey in the living room of their apartment in Beirut, Lebanon, 1979 | 200

Figure 21. Ken Bailey at the Tantur Ecumenical Institute, Jerusalem, Israel, circa 1985–90 | 232

Figure 22. Kenneth E. Bailey promotional photo, circa 1985 | 233

Figure 23. David, Leslie, and Sara Bailey, circa 1992 | 268

Figure 24. David Bailey and his music partner, Doug Ebert, in Not by Chance, circa 1997 | 280

Figure 25. Ken and Mickey Bailey in New Wilmington, PA, circa 1996 | 286

Figure 26. Kenneth E. Bailey promotional photo, June 18, 1997 | 286

Figure 27. Ken Bailey, circa 2005 | 294

Figure 28. Sara Bailey, circa 2005 | 303

Figure 29. Victor Makari and Sara Bailey Makari at the Palm Beach Hotel, Larnaca, Cyprus, on their wedding day, August 14, 2006 | 304

Figure 30. David and Ken Bailey, circa 2007–8 | 313

Figure 31. Kelcey, David, Cameron, and Leslie Bailey at Cam's confirmation, May 31, 2009 | 313

Figure 32. Ken relaxing in the living room of the Baileys' New Wilmington home, February 2004 | 342

Prologue

With many such parables he [Jesus] spoke the word to them [the crowds] as they were able to hear it; he did not speak to them except in parables, but he explained everything in private to his disciples.

—MARK 4:33–34

THE BLACK CAB PROCEEDED unhurriedly through the serene 5,000-acre Windsor Great Park, located about twenty-five miles west of central London. Passing by three-hundred-year-old oak trees, bridle paths for "smartly dressed" equestrians, and a deer park, the taxi stopped at Cumberland Lodge. A stately and spacious structure, it was originally built in 1650 as a country house by John Byfield, a captain in Cromwell's army, but in 1947 was converted into a conference center. A tall, sturdily built man with a fringe of grey wavy hair around a bald pate emerged from the taxi, briefly took in his surroundings, and then made his way, bag in hand, to a side building of the main lodge. After checking in that morning of March 10, 1995, he climbed the stairs to an austere attic room, equipped with antique furniture, a hard bed, and a wash basin. The "loo," at the other end of the hallway, had a bath but no shower and was to be shared with four other guests staying in the cramped attic accommodations. Clearly, he had been relegated to an overflow room. Later in the afternoon, he entered the main hall of the lodge, finding thirty-nine archbishops of the Worldwide Anglican Communion from around the world. Also present were about ten of their wives and a small number of functionaries, including five staff members from Lambeth Palace and five translators, two for the archbishops from Korea and Japan and three for the francophone archbishops from Africa. Conscious of being amid a distinguished assemblage, the man threaded his way carefully through the crowd and chose a seat near the front of the hall to listen to the opening address to be given by the Archbishop of Canterbury, George Carey. A Presbyterian missionary from Cyprus and distinguished scholar of the New Testament, the man was Dr. Kenneth E. Bailey.

During the week-long conference, each day began at 9:00 with morning prayers, Holy Communion, and an hour-long presentation by Bailey. Despite his lowly designation as "consultant" at the conference, this was more time than was given to anyone else to speak. Bailey at this time was well known among Protestant pastors and in Christian intellectual circles as the author of four groundbreaking books on the parables of Jesus, especially those of Luke 15: the parables of the lost sheep, the lost coin, and the prodigal son. For centuries scholars had interpreted these stories as allegories, assigning fascinating if fanciful meanings to each of the various elements to be found there. Scholars in the late nineteenth and early twentieth centuries had debunked this approach, but it was left to Bailey to reinterpret the parables according to his knowledge of Middle Eastern culture and perception of an underlying Hebraic structure to the stories that scholars had previously overlooked. Drawing on his profound understanding of these first-century tales, Bailey spoke that week on the theme of "Leadership in the New Testament." He spent three hours each day preparing his presentations and the rest of the time writing three radio scripts that, before leaving England, he would read on the BBC program "Words of Faith," which had a Sunday evening listening audience of about 30,000 throughout the English-speaking world. The conference concluded each day with evening prayers at 9:30, with the participants seated on chairs first crafted for Queen Victoria's coronation in 1842.

The second day of the conference being a Sunday, the conferees were transported by bus to St Martin-in-the-Fields, a historic church on Trafalgar Square dating back at least to the thirteenth century. The service that day was broadcast live by the BBC, and afterwards the archbishops were photographed in the square. After lunch at Lambeth Palace, they all returned to the lodge for a brief respite before moving on to nearby Windsor Castle for a reception given by Queen Elizabeth and Prince Philip, the Duke of Edinburgh. Upon entering the castle, whose first iteration was built by William the Conqueror in about the year 1075, each conferee was properly announced and then proceeded to stand in a queue to be formally greeted by the queen and prince. After tea, the archbishop of Central Africa gave a short speech, Prince Philip intoned a polite response, and the queen invited the group to view the paintings in the magnificent, 180-foot St. George's Hall. Bailey enjoyed the paintings, which in some places covered the walls from floor to ceiling, and he even spotted two Venetian paintings that he recognized, one being an image on a pencil case that he kept in his desk. It is customary for bishops to walk very slowly to underscore the dignity and solemnity inherent in their office, but Bailey as a mere canon in the church was under no such restriction. Taking long strides as he viewed the paintings in rapid succession, he soon found himself at the head of the group, where he enjoyed a brief chat with the entirely relaxed and approachable sovereign of the United Kingdom. They were contemporaries, the queen being born in 1926 and Bailey in 1930, and they each enjoyed long careers. Bailey at sixty-four would return to the United States during the summer and before the end of the year begin a highly productive retirement that would continue for two decades.

Stepping into the queen's private chambers overlooking the Long Walk, a two-and-a-half-mile tree-lined avenue ending on a small rise with an equestrian statue of King George III, someone in the group asked her majesty, "Is it pleasant living here at Windsor Castle?" "Oh, yes," she replied. "The only difficulty is that the planes approaching Heathrow Airport from the west fly fairly low over the castle and are a bit noisy. As one American tourist was heard to say, 'Isn't it a shame that they built the castle so close to the airport?'" Bailey, who stood about five feet from the queen, laughed lustily at the royal bon mot, which pleased her highness. He later mused to his family that the ill-informed American might have been from California but "definitely not from Pennsylvania!" his native state. The evening's event at Windsor Castle was followed by a group photo on the grand stairway, this one including not only the archbishops but the entire group—even common "consultants," Bailey airily noted.

On Wednesday morning, Bailey spoke on "The Christian Leader as a Father." He had written his first book, *The Cross and the Prodigal*, on the parable of the prodigal son, which was not only a tale of two sons but also of a supremely loving father. Bailey had given many presentations that expounded the meaning of the parable, and his learned if well-worn words that day struck a chord with many of the listeners. One of these was the archbishop of South Africa, Desmond Tutu. Bailey later recalled, "Tutu came up to me afterward and told me in very moving terms how much he appreciated the Bible studies in general and that morning in particular. I had an opportunity then to tell him how scared I was to be teaching the Bible to him, feeling that I had nothing to say to Desmond Tutu." Archbishop Carey, who was also moved by Bailey's morning presentations, took the opportunity to approach him about presenting a lecture at the next Lambeth Conference to take place in 1998.[1] These three-week-long conferences that meet every ten years are for the 850 bishops and about 2,000 others in the Worldwide Anglican Communion. Bailey was flattered but noncommittal. Later that day during the tea break he spoke with the archbishop of Scotland, Richard "Dick" Holloway, with whom he had grown close during the conference. Bailey mentioned Carey's invitation and his own sense of terror at accepting the invitation. Holloway responded, "Ken, under the purple shirts the bishops are all hurting, lonely people who need badly to hear what you are saying. You must accept." When Bailey completed his presentation the following day, Holloway commented to him, "Ken, it is good that your series is now finished. I don't think we can handle more of what you are telling us. Another of these sessions and we would all implode!" Both men enjoyed a hearty laugh.[2]

Bailey, who so impressed the archbishops that week at Cumberland Lodge, was a generally humble man, but at times in his career he had stood on his dignity and refused to remain silent in the face of injustices or misguided actions that he felt would ill serve the work of God's kingdom in the world. His outspokenness had occasionally landed him in trouble with the powers that be and resulted in propelling his career in unexpected directions—in Egypt, Lebanon, Israel-Palestine, and finally Cyprus—giving him an experience of Middle Eastern culture that was both broad and deep. Though the novel interpretations of the New Testament that he developed were due in part to his familiarity with the relevant scholarly literature, more important was his immersion in the culture of the region in which the Bible had emerged, which included his knowledge of its historic languages: Hebrew, Greek, Aramaic, Syriac,

---

1. Carey later wrote to withdraw the invitation because his "design committee" said that there would not be time for presentations by Bailey. See Ken to Leslie and David, April 9, 1995, Kenneth E. Bailey Papers, RG 274, box 28, folder 2, Yale Divinity School library. Henceforth this collection will be referred to as the Bailey Papers.

2. Ken to Leslie and David, March 25, 1995, Bailey Papers, box 28, folder 2. Ken described his entire trip in a six-page single-spaced typed account, which he sent to his son and daughter-in-law but also later made available to other members of the family. He clearly enjoyed the experience. My account closely follows his essay.

Prologue

and Arabic. His forty-year career as a Middle Eastern missionary, with all its unlikely twists and turns, was essential to his scholarship in that it led him to penetrating new insights into the New Testament that he could not otherwise have attained—insights that were not conclusively formed and published until his retirement. To appreciate Bailey's hard-won understanding of the Scriptures, one must examine his long conflict-scarred career and recognize, as Bailey himself understood, that an eventful career may simply be a prelude to the full flowering that comes only in the maturity of one's latter years. As such, Bailey in his retirement was fond of quoting Robert Browning's poem "Rabbi Ben Ezra":

> Grow old along with me!
> The best is yet to be,
> The last of life, for which the first was made . . .

1

The Bailey Family and the American Mission

We should not begrudge missionaries their achievements lest we pander to our own uncritical scruples.

—Lamin Sanneh, *Translating the Message*

Alexander Bailey was born in 1719 in the town of Northton, Scotland, fourteen miles north of Inverness-shire. He married Jane Brown in Ireland, and in 1759 the couple voyaged across the Atlantic to try their luck in the New World. Alexander and Jane Bailey were part of the great migration of the Scots and Scots-Irish—the people of Northern Ireland—who braved the stormy Atlantic to begin a new life in the British colonies of North America. This migration began as a trickle of people in the 1660s, but after 1710 the number of emigrants began to increase significantly until, by 1730, it had become a flood, with some three thousand to six thousand arriving every year.[1] The reasons for the immigration were largely economic. Scotland was poor and the opportunities for advancement few. In America there was the possibility for immigrants

---

1. Dwight R. Guthrie, "Presbyterian Beginnings in the West," in Walther, *Ever a Frontier*, 33.

to own their own land, unimpeded by distant landlords and oppressive laws. Consequently, they came by the tens of thousands, primarily to the middle colonies of New York, New Jersey, and Pennsylvania—and in lesser number to the Carolinas.[2] Alexander and Jane Bailey sailed to the colony of Maryland and established themselves in Frederick County, in the north central part of the colony near the Pennsylvania border. Between 1749 and 1765 they had eight children, the last being John Bailey, who was born in Emmitsburg, Maryland.

The Baileys had arrived in North America just as the conflict between the British colonies and the British government was heating up, leading to the American War of Independence, 1775–83. The Baileys' participation in this event is uncertain. John Bailey, Alexander's youngest son, grew up during the exciting time of the American Revolution, but he was most likely too young to participate as a soldier, being eighteen years of age when the war ended. In 1786 the Supreme Executive Council of the Commonwealth of Pennsylvania granted John, in lieu of monies he had paid into the Receiver Generals Office, "a certain trail of sand called 'Disappointment'" that came to a total of 162 and 7/8 acres of land in the county of Washington. In 1799 John married Margaret Gailey. The couple settled on John's land in Washington County, and over the next two decades they would have ten children. The following two generations of John Bailey's progeny remained in Pennsylvania, working as farmers and producing, in the case of Kenneth E. Bailey's immediate forebearers, large families of seven and eight children successively.

The first Bailey to give up a life on the land was Austin Smiley Bailey (1863–1935), John Bailey's great-grandson and Kenneth E. Bailey's grandfather. Born in Candor, Washington County, Pennsylvania, he attended Westminster College, graduating in 1890. He was licensed as a minister by Xenia Presbytery on April 12, 1892, and ordained by First Ohio Presbytery on September 6, 1893. Austin married Carrie Patton (1865–1951) on June 27, 1894, and between 1896 and 1907, the couple produced four children, two boys and two girls: Ewing (1896), Marian Alice (1899), William (1901), and Lois (1907). Over the course of his forty-one-year ministerial career, Austin served ten churches in the Midwestern states of Ohio, Indiana, Iowa, Kansas, and Illinois.[3]

2. Armstrong, "English, Scottish, and Irish Backgrounds," 3–18; and Drury, "Presbyterian Beginnings," 19–35. See too Bailey Papers, box 28, folder 12.

3. The brief biographical information on Austin Smiley Bailey and a list of the churches he pastored are given in Kelsey, *United Presbyterian Directory*, 79–80. The

The Bailey Family and the American Mission

Austin was a minister in the United Presbyterian Church of North America (the UPCNA or, as it was more commonly known, the UP Church or simply the UPC). The United States had been host to a variety of different Presbyterian churches, but they all originated from Scotland and Northern Ireland as the Scots and Scots-Irish emigrated to the American colonies. Though they shared a common heritage in the Scottish Reformation that saw the establishment of the Church in Scotland in 1560 as a national and presbyterian church, they arrived on the shores of British North America divided into a variety of different denominations, and they succeeded over time in the United States to find new reasons for further divisions and only occasionally for reunions. Following the American Civil War, the two largest Presbyterian bodies in the United States were sundered by region: the Presbyterian Church in the United States (the PCUS, a predominantly southern church, founded in 1865) and the Presbyterian Church in the United States of America (the PCUSA, a predominantly northern church, founded in 1869).

The third largest Presbyterian church was the UPC to which Austin Bailey, and later Kenneth E. Bailey, belonged. It was formed in 1858 by the union of two churches that had been dissenting Presbyterian churches in Scotland: the Associate Reformed Church (the ARC, also known as the Covenanters) and the Associate Presbyterian Church (the APC, also known as the Seceders). It was inevitable that the two churches would unite since the reasons for their dissension in Scotland had never had any relevance in the United States and because they had much in common. The theology of both churches was that taught by the reformer John Calvin as his Bible-based theology was expressed in the Westminster Confession of Faith and its Longer and Shorter Catechisms. Both churches fervently believed in presbyterian polity, the complete separation of church and state, infant baptism, closed Communion, and strict Sabbatarianism. Also, they both practiced exclusive Psalmody—that is, only the Psalms of the Bible were to be sung in the worship service, not modern hymns. In their worship services, musical instruments and choirs were strictly forbidden, and these latter restrictions on music would remain in force until the adoption of a new confession of faith in 1925. At the time of the union in 1858, the UPC had 54,789 members, 660 congregations, 49 presbyteries, and 5

UPC churches he served include the following: Sycamore and Hopkinsville, Ohio, 1893–95; Idaville, Indiana, 1895–1900; Service Congregation, Albia, Iowa, 1900–1904; Ainsworth, Keokuk, Iowa, 1904–1910; Eskridge, Garnett, Kansas, 1910–11; Tilden, Southern Illinois, 1911–14; Viola, Illinois, 1914–23; Atlantic, Iowa, 1923–27; and La Prairie, Sparland, Illinois, 1927–35.

synods; and its members were largely concentrated in New York, Pennsylvania, Ohio, Indiana, Illinois, and Iowa.[4]

Austin and Carrie's eldest child, Ewing McCready Bailey, was born on April 14, 1896, in Idaville, Indiana. During his youth, Ewing's father served six different churches in succession in the towns of Idaville, Indiana; Albia, Iowa; Keokuk, Iowa; Garnett, Kansas; Tilden, Illinois; and Viola, Illinois. The regular moving that this entailed interrupted Ewing's education, putting him a year behind his peers. In 1915 he matriculated at Monmouth College, a Presbyterian institution in Monmouth, Illinois, completing his freshman and sophomore years there by the spring of 1917. Ewing Bailey, Kenneth E. Bailey's father, was twenty-one years old on April 6, 1917, when the United States declared war on Germany and entered World War I. On May 18 President Woodrow Wilson signed into law the Selective Service Act, requiring all American men between the ages of twenty-one and thirty to register for the draft on June 5, 1917. Ewing signed up for the draft as required by law. Following the completion of his sophomore year in college, he served for two years in the US Navy, 1917–19. The family has preserved a photograph of Ewing wearing a naval uniform, including a seaman's cap emblazoned with the name *USS West Coast*, a ship that was commissioned by the navy in 1918 and on which Ewing presumably served. Ewing attained the rank of quartermaster second class before beginning discharged in the summer of 1919. He reentered Monmouth College in the fall of 1919 and completed his BS degree in chemistry in the spring of 1921. While studying at Monmouth, Ewing earned money by working on farms and holding odd jobs as a carpenter, janitor, waiter, and photographer. In his last year at Monmouth, he was given an assistantship in chemistry. By means of these various jobs, he paid his own way through school and graduated without debt. If he had graduated on time, he would have completed his education in 1918. Instead, he did not graduate until June 1921.[5]

Though Ewing does not seem to have been moved to follow his father's ministerial vocation, he was drawn to the life of a missionary, an interest he acquired at Monmouth College where mission was actively

---

4. Jamison, *United Presbyterian Story*, 58.

5. That Ewing was a veteran is clear in that he wrote to his parents on April 10, 1927, that he was sending a form to the United State Veterans Bureau, Insurance, Division, Washington, DC, to make Annette the beneficiary of his insurance policy. He also asked his parents to send the bureau his policy, K-297727, and to ask that a copy of the revised policy be returned to them. His file reference number was FBBC. See Ewing Bailey to folks, Ewing Bailey Papers, Vol. 1, 28.

promoted. During his junior year, Ewing listened to an address by Dr. Samuel Zwemer, a well-known missionary in the Middle East. Ewing later recalled that Zwemer's "message challenged me to think of my own duty as I had not done before. There seemed to be no reason why I should not go in person. I joined the Student Volunteer Band that year." The Student Volunteer Movement for Foreign Missions (or SVM) was the primary recruiting organization for Protestant missions on college campuses during the first third of the twentieth century. It reached its highest recruiting numbers in the years just after World War I, when in 1921, 637 student volunteers sailed abroad to serve as foreign missionaries, the apogee of new missionary volunteers sent from the United States in a single year that were recruited by the SVM.[6] Student volunteers usually signed a pledge card and then joined the college SVM band on campus, where they studied missions with like-minded students and listened to occasional mission speakers. During Ewing's senior year at Monmouth, Dr. Charles Archibald Owen came to the college campus to recruit missionaries for Assiut College, a UPC institution in Upper Egypt. Ewing had written to the UPC Mission Board the previous spring but had not received a definite response. He decided, therefore, to take up Owen's call to service, but before committing himself to serve as a full-time missionary, he would test the waters by becoming a short-term missionary in Egypt, where the UPC was well established.[7]

Presbyterians first arrived in Egypt in 1854, being sent as missionaries of the Associate Reformed Presbyterian Church. Just four years later, this church united with the Associate Presbyterians to become in 1858 the UPC. American Presbyterians who went to Egypt were inspired by the hope of world evangelization. Initially, they imagined that they would convert Muslims in Egypt, who comprised about 93 percent of the population. They soon discovered, however, that this would be very difficult. Therefore, changing strategies, they decided to focus on converting Coptic Orthodox Christians, then about 7 percent of the population, with the hopes of setting off a Coptic reformation. Emphasizing the Bible, education, and lay participation, they were able to organize the Egyptian Evangelical Church in 1870. They also succeeded in spurring Coptic Orthodox leaders to begin a tentative reform movement that was called the *nahda*—the Arabic word for "enlightenment" or "awakening."

6. Parker, *Kingdom of Character*, 190–91.

7. Ewing Bailey wrote of his military service and college education in a letter to the UPC Board of Foreign Missions, March 9, 1925, Ewing M. Bailey, vertical file, RG 360, Presbyterian Historical Society.

In 1860, as civil war impended in the United States, these Presbyterian missionaries purchased the river boat *Ibis* and began visiting villages in Upper Egypt for the purposes of evangelism. Hence, they became known as the "American River Boat Missionaries." The work went so well that in 1865 they established a permanent mission station in Assiut, a major city in Upper Egypt.

The UPC was part of the anti-slavery movement in antebellum America, and following the Civil War, it sent missionaries to the South to establish "Freedmen's missions." As Protestants they believed that the ability to read the Bible was crucial to conversion and discipleship. For them, therefore, home mission in the American South usually took the form of providing schools for former slaves. When these same folk arrived in Egypt, they naturally emphasized education, building schools in places like Alexandria, Cairo, Luxor, and Assiut. In 1870, they formed the American Mission as an organization for themselves in Egypt, and in the same year, believing that churches should be self-governing, they held the first presbytery meeting of the nascent Egyptian Evangelical Church. Since they also believed that vernacular language should be used in worship, in 1871 Arabic became the church's official language.

The British, in order to defend their economic interests and the recently built Suez Canal, invaded Egypt in 1881, making it a colony. The influence of the missionaries coincided with the era of British imperialism in Egypt, and when this imperialism faded so too did the influence of the missionaries. By 1897 there were 50 missionaries and 5,335 church members. By 1924, the number of missionaries had grown to 217. By this time, too, the American Mission was operating over 200 schools throughout the country and, in 1920, had established the sparkling jewel in the crown of its educational system, the American University in Cairo (AUC). Given the mission's specialization in education, a missionary with advanced degrees in education would be highly desirable—a fact Ewing Bailey seems to have understood.

During Ewing's short-term missionary experience in Egypt, 1921–24, he worked at Assiut College, teaching in the chemistry and physics department and also serving as a general maintenance man for the facility.[8] During this time, he met Annette Meader, whom he would marry a few years later. Although British, she was also working for the UPC as a missionary, serving as a nurse at Assiut Hospital. Annette later recalled

---

8. Ewing Bailey to UPC Board of Foreign Missions, March 9, 1925, Ewing Bailey, vertical file, RG 360, Presbyterian Historical Society.

that they met sometime during her first year in Egypt, which would have been 1923. After the end of Ewing's term in 1924, he returned to the United States to attend classes at Harvard University, graduating on June 18, 1925, with a master's degree in education.

Sometime during this year at home in the United States, Ewing was hired by the UPC to be a full-time missionary in Egypt in the area of education. However, he did not receive the usual publicity accorded to new missionaries. Ewing later wrote, "since the Board [of missions of the UPC] sort of sent me out under cover, I do not have any such publicity as the [other missionaries] had."[9] In 1926, historian Heather J. Sharkey wrote, "the UPCNA announced a 34 percent cut in the foreign mission budget, along with the recall of fifty missionaries from the Nile Valley and northern India."[10] It was most likely that, anticipating this cut, the board suspended the hiring of new missionaries in 1925 but made an exception in Ewing's case because it needed his special skills in education. This decision, however, would later cause him some pangs of conscience.

Ewing probably returned to Egypt at the end of the summer of 1925 to begin his first year of service as a full-time missionary and, possibly, to renew the romance that he had begun two years earlier with Annette Meader. Annette's family lived on the Isle of Wight, which lies in the English Channel about two to five miles south of the main British island. Family records go back to 1617 when the first Meader baptism was recorded.[11] Annette's great-grandfather Charles Colunette was the mayor of the town of Ryde on the Isle of Wight during the mid-Victorian era. Since his position required that he preside over large formal banquets, he ordered a set of stone china from Stoke on Trent. Colunutte willed this china set, then thirty-six settings, as well as many of his furnishing to Annette. They were passed down to Kenneth Bailey, but due to strict laws of foreign export, he had to leave many of them behind when he left Egypt. Nonetheless, Bailey wrote, "we managed to bring out two tables, a number of smaller items, and twelve place settings of the famous Stoke on Trent china." Elaborating further, he wrote, "These dishes have been used with pride in our family now for four generations and a word of gratitude must be expressed by us to the artisans and craftsmen of Stoke

---

9. Ewing to folks, May 8, 1927, Ewing Bailey Papers, Vol. 1, 36.

10. Sharkey, *American Evangelicals in Egypt*, 97.

11. The date appears in the records as 1616/17. The year 1616 is the date according to the old Julian calendar, and the date 1617 is the date according to the modern Georgian calendar, which was adopted by Britain in 1752. See Miscellaneous Bailey Family Documents.

on Trent who produced these beautiful examples of the potter's skill." The registry mark on the china is December 1, 1869.¹²

Figure 1. Ewing Bailey in the US Navy during World War I, 1918.

In January 1975, Bailey wrote to his mother to urge her to write an essay on her early life so that it could be enjoyed by the family.¹³ She obliged with a handwritten forty-five-page essay, which when typed doubled-spaced was thirty-three pages.¹⁴ This is a beautifully written memoir. Though it is too general and lacks dates, it is full of telling details, interesting stories, and occasional flashes of dry British wit. It reveals a woman of charm and intelligence, and it paints a colorful portrait of what it was like to be a British nurse in Assiut in the 1920s. She wrote little of her parents or siblings—her brothers Henry James, John Harold, and William Campling; and a sister, Phyllis Mary (Jane)—except that they lived in the small seaside town of Ryde, located on the northeast coast of the Isle of Wight. In her early teens her brother Jim had his appendix

---

12. Kenneth E. Bailey, Bailey Papers, box 28, folder 12.
13. Ken to Mother, January 19, 1975, Bailey Papers, box 29, folder 2.
14. Biographical Memoire [of Annette Bailey], Bailey Papers, box 29, folder 3.

removed and she visited him during his recovery. It was her first experience of a hospital, and she was so impressed with what she saw that she decided to become a nurse.

Figure 2. Annette Meader, circa 1914.

Born on January 12, 1893, Annette when she was fifteen moved with her family to Freshwater, a village at the west end of the isle. She attended a private school that was located in the nearby village of Totland and run by a Belgian Catholic, a Mr. Buissertet. After two years, she earned a secondary certificate from the College of Preceptors, and passing her exams qualified her to serve as a practical nurse. After a year serving as a nursery governess to three children on a farm, she decided to continue her education and obtained a first-class certificate. She then taught at a girls' boarding school in Eastbourne, located on the south coast of England nineteen miles east of Brighton. When the school closed a few years later, she secured a position at another girls' school, this time at Banstead Downs, twenty-five miles south of London, where she taught during the last three years of World War I. She called this school "The Larches," a name derived from the tall pine trees in the area.

In 1918, after the war had ended, Annette began a three-year course of study at the Royal Isle of Wight Hospital. She probably felt that her decision was vindicated the next year when in December 1919 Parliament passed the Nurses Registration Act, formalizing the three-year training program required to become a professional nurse, establishing a formal register of approved nurses, and minting a new term for this latest specialty, *registered nurse*. Annette's original intention was to become a missionary nurse in India, but when there was an opening for a nurse at the American Mission Hospital in Assiut, Egypt, she applied and was accepted. She completed her nurse's training in June 1921 at Ryde Hospital, but she took an additional fourteen-month course in midwifery at Middlesex Hospital in London. Completing this course in December 1922, the Central Midwifery Board (CMB) certified her as a midwife. Early in 1923, she arrived in Alexandria, Egypt, and then made her way to the hospital in Assiut where she would be on staff for the next three and a half years, from early 1923 to the summer of 1926.

Although Annette worked as a nurse, she was also assigned to teach Egyptian women to be nurses. Lacking teaching aids, she improvised. For example, needing a human skeleton to conduct her training sessions, she assembled one from the dried bones in a place she dubbed "valley of dry bones," a wry allusion to Ezekiel 37. The bones originated in nearby caves that had once served as a burial place. When thieves robbed the tombs, they cast the unwanted skeletons into the valley below, leaving an assortment of bones ideal for Annette's purposes.

In 1922, not long before Annette arrived in Egypt, the British archeologist and Egyptologist Howard Carter discovered the tomb of Pharaoh Tutankhamun in the Valley of the Kings outside the city of Luxor, which was about a five-hour drive from Assiut. It is now commonly believed that, in the weeks after Carter's discovery and the arrival of Egyptian officials who would oversee the opening of the tomb, Carter secretly opened the tomb, removed a number of precious artifacts, and then resealed it. Once the tomb was officially opened, he and his team spent the next eight years cataloging its contents. Though Carter was accused of illegally removing articles from the tomb, he always denied it. Yet when he died in 1939, a number of items from the tomb were discovered among his effects, revealing that he had indeed been an antiquities thief. During the period of cataloging, one of the archeologists working with Carter become ill and was taken to Assiut hospital, where Annette nursed him back to health. Grateful for her services, he gave her two items that he had, following Carter's example, apparently pilfered from the tomb: a small porcelain vase and a mummified hawk. Hawks were the symbol of the god Ra. If, however, the bird was actually a falcon, it would have been the symbol of the god of Egypt, Horus, who was considered the protector of the pharaohs. The two artifacts Annette received from one of Howard Carter's grateful assistants were later given to her son, Ken, and remain in the possession of the Bailey family to this day.[15]

After Ewing Bailey returned to Egypt in September 1925, he and Annette renewed their relationship. About a year later, in late July 1926, they traveled together to Annette's family home in Freshwater, Isle of Wight, and were married on August 2 in the Meader family church in Freshwater, where her father served as a warden. Because Annette's father held this position of honor in the Church of England, her wedding service enjoyed a full choir and bell ringers. "It was quite an emotional experience," Annette recalled, "to have bells peal out as one approached the church."[16] As was customary for the groom awaiting his bride, Ewing sat in the front pew of the church, which he felt to be a special honor because this pew had been used by the renowned British poet Alfred Lord Tennyson, and it continued to be occupied by his family. Tennyson's daughter-in-law added to the splendor of the day by lending her car to the wedding couple for their use to and from the church. Ewing and Annette enjoyed a two-week honeymoon at the Larches in Banstead Surrey. This no doubt brought a flood of happy memories to Annette, who had studied there during the war. Banstead Downs is known for its beautiful woods and open fields, ideal for sports and the strolls of young newlyweds basking in the warmth of new love. The happy couple then took a leisurely six weeks to travel through Europe before arriving in Alexandria and then continuing on to Cairo, where they took up lodgings at the home of the Presbyterian missionary Earl E. Elder.[17]

In the fall of 1926, the Baileys began the study of Arabic in earnest—a language with which Ewing in particular would struggle. Ewing quipped in his second letter home, "they say the first fifty [years] are the hardest in the study of Arabic."[18] They took courses at the School of Oriental Studies (SOS), an organization located at the center of Cairo off

---

15. This story is not included in Annette's Biographical Memoire but was told to me by Mickey Bailey.

16. Biographical Memoire [of Annette Bailey], Bailey Papers, box 29, folder 3, 30.

17. Biographical Memoire [of Annette Bailey], Bailey Papers, box 29, folder 3, 30–31.

18. Ewing to Lois, November 7, 1926, Ewing Bailey Papers, Vol. 1, 13.

of Tahrir Square that was part of the American University in Cairo but directed by the American Mission. SOS offered two semesters of study a year, beginning in the fall and ending in the late spring. The students were first taught conversational Arabic, using a phonetic Latin alphabet for Arabic words. The UPC required that every missionary take a two-year study course in Arabic and successfully complete four exams. After this, missionaries were to continue to study Arabic while beginning their work for the mission. They had to pass an additional three exams, which Ewing said few actually did by the end of their first five-year term.[19] In April 1928, Ewing received his grades for his third exam, which he listed using the Arabic grading system, explaining that he passed with about the lowest grades possible. "They make me wonder," he commented woefully to his parents, "if after all I did not make a mistake when I wanted to be a missionary." However, he did not feel that the grades were a good representation of his ability in Arabic. "If I were sure they had a fair standard and that those grades represented an honest measure of my ability, I would feel that the only fair thing I could do would be resign and go home. It is not fair to the Board to have them spend any more money on me. However, as you may have gathered from my remarks on the subject, I have doubts on both questions and will stay for a time at least."[20] Ewing soldiered on, taking his fourth exam in the late fall of 1928. He passed them all, but he thought that he had done so "by the skin of my teeth in most of them."[21] However narrowly he may have passed, Ewing at age thirty-two was now ready to begin his work as a missionary in Egypt.

In some ways this was an inauspicious time to launch a missionary career in Egypt as the height of mission effectiveness in the country was then waning with the end of the British colonial period in 1922. Though the British remained in Egypt until 1956 in order to protect their interests in the Suez Canal and other concerns and though they continued to wield much influence in the government, after 1922 the Egyptians were generally autonomous. The heyday of missions had passed, and a long, slow decline had begun.

The 1920s was a period when Egyptians began to assert their sense of nationalism not only by restricting British rule but also be creating ever-tightening restrictions on Christian missionaries. In 1928 Hasan al-Bana founded al-Ikhwan al-Muslimum ("the Muslim Brotherhood"), an

---

19. Ewing to folks, January 1, 1928, Ewing Bailey Papers, Vol. 1, 79.
20. Ewing to folks, April 22, 1928, Ewing Bailey Papers, Vol. 1, 96.
21. Ewing to folks, November 11, 1928, Ewing Bailey Papers, Vol. 1, 141.

organization that united the themes of Islam and Egyptian nationalism and often employed anti-missionary rhetoric as a way of rallying support. Since the Brothers tied Egyptian identity to the Arabic language and Islam, they naturally perceived Christian missionaries, whose educational institutions were generally conducted in English, as posing an existential threat. An opening salvo in the conflict between the two was a controversy over the work of missionary Dr. Samuel Zwemer, the speaker who had first interested Ewing in a career as a missionary as well as a prolific Christian writer of books hostile to Islam. His style of evangelism was to attack Mohammad as a false prophet and the Qur'an as a poor imitation of the Judeo-Christian scriptures. For him, Islam was not so much a new religion as a concoction of other religions, with little new to say.[22] Visiting al-Azhar University in 1928, he distributed some Christian tracts to earnest Muslim students. Though this was customary behavior for Zwemer, who had been distributing tracts in al-Azhar from time to time since 1915, the Muslim response of protest and outrage at the time was new, and Zwemer soon felt compelled to leave the country. In this dispute, Ewing took al-Azhar's side, explaining in a letter to his parents that the issuing of a ticket to Zwemer to enter al-Azhar was a courtesy that he should not have taken advantage of to distribute anti-Muslim tracts. "You can imagine to yourself the feelings that would be roused in case a Mormon came into Xenia Theological Seminary reading room and interspersed some of their books there with anti-Christian literature. I rather fear Zwemer is looking to the gallery at home too much." An unabashed Zwemer returned to the United States to take up the position of professor of missions at Princeton Theological Seminary.[23] Ewing believed that much of the publicity given to this incident was due to a single newspaper that had earlier supported the literary scholar Taha Hussein whose 1926 book, *Fi al-Shi'r al-Jahili* ("On Pre-Islamic Poetry"), had questioned the existence of a historical Abraham and Ishmael, whose historicity Muslims assumed simply because they appeared in the Qur'an. Taha was acquitted by the courts of heresy, but the newspaper that had supported him later took up the cause against Zwemer as a way of reasserting its loyalty to Islam.[24]

---

22. See for example Zwemer, *Islam: A Challenge to Faith*.

23. Ewing to folks, April 22, 1928, Ewing Bailey Papers, Vol. 1, 97. See Sharkey, *American Evangelicals in Egypt*, 108–16.

24. Ewing to folks, May 26, 1928, Ewing Bailey Papers, Vol. 1, 97. See too Sharkey, *American Evangelicals in Egypt*, 100–102.

Other incidents soon followed the Zwemer affair. Ewing observed that the Young Men's Muslim Association (YMMA), established in 1927 in Cairo as a Muslim copycat organization of the YMCA, called on Muslims to remove their children from mission schools and avoid mission hospitals.[25] The conflict between Muslims and Christians in Egypt further intensified in April 1930 when the Presbyterian evangelist Kamil Mansur was arrested on charges of *tatwul* ("insolence") toward Islam. Kamil was a Muslim Egyptian convert to Christianity who, on April 7, 1930, had given a lantern-slide lecture on the life of Christ in which he had allegedly disparaged Mohammad. In the course of the lecture, it was said, he had asserted that Islam was a religion of superstitions and that Mohammad was a prophet who, unlike Jesus, could perform no miracles. Ewing believed that the underlying issue of the case was that of freedom of religious discussion.[26] The church agreed and enlisted for Kamil's defense representatives of the US State Department, the British Foreign Office, and the Church of England. The court cleared Kamil of all charges, and he was able to resume his career as an evangelist for the Evangelical Church, a vocation he continued to pursue until as late as 1954.[27] Ewing did not believe that the agitation against Christians would be long-lasting, but in this he was mistaken. In fact, nationalist feeling tied to an Arab and Muslim identity in Egypt would continue for decades to come, eventually forcing the dissolution of the American Mission.

In the January 1929 meeting of the Egyptian Association of the Missionaries of the UPCNA, Ewing and Annette were given their new assignments for the year. Ewing would take over Earl E. Elder's work directing the school in Cairo when Elder went on furlough in the spring; he would be the chairman of the publicity committee, which meant responsibility for writing for the denomination's publications in the United States (*The U.P.* and *Christian Herald*) as well as producing promotion material in Cairo; he would serve on the committee overseeing the boys' orphanage in a town outside of Cairo; and he would continue to serve as the secretary of the Cairo branch of American Christian Literature Society for Moslems (ACLSM), an organization started by Zwemer to publish evangelistic material for Muslims.[28] These various tasks were to take up half of his time, and for the other half he was to continue his

25. Ewing to folks, May 6, 1928, and Ewing to folks, May 13, 1928, Ewing Bailey Papers, Vol. 1, 102–4.
26. Ewing to folks, April 20, 1930, Ewing Bailey Papers, Vol. 1, 225.
27. Sharkey, *American Evangelicals in Egypt*, 117–19.
28. Ewing to folks, October 23, 1927, Ewing Bailey Papers, Vol. 1, 69.

study of Arabic. In October 1928 Annette had already been asked to run one of the clinics in Cairo. Ewing wrote at the time, "Annette had gained quite a reputation for being the matron of a hospital and I rather expect that soon I will be known as the husband of Mrs. Bailey."[29] She had in fact done well enough that the Association assigned her a second clinic to run as well.

The Association meeting also dealt with the ongoing issue of finances. As early as 1926, Ewing had learned of the mission's budget constraints. He wrote to his parents at the time to explain that he was not concerned because the shortfall would be absorbed by attrition—that is, by not replacing missionaries as they retired.[30] But he became more apprehensive in May 1927 when the Board of Foreign Missions wrote to the Association to inform it that the board members had recommended a 15 percent cut in the mission budget for the year 1928. This prompted Ewing to consider the possibility of doing educational work in Beirut.[31] But at the July 1928 Association meeting, the missionaries decided that the cuts would be handled in the usual way, through attrition.[32] By the January 1929 meeting, however, it was clear that attrition alone would no longer be sufficient to meet the shortfall. A list of missionaries that would retire or be downsized was reviewed, and this list was published in a UPC journal in March 1929.[33] Ewing felt secure because only those retiring or going on furlough were being dismissed. The Board of Foreign Missions did not want to fire missionaries currently on the field as this would entail the extra expense of their travel home. One of those to be dismissed was a Mr. Work, an ordained missionary who had been in Egypt for twenty years, who Ewing recognized would probably have difficulty obtaining work in the United States because he had been abroad for so long.[34] Remembering that the circumstances of his employment by the church had not been entirely forthright, Ewing unselfishly offered to go on furlough in his place, thus facing the clear prospect of losing his employment. The board agreed to consider this if Work was willing to complete Ewing's

---

29. Ewing to folks, October 7, 1928, Ewing Bailey Papers, Vol. 1, 132.
30. Ewing to folks, January 16, 1926, Ewing Bailey Papers, Vol. 1, 13.
31. Ewing to folks, May 29, 1927, Ewing Bailey Papers, Vol. 1, 39.
32. Ewing to folks, July 10, 1927, Ewing Bailey Papers, Vol. 1, 47.
33. Ewing to folks, March 10, 1929, Ewing Bailey Papers, Vol. 1, 160.
34. The UPC records do not have a Mr. Work listed. However, they do list a Miss Ruth A. Work of Fort Morgan, Colorado, who began mission service in Egypt in 1904. See for example the Seventy-Sixth General Assembly of the United Presbyterian Church of North America (1934), 890.

term, which would require that he stay in Egypt an additional two years. Ewing explained to his parents, "I am sure that had I known how soon experienced missionaries would be recalled I would not have accepted the appointment as I did. Being allowed to slip through under the wire that way after the gates were shut to new appointments makes me feel all the more like I am usurping a place now."[35] Ewing wrote to Work, making the offer, but Work declined to accept it.[36] Ewing therefore reasoned that his place was secure through the end of his term, which would be the spring of 1931. By then he hoped that the shortfall in mission giving would have abated and that the members of the UPC would begin to support the mission budget again with their usual generosity. Then he would be able to return to Egypt. On the other hand, he reasoned that by then there would be so many missionaries languishing at home that it might be difficult for the mission to reassign him, especially given his poor performance in the Arabic examinations.[37] All of his calculations, however, were made in early 1929, at least six months before the Stock Market Crash on Wall Street in the autumn of 1929, which reinforced the downward trend in mission giving for the next decade.

The Baileys, despite being missionaries in a challenging field of service in which both spouses participated in the work, held traditional views about marriage. Annette took language classes with Ewing during his first four semesters at SOS, but then she seems to have stopped. Presumably she passed her exams, but Ewing never comments on her performance. Was his wife's success (or failure) not important to him? Annette was a trained nurse who was thought capable enough to direct two clinics simultaneously, but she retained conventional ideas about gender roles. In the 1920s women missionaries were not yet able to vote at Association meetings, which was considered an afront by some women. Ewing shrugged off the issue, explaining that the women living in the area of the meetings—in Cairo, Tanta, or Assiut—would predominate in any vote. Therefore, he believed that it would be unfair to grant them a vote. He wrote this as though he could imagine no solution to the problem. When pressed on the issue of women's suffrage in the mission, Annette said that she did not believe that women should have the vote, and if they did, she would vote as her husband directed her.[38]

35. Ewing to folks, January 20, 1929, Ewing Bailey Papers, Vol. 1, 152.
36. Ewing to folks, April 28, 1929, Ewing Bailey Papers, Vol. 1, 166.
37. Ewing to folks, March 10, 1929, Ewing Bailey Papers, Vol. 1, 160.
38. Ewing to folks, March 11, 1928, Ewing Bailey Papers, Vol. 1, 89.

During their first year of marriage, the Baileys had been trying to have children but had been unsuccessful. Early in 1928 when Annette learned that her failure to become pregnant was due to a physical problem, she checked into Assiut Hospital to have "a slight uterine trouble" corrected, which the Baileys hoped would allow her to conceive.[39] Annette remained in the hospital for two weeks for recovery and observation.[40] In January 1929, Ewing wrote home to announce that Annette was pregnant, and on July 20, 1929, she gave birth to James Bruce Bailey, who would generally go by his middle name.[41] Ewing wrote to his parents again in May 1930 to announce that Annette was once more pregnant, explaining that they "wanted the second baby to come as near Bruce as possible so that the two would grow up together and with our furlough year just ahead it means that it must be this coming winter." Their doctor recommended that Annette should leave Egypt for the summer to avoid the searing heat. The Baileys planned on traveling to Switzerland, where they would spend the summer. The doctor, however, changed his mind, though the reasons that Ewing gives for this are not medical but financial. The doctor explained that the costs to the mission of the Baileys going to Switzerland for the summer, returning to Cairo, and then going on furlough in September 1931 were too high. The cost of their proposed trip to Switzerland would increase the total cost to the mission by half. Therefore, the Baileys were told simply to leave for their furlough a year early so that Annette could have the second baby either in the United States or United Kingdom. Ewing and Annette left Egypt in mid-June 1930. After staying at the Meader family home in Freshwater for several weeks, they sailed to the United States in the first week of August 1930. They lived for a time in Paxton, Illinois, staying with Ewing's sister, Lois Bailey Moffett and her husband Clair Moffett.[42] Their second son, Kenneth Ewing Bailey, was born on November 24, 1930, in Bloomington, Illinois.

---

39. Ewing to folks, February 19, 1928, Ewing Bailey Papers, Vol. 1, 87.

40. Ewing to folks, March 4, 1928, Ewing Bailey Papers, Vol. 1, 88.

41. Ewing to folks, January 20, 1929, Ewing Bailey Papers, Vol. 1, 151. James Bruce Bailey was generally referred to by his middle name, Bruce. However, the US Army assigned him the name James when he served in the military during World War II. This resulted in a confused record in the Bailey Papers where he is sometimes referred to as James and sometimes as Bruce. For purposes of clarity, he will be referred to as Bruce in the narrative and subsequent footnotes.

42. Bruce Bailey to Ken & Mickey, June 7, 2003, Bailey Papers, box 28, folder 14. He comments that "it was Marion not Lois in Paxton."

Bailey Family

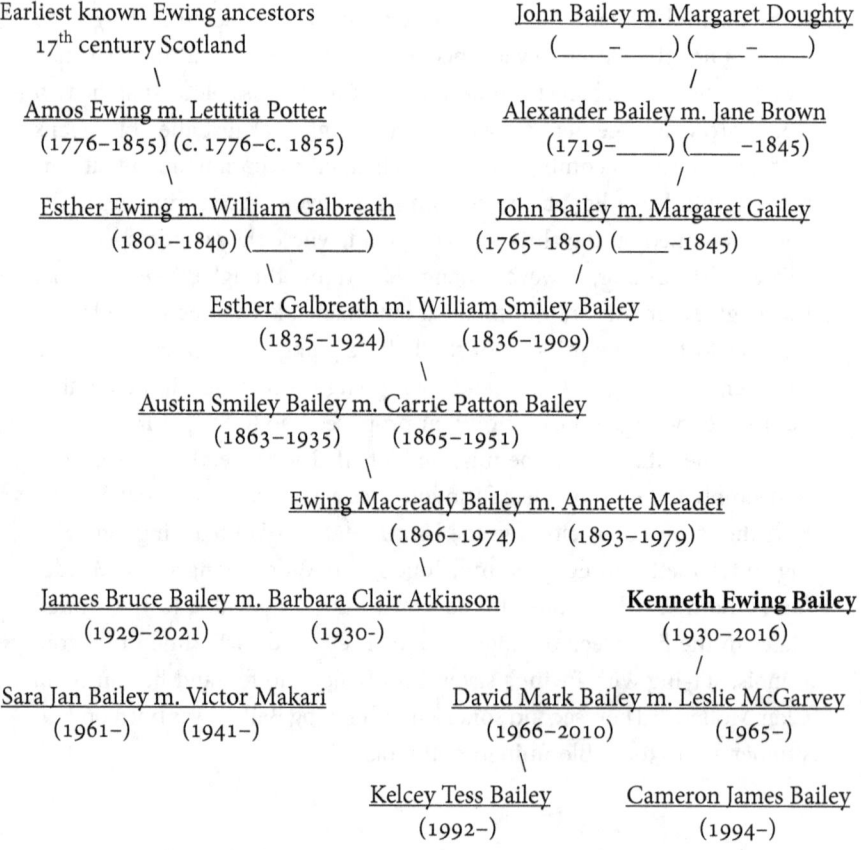

Earliest known Ewing ancestors	John Bailey m. Margaret Doughty
17th century Scotland	(____-____) (____-____)
\	/
Amos Ewing m. Lettitia Potter	Alexander Bailey m. Jane Brown
(1776–1855) (c. 1776–c. 1855)	(1719-____) (____-1845)
\	/
Esther Ewing m. William Galbreath	John Bailey m. Margaret Gailey
(1801–1840) (____-____)	(1765–1850) (____-1845)

Esther Galbreath m. William Smiley Bailey
(1835–1924)   (1836–1909)

Austin Smiley Bailey m. Carrie Patton Bailey
(1863–1935)   (1865–1951)

Ewing Macready Bailey m. Annette Meader
(1896–1974)   (1893–1979)

James Bruce Bailey m. Barbara Clair Atkinson   **Kenneth Ewing Bailey**
(1929–2021)   (1930-)   (1930–2016)

Sara Jan Bailey m. Victor Makari   David Mark Bailey m. Leslie McGarvey
(1961–)   (1941–)   (1966–2010)   (1965–)

Kelcey Tess Bailey   Cameron James Bailey
(1992–)   (1994–)

*The three couples asterisked here are Ethel Jean Milligan's siblings and in-laws, who are listed vertically due to lack of space.

Genealogy

Edward Meder, br. March 2, 1616/1617
Earliest known Meader ancestors
17th century Isle of Wight, England
/

Henry Meader m. Harriet Margaret
(1867–1940)   (1870–934)
         /
            William Calvin Milligan m. Margaret Elvira Turnbull
                  (1855–1937)   (1855–1931)
                                /
       Leslie Mason Milligan m. BerthaJanetta Kilpatrick
              (1888–1974)   (1897–1988)
                        /

m. Ethel Jean Milligan   Bruce Edward. Milligan m. Dorothy. Patricia Reid
     (1929–2023)   (1919–2007)   (1921–2015)

                    Floyd Wilmer Milligan m. Margaret Augusta Swaine*
                         (1920–2011)   (1920–2006)

                         Merle W. Milligan m. Emmy Louise Hoog*
                           (1922–2013)   (1925–2017)

                              Dale K Milligan m. Doris Eileen Hipple*
                                (1924–1998)   (1926–2016)

25

2

Childhood and Education
1931–55

I am a part of all that I have met.

—Alfred Lord Tennyson, "Ulysses"

Between 1931 and 1935, the Bailey family lived at the Home Mission High School in the town of Frenchburg, the county seat of Menifee County in eastern Kentucky. The school campus is at the junction of US Route 460 and Kentucky Route 36. At an elevation of 873 feet, it is nestled among the hills and dales that approach the Appalachian Mountains in an area known as the Cumberland Plateau. The region was poor and sparsely populated, making it ideal for a home mission project. In the early years of the twentieth century, Dr. Edward Ownings Guerrant recommended the establishment of the school to the Women's General Missionary Society (WGMS) of the UPC.[1] The women agreed, and by 1910 the UPC had purchased eleven acres of land for the school campus and erected a school building in the Georgian Revival style popular in the period, with other buildings added in later years, including the Jane Cook Hospital in 1915.

The details of the Baileys' residence there in the early 1930s are not known. However, the UPC's General Assembly minutes for 1932 and 1933 list Ewing Bailey as a home missionary under the category of

1. See McAllister, *Edward O. Guerrant*.

Childhood and Education

"Mountain Missions" to Frenchburg, Kentucky.[2] While Annette does not appear in the minutes, it seems likely that the church assigned her to serve at the hospital as a nurse while her husband, Ewing, continued his education in preparation for a return to Egypt.[3] The Bailey boys, Bruce and Ken, were too young to retain clear memories of Frenchburg, but one can imagine that they enjoyed exploring the rustic setting in the relative safety of a school campus and under the watchful eye of their mother.[4]

In 1931 Ewing began doctoral studies at Harvard University's Graduate School of Education, graduating on February 6, 1934. His doctoral thesis, *Problems in the Education of Teachers for Egypt with Special Reference to the American Mission*, was ideally suited to establish his bona fides as an expert in Egyptian education. Despite being in the depths of the Great Depression, the UPC rehired the Baileys as missionaries to Egypt in September 1935.[5] The couple, with their two children, now ages five and four, departed in October for Egypt, where Ewing would serve in the mission's educational work.

The family's first home during this second term of service was the west front apartment in the Azbakeya Mission Building in Cairo, where they stayed for most of 1935. Around early November, they moved to the city of Minia in Upper Egypt, which had a population of 60,000. They lived in a house on Sharia al-Ansha, where they stayed until sometime in 1940. The mission assigned Ewing the task of establishing a rural school in Minia that would respect local customs and values, unlike government schools that, Annette observed, "had a tendency to alienate the children from their environment."[6] Ewing spent his first months in Minia visiting the pastors and schools in the villages surrounding the city, attempting to

---

2. *Minutes of the Seventy-Fourth General Assembly of the United Presbyterian Church of North America* (1932), 282; and *Seventy-Fifth General Assembly of the United Presbyterian Church of North America* (1933), 588. Curiously, he is not listed in either the 1934 or 1935 minutes as a home or foreign missionary.

3. Kenneth E. Bailey, "Profile," ca. 1972, RG424, Presbyterian Historical Society. Years later in a mission "profile" of his life for the Presbyterian Church, Bailey noted that both of his parents served as home missionaries in Frenchburg.

4. The school was closed in 1957 and the hospital in 1969, but the campus still exists, and in 1978 it was admitted into the National Register for Historic Places. Abandoned and derelict, all the ancillary buildings slowly crumbled to dust or were torn down, and now only the main school building remains. A red-brick ruin, it can still be seen from Frenchburg's main road just behind the Family Dollar store.

5. Ewing M. Bailey, vertical file, RG 360, Presbyterian Historical Society.

6. Annette Bailey, "A Memorable Christmas Day," ca. December 25, 1935, in Ewing Bailey Papers, Vol. 1, unpaginated letter inserted into the front of the bound volume.

locate the best venue to establish an experimental school. He eventually chose the village of Edmu, just outside of Minia.

Figure 3. Ewing, Annette, and Bruce Bailey, 1929.

Figure 4. Bailey family—Ken, Ewing, Annette, and Bruce—circa 1935, at work on their annual Christmas cards, Cairo, Egypt.

Childhood and Education

Figure 5. Bailey family mid-1930s.

Minia had a large Christian population, and the Baileys had the choice of three Evangelical churches to attend. They tried to make the acquaintance of the church members, but as outsiders it was difficult. Bruce and Ken, at the ages of seven and five respectively, had an especially difficult time making friends as they did not speak Arabic and there were no public schools to attend. They were receiving private instruction from one of the mission mothers, who Annette said was doubling as a teacher.[7] As Christmas approached, Annette worried that the boys would not find the season a joyous one, and she determined that she would do her best to give them an American-style Christmas, making stockings and Santa suits for the boys. Bruce was to be Santa and Ken, Santa's helper. She purchased a turkey for Christmas dinner but confessed that it "could barely claim relationship with its American counterpart, as the poor thing had had to work too hard for a living and had somewhat the 'lean and hungry' look of Cassias.[8] Since the Baileys were foreigners

7. Annette Bailey, "A Memorable Christmas Day," Ewing Bailey Papers, Vol. 1.

8. Annette Bailey, "A Memorable Christmas Day." Ewing Bailey Papers, Vol. 1. For quotation see Shakespeare's *Julius Caesar*, Act 1, scene 2, 190–95.

new to the area and celebrated Christmas on December 25 rather than January 7 as Egyptians do, Ewing and Annette did not anticipate many guests on Christmas day. But despite their forebodings, guests began arriving as early as 9:30 a.m. and continued to appear in steady numbers throughout the day. Bruce and Ken, for their part, enjoyed being the center of attention in their Santa suits. Annette concluded the story: By the end of the day the Baileys were exhausted "but joyous and very thankful as our stream of visitors spelled for us acceptance in the community. We were no longer strangers in a strange land, and we had friends."[9]

Bruce began his formal education at the Schutz American School in 1936 or 1937, and Ken, who was about sixteen months younger, followed him there in 1938.[10] Located in Alexandria and named after an Anglo-Dutch businessman who had owned property in the area, the Schutz School had been established by the UPC in 1924 as a private institution for the children of its missionaries in Egypt, Sudan, and Ethiopia—though the largest number of students came from Egypt. The school was a combination elementary, middle, and high school as it held classes for grades one through twelve. Its teachers were young American women who had recently graduated from college, and the curriculum included the standard subjects of math, English, history, and geography. There were also two French teachers, and the students were required to speak French during evening meals.

During the summer break the children of missionaries would stay at Sidi Bishr, a ten-acre camping area for missionaries that was only a few miles away and on the Mediterranean coast. Their mothers stayed with them while their fathers continued working and only occasionally visited for short periods of time. This was rustic living as families resided in huts that had wall planking three feet up from the floor, matting and chicken-wire above the planking, and thatched roofs. Also, since there was no indoor plumbing, residents had to make do with a water pump and an outdoor privy.[11]

---

9. Annette Bailey, "A Memorable Christmas Day." Ewing Bailey Papers, Vol. 1.

10. Bruce Bailey, essay on youth. Bailey Papers, box 28, folder 13. This essay begins on page 16, and the title is not given. However, it has three subsections: "Life at Schutz School: 1936–1942," 16–19; "The War," 20–21; and "The Flight from Egypt: 1942," 22–24.

11. Bruce Bailey, "Life at Schutz School, 1936–1942," Bailey Papers, box 28, folder 11.

Childhood and Education

When World War II began on September 1, 1939, the British army was stationed at Alexandria, a strategic location from which it could defend North Africa and also launch assaults on Southern Europe. Bruce remembered that British, Australian, and New Zealander soldiers and airmen stayed at Sidi Bishr. He also met many British Commonwealth soldiers at church, and some visited the Baileys in their home. To protect the children, their fathers built several rudimentary air raids shelters, which consisted of deep trenches that were protected with a roof of planking that was covered with sand. The trenches were big enough to shelter everyone in the camp, but being open at either end meant that even a near miss might have had catastrophic results. The real danger, Bruce recalled, was the shrapnel from the aircrafts' shells that fell all around them. When the air raid sirens sounded, the boys fled to the air raid shelters and stayed put until they heard *the all clear*. Bruce remembered watching the search lights scan the sky until they spotted a plane. Then all the lights converged on the plane and the anti-aircraft guns began to blaze away.

Despite the increasing danger of living in Alexandria from the fall of 1939 through 1940, it was not until the fall of 1940 that Schutz School was moved to Assiut College, about 200 miles south of Cairo. On December 8, 1941, the Shultz students at Assiut College were playing soccer at recess when someone came onto the field to announce that Japan had attacked the American naval base at Pearl Harbor the day before. During the spring term of 1942 many of the American missionaries in Egypt returned to the United States, and by the end of the term there were only six American students left at the school. The Baileys chose to remain in Assiut through the academic year of 1941–42, and in the summer, they returned to Alexandria where they took up residence at Shultz School. Ewing recalled that German warplanes kept the British fleet in Alexandria under frequent attack, which had the effect of hardening the city's residents to the danger. However, when the British forces at Tobruk, Libya, fell on June 21, 1942, to German Field Marshal Erwin Rommel, the commander of the two panzer divisions of Germany's Afrika Korps, the missionaries recognized that it was time to beat a hasty retreat. The American Mission's executive committee ordered that the American missionaries who had remained in Egypt should proceed immediately to Sudan.[12] Ewing wanted to remain at his post, but Annette had other

---

12. Ewing Bailey wrote a five-page doubled-spaced typed account of the family's flight from Egypt. It is undated and included loosely in *Occasional Letter of Ewing Bailey Sent to Friends, retired missionary & former short-terms, 1945–1960*, Ewing Bailey

ideas. Bruce later wrote, "If Mother had not put her foot down, we might have ridden out WWII in Egypt."[13]

The Baileys left the family car at the mission school and then boarded the train to Luxor where they rendezvoused with the other missionaries evacuating the country. On Wednesday morning, July 1, the Baileys boarded the train at Luxor, bringing the total number of missionaries on the train to forty-nine. They made it as far as Aswan when they discovered that their tickets, which Ewing bitterly disparaged as "Cook's tickets," were no longer valid, being trumped by tickets held by others that had been issued directly by the Sudan Railroad. The 139 pieces of luggage held by the evacuating missionaries were piled unceremoniously on the bank beside the rails while other arrangements were made. The missionaries eventually obtained permission to take the steamer on the Nile as far as Wadi Halfa, a city just over the border in Sudan. However, since the steamer was scheduled to be pushing four barges that were loaded with, as Ewing noted with grim precision, "high test aviation gasoline," the missionaries were required to sign waivers in case they were all blown up. Given the options, they did not demur. As the steamer passed the Great Temple of Ramses II at Abu Simbel, Ewing imagined that the four gigantic statues of Ramses II, which had gazed upon the Nile for over three millennia, had a reassuring word for him: "We have watched refugees fleeing for their lives before invading armies. You are more fortunate than many." At Wadi Halfa, there were few provisions for the travelers. Bruce recalled that the family did not eat for several days, but eventually the train stopped at a *wadi* (a generally dry ravine) where they were able to purchase "a few scrawny chickens, which were cooked up for us."[14]

When they arrived in the Sudanese capital on Sunday, July 5, the Secretary of the Sudan Mission met them at the train station to report that he had arranged accommodations for all of them in the city. The Baileys were housed in the home of two missionaries who had vacated the premises. When they learned that Rommel had not succeeded in capturing Alexandria after all, Ewing seems to have considered returning to Egypt. However, the US Consul in Khartoum would not validate their

---

Papers, Vol. 2. There is another account of this event written by James Bruce Bailey, but it was written in 2010 and varies in many details with his father's account. See James Bruce Bailey, "Flight from Egypt," Bailey Papers, box 28, folder 13. I generally follow Ewing's account, but supplement it with details from Bruce's version when they seem reliable.

13. Bailey, "Life at Schutz School, 1936–1942," Bailey Papers, box 28, folder 13.
14. Bruce Bailey, "The Flight from Egypt, 1942," Bailey Papers, box 28, folder 13.

Childhood and Education

passports for travel back to Egypt and thus they had no option but to return to the United States.

The Baileys spent the rest of July in Khartoum and, around August 1, boarded a DC-3 prop plane, owned by the US Army but flown by Pan American Airways pilots, to begin the journey across Africa to Brazil and finally to the United States. Bruce recalled that they sat on aluminum benches along either side of the plane, and "the back of each seat was the ribbed wall of the airplane."[15] The US government enlisted the aid of Pan Am to establish an air route from the United States to Natal, Brazil, across the Atlantic to the Gold Coast of Africa, and from there across the breadth of Africa to Khartoum, Sudan.[16] The Baileys were the grateful beneficiaries of the unlikely alliance between Pan Am and the US Army in establishing this trans-African route to safety.

It took the Baileys several days to cross Africa, staying in barracks at the air strips along the way. Bruce recalled that at one stop they were visited "by a local African tribal chieftain and his retinue. They were very impressive in native dress." Their last stop in Africa was Monrovia, Liberia. From there they took a Pan American Clipper Ship across the Atlantic. Bruce recalled, "The clippers were the luxury airliners of the day," being seaplanes that landed and took off from the water.[17]

Upon arriving in Florida, the family traveled to Monmouth, Illinois, where they settled down. In August 1942, just a few weeks after returning to the U.S., the Baileys attended the New Wilmington Missionary Conference in the little town of New Wilmington in western Pennsylvania, fifty-eight miles north of Pittsburgh. This was Ken's first experience of a conference that he would attend many times in his life. Less than two years later, after seeing his family settled in Monmouth, Ewing returned alone to Egypt for a third term of mission service, from June 14, 1944, until his return to the United States on March 10, 1947, leaving his family in the United States for a period of nearly three years.[18] During the war years, the boys observed the scrap metal drives; the rationing of sugar, meat, and gasoline; and the families that proudly put a blue star in the

---

15. Bruce Bailey, "The Flight from Egypt, 1942," Bailey Papers, box 28, folder 13.

16. Vaz and Hill, *Pan Am at War*, 230–49. See also "Pan Am at War," 73–74, and the film Nagel, *Clippers at War*, which Pan American Airways released to publicize its war effort and that of its pilots and engineers.

17. Bruce Bailey, "The Flight from Egypt, 1942," Bailey Papers, box 28, folder 13. For more on the Pan American clippers see Vaz, *Pan Am at War*, 250.

18. "Record of Service—Ewing Bailey," in Ewing M. Bailey, vertical file, RG 360, Presbyterian Historical Society.

front windows of their homes to indicate that a son was serving in the military, which was replaced with a gold star if that son were killed. There were three rankings for gas rationing: A, B, and C. Those who received As and Bs were engaged in the war effort and received larger amounts. Those with a C rating had to make do with very little. The Bailey boys walked a great deal and joined carpools whenever they could.

Figure 6. Presbyterian missionaries at the New Wilmington Missionary Conference, August 1942. Ken is in the first row, third from the left. Annette and Ewing are behind him. Bruce is in the back row, second from the right.

Ken Bailey lived in Monmouth from the age of twelve until he started college, the period from 1942 to 1948. Here he completed middle school and high school. It was probably in these years that he discovered that he suffered from dyslexia. The affliction does not seem to have been particularly severe, and the only clear manifestation of it was a persistent inability to spell accurately—a problem that plagued him at least until the advent of computers in the 1980s. Curiously, in all of the Bailey Papers, Bailey only mentioned it once. He was not one to complain or to make excuses, but his reticence to speak about the problem makes its severity difficult to assess. By all accounts, he enjoyed a typical boyhood in America. He and Bruce joined the Boy Scouts, Troop 55, and on November 6, 1944, the brothers both became Eagle Scouts. No doubt they had been scouts in Egypt and continued in the scout system in the United States.[19]

Figure 7. Bruce and Ken Bailey, Monmouth, IL, circa 1947.

At the end of Bailey's junior year in high school in 1947, his parents prepared to return to Egypt to continue their mission work together with the intention of leaving their children behind in the States. Ken and Bruce moved in with John and Shirley Eastwood, who were family friends. John was also a UPC pastor. The Eastwoods, however, did not really serve as a surrogate family for the Bailey brothers, as the boys cooked

19. Ken to Mother and Dad, February 28, 1965, Black Volume, 292. Ken's mother had asked him about his becoming a scout, and he responded: "I got out my scout scrapbook Mother and the facts are as follows. Kenneth Bailey, Monmouth, Illinois, Troop 55, Nov. 6, 1944, Norwood G. Wright Scout Executive, Prairie Council. [I] also have a personal letter from Elbert K. Fretwell, Chief Scout Executive, 2 Park Ave., N.Y. 16, N.Y., dated Nov 9, 1944, [giving] congratulations on becoming an Eagle Scout. It seems that troop was without a scoutmaster at the time. We have the account of the award granting ceremony, but the scoutmaster is not mentioned. Leo Bricker gave us the awards, but that was as our former scoutmaster. Malcolm Ried [Reed?] was there but no scout master is mentioned. I expect that Bruce's date is the same in that we were awarded the badges at the same time."

their own food and generally took care of themselves. When Ewing and Annette departed for Egypt on September 11, 1947,[20] Ken would not see them again for another five years—that is, until his last semester in college. The separation was a doleful experience for Ken, who always felt close to his mother but saw his father as taciturn and emotionally distant. Reflecting in later years on his feelings of isolation and abandonment when his parents returned to Egypt, he resolved that, given the chance, he would be a more available and proactive parent.

Ken, like his brother, chose to enroll at Monmouth College, a small Presbyterian liberal arts school, which their father had also attended. Founded on the prairie lands of western Illinois in 1853 by the Associate Reformed Presbyterian Church, by the 1940s it had become a thriving Christian institution that emphasized the humanities, arts, and sciences. With the postwar GI Bill, the college enjoyed a bump in enrollment, reaching its peak of 900 students in 1948, the year that Bailey matriculated. Monmouth's curriculum was that of a typical liberal arts college. Students were required to develop a reading knowledge of one foreign language, study a year of laboratory science and an additional year of either general science or mathematics, take two credit hours of speech, six hours of English, and four of social studies. When these general requirements were met, they were to complete forty hours in a major field of study. Bailey chose philosophy as his major. Though the moral standards of the college were strict, it was not a dreary life. The students could join fraternities and sororities, participate on sports teams, play tennis, sing in quartets and choral groups, and join the theater department, whose plays were presented in the town theater, the Crimson Mosque. Bailey had never developed the skills needed to play team sports, but he did enjoy playing tennis. He also joined a quartet in which he sang bass. And he played various roles in the college drama productions.

The Christianity practiced at the college was more than formal or nominal. The president, James H. Grier, who led the college from 1936 to 1952, was a deeply committed Christian who had served as a pastor and as Professor of Old Testament at Pittsburgh Seminary. He emphasized at Monmouth what he called "Christian idealism," which was manifest

20. "Record of Service—Ewing Bailey," in Ewing M. Bailey, vertical file, RG 360, Presbyterian Historical Society.

in worship services, weekly prayer meetings, and devotional hours. The school also emphasized missionary activity, and over the years it had developed a special relationship with Assiut College in Egypt. This school had been founded by the Scottish missionary Dr. John Hogg in 1865, and Monmouth alumni had been active subsequently in further developing the institution. Given this connection, Annette's work at Assiut Hospital in the 1920s, and Ewing's work at Assiut College and his ongoing participation in the educational institutions in Egypt, Bailey felt a keen gravitational tug toward mission service in Egypt.[21]

In Bailey's freshman year, he wrote a six-page paper entitled "Judgment with Justice" in which he took up the cause of the Palestinians in the Palestinian-Israeli conflict.[22] In the same year he expanded this into an eight-page essay, which in the table of contents of his bound collection of college papers he titled "I Side with the Arabs" and noted that it was a "college oration, [in my] freshman [year,] 1948." Perhaps, he delivered it in a speech class. He argued that this was not a racial or religious conflict but a nationalist clash between Arabs and Jews, and he compared the Jews to the Germans under Hitler. Both sought the return of land that had been taken from them. The Germans sought land in Austria that was lost to them in 1919, and the Jews sought land they had lost 2,400 years before. If Americans accepted this argument, Bailey insisted, they should return the land they had taken forcibly from Native Americans. He cited the Balfour Declaration to show that the British had promised only a homeland to the Jews, not a political state. The document, he averred, also stipulated that "nothing shall be done which may prejudice the civil and religious rights of existing non-Jewish communities in Palestine." Following World War II, he continued, there were many displaced peoples, but the Arabs have been forced to take in more than all the rest of the world combined—350,000 from Europe. It is true that the Jews have worked hard to develop the land, but this is not a reasonable argument for taking land that is not theirs. Such a rationale, however, is typical of aggressors—"Mussolini in Ethiopia, Japan in Manchuria, Hitler in Europe." He warned that Arabs, who had previously admired the British and Americans, were now seeing them as enemies because of their stance toward Israel. Finally, American policy toward Israel should reflect the interests of the American people, not American politicians attempting to capture the Jewish vote. In these views, Bailey was so much out of step

---

21. See Davenport, *Monmouth College.*
22. Personal lectures [a bound volume], Bailey Papers, box 1, folder 2.

with his times that his fellow students may have seen him as eccentric or dismissed him as a crank or perhaps even an antisemite. And his comparison of Israeli policy to Nazi Germany's aggression would have been seen, at the very least, as immoderate. Yet Bailey would continue to be critical of Israeli policies and actions over the years until, by the 1980s and 1990s, many Americans would come to find them as well within the acceptable range of opinion. His experience abroad and among Arabs had simply given him a perspective that, among Americans, placed him decades ahead of his time.

As a philosophy student at Monmouth College, Bailey worked under Monmouth's Professor of Philosophy, Sam Thompson. Having kept his notes from his years as an undergraduate, Bailey organized them under major headings, which were undoubtedly the titles of his classes: Philosophy of Religion, Introduction to Philosophy, Modern Philosophy, Nineteenth-Century Thought, and Social and Political Ethics. Under Thompson's instruction, Bailey encountered the major themes of the philosophy of religion: the relationship between religion and philosophy, a Christian view of history, and natural law. He also studied the major philosophers, including Plato, Aristotle, Descartes, Hobbes, Spinoza, Leibniz, Locke, Hume, Rousseau, Kant, Mill, Darwin, Marx, Nietzsche, and Kierkegaard.[23] At the end of his college program, he wrote a fifty-two-page senior research paper on philosophy that he submitted in the spring of 1952, entitled, "Saint Augustine and Plato: A Discussion of the Influence of Plato on the Thought of Saint Augustine." Writing to Gary Burge in 2005, Bailey recalled, "I majored in philosophy in college and have always been grateful that I did, even though I have done very little with it. The subject taught me how to think in a clear, rational fashion and that training has been invaluable."[24] Studying philosophy was a wise decision for an undergraduate intent on the ministry, which Bailey certainly knew when he selected it.

Bailey was clearly a dedicated student at Monmouth College, but he was never a library recluse. During his freshman year, he toured with a choir, and one night in Des Moines, Iowa, he happened to be assigned accommodations with the family of Ethel Jean "Mickey" Milligan, who was also a freshman at Monmouth College though one majoring in biology. Although she was a year older than Bailey, they began their undergraduate studies together in the 1948–49 academic year. She and Bailey were both sincere and devoted Christians who soon developed a rapport. In

23. Philosophy Notes [a bound volume]. Bailey Papers, box 1, folder 1.
24. Ken to Gary Burges, July 7, 2005, Bailey Papers, box 28, folder 5.

the first extant letter between them, dated December 25, 1949, it is clear that they had been dating for some time and were very much in love.

Mickey's parents, Leslie and Bertha Milligan, had married on December 13, 1917, in a ceremony conducted in Leslie's parents' house near Idana, Kansas.[25] Leslie worked as an automobile mechanic for the Drake Auto Service Company and then for the Wood Brothers Threshing Machine Company. The Milligans had four boys: Bruce (1919), Floyd (1920), Merle (1922), and Dale (1924). Ethel Jean was born on January 14, 1929, the fifth child and only girl. In 1930, when the Great Depression ravaged the US economy, Leslie lost his job. The decade of the 1930s was a hardscrabble period in the Milligans' lives as it was for many in a time when a quarter of the nation's workforce was unemployed. The Milligans planted a garden to grow their own vegetables, acquired a goat for milk, and kept a chicken coop, which supplied the family with eggs and occasional meat. Unemployed, Leslie repaired cars in a shed behind the house, and Bertha hired herself out as a maid. During these years, Mickey would grow closest to Floyd and Dale, and they remained close throughout their adult lives. As a child at about age five, she remembered that an elderly man at church on Sunday dubbed her *Mickey*, a nickname that stuck for the rest of her life. Years later, Mickey remembered the hardships the family endured during the Depression. Usually, she recalled, the family bought one bucket of coal at a time because that was all they could afford, but perhaps the Milligans' worst luck came in January of 1941 when the garage in the backyard where Leslie worked burned to the ground. Leslie kept a potbellied stove there and speculated that embers from the stove must have ignited some of the gasoline-soaked rags that he kept lying around, leaving twelve-year-old Mickey with a vivid and lasting memory. In such stressful times, Mickey's mother reminded her children that "His everlasting arms were around us," a loose quotation from Deuteronomy 33:27. It was one of her mother's favorite Bible verses, one that Mickey confessed that she did not fully appreciate at the time but that stayed with her throughout her life.[26] In the 1940s when America was at war, Leslie was able to find work again, and he eventually opened his own auto repair garage. The Milligans regularly attended the Westminster United Presbyterian Church of Des Moines, and Leslie and Bertha raised their children to be devout Christians. All five of their offspring graduated from college, and Bruce and

---

25. This account is based in part on interviews with Mickey and on Floyd Milligan, "Floyd and Family," in Safris, *Milligan Stew*, 147–85.

26. Mickey to Leslie, January 24, 1987, Bailey Papers, box 27, folder 8.

Dale became ministers in the UPC. As a teenager, Mickey prayed that God would allow her to become a foreign missionary and make a lasting contribution to the world.[27]

Figure 8. Leslie Milligan, circa 1913.

Mickey graduated from Theodore Roosevelt High School in January of 1947 soon after her eighteenth birthday. She had applied to Monmouth College and was accepted but did not receive the scholarship she needed to meet expenses. Her brother Dale wrote to say that he wanted to help her financially. He normally gave a tithe to the church, but he decided to give a portion of this to Mickey as a scholarship in place of the one that he felt she should have received.[28] Before entering college, Mickey worked for a year at Sentra Insurance Company, doing clerical work—mostly filing, she remembered. During this time, she took advantage of a company program to help her save money for school, setting aside $25 a month after the company had given her $75 to start.

27. Sara Bailey recalled this prayer at her mother's funeral service on February 4, 2023.
28. Dale and Doris to Mickey, October 12, 1948, White Volume.

Childhood and Education

Though Bailey missed seeing his parents while he was in college, he recalled years later that he never fully realized how much he was missing out on familial experiences until he came to know Mickey. When she came into his life, he said, "gradually I discovered all that I had missed because she had a family and friends and a home and I had none of these." Bailey recalled that his parents, who had returned from Egypt during his final semester at college, "had not even met Mickey except just before the wedding [and] that Dad (my Dad) could not express his feelings and so getting close to him was a real problem and he was a kind of a stranger to everyone."[29]

Figure 9. Bertha Kilpatrick, high school graduation, 1916.

In October 1950 during their junior year at Monmouth College, Bailey proposed to Mickey, and she accepted. Mickey purchased the material for her wedding dress, which was on sale for nine dollars, and she returned home many weekends in the second semester of her senior year to sew the dress so that it would be ready in time for their wedding on June 12, 1952, the week after she and Ken graduated from college.[30]

29. Ken to Dave, October 9, 1986, Bailey Papers, box 27, folder 8.
30. That Mickey sewed her own wedding dress is a story related to me by Sara Bailey Makari.

Figure 10. Ethel Jean "Mickey" Milligan, high school graduation, Des Moines, IA, 1947.

Figure 11. Ken Bailey as a student at Monmouth College, Monmouth, IL, circa 1950.

Childhood and Education

Figure 12. Mickey, in the wedding dress she made, and Ken Bailey, just married, June 12, 1952.

That summer the newlyweds moved to Pittsburgh, Pennsylvania, so that Bailey could attend Pittsburgh-Xenia Theological Seminary. Mickey applied to work in the Virus Research Laboratory at the University of Pittsburgh's School of Medicine and was accepted on the spot by Dr. Jonas Salk. She would work as a technician in Salk's famous study of poliomyelitis—more commonly known as polio. The nation's first great polio epidemic occurred in 1916 when over 25,000 polio cases were reported, mostly of children under the age of five, and 6,000 died. In the 1920s and '30s the occurrence of polio stabilized at the relatively low rate of about four cases per 100,000, but in the 1940s these rates quadrupled. By 1949 there were 42,000 recorded cases, and in 1952 those numbers soared to the highest on record, some 57,000 cases, among whom 3,000 died and 21,000 were permanently paralyzed, some reduced to crutches and leg braces, others restricted to wheelchairs, and—most dreaded of all—a small number consigned to iron-lungs.

Figure 13. Leslie Milligan with Mickey on her wedding day, June 12, 1952.

Beginning in 1947, Salk sought to produce a killed-virus vaccine. Through the diligent work of a staff of twenty-one, including seven technicians among whom Mickey was numbered, the Salk vaccine was ready for mass testing in 1954.[31] By today's standards the laboratory Mickey

---

31. This account generally follows the story of the development of the Salk vaccine as it is presented in Oshinsky, *Polio: An American Story*. The safety and efficacy of the product were certified in the largest field test of a vaccine in American history, involving 1.5 million school children. The result was an impressive 60 to 70 percent effective rate. Salk, however, persisted in improving his vaccine. During the years when it was exclusively administered to American children, 1955 to 1961, it achieved a 90 percent effective rate, reducing the number of new polio cases in the United States to less than 1,000 in 1961. Later use of the Sabin live-virus vaccine succeeded in virtually eliminating polio in the United States. In July 1961, the American Medical Association endorsed Sabin's live-virus vaccine, and a month later, the Department of Health Education and Welfare (HEW) licensed Sabin's vaccine. By 1963 Sabin's vaccine had completely replaced Salk's. Sabin's live-virus vaccine eliminated the polio virus in the wild in the American environment, but it had a weakness. One in every million recipients of Sabin's vaccine contracted polio from it. Ironically, by 1980 the dozen or so new cases of polio reported annually in the United States were all attributed to the Sabin vaccine. Since polio persisted in America only because of the Sabin vaccine, the Center for

and the other lab technicians worked in was primitive and even dangerous. Mickey recalled transferring various samples of polio virus to test tubes by drawing the serum up through glass pipettes by sucking on one end as one would siphon gasoline through a rubber hose. However, if she sucked too hard, she would be in danger of getting a slurp of the polio virus in her mouth.

While Mickey was working in the laboratories of the University of Pittsburgh, Bailey was a seminarian at Pittsburgh-Xenia Theological Seminary. The committee on Seminary Training of Monmouth Presbytery recommended Bailey to be a student at the seminary, and the presbytery accepted the recommendation.[32] Bailey began his seminary studies in the fall of 1952 and completed them three years later, in May 1955. During Ken and Mickey's first two years at the seminary, they lived in married student housing, but during the third year they moved to a building that had been recently acquired by the seminary.

Pittsburgh-Xenia Theological Seminary has a distinguished number of seminaries that were its forerunners, the earliest of which was established in 1794.[33] These were the seminaries of the Associate Presbyterian Church (APC) and the Associate Reformed Presbyterian Church (ARP). By 1921, these various seminaries had consolidated into one institution, the last merger being between Pittsburgh Seminary in Pittsburgh, Pennsylvania, and Xenia Theological Seminary in Xenia, Ohio. Being the child of the Covenanter and Seceder traditions, the new seminary was theologically conservative, but it avoided the extremes of fundamentalism that seared the northern Presbyterian Church in the 1920s and '30s. At the time of the merger, it had been the intention of the church leaders that the seminary be relocated, but this was delayed due to the exigencies of the Great Depression. When, however, the number of students at the seminary tripled between 1923 and 1950, it was clear that the old campus in North Side, Pittsburgh, was no longer adequate and that a move should not be delayed any longer. The General Assembly of the church,

---

Disease Control recommended in the year 2000 that the United States revert to the Salk vaccine. Today the Salk vaccine reigns in America, while the Sabin vaccine continues to be used in the developing world. In the clash between the titans of science—and their titanic egos—it turned out that both sides had been right, and both had been wrong. To eliminate polio in America, both approaches, the live- and the killed-virus vaccines, had been needed. Oshinsky, *Polio: An American Story*, 265–68, 272–73, and 278–79.

32. J. Ralston to Kenneth Bailey, July 6, 1952, White Volume. Ralson wrote to Bailey to confirm the committee and presbytery's decision to recommend him.

33. For the background and history of the seminary see Walther, *Ever a Frontier*.

therefore, voted to relocate the seminary somewhere in Pittsburgh, and a General Assembly committee later selected a ten-acre site in East Liberty, Pittsburgh. Buildings were quickly erected, and the seminary moved to its new site in the summer of 1954. The first two years of Bailey's seminary classes were held at the old site, but in his final year, 1954–55, they were held at the new East Liberty campus.

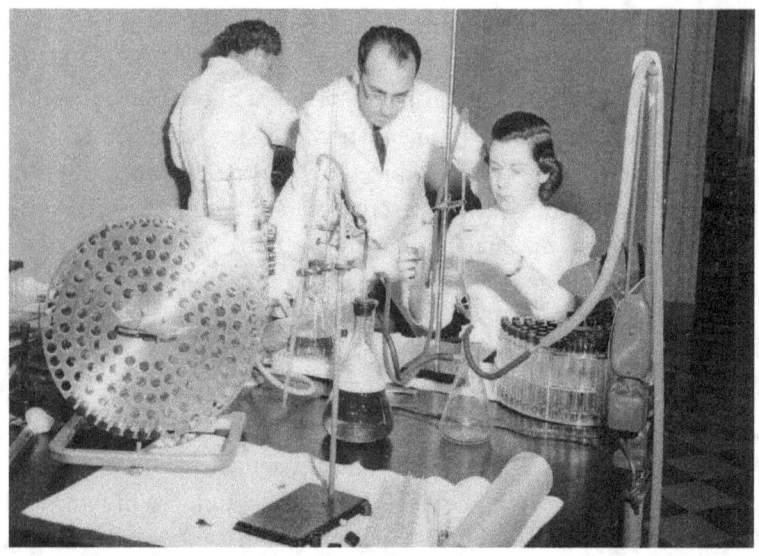

Figure 14. Mickey Bailey with Jonas Salk in the Virus Research Laboratory at the University of Pittsburgh's School of Medicine, circa 1952–55.

In the early twentieth century, most seminary students were single, delaying marriage until they had completed their studies and were ready to begin their ministerial careers. In the middle decades of the century this steadily changed as increasing numbers of students married before graduation. By 1955 the majority of seminarians in the United States were married, and in this year ninety-eight of Pittsburgh-Xenia Theological Seminary's students had also wed. Making the adjustments necessary for married life is a common challenge, but doing this amid the stresses of a seminary life, with its demanding class work, Spartan living conditions, and uncertain future, created additional pressures. Ken and Mickey would always have a strong marriage, and in later years Ken would praise his wife for sharing his calling to mission and selflessly and steadfastly standing by him through many trying times, but as newlyweds they had plenty to learn and much room to grow. Decades later,

Mickey wrote to her son and daughter-in-law of the difficulty of her early years of marriage:

> I remember the years of moodiness I spent early in our marriage over hurt feelings. I could go for several days without speaking, and part of it was that once into the situation I didn't know how to get out of it. I knew the adage, "Let not the sun go down on your wrath" [Eph. 4:26 KJV], but somehow, I couldn't seem to smooth things over that easily. Perhaps with some good advice I might have done better, or done it more quickly. In any case, I wasn't that great to live with in those early years, beside it being hurtful to Dad.[34]

When Ken and Mickey applied for mission service with the UPC in the early months of 1954, Ken noted on his application form that he was six feet tall and weighed 160 pounds, and Mickey wrote that she was five feet, four and three-quarters inches and weighed 125 pounds.[35] At this time, he was twenty-five years old, and she was twenty-six. The Board of Foreign Missions subjected them to a battery of psychological tests. The Reverend C. R. Thayer, PhD, summed up the results in a few lines. Both were well-balanced, self-confident, self-sufficient people. Ken tended to be socially extroverted and Mickey a little more reserved. Neither were moody or easily discouraged. Both were "dominate and aggressive [i.e., assertive] in personal relations." In the face of such normal, well-adjusted people, the evaluator strained at the end of the evaluation to find something negative to include in his evaluation, writing, "It is barely possible that they are too stable, too aggressive, too well-adjusted, too insensitive to [i.e., unaffected by] the feelings of others."[36]

Bailey almost certainly received a recommendation from Monmouth Presbytery to the UPC mission board, but there is no copy of it in his personnel file. Mickey received a recommendation from her employer, Jonas Salk, who assured the UPC mission appointments committee that Mickey was healthy, well liked, and had a fine perceptive mind—traits that would serve her well on the mission field.[37] Given Salk's celebrity status at the time, it is curious that no one remarked on the incongruity

34. Mickey to David and Leslie, September 28, 1987, Bailey Papers, box 27, folder 9.

35. Kenneth and Ethel Bailey, vertical file RG 424, Presbyterian Historical Society.

36. Psychological evaluation of Kenneth and Ethel Bailey by C. R. Thayer, 1955, is in vertical file RG 424, Presbyterian Historical Society.

37. Dr. Jonas Salk, UPC Reference form for candidate as a "foreign Missionary." Bailey Papers, box 28, folder 12.

of a Christian mission board receiving a missionary recommendation from a Jewish scientist.

In March 1955 the United Presbyterian Church of North America sent Ken and Mickey a formal letter appointing them to be missionaries to Egypt. Mickey quit her job at the Salk laboratory in April, after three years of employment there and when Salk was near the completion of his work on developing a cure for polio. Bailey graduated from Pittsburgh-Xenia Seminary on May 13. That summer the couple spent six weeks in the denomination's training conference for new missionaries in Meadville, Pennsylvania. They found the studies valuable but undemanding. Ken found time to play tennis two hours every afternoon, and the couple usually played golf together twice a week. When the conference ended, Ken and Mickey did their final packing, made a hurried trip to Iowa to say goodbye to Mickey's family, and then made their way to New York City where they embarked for Egypt.

3

Learning the Heavenly Language
1955–57

> A missionary or an anthropologist who really hopes to understand and enter into the adopted culture will not do so by trying to learn the language in the way a tourist uses a phrasebook and a dictionary. It must be learned in the way a child learns to speak, not by finding words to match one's existing stock, but by learning to think and to speak in the way the people of the country do.
>
> —Lesslie Newbigin, *The Gospel in a Pluralist Society*

On the afternoon of August 24, 1955, Ken and Mickey left from New York harbor onboard the ocean liner *Independence*. Mickey's brother Dale and sister-in-law Doris came to see them off, and Ken and Mickey waved goodbye as long as they could see them on the dock. They gazed at the Statue of Liberty as the *Independence* cruised by, and soon they were out to sea, the New York skyline quickly receding behind them. In those days an Atlantic crossing on an ocean liner took three or four days. The Baileys enjoyed a comfortable cabin on the ship. "Our ship," Mickey wrote, "was the essence of modern living—bunks folding down out of the wall, plus a couch which made a bed, private bath with a shower that hit on all '8' [cylinders], lots of drawer and closet space, good sized deck and comfortable deck chairs, huge lounge and big bar too, swimming pools, clothing shops, barber shops and beauty shops, elevators, auditorium with comfortable self-reclining chairs, etc.!" They also enjoyed dining as Mickey remembered that the ship had a "fabulous menu." While missionaries in past centuries may have dreaded a long sea voyage, Mickey wrote that their voyage was "a wonderful vacation, another honeymoon, full of rest and good food and new sights."[1]

On Sunday, the fourth day out from New York, they passed the Azores and Ken conducted the Protestant service on the ship, which the captain attended. Soon they moored for two hours at Gibraltar to let some of the passengers off. This was the first of many ports of call, including Genoa, the ruins of Pompeii, the famous Amalfi Drive, Sorrento, and Syracuse, before the Baileys sailed on to Alexandria, Egypt, to begin their new lives.

For Ken, who had spent his earliest youth in Egypt, this was a joyous and nostalgia-tinged return; for Mickey, who had never been to Egypt, arriving in Alexandria was a time of uncertainty and self-questioning. The tasks ahead loomed large before her, and she wondered if she would be equal to the challenge. The ship dropped anchor in the outer harbor, and Egyptian officials motored alongside and came aboard. As the ship proceeded to the inner harbor and docked, Ken spotted his parents waiting for them on the dock and waved. When they were allowed to land, Ewing and Annette welcomed them warmly and came with a wagon drawn by a donkey to transport their belongings to the Shultz American School, which at the time was not being used as a school. It housed two families and was also commandeered for guest housing and missionaries on vacation. On their second day in Alexandria, the Baileys obtained drivers' licenses so that they could legally drive the 1947 Ford sedan the mission assigned to them. Then they drove on the desert road to Cairo, which lay a few hours to the east. For Mickey everything was new—donkeys braying at 6:00 in the morning, desert mirages that reared up in the distance only to disappear as they approached, and women walking gracefully with heavy baskets carefully balanced on their heads.

Ken and Mickey moved into Ken's parents' home in Heliopolis, then a suburb of Cairo. They had a study, bedroom, and bathroom to themselves but shared the living room, dining room, and balconies. They also shared the cook, who prepared all the meals. Mickey never complained

---

1. Mickey to family, September 18, 1955, Black Volume, 596.

about living with her in-laws and no cross words ever seemed to have passed between them.[2] Ken and Mickey's baggage arrived from Alexandria that Saturday, which included a few pieces of furniture and a large number of boxes filled with Ken's books. They unpacked right away and settled in. On the following Monday they began to attend Arabic language classes, which were conducted by the School of Oriental Studies (SOS) of the American University in Cairo, where Ken's parents had learned Arabic three decades earlier. They were in classes Monday through Friday from 9:00 a.m. to 1:00 p.m. Being the only students in the classes put considerable pressure on them to preform, especially in reciting. Arabic studies are particularly hard for English speakers in that Arabic and English belong to different language families. Missionaries sometimes quip that Arabic is the heavenly language because it takes an eternity to learn. Having their afternoons unencumbered with classes gave the Baileys plenty of time to visit the various sites that tourists commonly frequent in the city, including the mandatory visit to the pyramids on the edge of the city where just the year before archeologists discovered a solar boat, which is now housed behind the great pyramid for visitors to enjoy.

The Baileys arrived in Egypt on September 7, and a little over a week later, on September 18, Mickey typed the first of many long letters to her family, beginning a letter-writing practice that the Baileys continued throughout their forty-year career as missionaries. During the Baileys' first mission term, from 1955 to 1960, Mickey wrote the only surviving letters home. In their second term Ken began to contribute to this effort, but the bulk of the letters home remained the work of Mickey until the 1990s when Ken did most of the writing. In her second letter home, written on September 29, Mickey explained that she knew her letters would be read and censored; therefore, she would be circumspect in what she wrote. She would not, for example, describe in detail the poverty and difficulties of the lives she saw in Egypt. She wrote only, "One coming from the States cannot help but notice and be a bit taken back at first. The conditions of women have been greatly improved in the last decades and yet . . . women seem to look older here much sooner. And their life is hard." Much more common were her references to food. They ate plenty of meat, including veal, lamb, and water buffalo beef. Pork, however, was forbidden because of Islamic restrictions. Salads were not the lettuce salads popular in America; rather, they consisted of tomatoes

---

2. Mickey to ___ [probably family], March 24, 1957, Black Volume, 527.

and cucumbers. Historians have observed that nineteenth-century letter writers in America often filled their correspondence with the intimate details of day-to-day life in order to create a *tableau* of their lives for family and friends whom they had left behind when they went to live in distant parts of the country.[3] Mickey often wrote in this vein, emphasizing local color and the minutiae of their everyday lives. She described in loving detail, for example, the family Thanksgiving meals, the gifts exchanged at Christmas, the flowers then blooming in the garden. Ken, on the other hand, would usually write of his work, his coworkers on the field, and his experiences of Middle Eastern culture and society. Together they left a vivid, intimate, and insightful account of their years abroad.

The Baileys' first two years in Egypt were centered on taking Arabic classes, but they also took other courses on Islam as they went along, including in their first semester a two-month course in Islamics that met from 5:00 to 7:00 three evenings a week. They continued to visit sites in Cairo too, such as the historic mosques, some of which date back to the ninth and tenth centuries. Mickey wrote home about the wall-to-wall carpets and numerous chandeliers in the old mosques, but she made no mention of the beautifully carved columns that the early Muslims had appropriated from Christian churches.

Mickey and Ken enjoyed their first Thanksgiving in Egypt that fall. Since Thanksgiving often coincided with Ken's birthday, the two events were frequently merged in the Bailey family. Mickey faithfully recalled the scene on the evening of Thursday, November 24, in a letter home. Fifteen people gathered around the table, which was lit by candlelight and decorated with corn ears and fall flowers. After dinner, the missionaries entertained themselves. The musical instruments present included the autoharp, accordion, violin, piano, and marimba. The men formed a quartet, and there were other singing groups. Mickey and Ken sang as a duet "Mountain Dew," a bluegrass song from 1947, performed by Grandpa Jones, that made light of illicitly distilled liquor, commonly known as moonshine or mountain dew. They sang it in a deadpan manner, but Mickey had trouble not laughing when she looked at Ewing. Ken's normally reserved father, she later commented, "was sitting on a hassock shaking up and down and looking as tho he would burst—that was too much and I started laughing! But we finished."[4]

---

3. For example, see Hedrick, *Harriet Beecher Stowe*, 79–80.
4. Mickey to family, November 27, 1955, Black Volume, 582.

This was the first of many descriptions of holiday festivities. The Baileys enjoyed this one with Ken's parents' help, but Mickey would orchestrate many such joyous occasions in the years to come. For Christmas that year, the Bailey house was no doubt decorated with poinsettias as Mickey said that she counted over two hundred of them from her home window. On Christmas morning Mickey was up at 6:00 in the morning, ringing sleigh bells that her mother had given her for the purpose. The family gathered around a five-to-six-foot tree, decorated with lights and homemade ornaments fashioned from flashbulbs that Ken's mother had saved and painted. Ken began the celebration with a short devotional and then they exchanged gifts, which were mostly homemade items.

Early in the new year of 1956, they traveled to Assiut for the annual Association meeting of the American Mission. Ken and Mickey stayed at the accommodations available at Assiut Hospital with Jack and Mary Lou Lorimer, fellow missionaries who were also friends of Dale and Doris Milligan when Jack and Dale had been in seminary together. The meeting continued for a week, and Mickey wrote of her first experience of an Association meeting: "It was a thrilling experience for us both to be there and not only to meet all the other members of the mission but to learn of the work of the whole mission in each phase of its program."[5] The missionaries were then considering the need to train Egyptians to assume places of leadership and teaching positions in the mission schools. This was in response to Egyptians who, in this post-colonial era, were seeking greater autonomy. But it was also due to pressure from the UPC mission organization as well as from the Egyptian government. With this in mind, the meeting received a report from a committee that had been formed the previous year to evaluate the effectiveness of mission programs. The missionaries also recognized that autonomous leadership was needed in the church. Consequently, they discussed forming a six-member team that would be dedicated to training church leaders in the coming year.

In a letter home on January 21, 1956, Mickey wrote to explain that a new law required the teaching of Islam to Muslim students. With Egypt's rising nationalism in the 1930s and the identification of Egyptian nationalism with Islam, the Egyptian legislature passed a number of laws regarding mission schools meant to curtail Christian evangelism. In 1934 the parliament passed the first of these laws, Law 40, which required mission schools to be inspected to ensure that laws regarding sanitation

---

5. Mickey to friends, February 22, 1956, Black Volume, 46.

and the separation of boys and girls were being followed. Missionaries did not find the law objectionable though they felt it was being selectively enforced in a way intended to limit mission activities. More ominously, the law stipulated that schools could only teach children their own religion. Missionaries circumvented the law by allowing Muslim students to be excused from attending classes in Christianity. In 1948, Parliament passed Law 38, which reiterated the 1934 law, and in December 1955, Parliament passed Law 583, which declared that schools must teach children their own religion, following the syllabus established by the government. The missionaries would have to make a definitive decision in the summer of 1956, a year and a half later, about how to respond to this governmental intrusion into their educational work. Naturally, they agonized over the decision, finding the new governmental requirements inconsistent with the raison d'être of a mission school.[6]

After the annual Association meeting, the missionaries were offered a choice between an excursion to the Red Sea or a four-day camel ride into the desert. Ken and Mickey chose the desert trip, which they took with fifteen other missionaries, fourteen Arabs, and twenty camels. Mickey described the event in great detail in three pages of single-spaced type in a letter home. The Baileys enjoyed both riding camels and the austere beauty of the desert. Mickey wrote, "All day long we saw more beautiful scenery—mountains, sand, and rocks. There were places where there were only narrow passes between the hills and dunes and other places where there was no escape from the noon day sun across vast expanses of barren, rocky and black desert." When they returned, Ken obtained a book on camel caravans in the desert, with Mickey commenting, "He really has the bug."[7] Ken would take similar trips in the future.

Following this trip, Ken reported to the hospital in Assiut to have a cyst removed from his tailbone. He spent ten days in the hospital and the next month recuperating. This operation left a hole in his back that needed to be dressed every day. This did not prevent him from occasionally walking around. However, he had to spend most of his time sitting on a rubber ring while the opening in his back slowly healed. "Of course,"

---

6. Minutes of the Association meeting of the American Mission, 1956, Presbyterian Historical Society, vertical file RG 209, Box 18A, file 10.

7. Mickey to family, January 15, 1956; see too Mickey to friends, February 22, 1956, Black Volume, 573–75, 46–47.

Mickey commented, "it keeps me from [giving him] an occasional whack on the derriere, which hampers me! But I find other vulnerable spots."[8]

Mickey reported that in late February she and Ken received their grades for their first semester of language exams. There were ten exams and both received a cumulative grade of B. Mickey did not give their exact scores, but she did suggest that hers were one point higher than Ken's. The bound Bailey Family letters include their report cards for the second term of language study, which ended in June 1956. The subjects graded were grammar, composition, translation (Arabic to English, English to Arabic, impromptu English to Arabic, and colloquial to classical), and dictation. Mickey received a cumulative grade of 156 out of 200, which was a B, while Ken received a cumulative grade of 139 out of 200, which was a C+.[9] Mickey acknowledged the mediocre results in a letter home: "Incidentally, we got our grades and we didn't do so hot. But, then, grades don't tell all."[10]

While Mickey at this point was the better student, Ken was regularly practicing Arabic by speaking with as many people as he could and preaching as often as he found opportunities. During the Christmas season he assembled what he called a "flannelgraph"—a large board with pictures depicting the Christmas story or perhaps the gospel story in general. He used this to give presentations at churches as a way to compensate for his halting Arabic. In the new year he gave regular children's sermons in one of the Cairo churches. Mickey also reported that he was preaching in Tanta and Alexandria. She did not say if he was being translated or not, but possibly he was giving short presentations in Arabic.[11] It is clear that from his first year in Egypt as a missionary he was striving to master Arabic. Mickey occasionally seemed to marvel that he spoke to as many people as he did, commenting, "He talks all the time [in Arabic], and if you can't find him, look for an Egyptian and you'll find him talking to him."[12] A few weeks later she commented on Ken's children's sermons: "He does quite well, so they tell me. And he thoroughly enjoys it, tho frightened at the time."[13]

8. Mickey to ___, February 15, 1956, Black Volume, 567.

9. Mickey to friends, February 22, 1956, and Mickey to ___ March 3, 1956, Black Volume, 47, 562, 566.

10. Mickey to family, July 3, 1956, Black Volume, 555.

11. Mickey to family, March 3, 1956, Black Volume, 566.

12. Mickey to family, March 20, 1956, Black Volume, 565.

13. Mickey to friends, April 18, 1956, Black Volume, 45.

In the Association meeting of the American Mission in the summer of 1956, the issue of compliance to the new law requiring the teaching of Islam could no longer be avoided. While in the past missionaries had been able to ignore or circumvent such laws, the government was serious about the enforcement of the new law it had passed in 1955. At the Association meeting that took place in June, the missionaries initially voted not to teach Islam in their schools, a defiance of the government that would probably mean their expulsion. However, they reversed this decision at the behest of the Evangelical Church and the urging of the two UPC mission board secretaries, Don Black and Glen Reed, who attended their meeting that year. Reed gave a thoughtful speech on the need for Christians to remain in contact with Muslims. He observed that a great spiritual barrier had long existed between the Muslim and Christian worlds and that Christians had been part-builders of this barrier, which could only be demolished through the communication of the gospel.[14] After much debate and hand wringing, the missionaries voted thirty to twelve to comply with the new law.[15] Mickey wrote, "I suppose it was Glen Reed who swung the tide if we may say anyone did. Never have I been in such a situation of anguish and torment and seeking for the right answer—and all said the same thing." Ken and Mickey were relieved that, since they had not yet completed their first full year as missionaries, they were not eligible to vote.[16] The Association's decision that summer meant that the mission had acquiesced to the government's desire to block the last major avenue of evangelism available to Christians in the country. Church and mission alike had been maneuvered into focusing almost exclusively on the improvement of their own people through educational and economic self-development programs and institutions—areas in which, as it turned out, Ken and Mickey would excel.

The Association also voted to agree to Ken and Mickey's request that they be allowed to skip the next term of language study in order to live in Assiut and practice what they had already learned. Ken, who was now twenty-six years old, had been a perpetual student since the first grade. He felt that, in Mickey's phrase, he had "reached the saturation point"

---

14. "Memorandum on Remarks made by Dr. Glenn Reed before the Association of the American Mission in Egypt concerning compliance with the law requiring schools to teach Islam to Muslim pupils. Egypt Mission," Schools and Government, 1956, RG 209-26-24, Presbyterian Historical Society.

15. Sharkey, *American Evangelicals in Egypt*, 131–32, 183, and 198–201.

16. Mickey to family, July 3, 1956, Black Volume, 555.

and needed a break.[17] Moreover, Ken wanted to be sure to acquire a solid grasp of colloquial Arabic before beginning the study of classical Arabic in the fall. They proposed to occupy the home of a missionary who had just left Assiut. Being close to Assiut Hospital, Ken could give regular sermons there as well as speak daily with patients. Ken and Mickey also asked to be allowed to sail on the *Ibis* beginning in October in order to visit as many villages as possible for the purposes of both language acquisition and ministry. This request, too, was granted. Mickey wrote that, in effect, Assiut would be their home base from which they would venture out into the region. She looked forward to using this opportunity to do her own cooking. Explaining that missionaries hire cooks ostensibly so that wives would have more time for ministry, she commented that she had "not seen wives more engaged in mission because of it."[18] The Baileys would move to Assiut in mid-September and stay until the end of January.

With no Arabic classes offered in the summer, Ken and Mickey enjoyed living in a cabin at Sidi Bishr for most of the summer. But the summer was not all relaxation since they also participated in two work projects for the church at that time. The first was a two-week work camp to construct Beit el-Salam ("House of Peace") that would be the Evangelical Church's youth conference center on the Mediterranean. Joined by Egyptian college and medical students, the Baileys helped to dig foundations, removing heavy rocks by hand. They also mixed, carried, and poured cement to form the foundations of the buildings. The second project was to improve the Evangelical Theological Seminary in Cairo. The seminarians' rooms lacked desks, lamps, and chairs; and the dining area lacked a sufficient number of plates and chairs so that all twenty students could dine together. Ken was particularly keen to participate. Having recently graduated from Pittsburgh-Xenia Theological Seminary, with its spanking new buildings, the shame of working in such poor and dilapidated facilities was especially uncomfortable and discouraging for him. The seminarians returned to the institution in early October, three days before the formal semester was to begin. They joined in constructing desks, lamps, tables, and benches; painting classrooms and halls; and cleaning and renovating the prayer room, student lounge, kitchen, and roof. Finally, they repaired the seminary courtyard and remodeled it for

17. Mickey to friends, August 27, 1956, Black Volume, 42–43.
18. Mickey to family, May 15, 1956, Black Volume, 559.

volleyball, basketball, tether ball, and horseshoe tossing. Some of the money for these projects was raised by the Baileys, who wrote home to family and friends for funds.

Ken and Mickey moved to Assiut in mid-September. Since the house they had intended to occupy would not be available until October when the missionary couple then living in it would be going on furlough, they moved into the hospital guestroom on the third floor. To get the lay of the land, they visited six village communities where they observed the *fellaheen* ("peasants") picking cotton and tending dura and maize crops. They also met pastors and visited churches to observe what Christian life was like. Though Christian and Muslim villages were similar, they could be assured that they were in a predominantly Christian community when they observed hundreds of pigs roaming around and scavenging to survive.

Perhaps most important for Ken's future, they visited the Christian village of Deir Abu Hinnis, near Mallawi. Here they met Miss Davida Finney and Miss Marjorie Dye, Presbyterian missionaries who had conducted a literacy campaign there over the previous year. Finney at nearly seventy years of age was soon to retire and was therefore looking for someone to take up the work in her stead. Ken was intrigued, being convinced that literacy in the villages was essential to the advancement of Christianity in Egypt. In fact, he had come to this village to investigate what was happening with the intention of participating if he liked what he saw. While spending four or five days there, Ken preached on Sunday and gave many other talks as well. The Baileys observed the literacy classes, the women's classes being in the afternoon and the men's in the evening.

In early October, back in the hospital guestroom in Assiut, Ken was diligent in continuing to develop his colloquial language skills as well as immerse himself in the culture of Upper Egypt. From this base he regularly visited the hospital patients to minister while speaking in Arabic. He also gave regular sermons or meditations in the chapel and told stories to the children. Soon he was visiting the churches in the nearby villages, becoming acquainted with pastors, congregations, and village life. The day after the Baileys had settled into their new home in mid-October, they drove eight and a half hours on uneven dirt roads to visit Luxor, 200 miles to the south. The villages they saw along the way were generally isolated, but in that time of year they were more isolated than ever because it was the flood season when villages became small islands surrounded by water that often rose as high as the doors of houses.

Learning the Heavenly Language

Indefatigable tourists, Ken and Mickey enjoyed seeing Karnack with its 134 columns and its impressive cartouches.

Ken and Mickey paid a price for their ceaseless activity. Mickey said that Ken was sick for most of the summer, and in the last weeks of October, they both succumbed to what Mickey described as either "influenza or virus pneumonia." Ken's temperature rose to 105 degrees, and Mickey's at one point reached 104. When Ken's mother, Annette, came to stay with them and nurse them back to health, Mickey was grateful and relieved, commenting with her customary reserve, "She was a most welcome sight."[19]

Their illnesses coincided with the Suez Crisis in the autumn of 1956. Four years before, on July 23, 1952, the Free Officers led by General Muhammad Neguib had overthrown King Farouk of Egypt in a coup. Neguib, who became the nation's prime minister in 1952 and its president in 1953, implemented a series of socialist reforms meant to improve the lot of the Egyptian peasants. Gamal Abdel Nasser soon replaced him, becoming prime minster in 1954 and president in 1956. Appealing to nationalist sympathies, he seized control of the Suez Canal Zone on July 26, 1956, which the British and French had controlled since its construction in the period 1859–69. This precipitated what has been variously called the Tripartite Aggression, the Second Arab-Israeli War, and the Suez Crisis. An attempt to regain the canal zone, it was an invasion of Egypt by Britain, France, and Israel on October 29, which lasted until November 7, 1956. Later in the year, the three powers were forced to withdraw under threats from US President Dwight Eisenhower, signaling the decline of British power in the region and the rise of the United States. Mindful of Cold-War-era geopolitics, Eisenhower had turned on his NATO allies, Britain and France, because he feared that appearing to side with European colonialism would push the Arab world into the arms of the Soviet Union. Nasser was seen as having won a great victory, but actually it was a victory handed to him by the United States. When Nasser quickly pivoted to the Soviet Union despite American goodwill and promises of aid, Eisenhower came to see his handling of the Suez Crisis as his greatest blunder.[20]

When Ken and Mickey learned of the invasion, they were ill in Luxor and awaiting a boat to take them to Cairo. Instead, they took the train back

---

19. Mickey to friends, December 2, 1956, Black Volume, 40.
20. Doran, *Ike's Gamble*, 239–43.

to Assiut, arriving in time for the first night of blackouts. The short-term missionaries in Egypt at this time traveled to Cairo, took the train to Alexandria, and were then evacuated to Europe to await events. Ken's parents in Cairo asked Glen Reed to order Ken and Mickey to return to Cairo and then leave the country. They received this message on October 29, but by this time the ships to Europe had already departed, eliminating that means of transport as an option. Ken and Mickey were uncertain of the best course, but they reasoned that if others could stay so could they. Moreover, their presence would be an important show of solidarity with their Egyptian friends and coworkers. "At any rate," Mickey wrote home, "we are going to sit it out and pray that it might be ended very soon."[21] Since there was a military base at Luxor, it was feared that it might be attacked. As a result, the city of Assiut was in blackout every night of the conflict and Assiut Hospital, which was the only major hospital in Upper Egypt at the time, prepared to receive the wounded. Fortunately, this was not necessary as the conflict soon ended. Ken and Mickey believed that Egypt had gone too far in fomenting this conflict, but they also considered the tripartite invasion to be an inappropriate response.

By early January 1957 Ken and Mickey were again living in Cairo, sharing a home with Ken's parents. With the adventure in Upper Egypt over, they also returned to the School of Oriental Studies (SOS) at the American University in Cairo. They needed to complete four semesters of language study in two years in order to meet the mission's requirement. The next term began just after Christmas and would continue through March 4, and there would also be a summer term beginning in June. Taking the second semester so soon proved too demanding, and they eventually decided to complete their requirements by taking the fall term, which ended before Christmas. Despite the stress they felt for having to make up for the five months of language study they had missed by living in Assiut, they felt that their time there allowed them to make much progress in colloquial Arabic. "Ken's Arabic," Mickey observed, "is so much improved, and he talks almost as fast as they do."[22]

Although Ken and Mickey were making strenuous efforts to complete their language requirements, they were careful to give themselves plenty of leisure time. Reviewing Mickey's letters home during their first term in Egypt, it is clear that they were inveterate and insatiable

---

21. Mickey to family, November 4, 1956, Black Volume, 543.
22. Mickey to family, January 13, 1957, Black Volume, 536.

tourists. They visited the Great Pyramid in Giza numerous times, and Ken climbed it at least twice, which was still allowed in those days. They also visited the Citadel at least twice, the Mokattam Hills, the palace of Muhammad Ali, several of King Farouk's palaces, the Sakkara pyramid at least twice, the mosques and churches of Old Cairo, and the World War II battlefield of El-Alamein, which was just west of Alexandria. They visited the museums in Cairo and Alexandria too, as well as Pompey's Pillar in Alexandria. When people visited them, the Baileys did not hesitate to revisit sites again and again.

In the spring of 1957, political tensions due to the Suez Crisis began to relax. US ambassador Raymond A. Hare returned to Cairo early in the new year, and the travel ban in place since the conflict began was lifted in April with the first evacuated missionary returning on April 14.[23] In March, Ken and Mickey began another term of language study that included grammar, reading, public address, and Egyptian history since the Muslim conquest. They realized at this point that they would never successfully complete their language requirements by June, but now knowing that they had until January they felt relieved of much of the pressure. Nevertheless, in May Mickey wrote that she and Ken had hit their lowest point, with tempers on edge. The main source of irritation was the pressure of two years of language study, but the desert heat and Arab culture played a part, too. As they prepared for their written exams at the end of May, Mickey observed, "The last week has seen us cramming as in college days."[24] In June they learned that they had passed all but their composition exams, but their overall grades were still passing. Mickey signed up for extra courses in preparation for the oral exams in Arabic that lay ahead. They took these exams on June 24, which they passed.

Immediately after the Baileys completed their language exams, the American Mission held its Association meeting, which was stressful and contentious because work assignments were being made. Ken asked to be assigned to the city of Minia in Upper Egypt to work on the literacy campaign launched by Davida Finney. Others argued that this campaign was already well staffed by Egyptians and had its quota of missionaries as well. Moreover, the assignments committee had determined that other areas, especially in the Delta region, were understaffed and therefore needed to receive more missionaries. One missionary contended that

---

23. Mickey to family, April 14, 1957, Black Volume, 525.
24. Mickey to family, May 20, 1957, Black Volume, 522.

missionaries should simply accept the assignments given by the Association as a matter of duty, while Ken insisted that a missionary's affinities and sense of calling were also important. After a great deal of posturing, arguing, and dickering, Ken received the assignment he wanted, and those who disagreed had to content themselves with a promise that in the future there would be a better balance of staff assignments due to the implementation of a five-year plan.[25]

Figure 15. Christmas in Cairo, Egypt, 1956:
Ewing, Annette, Mickey, and Ken Bailey.

From July 16 to about mid-September 1957, Ken and Mickey traveled in Sudan, Eritrea, and Ethiopia in order to learn more about the East African region commonly known as the Horn of Africa where many UPC missionaries were stationed and conducted their work.[26] The

25. Mickey to family, July 12, 1957, Black Volume, 517–18.

26. This trip included visiting mission sites in Sudan, Eritrea, and Ethiopia. They spent time with frontier missionaries such as Charles and Lois Haspels, Joan Yuilek and Niles Neimer, and Harold and Polly Kurtz. They also visited the Anuak mission project launched by legendary missionary Don McClure—see Partee, *Story of Don McClure*. For Mickey's account of the trip see Mickey to family, September 15, 1957, Black

Baileys, inspired and refreshed by their trip, were back in Cairo by mid-September and soon plunged again into Arabic studies. It would be their last term of language classes. Mickey quickly became discouraged, but Ken goaded her on by arguing that she could not quit because then he would have no one to explain Arabic grammar to him. Despite intensive study, Ken found time to preach regularly on the weekends, sometimes traveling as far away as Tanta, Alexandria, and Fayoum. In the last week of January 1958, the Baileys crammed for their final exams while also packing for Minia. Although they did not mention the results in any of their letters home, they apparently passed their exams. Language study, however, was not entirely behind them. While engaged in the literacy campaign in the villages around Minia, they were supposed to spend half of their time in the continued study of Arabic.

Figure 16. Ken Bailey in Asmara, Ethiopia, April 1959.

Volume, 511–14; and Mickey to friends and family, Christmas 1957, Black Volume, 38–39.

4

Mission in Minia

1957–60

> In a pioneer situation the missionary was faced either with complete ineffectiveness or with a course which, if it did not make him a scholar, would give him, in spite of himself, scholarly instincts and disciplines.
>
> —ANDREW F. WALLS, *THE MISSIONARY MOVEMENT IN CHRISTIAN HISTORY*

THE BAILEYS WERE GENERALLY pleased with their new apartment in Minia, though Mickey complained that it lacked curtains and that the kitchen was too small. But whatever the inconveniences and deficiencies of the apartment, it had the unassailable virtue of being the first home that was entirely theirs.[1] Unfortunately, they did not have long to enjoy it before calamity was upon them. On February 3, 1958, while Ken and Mickey were traveling by automobile from Minia to Cairo, they had an accident. The driver was going too fast, and Ken had asked him to slow down. Nevertheless, the young man pushed the car to over 80 kilometers an hour and screeched around a sharp turn. The car flipped over and landed upside down, throwing the passengers from the car. Mickey was hurled forty feet. Ken cracked a rib. All were in shock. They were treated

---

1. Mickey to family, October 11, 1957, and May 25, 1958, Black Volume, 507–8, 487–88.

at a nearby government hospital but later transferred to the mission hospital in Tanta, which was of a higher standard. There they spent a week recovering from cuts, bruises, scrapes, and gashes. Mickey believed that the accident was filled with miracles because they had not hit a pedestrian or a tree or a house or fallen into a canal. The car had also landed on plowed ground, which cushioned its landing and slowed it down.[2]

Ken and Mickey faced another health issue the following month. They had been trying to start a family for some time but had been unsuccessful. After seeing several doctors, Mickey finally consulted with Dr. Norman Kraft, a mission doctor who discovered a possible cause for her infertility. She scheduled a surgery at Assiut Hospital for the end of March 1958. On being moved from the operating room to her room in the hospital, she gained consciousness for a moment and heard Ken say, "I think I'm going to faint." He lay down, and one of the nurses brought smelling salts, which averted what would have been an embarrassing episode. Mickey graciously commented, "I'm sure it was harder on him than on me!" She was in the hospital for two weeks recovering, while Ken's mother came to stay to help in her absence.[3] Despite the time, expense, and pain of Mickey's hospital stay, she was unable in the years immediately following her surgery to conceive.

The literacy program to which Ken and Mickey had been assigned by the Association in June 1957 had been launched by UPC missionary Davida Finney in 1947 as a joint program of the Literature Committee of the Evangelical Church and the American Mission. To promote literature in Upper Egypt, Finney established small libraries in village churches. In 1950 she was joined in this work by Samuel Habib, who had graduated from the Evangelical Theological Seminary in Cairo that year. In the early 1950s, while working on the literacy project, he also obtained two additional bachelor's degrees from the American University in Cairo in social science and journalism, and in 1955 he earned a master's degree

---

2. Mickey to family, March 9, 1958, Black Volume, 492–93.

3. Mickey to family, March 9, 1958, and April 26, 1958, Black Volume, 493, 490. Mickey told me that she had two surgeries to correct whatever problems were preventing her from become pregnant or inducing spontaneous abortions; this must have been the first of them.

in journalism from Syracuse University in New York.[4] In 1952, after five years of effort, the literacy program showed little progress, and the funding organization, the World Literacy and Christian Literature Committee of the National Council of Churches of Christ in the United States, threatened to end its funding in one year's time if progress was not soon evident. Finney and Habib decided to focus their efforts on the single village of Herz, and after one year, remarkably, 12 percent of the population became literate, and after two years this doubled to 24 percent. The story was reported in an article in the *Reader's Digest*, which gave publicity to the work around the world. Because of this success, the National Council of Churches renewed Finney's funding, and the work in subsequent years was extended to surrounding villages in Upper Egypt.[5]

In late April 1958, Ken assembled the literacy staff to train them in a new book to be used in the literacy campaign. The staff included Mickey, Eleanor Gersiek, and Amir Gayyid, who had been appointed by the Evangelical Church. They would introduce their literacy program in Deir el-Barsha, where there had already been a literacy campaign the previous year, and they would also use it in a new village, al-Kom al-Akhdar. Ken and Mickey began their work together in the literacy campaign at Deir el-Barsha, an isolated village on the east bank of the Nile that was not easily reached. To travel there from Minia, the Baileys drove south along the Nile for about an hour and a half until they arrived at the city of Mallawi. From there it might take anywhere from a half hour to two hours to cross the river in a boat depending on the wind. Once across the river on their first excursion there, Ken, Mickey, and four others who were with them rode donkeys for an hour with the temperature above 100 degrees before reaching the village. There were eight donkeys for the six of them and their supplies. Ken fashioned stirrups for Mickey to make the ride more comfortable. "It was my first donkey ride since the operation," recalled Mickey, "and I got along quite well as long as the donkey didn't get in a hurry. Once it took off following another one and we had a merry chase." During the campaign conducted in the village the previous year, a new home had been constructed by a village elder for the literacy workers, with the intention that following the campaign it would become a manse for a new pastor. The beds in the house were wooden benches with thin mattresses on top. Though they looked uncomfortable, the group quickly

---

4. For a life of Samuel Habib see Virtue, *Vision of Hope*.
5. Lorimer, *Presbyterian Experience in Egypt*, 81–83.

became accustomed to them. They even discovered that their hardness was probably good for their backs. One night, recalled Mickey, tiny insects swarmed around the lights in the house. After a while, "they were stacked all around the lite like snow drifted on the window. We were literally crawling with them." During the day the temperatures hovered between about 105 to 108 degrees, but it usually cooled off at night. One night Ken and Mickey slept in a room known as "the oven" because it retained the heat throughout the night. This was a mistake they did not repeat.[6]

During the week the Baileys spent at Deir el-Barsha in April 1958, Ken preached often but much of his work was simply resolving problems that had arisen due to a lack of good supervision. The literacy classes were divided into groups of females, adult males, and boys. Apparently, the men did not want to study with the boys and declined to attend. However, when classes were segregated, the men decided to participate. In the spring when the wheat was ready to be harvested, the village men spent most of their time in the fields, sometimes working through the night. Generally, however, they worked in the fields by day and in the evening attended classes, which concluded with a church service at 10:00. Often the meetings were held outdoors because of the heat. All sat on the ground, the men on one side and the women on the other. The village elders kept order, paying special attention to the young boys. Discipline was maintained by wielding a stick, which, Mickey commented, "is not spared." With the day's activities completed, the villagers returned home to eat and sleep. In total about 500 villagers participated in the classes, each receiving about four and a half hours of class time each week. Though the teachers were using books especially prepared for the use of villagers, teaching was still often difficult because of the villagers' limited life experience. For example, Mickey recalled sitting with a group of girls one afternoon and flipping through a *Reader's Digest*. The girls were fascinated by the advertising pictures, but Mickey had to explain them at length.[7] Ken delighted in this work and in village life in general. When he expressed an interest in the wool that the villagers spun by hand as they walked around the village, the elder who built the house for the literacy staff showed Ken how to spin and even brought him a spinner and some wool so that he could try it himself. Ken promised to

---

6. Mickey to family, May 25, 1958, Black Volume, 486.
7. Mickey to family, April 26, 1958, and May 25, 1958, Black Volume, 486.

master the technique and was soon producing a coarse wool such as that used for rugs.[8]

After their first week in the village of Deir el-Barsha, the Baileys returned home but soon ventured out to another village that was just then completing the literacy program. The staff held a graduation ceremony for those students who had successfully completed the program. On the occasion, a number of the graduates demonstrated their newly developed skills by standing to read, even some of the women who were timid and embarrassed to perform in public. Several members of the staff delivered speeches, including Ken, and then Ken's father, Ewing, formally distributed diplomas to the proud recipients.[9] At this time, the staff and mission workers held a retirement party for Davida Finney, who had turned seventy and would soon return to the United States. There was also a second party held in Finney's home for all the village dignitaries in the places where there had been literacy campaigns. Finney had the flu on both occasions but attended anyway. The torch was to be passed to a new generation of missionaries and to the Egyptians themselves.[10] Samuel Habib now became the head of the program, and in 1960 under his leadership it was renamed the Coptic Evangelical Organization for Social Services (CEOSS), which over the years would continue to expand until it came to be regarded as the social action arm of the Evangelical Church.

Sometime during this first full year of ministry in Upper Egypt, Bailey had a revelation about the importance of understanding traditional Egyptian village life as a means to better interpret the New Testament.[11] He later traced this insight to a sermon he heard that year while serving on the Committee for Fighting Illiteracy.[12] In the village of Deir Abu Hinnis, on the other side of the Nile from the town of Mallawi, the Reverend Adib Qaldas preached on the story of the Woman at the Well in the fourth chapter of John's Gospel. A local pastor speaking in colloquial Arabic, Adib turned to the women in the congregation who were seated together on one side as is village custom. He asked them a series of questions intended, in Socratic fashion, to elicit from them the meaning of

---

8. Mickey to family, April 26, 1958, Black Volume, 489.
9. Mickey to family, April 26, 1958, Black Volume, 489–90.
10. Mickey to family, May 25, 1958, Black Volume, 487.
11. Bailey, "Kenneth Bailey's Inaugural Lecture."
12. In this lecture, Ken said that he heard the sermon in 1957. However, he was not employed in literacy work in Upper Egypt until 1958. Therefore, I believe he was mistaken and have changed the date to 1958.

the story. Though Egyptian women in traditional villages in Egypt go to the Nile for water, not a well, Adib believed that as Middle Eastern women they had a unique insight into the cultural context of the Gospel story. As Bailey recalled, Adib began,

> "This woman went to the well alone! Do any of you women go to the river alone?" The women together replied, "No." "Why don't you go to bring water at noon?" asked Reverend Adib. "It's too hot," came the answer. "When do you go to the well?" he asked again. "First thing in the morning and the last thing at night," they replied.
>
> Reverend Adib continued, "This woman went to the well alone! Do any of you women go to the [Nile] river alone?" "No," came a chorus of voices. "Why don't you go to the river alone?" "It wouldn't be proper," was the joint reply. "What do you think of this woman who went to the well at noon, alone?" asked Reverend Adib. "She's a bad woman!" was the unanimous conclusion.

Bailey was astonished at what he heard that day. Though it is eventually made clear in John's account that Jesus was speaking to a "bad woman" in that she had had five husbands and was then living with a man who has not her husband, the women of Deir Abu Hinnis had surmised from the cultural clues given at the beginning of the story that this was an immoral woman who had been ostracized by her community. Bailey later said of Adib's performance, "That sermon changed my life." Adib had been able to elicit from these simple village women insights into the meaning of the story unavailable to Western scholars or recorded in Western commentaries. After reflecting on the sermon, Bailey wrote, "My studied conclusion was that there is a layer of meaning in the stories from and about Jesus that can only be unlocked by a more precise awareness of the Middle Eastern culture that informs the text." This layer of meaning was lost to the Western church because it did not understand or appreciate Middle Eastern culture, and it was "blurred" for Middle Easterners because the scholars and pastors of the region had long assumed that the meaning of these ancient texts had already been revealed at length by the fathers of the early Greek-speaking church. In contemplating this sermon, Bailey slowly brought into focus what he later described as a "heavenly vision"—that is, a calling to be an interpreter of the New Testament from a Middle Eastern perspective. Alert now to this new task, he would begin to attend to the village culture of Egyptian Christians in order to open a window of interpretation that did not exist for the church at large.

Bailey's vision was confirmed that July at a three-week conference in Jerusalem taught by the British scholar of Islam Kenneth Cragg, the author of the seminal book *The Call of the Minaret* (1956) and later a bishop in the Anglican Church. Mickey enjoyed listening to the man, later writing, "He was simply wonderful—a deeply devotional and scholarly man. And talk of the King's English. He is a Brit and knows his language well." The morning sessions were taken up with the issues that Muslims might bring to the study of the New Testament: the unity of God, the nature of divine revelation, the extent of human sinfulness, the necessity of the cross, and the greatness of God—among others. They also studied various aspects of the Qur'an, some contemporary themes of Islam, basic Islamic concepts, and some of Islam's greatest scholars. Three afternoon sessions each week were conducted by the Rev. Eric Bishop who devoted the time to such issues as the Palestinian background of the New Testament writers. And one was led by a survivor of the Armenian genocide in the early twentieth century.[13]

In his 1992 book, *Finding the Lost: Cultural Keys to Luke 15*, Bailey wrote that his love affair of over thirty years with Luke 15 began at this conference. In one lecture Cragg discussed the Medieval debate between Christians and Muslims about how to interpret the parable of the prodigal son. Though this parable is generally considered a concise recapitulation of the gospel of grace, Muslims point out that the story does not include allusions to Jesus as the incarnation of God, the mediator between God and humanity, or one who suffered and died on the cross. The prodigal son, they conclude, did not need the incarnation, mediation, or cross of Christ to be reconciled to his father. Rather, he simply repented on his own volition and returned home, where he was warmly received. According to this interpretation, Jesus' telling of the parable shows that he had a Muslim theology of salvation. Bailey wrote, "As a young listener to the bishop's lectures I went into shock." Cragg's response to the Muslim challenge was to point out that throughout the parable the father endures the "agony of rejected love," which suggests that suffering is indeed at the heart of a true understanding of the salvation taught by Jesus. Bailey

---

13. Mickey to family, September 8, 1958, Black Volume, 479–80.

found Cragg's "hints of the cross" to be helpful but inadequate. So began Bailey's lifetime of study and reflection on this crucial parable.[14]

Following the conference in Jerusalem, Ken and Mickey enjoyed the last week of July in Beirut and then the month of August at Sidi Bishr before returning to Minia to continue their work on the literacy campaign. At this time, they learned that the women of the newly formed United Presbyterian Church USA (UPCUSA) had decided to make the literacy campaign in Egypt their special project for the year 1959. That would mean a substantial expansion of the budget and of the program for the Committee for Fighting Illiteracy, which at this time consisted of the Baileys, Samuel Habib, and perhaps a few others. They would be joined in this work by the Rural Church Service Team, which operated under the supervision of the church and included three trained Egyptians, six village workers, and two servants. The Executive Committee of the American Mission as well as the committee for the Rural Church Service Team met in October to plan for the expansion and the assignment of new personnel to staff it. In November Bailey met with Synod leaders to discuss the project and to make sure that the church was in accord with the mission's plans. Though principally concerned with literacy, the two organizations were also engaged in Bible study, ministry among women and children, family health and nutrition, and the improvement of agricultural techniques.[15]

From October through the middle of November 1958, Ken and Mickey worked in the Coptic Orthodox village of Mallawi while living on the houseboat *Ibis* since no living quarters were available in the village. Many villagers came to see Ken on the boat, and Mickey provided the requisite tea and snacks. Mickey recalled one uncomfortable meeting between Ken and three Coptic Orthodox priests. Being used to much deference in the village, they asked for frankness without really anticipating that they would receive it. But Ken spoke with his customary bluntness, which left them perturbed and restive—a portent of Ken's coming troubles in Assiut in 1964 and Beirut in 1985.[16]

---

14. Bailey, *Finding the Lost*, 9.

15. "Budget for the Rural Church Service Team 1959," Presbyterian Historical Society, vertical file RG 68.0217 box 5. Mickey to family, September 8, 1958, Black Volume, 479. Mickey to family, November 20, 1958, Black Volume, 475. *Minutes of the General Assembly of The United Presbyterian Church in the United States of America. Part II* (1960), 80.

16. Mickey to family, November 20, 1958, Black Volume, 474.

At the Association meeting of the mission in the second week of January, the missionaries discussed the enlargement of the literacy program. At that time the Baileys were the only mission personnel assigned to the campaign, and they were still supposed to be spending half of their time on Arabic studies. The program would have to have a new full-time director from the mission as well as additional Egyptian staff workers. Bailey hoped that the new director would be an older missionary who could bring experience and wisdom to the task. Instead, the Association appointed Jack Lorimer to direct the team. Though he was a young man, Bailey was initially delighted with the choice, seeing Jack as a like-minded missionary and friend. Later, in September 1961 when he returned to Egypt after a furlough in America, he expressed to Mickey some uncharitable feelings about Lorimer: "I just don't feel the same way I did about Jack. I sincerely hope I am not being resentful. I don't want to be. But I guess I'm just more disappointed than I know." Perhaps this was inevitable. After all, Lorimer was appointed to lead a project pioneered by Bailey. But whatever misgivings Bailey had about Lorimer, he was still committed and enthusiastic about teaching literacy and the Bible, seeing these as providing a firm foundation on which to build. He agreed with Samuel Habib that the literacy program's greatest immediate need was developing literature appropriate for simple villagers, which would take into account their culture and thought patterns.[17] The Rural Church Service Team now believed that the time had come to expand their work to include health, agriculture, and Christian education. To achieve this end, the team would be expanded to include new Egyptian personnel in the fields of agriculture and home life. Bailey's work on the staff would continue to involve teacher training and would eventually include the development of Arabic literature of his own making.

From the outset, Mickey was appointed the treasurer of the project. The first book they translated was Lesslie Newbigin's *Sin and Salvation* (1956), but Mickey soon wrote to supporters for funds to translate books to meet the needs of young pastors, Bible study instructors, and literacy teachers. In addition to publishing costs, they also needed funds to provide medical care for the staff and for pastors to attend summer conferences. Mickey wrote to her family that, should they or others be interested in this work, they should give through the regular channels of

---

17. Mickey to family, December 19, 1958, Black Volume, 473. Ken to Mickey, early September 1961, White Volume. Mickey and Ken to friends, Christmas 1958, Black Volume, 36–37.

the church. However, she quickly added that she would receive money however it came.[18]

Over the next year and a half, from February 1959 to early June 1960, Ken and Mickey worked in various villages to promote literacy, Bible study, and socioeconomic development. These villages included Deir el-Barsha, Deir Abu Hinnis, and Mallawi. They were frequently on the move between various villages where the program had been established, often crossing the Nile in traditional boats pulled by ropes from the shore. While at the village of Deir el-Barsha in March 1959, Ken alternated between sleeping on the *Ibis* and sleeping in the village, traveling between boat and shore on the *Ibis*'s small motor-powered dinghy. Throughout it all, they lived in primitive conditions, riding camels and donkeys to and from isolated villages, lighting the nights with kerosene lamps, and living on the local diet. In their home in Minia, the Baileys had quickly installed mosquito netting on their windows to keep flies and mosquitos out of the house, but in October 1959 they also began sleeping under a mosquito net. Mickey feared that the standing water at flood time was increasing malaria levels in the city, and she hoped that the netting would not only keep them healthy but also help them sleep more soundly as the whir of mosquitoes would be kept at bay.[19] But despite their best efforts, Ken and Mickey were frequently ill with dysentery from the food and water, or had flu from the cold and wind in the winter. Once when Mickey's mother spent time with them on the *Ibis* and fainted and fell ill for a time, Mickey felt as if she was running an infirmary. In addition to meeting physical challenges, the Baileys had to withstand other types of assaults. Mickey endured unscrupulous church officials who tried to wring as much money from her as possible; and Ken dealt with Orthodox priests who resented his presence in villages in which they believed that they had proprietary rights. There was also crime that nettled or even endangered the work. For example, one Christian village produced beer from sugar cane and dates that it sold illicitly across the river, and occasionally villages would engage in blood feuds that made their Egyptian staff fearful.[20]

Despite irksome inconveniences, the Baileys' literacy program was both successful and popular because, at least in part, it was always the

18. Mickey to family, January 25, 1959, Black Volume, 470.

19. Mickey to family, October 4, 1959, Black Volume, 452; Mickey to family, September 6, 1959, Black Volume, 457.

20. Baileys to friends, May 8, 1959, Black Volume, 33–35.

best and generally the only show in town. In these traditional villages, Mickey pointed out, the church "is the cinema, town hall, 4-H [club], community club, [and] coffee shop."[21] While a literacy program was in process, there was a church program every night. As many as one thousand people might sit on freezing ground to watch Bailey make his flannelgraph presentations, which had formerly been reserved for child audiences but now were adapted for presentations intended for an entire village. He also showed slides of his trips to the Holy Land, which were both educational and entertaining. And, of course, the literacy program not only taught reading and the Bible. Its various subsidiary activities had an immediate economic impact on a community. For example, Bailey introduced a brickmaking machine so that villagers could erect permanent buildings. In one village, when they were finally able to make a brick that did not break, they decided to erect a new brick church. Bailey also introduced a shoe-repair kit provided by the humanitarian agency CARE (Cooperative for Assistance and Relief Everywhere) and taught simple carpentry skills so that unemployed young men could use the stems of palm branches, which are quite strong, to produce furniture to sell. The young men at Deir el-Barsha quickly embraced furniture making. Mickey wrote that it is said in the village that there is now at least one chair per house and there was a growing demand for beds. She hoped that the latter would make a significant difference in the health of the villagers, especially in the winter.

Without necessarily always being conscious of it, Bailey was also observing and absorbing village culture. Later, as he studied the parables and stories in the New Testament, he would use what he had learned to provide fresh interpretations. For example, in 1959 he attended a village wedding in which the young men celebrated together before going off to collect the bride and return with her for the wedding ceremony at the house of the groom's father, where there was an evening feast and a room prepared for the newlyweds. Observing these communal practices later helped him to interpret Jesus' account of the ten virgins awaiting the arrival of the groom (Matt 25:1–13).[22]

Ken and Mickey were still required to spend half of their time in language study, but they found this obligation difficult to fulfill while engaged in full-time work in the villages. The Association, therefore,

---

21. Mickey to family, February 8, 1959, Black Volume, 467,

22. Mickey to family, February 8, 1959, Black Volume. For Bailey's exposition of the parable of the ten virgins see Bailey, *Jesus through Middle Eastern Eyes*, 269–75.

asked them to return to Cairo in June in 1959 in order to continue their language courses. Mickey explained that they had to complete one more term of language study in order to qualify for their furlough. It may also be that, aside from meeting formal language requirements, the Association recognized Ken's growing facility in Arabic and wanted to encourage it. The Baileys left their home aboard the *Ibis* around May 10 to return to Cairo for this purpose. Following the Association meeting of the mission in Sidi Bishr toward the end of June, they planned to attend another study conference in Jerusalem while staying at St. George's Hostel. They would also take six Egyptians, if it was possible to obtain visas for them. After returning on August 1, Ken intended to spend the month studying Arabic.

In the event, Ken's parents, Ewing and Annette, accompanied them to Israel. The two couples enjoyed sightseeing, and Ken and his father had the pleasure of participating in an archeological dig at King Saul's village of Gibeon. It was fortuitous that Ken and his parents could spend this time together as Ewing and Annette would soon be leaving Egypt. Ewing had accepted a new position as the Area Representative of the mission for Egypt, Sudan, and Ethiopia—the Horn of Africa—replacing Glen Reed. He would spend September in New York for orientation and travel in Sudan during the fall. Ken's parents would then move in January to Asmara, Ethiopia, where they would spend the last two years of their professional ministry.

Back in Egypt in August, Mickey checked into the American Hospital of Tanta to undergo surgery to remove an ovarian cyst. Her doctors removed a cyst the size of a softball as well as one of her ovaries. She was sanguine about the matter as she felt she was receiving excellent medical care.[23] At this point Ken and Mickey had one more year to go to complete their first five-year term, which was to be followed by a year's furlough with an extra month for traveling. Deciding that he wanted to obtain his master's degree from Pittsburgh-Xenia Theological Seminary, Ken applied and was accepted. He learned in October that he had been allotted the seminary's housing for visiting missionaries.

Ken and Mickey spent six weeks in the fall living on the *Ibis* and working in the village of Deir Abu Hinnis, and they planned to finish up there early in 1960. In the last week of November, they were back in Minia but, because in Egyptian society business must be handled tête-à-tête, Ken found himself traveling to a different village every day. In December they

---

23. Mickey to family, August 22, 1959, Black Volume, 458.

completed the literacy training in three villages. The closing program at Deir Abu Hinnis was particularly memorable for Mickey. Despite months of acculturation in classroom decorum, the audience of 1,000 to 1,500 enjoyed an evening of wild, unrestrained exuberance. Mickey wrote, "Never have we seen the like, and never hope to again." Though the audience listened submissively to an older, respected member of the community, Jack Lorimer's slideshow presentation on his recent trip to India and Pakistan produced a response of "bedlam." Other speakers presumably met with mixed responses. When the leaders attempted to bring the program to a conclusion with the awarding of certificates and prizes, the audience simply could no longer be contained. Mickey remembered, "The place broke up, the dust rose, sticks were flying to beat the people down, [but] to no avail. Ken told the preacher to pronounce the benediction. We got two of the club pressure lights put out. We left, and the people followed. What a nite! There is no other village like it. Thank goodness!"[24] Despite this inglorious denouement to months of patient effort, the villagers of Deir Abu Hinnis, as well as those of Deir el-Barsha, were beginning to organize Christian education programs utilizing their own teachers. The task remaining for the literacy team was to supply them with literature that they could use in their ongoing studies. To this end, the team proposed to produce four new Bible study pamphlets each year. In addition, before Christmas they planned to open literacy projects in three new villages near Minia—one of these being in a village that the team had not yet visited. Because Jack Lorimer was still new at the job and Eleanor Gerseik as a woman was ineligible in Egyptian society for a leadership position, Ken was in charge of all three projects.[25]

The mission's Association meeting in January 1960 included the usual serious mission business but also some frivolity. One evening they had a skit and music night. Mickey wrote, "Ken and Jack Lorimer did one [skit] together using long underwear and leotards for part of their costumes! Music night was quite varied from near professional voices to a musical saw! Ken did 'Sailor Men' for one of the numbers about three little boys who use a box for their boat and the backyard for the sea." One quartet sang, "Don't Throw a Lighted Lamp at Mother," while others performed more serious numbers that included violin solos and duets. On this occasion, Ken's parents were honored for their long service

---

24. Mickey to family, December 8, 1959, Black Volume, 448.
25. Mickey to family, December 8, 1959, Black Volume, 448.

in Egypt before traveling on to Asmara, Ethiopia. The missionaries presented them with a *mushribiya*-style picture frame (a Middle-Eastern window screen) and about $100 in Egyptian pounds for their own use. The next day Annette and Mickey went to Sharia Muski, a street in Cairo full of bargain-basement stalls and shops, to purchase a silver tray to go with her tea set, but they left some money for Ewing to purchase some supplies for his photography hobby.[26]

In February the entire literacy campaign staff moved to Assiut where they lived in a large house that they dubbed the palace. On completing their work at the village of Deir el-Barsha, there was a commencement celebration in which young men performed a play reenacting the conflict between Jacob and Esau (Gen 26–33). The men unconsciously performed their parts in a manner consistent with Middle Eastern village customs. For example, when Esau slept outside at night, he never failed to clutch his staff. And when Jacob bargained with Esau, he only revealed at the end of the negotiation his true aim, his brother's birthright. Ken was so impressed with their performance that he asked them to perform their skit in the nearby village of Ezziyya, where they intended to begin a literacy campaign that month. With these experiences in mind, Ken may also have begun to consider the potential of short plays to convey the gospel message in Egyptian villages.[27]

In March the Baileys moved to Ezziyya where they took up residence in a large house in order to be closer to work. Their house was wired for electricity, but it was not in working order; and the screening was so deficient that they had to contend with numerous flies. Mickey commented that there were so many that it "would have turned your stomach." But they put up curtains, which helped.[28]

In their last months in Egypt, Bailey plunged into the study of Arabic and then took a final exam, which he passed. Despite the pressures of language study, he still made time to continue to participate in the ongoing work in the villages as well as to train Egyptian teachers to carry out the literacy work. One week he took an early train to Cairo in order to give an hour lecture in Arabic at the Girls' College for three women who would become literacy trainers in the villages. Early in May Bailey traveled to the villages of Deir el-Barsha and Deir Abu Hinnis, where he and Mickey had spent so much time, in order to say farewell. The

26. Mickey to family, January 10, 1960, Black Volume, 445.
27. Mickey to family, February 4, 1960, Black Volume, 443.
28. Mickey to family, March 15, 1960, Black Volume, 438.

Baileys departed Cairo on May 23 and took a leisurely month traveling through Europe before boarding the *Queen Mary* bound for New York. They would now enjoy a much-earned furlough during which Ken would focus on his master's studies at a newly formed seminary in Pittsburgh.

5

Master's Degree and Work with CEOSS in Minia

1960–61

> Always be prepared to make a defense to any one who calls you to account for the hope that is in you, yet do it with gentleness and reverence...
>
> —1 Peter 3:15

In 1958 while Bailey had been away in Egypt, the Presbyterian Church in the USA (PCUSA) and the United Presbyterian Church in North America (UPCNA) combined to form the United Presbyterian Church in the USA (UPCUSA). The newly merged churches established a new mission organization, the Commission on Ecumenical Mission and Relations, known by its acronym COEMAR, under which Ken and Mickey would now work. It was under COEMAR's auspices that Bailey used his furlough in 1960 and 1961 as an opportunity to obtain a master's degree before returning to Egypt to continue his mission service.

Bailey would do his graduate studies at the new seminary that came about with the merger of the UPCUSA's two Pittsburgh seminaries: Western Seminary, formerly of the PCUSA, and Pittsburgh-Xenia Theological Seminary, formerly of the UPC and the institution where

Bailey had obtained his degree in divinity.[1] Those became Pittsburgh Theological Seminary (PTS) and in the fall of 1960 operated as one on the Pittsburgh-Xenia campus in East Liberty, which was only six years old and with ten-acres provided plenty of room for expansion. It was also near to the University of Pittsburgh, Carnegie Mellon University, and Chatham College. The combined faculty of the two seminaries gave PTS twenty-three professors. The biblical department alone had nine professors and would soon expand to twelve. The combined library boasted 102,693 books, but a new library building to house them would not be built until 1964.

Bailey arrived at the newly united seminary in the fall of 1960, the first year the two seminaries operated together. He studied with New Testament professor Addison H. Leitch, who at the end of the academic year of 1960–61 would leave in order to teach at Tarkio College, in Tarkio, Missouri. Leitch's employment at Pittsburgh-Xenia Seminary had begun in 1946 when he served as the Professor of Philosophy and Education. In 1949 he held the Chair of Systematic and Biblical Theology, and he was also the president of Pittsburgh-Xenia Seminary from 1955 to 1959. In addition to having a love of the New Testament in common, he and Bailey shared a love of mission and an understanding of Egypt. "Ad," as he was known to his friends and later to Bailey, had taught briefly at Assiut College in Egypt.[2] Under Leitch's guidance, Bailey was able to complete his master's in theology in the field of systematic theology during the academic year of 1960–61.

Bailey's master's thesis was *THE DOCTRINE OF GOD for Village People (A Series of Twenty Plays on the Doctrine of God Using Village Characters)*.[3] In the preface, Bailey explains that the plays are intended to be used in Egypt to present the fundamental doctrines of Christianity in a form appropriate for traditional villagers. His thesis was written in English, but once Ken was back in Egypt, he had it translated and published in Arabic. Since the thesis was intended for translation, Bailey explains, "In many places the style is a bit awkward in English. Sentences are kept purposely short.

---

1. For more on the new seminary see Walther, "Pittsburgh: Where the Streams Meet," in Walther, *Ever a Frontier*, 159–80.
2. Kelley, "Pittsburgh-Xenia Seminary," in Walther, *Ever a Frontier*, 129.
3. Bailey, *DOCTRINE OF GOD*.

Words and phrases are often rather monotonously repeated." Though English-speakers may find this tedious, he explains that short sentences and much repetition would be welcome to a "newly literate" people.[4]

Bailey set his play in the context of a traditional village in the Middle East that is influenced from above by Islam and below by the "spirit filled superstitious village world." Having written it, in part, with an Islamic audience in mind, he suggests that it might have been titled *Beginnings in the Doctrine of God for the Village Church in an Islamic Context*. Since he is concerned with doctrinal matters, he admits that it may be "a bit over the heads of many laymen but just hits the spot for many pastors." "Insights for the Islamic background of the book," Bailey writes, "are almost without exception from my teacher and friend, Dr. Kenneth Cragg."[5] By this time Cragg had written only two books: *The Call of the Minaret* (1956) and *Sandals at the Mosque—Christian Presence Amid Islam* (1959). Bailey may have read both books, but the insights he borrowed from Cragg were probably from Cragg's lectures that he had attended in Jerusalem in 1958.

The book is divided into four sections: God is Great, God is Light, God is Three in One, and God is Holy Love. Each section has four to six scenes comprising twenty scenes in all. Twenty-three characters appear in the book but only three characters engage in dialogue, which Bailey properly calls "trialogues." The three principal characters are based on village archetypes: Abdu, an earnest village farmer who is a seeker; Ba-seat, who lives up to his name, which means "simple," and provides some comic relief; and Yousef the Wise, who is the theologian of the group, a mouthpiece for Bailey. The character of Yousef, however, is based on Elder Musʿad of Deir el-Barsha, the village in Upper Egypt where Bailey had spent much time in literacy work in the late 1950s. Seeing Musid's life as "a living example of the holiness that is fulfilled in righteousness," Bailey dedicated the book to his memory.[6]

Bailey includes a number of parables in his thesis taken from the lives of common village people. For example, to illustrate the idea that human freedom is necessary if human beings are truly to love God, he tells the story of a mayor who lives in a town with the Bunyanesque name of the Hamlet of Ignorance. In the story the mayor rules that his people

---

4. Bailey, DOCTRINE OF GOD, ii.

5. Bailey, DOCTRINE OF GOD, i, iii.

6. In the book Bailey spells this Der al Barsha, but for consistency's sake, it is spelled Dier el-Barsha here. Bailey, DOCTRINE OF GOD, iii.

must love him, and so, of course, they come to hate him. Bailey's point is that God cannot simply command human beings to love him. Human freedom, therefore, is necessary. In explaining the nature of the new covenant, Bailey tells another story about the mayor of a small village. The mayor's garden has wild dogs guarding it at night so no one can pass. But the mayor can pass and anyone who is walking with him can pass safely. In the story, the garden is the world, the dogs are the devil, and the mayor is Christ who walks with human beings to keep them safe.[7] Both stories provide a frame of reference that Egyptian villagers would have easily understood and appreciated. Taking this approach, the book then attempts to explain concepts such as God's omnipotence, the Trinity, God's love and justice, grace, repentance, and restoration. To show how God can be both holy and love, Bailey has the characters in his trialogue perform a play within a play. It is a play about the second half of the parable of the prodigal son, which concerns the proud elder son who refuses to join the party. Bailey titles the play within the play "The Father and the Son Who is Not a Son."[8]

THE DOCTRINE OF GOD for Village People, being a master's thesis and not intended as a vehicle for new interpretations of the Scriptures or doctrine, was never reviewed in scholarly or popular journals. Bailey's underlying thesis is that villagers best understand theology that is presented in a story. Though his book includes a number of parables, playful dialogues, and a short play in the twenty scenes he presents, the theology in the book is generally simply placed in the mouth of the village elder, Yusef the Wise, who gives short lectures on key doctrines. In fact, there is no real story presented in this book. Its main strength is that it manages to pack a large amount of theology in twenty short scenes, but its approach would at times have been tedious and predictable for village listeners, and considerable discussion and instruction must have followed the presentation of the scenes for their lessons to be absorbed. On the other hand, his simple explanations of Christian doctrines, his attention to ideas relevant to Muslim and village listeners, and his inclusion of stories from village life would have been appreciated. Finally, in lessons eighteen and nineteen Bailey presents many of the ideas that he would later expound at greater length and depth in *The Cross and the Prodigal*.

---

7. Bailey, *DOCTRINE OF GOD*, 111.
8. Bailey, *DOCTRINE OF GOD*, 194–203.

Remarkably, he had already discovered in 1961 a number of key insights that he would continue to develop throughout his subsequent career.

~

Unsuccessful in their attempt to conceive a child, Ken and Mickey made the final arrangements in November 1960 to adopt a baby girl, Sara Jan, while she was still in her mother's womb. The Baileys never wrote anything specific about Sara's birth mother, and it is likely that they knew little or nothing about her. In 2005 or 2006, Ken wrote to Sara his only extant comment on the subject: "Your biological mother loved you so much she opted to carry you to full term and give you to people who could love you and take care of you. We started loving you three months before you were born."[9] On Monday, February 6, 1961, Ken and Mickey traveled to Columbus, Ohio, to collect their six-pound five-ounce infant, who had been born twelve days before on January 26. A heavy snowfall on the previous Friday had left the region paralyzed over the weekend. But by Monday the roads had been cleared and the Baileys were able to drive from Pittsburgh to Columbus, some 185 miles. On the return trip, they experienced another snowstorm in Ohio but fortunately soon drove through it, with little Sara resting comfortably in the back seat under a mound of blankets. Mickey, who worried on the way home about whether she was warm enough, kept reaching back and checking under the blankets to make sure that she was okay. It was a memorable day for Mickey, who recalled it vividly seventeen years later in a letter to her family.[10] Sara was baptized on April 21, 1961, in a ceremony performed by Mickey's two brothers in the ministry, Bruce and Dale, in Beulah Presbyterian Church, in Pittsburgh.

Ken and Mickey's furlough had begun in June 1960 and was intended to be a year and a half. Having completed his master's degree in a year, Ken began his return journey to Egypt around mid-August 1961, but Mickey stayed behind to complete a residence requirement for Sara's adoption and to have Sara put on her passport.[11] Consequently, she would not return to Cairo until late in October. Boarding a small ship at Hoboken, New Jersey, on August 16, Ken began the long sea voyage to Egypt. Though nine of his fellow passengers were also going

---

9. Ken to Sara, undated, ca. 2005 or 2006, Bailey Papers, box 28, folder 4.
10. Mickey to family, February 6, 1978, Bailey Papers, box 27, folder 5.
11. Mickey to friends, July 23, 1963, Bailey Papers, box 27, folder 1.

to Cairo and four of these were Presbyterian missionaries, Bailey was immediately overcome with loneliness and a desire to be with Mickey. During the course of the voyage, he would write to her virtually every day. To express his love, he twice quoted Shakespeare's Sonnet 29, wrote at least three love poems, and confessed that he was going to the upper deck every night to sing romantic show tunes to her. There was no one there to hear him, and the wind was strong enough to carry his voice away. The voyage included a visit to Barcelona where Bailey toured the Benedictine monastery of Santa Maria de Montserrat, settled in the crags high in the mountain of Montserrat above the city. But this did little to assuage his melancholy funk. The only time on the trip when he did seem able to shake off his loneliness and allow himself to enjoy the experience was in watching four bull fights in Barcelona. He filled two pages of single-spaced type to record the event and promised to take Mickey to the monastery of Montserrat and "maybe to a bull fight, if after this account you still want to go."[12] There is no record in the Bailey Papers that they ever attended a bull fight together. His ship moored in the inner harbor at Alexandria on September 3, and Bailey disembarked to move temporarily into an apartment at the Schutz School before moving on to Cairo and then returning to Minia.[13]

At a meeting with Jack Lorimer, Bailey asked about the progress of the publication of a book he had submitted to CEOSS before his furlough. Lorimer admitted that he had not even shown the book to Samuel Habib or Minis Abd al-Nur, the two leaders of CEOSS. Bailey had hoped that it would be translated by this time. Lorimer, who said he had not presented Bailey's book because he did not want to "prejudice the case one way or the other," seems to have realized before Bailey that CEOSS could afford to publish only a limited number of books. Bailey's book—perhaps an early version of THE DOCTRINE OF GOD—was in competition with other books written by Egyptians, especially it seems those by Samuel Habib. Bailey's ability to write effective books and plays, he eventually concluded, caused some jealousy and resentment among the Egyptian leadership.[14] Bailey soon learned that in his absence Samuel Habib had asserted his authority over the Literacy Campaign staff, which came completely under his sway. As a member of the *ancien regime*, Bailey

12. Ken to Mickey, August 28, 1961, White Volume.

13. This paragraph has summarized a series of letters that Ken wrote to Mickey during his return voyage to Cairo in August and September 1961, White Volume.

14. Ken to Mickey, September 10, 1961, White Volume.

was not sure how he would fit in with the new organizational patterns emerging. At the very least, he hoped to be left out of the administration of the program in order to avoid conflict.[15] After the worship service on Sunday morning, Jack spoke with Bailey about his relationship to the literacy campaign team. He concluded, "It is all very indefinite right now with the big thing unknown—Sam's feelings." The two concluded that Bailey should dedicate the winter period to a continued study of Arabic while they waited to see how the Egyptian leadership felt about him. In the meantime, Bailey found that the Egyptian staff seemed genuinely pleased to see him and that students were beginning to come to him to seek counseling about their spiritual lives, which he found both reassuring and rewarding.[16] Despite his agreement with Lorimer, Bailey worked with a church group to perform his play "The Father and the Son Who Is Not a Son"—the play within a play that he had included in his master's thesis[17]—which was to be presented in a church around the end of the first week in October. On October 9 he reported to Mickey that the play had gone well.[18]

In Bailey's sour mood, he took particular notice that the apartment where he was staying suddenly seemed noisy because of the family below. Soon he was also complaining that the family monopolized the stairway and roof, leaving their wash out to dry every day. Disgruntled, he decided to move to a new apartment. At this time, Menes Abd al-Nur had decided to move to an apartment across the hall from him in the same building. This made available his old apartment, which was on the first floor, overlooked the river, and was comparatively quiet. Bailey negotiated with the owner and came to an agreement. But later the owner tried to increase the rent and demand money up front. Ken, however, was adamant about the price and arrangements upon which they had agreed, and he eventually got what he wanted at the original price.[19]

On October 24, Mickey flew from New York with Sara and her parents, Leslie and Bertha Milligan, arriving three days later in Cairo. Ken met the plane, and he and Mickey showed her parents around Cairo

15. Ken to Mickey, September 13, 1961, White Volume.
16. Ken to Mickey, September 23, 1961, White Volume.
17. Ken's one-act play on the parable of the Prodigal Son is included in his master's thesis as "The Father and the Son who is not a Son." This can also be found under the title "Two Sons Have I not" in Bailey, *God Is . . . Dialogues*, 214–23.
18. Ken to Mickey, September 27, 1961, White Volume.
19. Ken to Mickey, September 13, 1961, and September 27, 1961, White Volume.

before departing for Minia. Her parents would remain with them for four months. Ken, Mickey, and baby Sara lived in an apartment on a short-term basis for three weeks before their new apartment was ready for occupation. When the Baileys and Milligans moved into the new apartment, it was full of mosquitos.[20] Over the next two months, with Leslie and Bertha's help, the Baileys fixed up the apartment. They installed a new bathtub and a sink in the bathroom. Since the window in the bathroom could not be opened, Ken and Leslie installed twelve shelves in the window space and painted them. Next, they tackled the large window in the dining room, which was broken and let in little light. Ken and Leslie installed shelves there too, giving them a coat of dark wood stain. They loaded a few books on them but mostly knickknacks. Placing a *Mushrabiyya* screen in the large main hall of the apartment, they separated the dining room from the living room. The living room was small and cozy, being furnished with a two-seat coach, chair, and piano. Sara, who had her own room that included a play pen, played there and in the sand pile behind the apartment building.[21]

The work assignment that CEOSS eventually decided to give Bailey fit well with his talents and interests. He wrote to his father, "I am to be a sort of freelance theological thinker, writer and preacher for the team. I am very satisfied and indeed pleased about it. Right now I am assigned the writing of six Bible study books."[22] The team he was working with included five others: Samuel Habib, the head of CEOSS; and Menes Abd al-Nur, who worked on translation and writing; Jack Lorimer, a fellow missionary who worked in the literacy and Bible study program in the villages; Harris, possibly the Egyptian pastor Harris Qeresa, who served in Minia at the Tahnasha church; and Fayez Faris, a local pastor in the area who had also recently served on the study committee for COEMAR. Feeling deficient in the area of modern philosophy and theology, CEOSS also assigned Bailey to teach a two-hour class every week on theology. This was not a mere sop to placate Bailey as Mickey commented that the students hardly knew the names of Karl Barth or Søren Kierkegaard. In addition to these activities, Ken spent every Sunday in the villages preaching and teaching, and much of his work week continued to be taken up with the study of Arabic.

20. Mickey to family, November 5, 1961; December 17, Black Volume, 432, 429.
21. Mickey to family, December 7, 1961, Black Volume, 428.
22. Ken to parents, January 14, 1962, Bailey Papers, box 27, folder 1.

Master's Degree and Work with CEOSS in Minia

At the beginning of the new year, 1962, Bailey began to teach a regular class on Kierkegaard for four students, using a room in a local Protestant school. When he saw that the school had lacked a bell for two years but that the church across the street had one, Bailey moved it to the house across the street, which took all of about ten minutes. He griped to his parents, "The complete helplessness and/or inertia of a certain segment of the country completely mystifies me."[23] In the same month a group of seven men came to Minia to hold a weekend conference among Protestant and Coptic church authorities, lay leaders, and youth to discuss a Christian radio project with a broadcasting station to be located in Addis Ababa, Ethiopia. Bailey was immediately drawn to the idea.[24]

The literature committee of CEOSS assigned Bailey the task of writing two books on the prophet Amos, one for the newly literate villagers and the other for pastors. There was then no book on Amos available in Arabic. Bailey began his study book on the prophet Amos perhaps by early March and was soon working assiduously at the task. Mickey commented, "You'd think he was going to write a commentary the way he is going at it, but I'm sure there will be new sermons from it as well."[25] By the end of March he was already trying out parts of it on the staff. In early April Mickey wrote that Bailey was visiting a nearby village to teach it to the literacy staff there and to try to discover areas that needed to be changed or improved before publication.[26] This village was probably Deir el-Barsha. Bailey wrote to his parents on April 26 that he had recently completed a study of the book of Amos with the CEOSS staff but had not completed the book itself. His deadline for submitting it for publication with CEOSS was April 26, but he missed it. He did not see any reason for rushing since CEOSS had not yet even begun to translate the book he had earlier submitted for publication.[27] Mickey was more forthright in her letter to the family on April 29. Ken, she explained, had asked the committee why they had set the deadline for April 26 when they had not yet begun to work on his previous book. He was told that his book was in the budget for 1963, but later in the meeting it became clear that Samuel Habib had revised one of his previously published books and wanted it reprinted that year though it was not in the budget or on the list of books

23. Ken to parents, January 29, 1962, Bailey Papers, box 27, folder 1.
24. Mickey to family, March 15, 1962, Black Volume, 426.
25. Mickey to family, March 15, 1962, Black Volume, 427.
26. Mickey to family, April 6, 1962, Black Volume, 424.
27. Ken to parents, April 26, 1962, Bailey Papers, box 27, folder 1.

to be published in 1963. It was apparent that they intended to use money for a book left unpublished to cover the costs of republishing Samuel's book. Bailey left the meeting deeply discouraged. Mickey summed up his feelings in a letter to the family: "One begins to have thoughts as to one's usefulness. I suppose integration is like adolescence—some make it and some don't. It certainly takes a certain type of personality for this type of thing. It is hard to be in a situation where you don't feel as tho you are really, deep down, wanted." Though Bailey was dispirited by his dealings with church leaders, Mickey commented that he was reenergized by working in villages. She wrote, "He always comes home in high spirits after being in Deir el-Barsha. It is so refreshing to be with simple people, who don't feel the need [to show], or even know, sophistication."[28] Ken and Mickey began to wonder if they were really wanted by CEOSS. The feeling of being superfluous—or worse, being an inconvenience or impediment—was further reinforced when Bailey's plans for touring the country with actors to stage productions of his plays was rejected by CEOSS.

Though CEOSS seemed to be strangely indifferent to Bailey's efforts at script writing, Dr. H. Kenn Carmichael showed real interest in his thesis. Carmichael had written the screenplay for *The Mark of the Hawk*, a 1957 movie starring Sydney Poitier, and was a scriptwriter for Radio Voice of the Gospel. The previous summer, Carmichael sought to interview Bailey in New York while he was on furlough, promising to pay the costs of the flight. When he traveled to Egypt that year to run a workshop on radio script writing, CEOSS did not invite Bailey to attend. Bailey, however, went anyway. As a result of this class, he wrote a radio play that was later recorded and, he wrote, "well received."[29]

At the Association meeting, which began on June 24, the Assignment Committee selected Bailey to replace Paul McClanahan as a teacher in the pre-seminary year program that operated on the Assiut College campus. McClanahan, who was being transferred to Cairo to work with a radio project, had begun a one-year pre-seminary course for students accepted at the Evangelical Theological Seminary in Cairo. Since the Synod would not be able to assume the direction and expense of the program, the mission decided to do so, believing the program to be vital for the preparation of students for seminary studies. A short-term

---

28. Mickey to family, April 29, 1962, Black Volume, 422.
29. Ken to parents, July 15, 1962, Bailey Papers, box 27, folder 1.

missionary named Daniel Gerhardt had been teaching the program for two years and would continue to do most of the teaching. The courses he taught were generally Arabic, English, and Greek. Though Bailey did not feel qualified to teach any of these, he did feel comfortable teaching other aspects of the program. He would work with Gerhardt while continuing to study Arabic. Since the program was not part of either the Synod's or the Mission's budget, Bailey would be responsible for raising funds to support it.[30] Given a list of names of interested donors, it would be his task to communicate with them as well as send out a regular newsletter about the program.[31]

The Association's decision to transfer Bailey, so far as he knew, was made to meet the needs of the pre-seminary program, but after he accepted the new position, he learned the embarrassing truth that he was no longer wanted at CEOSS, which confirmed his suspicion that he was not being encouraged as a writer due to jealousy of his talent and success. He wrote of the problem to his father, explaining that Jack Lorimer had informed him of Samuel Habib's "increasing hostility . . . to me and everything I was trying to do." That Habib expressed it behind his back made it all the more galling. Bailey was aware in May and June that he was becoming, in his words, "*persona non grata* in Minia with Sam and Minis," a hostility he continued to attribute to "professional jealousy."[32]

Bailey decided to accept the new position, perhaps with some regret but also with a conviction that the job might actually be better for what he hoped to achieve. "On the positive side," he explained to his parents, "the Assiut campus is a lovely place to live and raise one lively small girl. Then, too, the chance to teach and get to know the seminary students will be a rare privilege indeed; and I can continue studying and writing as I like—and get paid for doing it. What more could a man ask for?" More reflectively, he added, John F. Kennedy once remarked "that in politics you don't make friends you make allies. Basically, Sam [Habib] is a politician and allies are what he wants, not friends. I have offered him friendship but am not his ally in the party struggles of [the] Synod, and this has not been enough."[33] Though aware of the difficulties and frustrations

30. Mickey to family, July 2, 1962, Black Volume, 416.

31. Mickey to family, October 28, 1962, Black Volume, 401.

32. Ken to parents, July 15, 1962, Bailey Papers, box 27, folder 1. Also, found in the Black Volume, 412.

33. Ken to parents, July 15, 1962, Bailey Papers, box 27, folder 1. Also, found in the Black Volume, 413.

faced by her husband, Mickey also noted that there were some pleasant prospects that came with the new assignment. There would be a large mission house, a garden in which Sara could play, and children in the neighborhood whose company she could enjoy. There would also be fresh milk and vegetables, the nearby Assiut Hospital, and an English-language worship service.[34]

In the last week of July Bailey attended another workshop for radio script writing in Cairo run by H. Kenn Carmichael. Bailey made a point of getting to know the Carmichaels, both Kenn and his wife, Sue. After the workshop, Ken and Mickey went to stay at Sidi Bishr to take a break from the work in Upper Egypt. The Carmichaels were also in Alexandria, staying at the hotel that served as the headquarters for the moviemakers and actors who were then filming *Cleopatra* (1963), starring Richard Burton and Elizabeth Taylor, though only Burton was then in Egypt.[35] Ken and Mickey may have met with the Carmichaels at the hotel at this time to discuss radio scriptwriting. Kenn Carmichael was apparently aware of the hostile atmosphere in which Bailey worked at CEOSS; therefore, when Bailey wrote a ten-minute radio script, he gave it a private reading rather than insisting on the usual classroom presentation. Carmichael also asked Bailey to send any future scripts directly to him, bypassing the CEOSS committee. This was intended to avoid arousing Egyptian jealousies. Bailey saw the problem clearly, explaining to his parents, "As long as the attitude is 'anything you can do I can do better' deep resentments are built up when someone appears on the scene who in any area and anyway[sic], regardless of how limited, demonstrates this not to be true."[36]

Clearly, Bailey was caught between the rising need of Egyptians to assume leadership positions in their own country and the ongoing desire of missionaries to make significant contributions to the church, not simply recede into obscurity or, to use a biblical metaphor, hide their light under a bushel. Bailey, however, preferred to liken modern missionaries to medieval court jesters. They were required to make intelligent comments, but their observations could never be too shrewd or insightful. The modern post-colonial missionary faced a similar conundrum. If their contributions were innocuous and insipid, they were making no real contribution to the church. But if they proved themselves to be too helpful and even indispensable, they would be seen as attempting to

34. Mickey to family, July 2, 1962, Black Volume, 416.
35. Mickey to family, August 2, 1962, Bailey Papers, box 27, folder 1.
36. Ken to parents, August 19, 1962, Bailey Papers, box 27, folder 1.

Master's Degree and Work with CEOSS in Minia

return the church to the colonial era. Either tack could result in their marginalization or dismissal. This put Bailey in a deeply conflicted and frustrating position.[37]

**Figure 17. Mickey, Ken, and Sara Bailey,
Cairo, Egypt, summer 1962.**

---

37. Ken to parents, August 19, 1962, Bailey Papers, box 27, folder 1.

6

Immersion in Egyptian Culture and Ministry

1962–64

> For they [ancient Egyptians] conceived of their world as essentially static and unchanging. It had gone forth complete from the hands of the Creator.
>
> —Henri Frankfort, *The Birth of Civilization in the Near East*

Ken and Mickey moved to Assiut early in September 1962. Assiut College opened on September 15, but the pre-seminary course would not begin until October 9, giving Ken plenty of time to prepare. He would teach four hours a week, two hours on the Minor Prophets and two hours on homiletics in Arabic. Having spent much time preparing his book on Amos, he had ample material to teach the Minor Prophets. He planned, therefore, to concentrate on teaching homiletics in Arabic. There were only six students in the program, but later a seventh was added. They had been admitted to the seminary having met the minimum requirement of a secondary degree with an average grade of 55 percent (in the British system this was equivalent to a grade of C), but such a low standard meant that most of them would be mediocre students.[1] Bailey commented, "Two of them are quite good students and two others show some promise. In any case, I am enjoying the work immensely."[2]

In the February 1963 newsletter for the pre-seminary year at Assiut, Bailey wrestled with what it means to be a Christian servant in a foreign land where cultural assumptions are very different from ones' own. To illustrate his point, he told an amusing story of picking up some Egyptian hitchhikers in his car. Passing by a bus stand, a man called out, "Assssseeeeee-yeuuuuuut!" (Assiut). There was a crowd of village men at the stop, but Bailey in a kindhearted mood stopped his Volkswagen bug and offered to take three of them to Assiut, where he was headed. They agreed to his stipulation of three, but soon twenty men surrounded the car and eventually seven managed to pile in. Three were together and refused to be separated, and others had friends that they could not leave behind. Bailey fumed but he could do nothing as these were rough, unshaven men who would not take no for answer. Since there were still two hours of sunlight left, he felt himself to be in no physical danger. So, off they went down the road together. Bailey then asked the pertinent theological question: If a Christian chooses to become a servant, must he be a suffering servant? Moreover, in the servant-master relationship, who sets the rules? The answers came quickly. What kind of servant, he asked himself, sets the rules of his relationship with his master? Though he was infuriated with his passengers' deception and lack of consideration, he recognized that they were acting according to their own cultural rules, not his. He had no choice but to be a suffering servant.[3]

Bailey's May 1965 Pre-Theological Newsletter was titled "Moses and his Revolver," which recounted a student's presentation with which Bailey meant to convey the lack of historical perspective shown by many of his students in Upper Egypt. It began,

> "Moses was very angry," continued the student preacher. "He felt his blood hot within his veins. How could he be silent while this slave-driver beat one of his people? So, he drew his revolver out of its holster and shot the slave-driver dead."
> "Yes sir, he shot him dead!"

---

1. Mickey to family, October 8, 1962, Black Volume, 404.

2. Ken to family, October 21, 1962, Black Volume, 402.

3. Kenneth E. Bailey, "The Sun, the Road, and the Ride," *Pre-Theological Newsletter*, 3, no. 2, February 1963, in Bailey Papers, box 27, folder 1.

"I nearly rolled off my chair!" Bailey wrote. "Moses and his revolver—Hummmmm!" Yet the other students seemed to take it in stride: "No one batted an eye. No one laughed." Some may have suspected the presence of a historical incongruity, but they remained silent. None seemed in any way as stunned as their teacher. Bailey wrote that this lack of historical understanding was typical and perhaps was due to more than a failure of the educational system. It might be that, as Dutch Egyptologist Henri Frankfort explained in his recent book, *The Birth of Civilization in the Near East* (1951), ancient Egyptians lived in a static world with a worldview that included, Bailey paraphrased, "the implicit assumption that only the changeless was ultimately significant." Given this mentality, it was difficult for many Egyptians to imagine an ancient world that was radically different from their own.[4] When they read the Bible, they conjured up a biblical world in which characters "fight their enemies with guns, cook their food with kerosene pressure stoves in aluminum kettles, and tell time with Swiss watches."[5]

With his understanding of Egyptian culture and ministry deepening, Bailey resolved to avoid involvement in college affairs so that he could concentrate on preaching and teaching in the community. He explained to his parents as early as September 9, 1962, that he had already been asked to speak at the monthly meetings of the Mallawi Presbytery "for an hour and a quarter on any subject" as well as a monthly meeting of pastors, "and then the preaching dates are starting to roll in. So, it looks like I will not be idle."[6] On October 21, he wrote proudly to his family that he was already entirely booked through January. He estimated that, within a two-hour driving range of Assiut, there were at least 100 churches and that the actual number might be twice that.

Being much in demand, Bailey preached regularly—often every Sunday—in the surrounding villages. He also gave a monthly talk at the YMCA Club, and a fellowship group at Assiut University invited him to give a lecture five times that year.[7] Bailey did his best in these years to

---

4. Frankfort wrote, "For they conceived their world as essentially static and unchanging. It had gone forth complete from the hands of the Creator. Historical incidents were, consequently, no more than superficial disturbances of the established order, or recurring events of never-changing significance. The past and the future—far from being a matter of concern—were wholly implicit in the present. . ." Frankfort, *Birth of Civilization in the Near East*, 20–21.

5. Bailey Papers, Bailey Papers, Box 27, folder 1.

6. Ken to folks, September 9/16, 1962, Black Volume, 411.

7. Mickey to friends, July 23, 1963, Bailey Papers, box 27, folder 1.

Immersion in Egyptian Culture and Ministry

meet the needs of students, pastors, and lay people in new and innovative ways. For pastors, he formed a book club. Mickey wrote home in May, "His book club is going in high gear and it is really amazing the amount of money the pastors are spending for books out of their meager salaries, indicative of the need they feel."[8] With his father's help, Bailey ordered film strips from the Missionary Equipment Service in Chicago that would be helpful in the churches. There were four sets of "Moody Children's Bible Story Filmstrips in Full Color" and two extra bulbs for the projector.[9] He also prepared a panel of speakers to be recorded and broadcast over a radio station in Addis Ababa, The Radio Voice of the Gospel, which would reach the entire Middle East and Africa. Taking over a room in Assiut College, Bailey and the others "hung rugs, spread rugs, [and] put up a screen to try to approximate a studio."[10] Bailey was also involved in the ongoing effort to integrate the mission and the church. When he suggested that the two meet in a monthly social night in which they might learn what each other was doing, what assistance they might need, and to pray for one another, this was accepted, and Bailey was appointed the head of a committee to carry it out.

One area where Bailey was not successful was the establishment of a program for the 3,000 students of Assiut University.[11] He urged the establishment of a committee of laymen to review the needs of the youth and propose solutions, and he hoped to create a Christian center and hostel for them. He was thwarted, however, by two powerful elder clergymen in Assiut, the Reverends Girgis Grace and Badie Ibrahim. As these pastors were near retirement, they did not want Bailey's efforts in the university to upset their staid lives, and they regarded the rise of new leadership in the university as a possible threat to their power in the church. Therefore, they blocked every effort to advance youth work. Bailey believed that one of the two was particularly hostile—meaning Girgis. Bailey observed, "We have had some real heart-breaking committee meetings this past month in which all the fears, insecurities, jealousies and partisan spirit of

---

8. Mickey to family, May 19, 1963, Bailey Papers, box 27, folder 1.
9. _____, April 5 and 17 and May 15, 1963, Bailey Papers, box 27, folder 1.
10. Ken to Mother and Dad, November 11, 1963, Bailey Papers, box 27, folder 1.
11. Mickey to dear loved ones, Christmas letter 1963, ca. December 15, 1963, Black Volume. The number of students at the university is not certain in that, in her Christmas letter of 1963, Mickey said that there were 9,000 students.

the presbyters had a field day."[12] This would not be Bailey's last dealings with this man.

Figure 18. Ken with pre-seminary students in Assuit, Egypt, 1963. Pastor Emile Zaki is standing on the right.

Bailey's commitment to preaching in villages and other venues exposed him to Egyptian culture in a way that would come to radically transform his understanding of the New Testament. He explained, "It is trying but very rewarding to have this weekly opportunity to see and meet and talk with and learn from the village people."[13] These conversations became the basis for many of his insights into the village norms and customs depicted or assumed in the New Testament.

While Bailey was immersing himself in village culture, his Arabic was improving sufficiently that it was becoming difficult for native Arabic speakers to identify his accent. A group of absentee landowners, intrigued by an Arabic accent they could not place, encouraged him by asking if he were Lebanese.[14] Whether or not this was mere flattery, Bailey's command of the language was giving him a hard-won freedom to experiment. At an evening service in the village of Deir el-Barsha, where he had been going for years and felt comfortable, he tried a new approach. Instead of a traditional sermon, he engaged the congregation

12. Ken to family, November 11, 1963. Bailey Papers, box 27, folder 1.
13. Ken to family, October 21, 1962, Black Volume, 402.
14. Ken to family, October 21, 1962, Black Volume, 402.

Immersion in Egyptian Culture and Ministry

with questions and elicited their responses. This give-and-take method met his desire to learn more about what villagers thought, and it also demonstrated a growing confidence in his knowledge of Arabic.[15]

Bailey was committed to being in a village church every Sunday to deliver a sermon and to experience village life, but his attitude towards village society was one of ambivalence. He appreciated the warmth of fellowship among village people and the open-handed welcome they extended to guests. Yet he also despaired over the unchanging nature of village life. As he continued to reflect on the writings of Egyptologists, such as Henri Frankfort, his suspicions were increasingly confirmed: he believed that if he had visited Egyptian villages 5,000 years ago, he would have experienced the same norms and customs, with one exception.[16] The ancient Egyptians were a highly organized people, which they had to be in order to build the pyramids, temples, and palaces for which they are known.

To illustrate this point in a letter home, Bailey told of visiting a village church on a Sunday morning. He drove to the church, but the bridge crossing the canal was being repaired. Consequently, he had to leave his car and walk to the church, making him late for the service. However, it did not matter because the people were content to sing song after song while they waited. Though late when he arrived at the pastor's home, he was still served tea, and the pastor took time to feed his ducks. They arrived an hour late at the church where before entering the front door the two carried on the traditional competition as to who would allow the other to go first. As a visitor, Bailey was to go first. But since the pastor was senior, he should go first. This was repeated when they came to the pulpit regarding who would sit in the middle chair. And it was repeated again when they had to sit before the communion table. Though this was an important service because there was a guest preacher and a congregant was to be baptized, the church was not well organized. The church benches had been repaired during the week, but the carpenter had left a pile of wood scraps in the aisle. Behind the pulpit there should have been three chairs, but there were only two. Consequently, someone was sent to the pastor's home for a third chair. There should also have been three chairs behind the communion table, but there were none at all. The pulpit had not even been dusted, and Bailey imagined that he could have easily written his name in the dust that covered it. The problem was

---

15. Ken to Mother and Dad, November 4, 1962, Black Volume, 397.
16. Ken to Jack Lorimer, October 3, 1963, Bailey Papers, box 27, folder 1.

quickly, if indecorously, solved. Since there was water in the baptismal font in anticipation of the baptism planned that morning, the minister insouciantly dipped his handkerchief into the font and then wiped the pulpit clean. While the service was in progress, the minister requested that Bailey ask the baptismal questions. But since he did not have these questions in printed form, the minister had to write them out in Arabic for him to read aloud, and Bailey was forced to stumble though the questions, straining to read the minister's hasty scrawl. It was important that Bailey perform this service because then, he surmised, "the *'barala,'* the 'blessing,' the 'magical charm' of the sacrament will be more powerful if" administered by the distinguished foreigner rather than by their own spiritual leader. At the end of the service, all the women were required to leave the church before a single man could exit as it would be shameful for men and women to be seen leaving together. Despite the disorganization and adherence to antiquated ritual and superstition that Bailey experienced in the church, he believed that the service was conducted reverently and solemnly, that the congregants had worshiped in "spirit and truth," and that all came away inspired by the proceedings. Most important, Bailey found that the villagers' observance of ancient, unchanging customs shed light on the ancient world that would allow him to interpret the New Testament in terms of the customs and unspoken assumptions of this society. If for no other reason, he would continue to occupy his time with village life on Sundays, though the experience could often be tiresome.[17]

Thoroughly immersed in his ministry in Egypt, Bailey did not look forward to emerging, albeit briefly, to face the stiff deliberative winds of the mission's Association meeting held in late January or early February 1963. The main subject discussed by the missionaries was "integration"—their shorthand term for integrating the work of the mission with the Egyptian Church. There had been a conference in Lebanon to study the issue, and the Presbyterian mission board, COEMAR, had issued an advisory study. In his correspondence, Bailey never disagreed with the concept or the need for integration, but he did object to the animus behind it. He wrote, "There is a spirit loose in certain vocal circles that leads most such discussions into an overworked belaboring of the mistakes of the past and an attributing of everything that is or has ever been wrong with the church to some narrow-mindedness of the former generation of

---

17. Ken to family, December 16, 1962, Bailey Papers, box 27, folder 1.

missionaries, especially those who worked in the large institutions." He thought the missionaries were being used as "scapegoats" for contemporary difficulties in the church. Browbeaten by assertions of American activism and holding fast to a Western perspective, missionaries were reluctant to assert themselves or to fully employ their talents in the work of the church. Bailey was sufficiently vexed by the issue that he wrote a paper about it, which his colleague Ken Nolin subsequently toned down so that it could be circulated for reflection by the entire mission.[18]

Bailey enjoyed a brief respite from the pressures of mission and ministry in Egypt from March 22 to April 25 to help in the production of dramas to be performed in four Protestant churches in Jerusalem during Holy Week, April 7–13, 1963. The four participating churches were St. George's Cathedral, St. Andrew's, the Church of the Redeemer, and Christ Church. The play consisted of five episodes adopted from Don A. Mueller's play *Eyes upon the Cross: A Cycle of Plays for Lent*.[19] It was performed with two casts, one speaking English and the other Arabic. In each scene of the drama, a different set of people conversed at the foot of the cross. Financed by the fine arts department of COEMAR, the project was headed by Kenn Carmichael, with Bailey and Lorimer assigned by the mission agency to help with the dramas conducted in Arabic.[20] Bailey arrived a week before Lorimer and spent his time correcting the Arabic scripts, which had been translated from English. The productions were performed each night of Holy Week, the Arabic services at 5:00, and the English services at 8:00. Bailey noted that the churches were full each night. The productions were recorded and intended for presentation on television in the region, and Mickey hoped that someday they would be seen in Egypt.[21]

During Bailey's second term in Egypt, he published three books in Arabic.[22] The publisher Dar el-Thaqafa ("The House of Culture") does not

18. Ken to Mother and Dad, January 20, 1963, Bailey Papers, box 27, folder 1.

19. Mueller, *Eyes upon the Cross*.

20. Mickey to family, February 1963, and March 24, 1963, box 27, folder 1.

21. Ken to Mother and Dad, April 21, 1963, Black Volume. See too Carruthers, "Holy Week Drama in Jerusalem," 16–17.

22. Ken Bailey, "Suggested Plan for Writing for the Younger Churches" to Don Black, D. P. Smith, Willis McGill, and Ben Weir, received date stamp September 7,

have a record of these, but one at least was probably his master's thesis, THE DOCTRINE OF GOD for Village People (1964?). Another may have been a work he titled Reason & Christian Faith (1965?). There is no manuscript with this title among the Bailey Papers, and so it is probably lost. The third was a book on the prophet Amos, which he had been working on for over a year during the period of 1961–62. Fortunately, a full manuscript of this book has been preserved among the Bailey Papers. Having missed the deadline for submitting a manuscript for translation and publication set for April 26, 1962, an entire year was to pass before Bailey finished dictating the study into a tape recorder. The English version now in the Bailey Papers is entitled *The Roar of the Lion: A Study in the Prophecy of Amos the Shepherd*. Bailey included a note at the bottom of the title page, "Delivered to Menes Abd al-Nur, June 15, 1964."[23]

Bailey wrote the book in a clear, lucid style, using simple sentences that could easily be translated. Throughout the text, he strove to apply the teachings of Amos to the village life of contemporary Egyptians. To explain the sinfulness of the lavish lifestyles of the rich in the Israel of Amos's time, Bailey uses an Arabic proverb: "A man who has extra money buys a pigeon and lets it fly." In other words, the rich Arab flaunts and wastes his wealth.[24] And Amos's description of righteousness as an "ever flowing stream" becomes, in Bailey's hands, "like the Nile river that never runs dry," a stream of water that fills valleys, human hearts, market places, courtrooms, and the temple (Amos 5:24).[25] When Amos rails against those who idle their time away on ivory beds or singing trifling songs, Bailey asks his Egyptian contemporaries, "Do we sit with the men in the coffee shops or the women on the balconies who stare hour after hour into the street?"[26] Finally, Amos taught that God is the lord of all creation, history, and humanity. He is present everywhere—in the market, the courts, and home. And he is God alone, without any other gods. Bailey asks his Egyptian readers, "Is God for us God alone? Or do we worship other spirits? Are we afraid of evil spirits in the night and evil

---

1966, RG 424 Presbyterian Historical Society.

23. Kenneth E. Bailey, *The Roar of the Lion: A Study in the Prophecy of Amos the Shepherd*, typescript, Bailey Papers, box 12, folder 2. The pagination is confused, but I count 190 pages. To avoid confusion, I will reference chapters, not page numbers.

24. Bailey, *Roar of the Lion*, ch. 10.

25. Bailey, *Roar of the Lion*, ch. 15.

26. Bailey, *Roar of the Lion*, ch. 16.

spirits in the tombs and evil spirits in the abandoned well?"[27] Though Mickey wondered why Ken had lavished so much time on this book, *The Roar of the Lion* was clearly a labor of love for him, one that gave him an opportunity to write another book as well as to seek to find ways to make the message of Amos relevant for traditional villagers in Upper Egypt.

The second book that Bailey saw published in Arabic was his master's thesis, THE DOCTRINE OF GOD *for Village People*. The book has four sections, but only three were translated. With the book in print, Bailey recognized that the "moment of truth" had arrived in which the usefulness of his plays would be tested.[28] In a nearby village, Jack Lorimer staged some of the plays during a two-week period, and Bailey invited the players to perform in a church in Assiut, relieving him of the need to write at least one sermon.[29] In May, three of the plays were performed in the space in front of a village church as the crowds were too large for the church building. On the nights that Mickey was present, she guessed that there were from 500 to 700 people viewing them. Bailey anxiously watched the crowds to see how they would react to the performances.[30]

When president John F. Kennedy was assassinated on November 22, 1963, the Baileys did not learn of it until they listened to the radio the next morning. They were genuinely surprised and heartened by the Egyptian response of sorrow and the offering of condolences. Egyptian schools put their flags at half-mast in honor of the fallen president, and services of mourning were held in churches and mosques throughout the land. The week following the assassination, Egyptian papers devoted half their space to articles on Kennedy and coverage of the funeral at Arlington National Cemetery. With the entire country of Egypt in mourning for the American president, the missionaries cancelled their traditional Thanksgiving meal in the garden at Assiut College. No feasts of any kind are appropriate during a mourning period in Egypt and would have been interpreted as a sign of disrespect. Instead, there was a special service that evening, and the Baileys invited a few friends over afterwards. In lieu

---

27. Bailey, *Roar of the Lion*, ch. 20.
28. Ken and Mickey to Dear Loved Ones, Christmas 1963, Black Volume.
29. Mickey to family, April 28, 1963, Black Volume, 375.
30. Mickey to family, May 19, Bailey Papers, box 27, folder 1.

of a formal Thanksgiving meal, the missionaries went to the desert the following Friday for a picnic lunch.[31]

For Christmas that year, the Baileys put up a Christmas tree for which Ken crafted some handmade ornaments: decorated pine cones and walnuts, and also long wood curls that he made with his planer. Four-year-old Sara, who was fascinated with the tree, was given several "reindeers, stars, and bells" so that she could have the pleasure of hanging them on the lower branches of the tree. The Baileys had twelve guests over for Christmas to celebrate with them.[32] In a letter to his family, Ken explained that he was ambivalent about Christmas in Egypt. He appreciated the lack of commercialization of the holiday and that his colleagues were united in seeing Christmas as a religious event. But since Christmas is celebrated on January 7 in Egypt, he found himself teaching classes during the week before the celebration of Christ's birth. He declined to teach on December 25, but he was present in class on December 24 and 26. Though Egyptians did not recognize December 25 as a holy day, they scarcely celebrated Christmas even on January 7. Bailey observed, there were "no special customs, no gaiety, no gifts, no tree, no cards (for the most part)." When he was asked to talk about Christmas in Egypt while on furlough in the States, he declined, explaining that it is scarcely celebrated at all.[33]

The first half of 1964 held many frustrations for Bailey. At the Association meeting, which was held sometime in January or early February, the missionaries discussed the ongoing issue of integration. Writing to his parents, Bailey explained that the committee on integration had made no progress. Though the mission had invited the church to send members to participate and vote in its meetings, the church had declined because it feared committing itself. Bailey also noted that American missionaries in South Sudan would be expelled that year. But since the country seemed to be headed for civil war, their expulsions might be a blessing in disguise. He also groused about the church's seminary in Cairo, finding it deficient in leadership and scholarly commitment. In a separate letter, Mickey explained to the family that the Association had decided to sell the Sidi Bishr Camp property. This was an emotionally wrenching decision for the missionaries and the debate preceding the

31. Mickey to family, November, 24, 1963; Ken to family, December 1, 1963, and Ken to Mother and Dad, December 1, 1963, Bailey Papers, box 27, folder 1.

32. Mickey to family, January 12, 1964, Black Volume.

33. Ken to family, January 12, 1964, Bailey Papers, box 27, folder 1.

decision was heated since the camp held so many fond memories for them as well as being a place for rest and relaxation that did not require leaving the country. But the decision was made in response to the camp's mounting problems, not the least being its expenses. In lieu of the Sidi Bishr camp, the missionaries decided to make a campsite in Cyprus their summer vacation spot. Bailey was designated the manager of the camp, which would require a great deal of remodeling to make it practicable. Consequently, it would not be ready until the summer of 1965, giving missionaries one more summer to enjoy Sidi Bishr.[34]

Following the Association meeting, Bailey joined a group of nineteen expats on a camel trek into the Eastern Desert to visit the famous well of Bir Shaytoun.[35] He had been part of a similar expedition in 1960, but at that time there were only four present and the trip was poorly planned. Bailey described this earlier trip in his book *Jesus through Middle Eastern Eyes* (2008). On this occasion, one of the travelers' goat-skin water bags leaked, and the group soon ran out of water as the temperature in the Sahara Desert rose to 110 degrees Fahrenheit. For a day and a half they pressed on without water. "My mouth," Bailey wrote, "became completely dry, and eating was impossible because swallowing felt like the rubbing of two pieces of sandpaper together. My vision became blurred and the struggle to keep moving became harder with each step." He also worried that should the group find the well dry, their armed guards would seize their camels and leave them to die. Unfazed, Bailey quipped that the experience provided him with plenty of sermon material for his home furlough in 1960–61.[36] The group in 1964 included ten people from the Schutz School as well as ten missionaries. Mickey prepared food for four days, anticipating that the journey would require a day and a half out, a day at the well, and a day and a half back.

Beginning from Assiut, they drove to a village in the desert that would serve as their staging ground. Though they had registered with the local authorizes in advance, when the group arrived, they found that their intentions were a complete surprise to them. The Camel Corps needed to be notified to accompany them, and they were thirty miles away. Nevertheless, they arrived in the village at 10:00 a.m. Still, there were delays, and the group did not set out until 4:00 p.m. The whole

34. Mickey to family, March 8, 1964, Black Volume, 336.

35. There are a variety of ways to spell this in Arabic. I follow here the spelling Bailey gives in *Jesus through Middle Eastern Eyes*, 128.

36. Bailey, *Jesus through Middle Eastern Eyes*, 76–77.

village of about a thousand people came out to see them off—and to try to shake them down as well. "The Camel Corps here," Bailey explained, consists of "Sudan tribesmen from the desert tribes between Egypt and the Sudan [in other words, Nubians]. They are about as noble a race as inhibit the entire Middle East. Quiet, very polite, disciplined, considerate, conscientious, fearless, and with a great inner stability stemming from their pride in their tribe and its honor."[37] Since the corpsmen rode racing camels and the expats had only village pack camels, the corpsmen rode in circles around the group so that they would not soon out pace them. Bailey was at the head of the group. After two hours, he spied the cliffs that border the valley of the well that was their destination. In another hour, he located a dry riverbed that would be an ideal spot to spend the night. Exhausted from the day's journey, after setting up their pup tents and enjoying a brief meal, the weary travelers went to sleep at 8:00 p.m. Rising at 5:30 a.m., they were on the move again by 6:45 a.m.

Bailey was able to take in more of the scenery that he had missed or forgotten on the first trip. He wrote that he observed "all kinds of little valleys, dry river beds, interesting rock formations. The last time we couldn't think or see anything except the ever-beckoning pool of water." They traveled for eight hours that day, alternating between riding and walking. "Each in turn is a relief," Bailey explained. "It is a relief to get on the beast to ride a while and then after a while it is a relief to get off." On this second day, they came to Trippel Valley where the well of Bir Shaytoun lies "in a canyon in a canyon"—that is, there is an upper and lower valley. They camped in the upper valley to be near to the well. There are ancient steps leading down to the valley below, which Bailey surmised were probably craved out by the Romans. The steps, however, were worn, and rather than risk a slip or fall, the group lowered their supplies down to the valley floor by rope. The well is actually a pool fed by an underground source, and its water is 104 degrees Fahrenheit, too hot to swim in at the end of the day. Bailey was thrilled by the beauty around him: "the very barrenness of the desert, the surrounding canyon, and then this unspeakably beautiful pool that should be in Switzerland and for some reason is out here in the Eastern Desert, is really breathtaking. If this place were in the States, it would be a national park. I would guess that, aside from us, there are less than half a dozen Europeans who have ever seen it." The next day they swam in the pool. The trip back,

---

37. Ken to family, March 8, 1964, Black Volume, 338.

Bailey reported, was uneventful, but he was pleased to see the village, in its verdant surroundings, from which they had departed.[38]

When Bailey returned from his trip into the Eastern Desert, he soon learned that his fears for the missionaries in Sudan had been fully realized. On February 27, 1964, the Sudanese government issued a decree expelling all foreign missionaries in South Sudan. Between the date of issuance and March 9, about 300 missionaries departed Sudan. Many traveled to Cairo, where they remained for a time.[39]

While the young church in South Sudan was imperiled by the actions of the government, Bailey felt that the Evangelical Church in Egypt was hobbled by its own leadership. This feeling had been building in him for years, but it came to the surface while he was attending a synod meeting in the last week of March. These meetings, he explained to his parents in a letter home, consisted of about 200 men, both elders and pastors, and were held in churches. The men were informally ranked by age. The oldest members, about fifteen pastors between the ages of sixty-five and eighty-six, though most were between the ages of seventy and seventy-five, sat in the first four pews. The pastors in these front rows did almost all of the talking while the elders did not speak at all. Rows five through twenty held the men between ages thirty-five and sixty-five. Though they made up the majority of the synod, they had no power and were limited to an occasional comment. The last ten rows held the pastors and others who had graduated in the last fifteen years from seminary, and they had no voice or power whatsoever at these meetings. These men, however, enjoyed a good time of fellowship with each other while their elders droned on in the front. Few decisions were ever made at synod meetings because the losers would feel that their honor had been impugned. Also, when a vote was taken, the losers rarely took no for an answer, and the debate just continued but with greater fervor. After a period of debate, most issues were simply referred to committee where they underwent further study. The moderator of the synod, he said, was in his dotage and was also a hypochondriac.[40] In a letter in the previous week, he referred to him as an example of Egyptians' "crippling respect for age."[41]

---

38. For Bailey's entire account of the trip, see Ken to family, March 8, 1964, Black Volume, 338–40.
39. Mickey and Ken to family, March 29, 1964, Black Volume, 333.
40. Ken to family, April 5, 1964, Black Volume, 330.
41. Ken to family, March 29, 1964, Black, Volume, 333.

After four days of debate and discussion, little was accomplished. At the very least, wrote Bailey, the synod might have made the decision to hire the Reverend Faheem Aziz, who was soon to complete a master's degree at Louisville Presbyterian Theological Seminary in the area of New Testament Studies. He intended to return to Egypt in June but did not yet have a job. Nevertheless, the synod decided to refer the matter to a committee for further consideration. Bailey concluded with rash but understandable frustration: "The best thing that could happen to the church here would be a dozen good funerals!"[42] In another letter he concluded that the septuagenarians and octogenarians ruling the Evangelical Church were men living in the past who paralyzed the institution, preventing it from taking any action or initiative. Moreover, they limited the work of missionaries, providing them with little meaningful work to pursue and forbidding them from beginning new ventures. The result was that, in the past year, seven missionaries had retired and nine had resigned, but only seven new missionaries had been assigned to fill the depleted ranks. He concluded that missionaries, in their frustration with church inertia, were ready to leave Egypt and look elsewhere for meaningful work.[43]

Bailey believed that the problem of geriatric and ineffectual leadership was shared by the church's seminary, the Evangelical Theological Seminary in Cairo (ETSC). He wrote, "The [former] president of the seminary [Ghobrial (Gabriel) Rizqallah] is approaching ninety and is totally blind," having "gone blind only in his later years." Following his term as president, he was continuing to serve as the seminary's only professor of theology. ETSC was divided into three cohorts of students, and this professor regularly met with each of them. The students were required to come to class and read papers that they had written to which he would respond with comments. The result was crushing boredom. "Some students sleep," Bailey wrote, "others get caught up on the morning newspaper, some have breakfast, others play chess, and the remainder slip quietly out the door." Administrative decisions at the seminary had stood at a standstill for five years and records were not being kept. Three other professors at the seminary, he wrote, "are also well beyond retirement age and qualified to teach only by the wildest stretch of the imagination." The board of trustees responsible for the hiring of professors, being well

---

42. Ken to family, April 5, 1964, Black Volume, 331.
43. Mickey/Ken to family, November 22, 1964, Black Volume, 306.

aware of the situation, considered a committee report ten years before that recommended that the then-current president be given honorary status and that some of the older professors be replaced. The report was duly debated and then sent back to committee for further study, where it had languished ever since.[44]

Despite the frustrations Bailey felt with the synod and seminary, he continued to seek to do innovative work in the areas of his interests. In early March, he began to organize a trip for seminarians to visit the Holy Land, where he would conduct their tour. The trip would be financed by a surplus in the funds he was collecting for the pre-seminary program and by special appeals he was making to donors for this purpose. In the village of Deir el-Barsha, he organized an experimental conference for the entire local presbytery.[45] It began with a lecture on a biblical passage; then a panel of pastors discussed the passage; and finally, the people on the floor offered their comments. When everyone had had their say, the speaker presented a lecture on the next passage. The conference was held for three hours in the morning and succeeded in holding the attention of the congregation, which consisted of the leaders, nearly the entire population of the village, and thirty-seven delegates from other places who had paid to attend.

Bailey's greatest excitement was for directing university students in the performance of three scenes from Don A. Mueller's play *Eyes upon the Cross*, which he had also helped to direct in Jerusalem the previous year. They were performed in Arabic, but the narration was in English. These scenes were staged in an English service in Assiut but also in the village of Abu Tag, which was about an hour and a half drive from Assiut. In a letter home, he explained that theater and plays were new phenomena in Egypt and had only been introduced by Westerners in the twentieth century. Previously, actors did not fully memorize their lines and relied on prompters, who sat in the wings reading the entire play as the actors performed. Understandably, priests in the Coptic Orthodox Church did

---

44. Ken to family, April 5, 1964, Black Volume, 330. Ken wrote his account of Ghobrial Rizqallah as though he were still the president of the seminary. However, Emile Zaki, who graduated from ETSC in 1958, recalls that he served as president from 1947 to 1961 and then continued on as a professor of theology.

45. In this letter of Mickey and Ken to family, May 3, 1964, Black Volume, 326, Ken gave the name of the village as Hour. He seems to also have mentioned this conference in a separate letter to his father dated April 26, which is not in this collection. When questioned in this letter by his father about the name of the village, in a letter of Ken to Mother and Dad, May 4, 1964, he gave the name as al-Barsha.

not allow plays or scenes acted in their churches because they were seen as "entirely too frivolous for serious worship." But Bailey required that actors memorize and practice their parts, resulting in polished theatrical presentations that were beginning to change minds. "It was a brand-new experience for the actors," Bailey wrote, "and once having tasted it, they really were thrilled by it. They are really dedicated Christians, and once they became gripped by the play and saw its potential as a powerful message, they took it very seriously indeed as a spiritual responsibility."[46]

Though sometimes frustrated by the leadership in the church, Bailey at this time seemed to be hitting his stride as a missionary and was looking forward to years of creative and fruitful labors in Egypt. Moreover, he continued to pursue writing. The English version of his book on Amos had by this time been reviewed by two individuals, one a Dutch professor at the seminary. Having read their comments, he was preparing a final revision of the manuscript and looked forward to seeing it translated into Arabic and published. At this time, he had also been asked to write similar books on the First Epistle of John and on the subject of existentialism. Most important, he was working on a new interpretation of Luke 15, a project that would bring his village work in Egypt to an unexpected fruition and send his career in a new direction that he would follow for decades to come.[47]

---

46. Ken and Mickey to family, May 3, 1964, Black Volume, 326.
47. Ken to Mother and Dad, May 4, 1964, Black Volume, 324.

— 7 —

Expulsion from Egypt and Furlough in Pittsburgh

1964–67

Even though the Jewish authorities and those who followed their lead pressed for the death of Christ (see Jn 19:6), neither all Jews indiscriminately at that time, nor Jews today, can be charged with the crimes committed during his passion.

—*Nostra Aetate* (document of the Second Vatican Council)

BAILEY'S WORK AS A missionary had largely been concerned with popularizing Western scholarship in the area of biblical studies for Egyptians raised in a traditional culture. While doing this, he learned that Egyptians also had something to teach him. Writing to his parents in May 1964, Bailey explained that he was writing a short book on Jesus' parable of the prodigal son (Luke 15:11–31), which interpreted the story using the insights he had gained from Egyptian village culture. The book at this point was a hundred-page rough draft that he titled *Through Peasant Eyes* but that would later have the published title *The Cross and the Prodigal*. As he explained excitedly to his parents, "I look at the chapter [Luke 15] through the eyes of the villager and try to see just what the parable means in these terms. There is a lot of material hidden in the stories that I am quite certain has never occurred to any Westerner and to few Easterners." Having already presented this material to different groups in various forums, he was confident that his reinterpretation of the parable was an accurate reflection of the way it would be readily interpreted by perceptive Egyptian villagers.[1]

By June 25, Bailey had completed his essay.[2] While vacationing with the family in Cyprus, he sent fifteen copies of the text to Dale and Doris Milligan, his brother- and sister-in-law, asking them—but really Dale—to forward copies to four of his Pittsburgh Theological Seminary professors and to others he designated. Bailey confessed that the manuscript contained many mistakes but hoped that these would be overlooked since he labeled the text a draft. The question he wanted his readers to consider was whether the material he was presenting was new. He feared that it might already be present in biblical commentaries that he was not well-read enough to have encountered. He was confident, however, that his interpretation was valid. If it turned out that it was also unique, he was considering the possibility of producing a series of commentaries on Jesus' parables as they might be interpreted by Middle Eastern villagers.[3]

Unfortunately, Bailey would have to wait until 1973, a further nine years, before his book was published. His lack of academic qualifications no doubt was a hindrance, and this was one of the reasons—as he would later explain—that he decided to earn a PhD. In the very year he obtained this degree, his book was published—even before his dissertation. This book was substantially complete in 1964, and Bailey probably added the play *Two Sons Have I Not* the following year. Sometime in the summer of 1965 short-term missionary Elizabeth Hill typed the completed copy, which included the play. Though he continued to work on the text in 1966, he dated the preface to the book 1965, and when it was finally published years later, he keep the date of the preface as 1965 and located its provenance as Assiut, Egypt.[4] Clearly, he wanted the world to know that this work was a product of his years in Egypt.

The seminary in Cairo at this time acquired a new president, Labib Mishriky. At the beginning of the academic year, he was only the president-elect but was already assuming responsibility for the seminary.

1. Ken to Mother and Dad, May 4, 1964, Black Volume, 324.
2. Mickey to family, May 24, and June 25, 1964, Black Volume, 320, 303.
3. Ken to Dale and Doris, September 16, 1964, Black Volume, 314.
4. Bailey, *Cross and the Prodigal* (1973), 11.

He wanted to move the pre-seminary course in Assiut to the campus in Cairo in the fall of 1965, and he wanted Bailey to become a full-time lecturer at the seminary. Since the number of students in the pre-seminary program had dropped from eight to three, there was plenty of room on the Cairo campus for them. Though Bailey must have seen this as an affirmation of his work, he was reluctant to move to Cairo just nine months before he was scheduled to return to the States on furlough, and he considered commuting from Assiut to Cairo by train, a trip of about six hours. But Bailey was not anxious about moving. Given the slow pace of change in Egypt, he knew that there was time to work things out.[5] In the five years that the pre-seminary course was in operation from 1960 to 1965, thirty-six students in five classes had received instruction, and all but three had passed the course.[6]

While Ken and Mickey had been serving their second term as missionaries in Egypt, the leaders of the Roman Catholic Church had been meeting in the Second Vatican Council in St. Peter's Basilica in Vatican City. The purpose, as declared by Pope John XXIII, was *aggiornamento*, the "updating" or modernizing of the church for the twentieth century. Meeting in six- to eight-week sessions held in the autumns from 1962 to 1965, the council produced sixteen major documents that were intended to reform various aspects of the church's theology and practice. In the fall of 1964, the Second Vatican Council issued one of its most controversial documents *Nostra Aetate* (Latin for "In our time"), which sought to clarify the church's teaching on antisemitism and, specifically, the guilt of the Jews for the judicial torture and murder of Jesus. The document repudiated the long-held view that God had cursed the Jews because they had rejected and murdered his son. The Jewish people were not, it insisted, responsible for the death of Christ, and the descendants of first-century Jews did not the inherit their ancestors' guilt for Jesus' passion. The Egyptian government, interpreting this document in political terms as a pro-Israeli statement, decided to weigh in on the declaration by rejecting the church's position.

At this time, Bailey was teaching two Bible classes in Assiut for seniors at the Pressly Memorial Institute (PMI), the female equivalent of Assiut College. The girls took the opportunity to ask Bailey his opinion of

5. Mickey to family, October 18, 1964, and Mickey/Ken, November 22, 1964, Black Volume, 308, 306.

6. Ken to friends of the Pre-Seminary Course, November 3, 1965, RG 424, Presbyterian Historical Society.

Nostra Aetate. He explained that the issue addressed by the Second Vatican Council was not political, but theological. Since Jesus died for the sins of the world, it was not theologically correct to argue that the Jews alone were responsible for his crucifixion. One of the girls then asked about the passage in Scripture where the Jewish people took upon themselves and their descendants the guilt for the death of Christ: "His blood is on us and on our children!" (Matt. 27:25). Bailey explained that they had no power or authority to make this assertion any more than a convicted criminal today, being led to execution, could pass along his guilt to his descendants merely by making a declaration. Bailey then explained his position:

> The high priest at the time of Jesus was a bad man. He was a liar and a cheat, and a provider of false witnesses. He is the one to be blamed for the death of Jesus. The Pope has not exonerated him. Everyone in Pilate's court who was responsible for sending Jesus to the cross are still blamed by the Pope. But God, the righteous judge, will neither blame their children or their grandchildren, let alone their descendants 2,000 years later.[7]

Bailey had made a theological pronouncement, but it was interpreted politically because it took exception to the position declared by the Egyptian government. As an American missionary, his statement soon reached the ears of Egypt's State Security, who interpreted it as pro-Israeli and anti-Arab. The leading minister in Assiut, a Reverend Girgis Grace, pastor of the Second Evangelical Church in Assiut, decided to use the occasion of his Sunday sermon to disassociate himself from any position that an American in Egypt might take on the issue. He and Bailey met the following week, and Girgis informed Bailey that what he had said had embarrassed the church. At this time Bailey was speaking regularly to a university group that met on Friday mornings at his church. Girgis asked him to stay away from the church until the matter had blown over, a request to which Bailey acquiesced. Privately, however, Girgis assured Bailey that of course he agreed with his statement on the matter. The students meeting at Girgis's church in Assiut were incensed, and the long smoldering conflict between them and Girgis burst into flame during the winter.[8] Other pastors defended Bailey's statement, including the

---

7. Lorimer, *Presbyterian Experience in Egypt*, 172. Lorimer's quotation has no citation and it may simply be a paraphrase of what Bailey actually said. In any event, the book was published about nine years before Bailey's death, and there is no record that he ever repudiated it.

8. Ken explained this incident in a letter to Rodney A. Sundberg, the Secretary

chaplain of Assiut College, Emile Zaki, who courageously submitted a written statement to this effect to authorities. Bailey suffered no immediate repercussions because of his public position, but it would be used against him the following spring.[9]

In the meantime, Bailey would enjoy the holiday season with his family and friends. Thanksgiving Day and Christmas were always important holidays for the Baileys, and Mickey usually went to great lengths to make these events as much like traditional American festivities as she could. For Christmas 1964, the Baileys invited John and Nancy Davies to join them on Christmas Day. Nancy wrote a brief description of the event, which is preserved in the Bailey Papers and quoted here in full as it gives a rare outsider's glimpse into the Baileys' lives:

> After three days in Cairo, we took an early morning train to Assiut (four hours),[10] arriving in time for lunch Christmas Eve, December 24th. Our hosts were Ken and Mickey Bailey and children [sic]. They live on the mission compound next to Assiut College where Ken teaches, in a big stone house, high ceilings, huge rooms. There are some trees, shrubs and flowers around the house but Assiut, more than a village, less than a city, a town, I guess, seemed dusty and poor to me.
>
> Everything in the house was lovely and so Christmasy. They had three single gals for Christmas dinner (teachers). There was a fire in the fireplace, a tree with lights and poinsettias from the backyard. Turkey and all the trimmings. I don't know how Mickey manages. To find a turkey in the area took some doing. Mickey makes her own salad dressings, ketchup, and pickles. She even made marshmallows for a frozen fruit salad plus all her own candy: peanut brittle and candied orange peel. They had Christmas stockings for all of us with little presents.
>
> [On] Christmas Eve we gather[ed] in the living room and I read *The Night before Christmas*. Ken read the story from the Bible. [On] Christmas morning we had devotions before breakfast.[11]

---

for the Middle East of the Program Office, September 24, 1965, RG 424, Presbyterian Historical Society.

9. Mickey to ____ [first page missing, probably sent to friends and supporters], ca. September 1965. For another interpretation of the story see Lorimer, *Presbyterian Experience in Egypt*, 171–72.

10. The Cairo-to-Assiut train usually takes about six hours, not four.

11. John and Nancy Davies, a letter titled "Christmas with the Ken Baileys, Assiut, Egypt," January 7, 1965, Bailey Papers, box 27, folder 1.

In the first two weeks of February 1965 the annual Association meeting took place.[12] As the work of the Association was rapidly being turned over to the Egyptian Church, the number of things to be discussed by the missionaries was decreasing, and the meeting lasted only three days with no evening sessions. The only committees that had consequential work to report were those responsible for finance, property, and personnel, the latter being responsible for making missionary assignments. Bailey's immediate assignment was to return to his work in Assiut, but his job description was slightly reworded. He described it this way to his family: "I am as of now to continue in Assiut as a general church worker with special emphasis on preparing Bible study materials for village churches." This was fine with him, and he looked forward to writing more dramas for the churches. For the summer, the Association assigned Bailey to travel to Cyprus in June to repair the camp and replace some equipment. Since the camp had been broken into by thieves the previous summer, Bailey was asked to secure one of the rooms with a steel door and reinforced window so that camp property could be safely stored there. Electricity and a gas water heater were also being added, and he would supervise their installation as well. In addition to these assignments, Bailey was authorized to take another group of seminary students to Jerusalem in the second and third weeks of July, and he was assigned to teach the Bible at an Arabic language conference in the last week of July. In the fall of 1965, he was to work at the seminary, but the nature of his assignment had yet to be clarified. The seminary board of trustees wanted him to teach English, but Bailey protested that he was not qualified to be an English teacher. He wanted to teach the students biblical theology or philosophy. Another issue, remarkably, was what language he would use as the medium of instruction. American professors were teaching in English, but Bailey wanted to teach in Arabic, seeing no reason to create an artificial language barrier that, in his case, was entirely unnecessary. As it turned out, this was more a problem for the American teachers than it was for the Egyptians, who saw no difficulty in Bailey teaching in Arabic. The Association also agreed that Bailey could continue living in Assiut and commute by train to the seminary.[13] At the completion of the 1965–66 academic year, he would return to the United

12. Ken and Mickey to family, January 24 and February 14, 1965, Black Volume, 297–99.

13. Ken and Mickey to family, January 24 and February 14, 1965, Black Volume, 297–99.

States on furlough, during which time he intended to continue his studies in biblical theology at Pittsburgh Theological Seminary.

Much of Bailey's time in the first half of 1965 was taken up with a legal issue. During the month of October 1964, four German students had passed through Assiut and asked if they might sleep overnight in the Baileys' garden. Bailey was pleased to oblige, but he was careful to comply with the legal requirement that he report the presence of these overnight guests to the local police. When the students passed through Luxor, the passport office there determined that their stay in Assiut had not been properly reported and fined Bailey $500. Although Bailey had official documents from the police that he had complied and the police themselves admitted as much, he nevertheless had to make a court appearance in Luxor to clear his name. Given the lugubrious nature of the Egyptian court system, Bailey anticipated having to travel to the court in Luxor at least four times. Since Luxor was five hours away from Assiut by train, this would be a time-consuming affair. Writing in February to his parents, he said that he had already spent six days on the matter and had barely started to resolve it.

Bailey observed that, when he preached on fear the previous week, there was dead silence in the congregation, which he felt indicated that "the subject was really hitting home."[14] The Egyptian government of President Gamel Abdel Nasser was revered by many Egyptians, but it was also feared. Recalling the story of his conflict with the Egyptian judicial system in his 1992 book *Finding the Lost*, Bailey wrote that in the four months that transpired before his trial in March 1965, "I experienced the psalmist's plight. I became a 'horror to my neighbors, an object of dread to my acquaintances.' Literally some would cross the street to avoid me. Invitations to preach were canceled. Committees of which I was a member did not meet. The phone seldom rang. No one wanted to have their car seen parked in front of my house." His shunning, however, was not total. An elder in an Assiut church accompanied him on the train to Luxor on the weekend before his appearance before the court, and the pastor of the Evangelical Church in Luxor asked him to speak in the worship service on the Sunday before his trial. Also, both men, he recalled with relief and gratitude, "marched me down the center of the main street of Luxor, sat me down in a sidewalk café in full view of the

---

14. Part of this letter is missing, so the date and addressees are not given, but the letter was almost certainly sent to his parents sometime in February 1965, Black Volume, 294.

town and *fed me a meal*! They prepared a 'table before me in the presence of my enemies.'"[15]

On March 21, Mickey wrote home to the family that Bailey had been declared innocent in two of the four cases before the courts. The third was judged but the verdict had not yet been rendered. Later he learned that it had been decided in his favor. On the fourth count, he was judged guilty but intended to appeal, for which he had a court date in late April.[16] Writing from Cyprus in May, where he could express himself without fear of government surveillance, he explained that, in this fourth case, he had been tried but never given any notice of the court hearing. Because of the common people's genuine fear of government, rumors quickly spread that Bailey was in trouble with the authorities. The result, Bailey explained, was that "The rumors grew, and grew to incredible proportions and were scattered to the far corners of the country. The presbytery even had a debate over the matter (mercifully in my absence) and with two absenting votes gave us a resounding vote of confidence. All the 'he saids' and 'we answereds' and intrigue and suspicion and accusations involved would fill a book easily." By this point, however, Bailey was confident that the controversy would soon "blow over."[17]

In addition to this legal dispute, Bailey also had to deal with the ongoing conflict with the leading pastor of Assiut, the Reverend Girgis Grace, who opposed his efforts and that of the university students to establish a youth hostel and ministry. "He has tried to sue me," Bailey wrote, "as one more pawn in the battle and has not succeeded."[18] What this suit was cannot be known with certainty. However, in March 1965, Mickey also wrote of another case brought against Bailey, explaining that a church worker had brought the case against the mission but in Bailey's name. The court dismissed the case when it became clear that Bailey had no responsibility for mission affairs in the matter at hand.[19] This was probably a frivolous suit brought merely to put more pressure on Bailey. The controversy was actually between the students and the pastor. Bailey explained that hostility between them meant that the pastor had

---

15. Bailey, *Finding the Lost*, 207-8.

16. Mickey initially said the date was April 27; see Mickey to family, March 21, 1965. But she later reports the date as April 29; see Mickey to family, May 18, 1965, Black Volume.

17. Ken to friends, May 19, 1965, Black Volume, 10–12, 24–27.

18. Ken to Mickey to ___, undated letter (ca. late May 1965), Black Volume, 291.

19. Mickey to family, March 21, 1965, Black Volume, 302.

no ministry among them; and out of spite, Girgis refused to allow the students to invite him to participate at the university meetings held in his church. "Most people," Bailey wrote, "fear and despise him and leave the field for him to dominate." Nevertheless, after five years of discussion, the Youth Committee of the Synod finally authorized the establishment of a youth hostel on a vacant floor in one of the dormitories at Assiut University. Yet the decision had come so late that Bailey feared that the success of the proposal had been compromised. Nearly despairing of making any progress, Bailey wrote: "And I guess the work of the church is politics, and I am not a politician. Increasingly one is burdened with the almost crushing handicap of nationality. All the things that need to be said and done that I understand and can in some way handle seem to need to be said and done by a local leader. I am quite willing to follow the lead—just so someone will lead."[20]

Although Bailey would have avoided church politics if he could have, circumstances seemed to move ineluctably against him—beginning with the pre-seminary program. The number of students in the pre-seminary course he offered had been steadily shrinking. In the 1961–62 academic year there were seven; in the 1962–63 year there were six; and in the 1963–64 year there were only three—two Egyptians and one Sudanese. It was, in part, in response to this declining enrollment that the seminary had decided that the pre-seminary course should be moved to Cairo for the 1964–65 academic year. However, since Bailey would continue to live in Assiut while commuting to Cairo, in the spring the mission asked the two presbyteries around Assiut if they wanted Bailey to continue to work with them. Bailey had been active the entire time he lived in Assiut, often preaching in village churches. Consequently, he was a well-liked and well-respected minister in these presbyteries. As Mickey observed, Ken brought to their churches "fresh ideas and help." Had he been an Egyptian, they might have seen him as a threat, but as a foreigner he could be welcomed as a visitor coming only to assist.[21] One presbytery immediately endorsed Bailey's continuing to work with them. The presbytery that took in the city of Assiut, however, was dominated by the two church leaders, the Reverends Girgis Grace and Badie Ibrahim, who had opposed all of Bailey's efforts to establish a program for

20. Ken to Mickey to ___, undated letter (ca. late May 1965), Black Volume, 291.

21. Mickey to [probably friends and family], ca. September 1965, Black Volume, 268–69.

university youth in the city.[22] At the synod meeting in which the decision on Bailey's continued work in the community was made, the Reverend Girgis was the moderator. When Reverend Badie moved that the synod report that it had no need of Bailey's services, there was no second from the floor. Moderator Girgis, therefore, stepped down from his position in order to second the motion himself and then speak in its favor. To his surprise, the other members of the synod stood solidly behind Bailey and opposed him and Badie. When the motion came to a vote, it was overwhelmingly defeated, to the great chagrin and humiliation of these two church kingpins.[23]

After a summer break in Cyprus, Ken and Mickey returned to Egypt at the end of August as they needed to renew their visas and Ken's work permit, which were issued annually and expired on September 8. As required by law, Bailey submitted the forms to renew his work permit first, but when he went back to the government labor office, he learned that it had been rejected. The office had received a letter from the Ministry of Education in Cairo that it was not to be renewed because of a complaint about Bailey that had been made by a pastor in Assiut—Bailey's nemesis. The police summoned Bailey to their office on September 8 and informed him that he had one week to depart the country—that is by September 15.[24]

The Egyptian government never gave a clear reason for its decision not to renew the Baileys' visas and Ken's work permit. And when sympathetic church figures sought to investigate at the government ministry, they were told not to make any inquiries then as the time was not yet propitious and they would simply receive a "flat no." The Baileys, however, believed that they were able to piece together the reasons from various sources in the church. The pastor-patriarch of Assiut and his close ally in the ministry could not let their humiliating defeat at the synod stand without taking some action, however vengeful. The pastor complained to his contacts within the secret police about Bailey's activities, probably

---

22. In some versions of the story, Badie Ibrahim is presented as the President of Assiut College; however, I am informed by Emile Zaki that he became president after Bailey's departure from Egypt.

23. Mickey to [probably family], ca. September 1965, Black Volume, 268–69. This three-page letter, of which the first page is missing, is crucial because it explains the Baileys' expulsion from Egypt. Bailey tells the same story in a letter to Rodney A. Sundberg, September 24, 1965, GR 424 Presbyterian Historical Society.

24. Mickey to [probably friends and family], ca. September 1965, Black Volume, 268.

highlighting his response to the Vatican II decision regarding the guilt of the Jews for the death of Jesus. "Of course," Mickey wrote, "once the church pastors found out—and nothing remains a secret in Egypt—we had a steady stream at the house of callers. People were most concerned and kind and gracious. I don't think we had a meal at home the whole last week. And no one asked what had happened. All seemed to know the basis of it all. The Christian community of Assiut was upset as well as the mission group. If it is so easy to expel one, all are wondering who would be next?" Among the Baileys' visitors was the nephew of the pastor who was the source of their expulsion. No friend to his uncle and a friend of Bailey's, the man explained that, when his uncle was defeated at the synod, he vowed not to rest until he succeeded in having Ken Bailey and Ken Nolin[25] expelled from Assiut. Bailey later wrote, "It was a very trying time in the last two weeks in Assiut, in that the entire community was sure Girgis and Badie were responsible and I had to listen to a lot of very unpleasant *kalam* [gossip, but literally "words"]. I didn't care if it was true or not—I just had niffs [literally, an unpleasant odor] to even talk about it."[26]

Although the Baileys were scheduled to return to the United States on furlough in June 1966, they had moved up the date of their departure, purchasing airplane tickets to the States for September 14, 1965. They had planned to return early because Mickey was pregnant, and they were worried that given her medical history there might be complications with the delivery. Consequently, when they were ordered to leave by September 15, they were prepared to travel, though they had to completely rethink their packing. In the end, Mickey wrote, they took very little out of the country: "one trunk, two boxes of books, and a screen [*mashrabiya*], which we very much wanted."[27] Bailey saw the hand of a merciful God in their preparations to return to the States early. Nevertheless, they were greatly shaken by this turn of events as they ruefully set about packing their things to leave Egypt, not knowing if they would ever be allowed to return.

---

25. Mickey to [probably friends and family], ca. September 1965, Black Volume, 268–69. Although Ken Nolin had nothing to do with the immediate controversy, he was seen by the Girgis and Badie as uncooperative. This is based on an interview with Emile Zaki.

26. Ken to Carol Geren, October 2, 1965, Black Volume, 165.

27. Mickey to [probably friends and family], ca. September 1965, Black Volume, 269.

On October 18, Bailey traveled to Presbyterian Church headquarters at 475 Riverside Drive, New York, for the Middle East Task Force Consultations. The following day he met with Dr. Rodney Sundberg, the church's Secretary for the Middle East. They discussed the reasons for the Egyptian government's decision not to renew Bailey's visa and work permit and then, briefly, his future plans. Apparently, they agreed that he would take an early furlough and study at Pittsburgh Theological Seminary before beginning a new assignment.[28]

Bailey audited a number of classes at Pittsburgh Theological Seminary during the academic year of 1965–66, studying Koine Greek and Hebrew as well as the New Testament. He explained to his parents, "The big project for the year is to get some real command of the two biblical languages. I have forgotten, or perhaps never learned, so much grammar that it is pitiful. I don't see much light right now, but then I remember that I didn't see much light at many points in the Arabic studies as well." Though language study was grueling for him, he enjoyed auditing courses on the New Testament, studying what appealed to him without having the strain of preparing for exams. He particularly enjoyed a course on Paul's Epistle to the Galatians taught by Markus Barth, the son of twentieth-century Protestantism's most distinguished theologian, Karl Barth. Bailey considered it the best course he took that year. At the time, he wrote, Barth was working on a short commentary on Galatians, which was later published under the title "Justification: From Text to Sermon on Galatians 2:11–21" in the journal *Interpretation*. Barth's article began with the sobering insight that the struggle between good and evil is perennial, and often "The all-too-righteous turns out to be frivolous and unrighteous."[29] Bailey commented that Barth's words reflected his own experience in Germany of the Nazi nightmare.[30]

Ken's enjoyment of academic life at the seminary was interrupted on the night of February 25–26, 1966, when he had to take Mickey to the University of Pittsburgh Medical Center to give birth. By 2:30 a.m. the doctor determined that a caesarian section would be necessary. At 4:00 a.m. one of the doctors emerged from surgery to announce that Bailey

---

28. Ken to Dr. Sundberg, October 2, 1965, Black Volume, 267; and Ken to Carol Geren, October 2, 1965, Black Volume, 265.

29. Barth, "Justification," 147.

30. Ken to Mother and Dad, October 2, 1965, Black Volume, 264.

was a father. He did not get home that morning until 6:00. When he phoned his parents to announce the birth but received no answer, he sat down to write them a letter, explaining that he and Mickey "are the proud parents of David Mark Bailey, a pink screaming seven pound and four-ounce baby boy." He then explained all the complications and observed that it was probably better that he was writing because this way they would get the full story. He confessed, "I am quite unable constitutionally to communicate this kind of information over a telephone."[31]

During the first half of 1966, while enjoying his expanded family, speaking regularly in churches and other venues, and taking classes, Bailey was also revising his book on the prodigal son. He wrote to his parents in March that he had decided to stop auditing classes so that he could devote more time to his book. He was already waiting for the response of a publisher that his former advisor, Addison Leitch, had recommended, but in the meantime, he would continue to work on the manuscript. He explained to his parents, "I try to run down each Greek word as to all the shades of meaning and synonyms that were rejected to select the word that was used and so forth."[32] Later in the year, he began to revise it for the fourth time, but this time for a publication in Arabic. Since nothing came of this, at some point before the end of the year he must have put the manuscript aside to work on other things.[33]

In March Bailey continued to be in communication with the Egyptian Church and the American Mission in Egypt. Part of him hoped to be able to return to Egypt to continue his ministry there.[34] It was the American Mission and not the church in Egypt that was pursuing a visa for Bailey to return; and Bailey would almost certainly have returned to Egypt if a visa had been granted. But he saw this, correctly, as a "stab in the dark" and gave it about a 25 percent chance of success. Moreover, he recognized that it should have been the church in Egypt pressing for his visa. Otherwise, in any future crisis, the church might simply disavow him, claiming to have no responsibility for him. But if church officials had actively sought his visa, pled his case, and pressured the government, he would know that he belonged. When Bailey saw that this was not happening, he concluded that he would be better off serving

31. Ken to family, February 26, 1966, Black Volume, 290.

32. Ken to Mother and Dad, March 21, 1966, Back Volume, 270.

33. Ken to Mother and Dad, August 21, 1966, Back Volume, 285. Ken and Mickey to friends, Christmas 1966, Black Volume, 7.

34. Ken to Mother and Dad, March 13, 1966, Black Volume, 272.

elsewhere. Though his one-year furlough would conclude on September 6, he doubted that the visa would arrive in time. Therefore, he resigned himself to staying in the States for several months. "There will be plenty to do this fall," he wrote to Bruce and Barbara Bailey, "so we will not be twiddling our thumbs, but the uncertainty of it all is getting us down."[35]

While Bailey was giving much thought to how to return to work in Egypt, he also considered the possibility of working in Beirut, Lebanon, which would allow him to continue to use his Arabic-language skills as well as work in the Middle East. Writing in the summer to Presbyterian missionaries Ben Weir and Bill Davies in Beirut, he received an enthusiastic response. They suggested that he could write for Radio Voice of the Gospel as well as teach at the Near East School of Theology (NEST). Bailey had not considered the possibility of working at NEST because he assumed that its standards would require all of its professors to have earned doctorates.[36] Later Laurie Anderson, a professor at NEST, joined the conversation, suggesting that Bailey become a writer for the Near East Council of Churches (NECC), which was located in Beirut. Bailey wrote to his friend Albert Isteero, then serving as the new secretary of the NECC, about the organization's need for writers. As he considered the writing opportunities that might exist for him in Beirut, he wrote to his parents, "Actually, I am really getting quite excited about the possibilities up there."[37] When his visa to Egypt was definitely rejected in August, he resolutely set his face toward Beirut.

In early September, he wrote to his parents that he had definitely been offered a job at NEST in Beirut and that the other work he would do there—the writing of radio scripts, working for the Synod, and continuing his own scholarship—were all highly attractive to him.[38] The New York mission office informed Bailey that he should expect to receive visas for Lebanon by the end of the month. Ken and Mickey then began packing in earnest, knowing that life in Lebanon would be very different from what they had experienced in Egypt, and they would need to pack accordingly. For example, taking large appliances would be unnecessary as most of those would be available in Beirut. They could look forward to an easier life as they would be living in a modern city not in traditional

35. Ken to Bruce and Barbara [Bailey], August 20, 1966, Black Volume, 286; Ken to Mother and Dad, September 3, 1966, Black Volume, 282.
36. Ken to Mother and Dad, August 1, 1966, Black Volume, 287.
37. Ken to Mother and Dad, August 21, 1966, Black Volume, 284.
38. Ken to Mother and Dad, September 3, 1966, Black Volume, 282.

villages. Unfortunately, acquiring visas was harder than expected. On September 14, the New York office informed the Baileys that it would be at least another month before their visas arrived. A week later, they learned that the visa office in Beirut was overwhelmed and was not considering new visas submitted in September. The New York office eventually extended the Baileys' furlough to November 15.

Bailey did his best to redeem the time, attending a writers' conference in Montreat, North Carolina,[39] being the main speaker at the New Wilmington Missionary Conference, and preaching in churches and conferences across the country. By Christmas he estimated that he had given 250 sermons or talks during the year.

During his furlough, Bailey became concerned about the drafting of a new confession for the Presbyterian Church. The impetus for the confession came about due to the union of the UPC and the PCUSA in 1958. At that time the General Assembly established the Special Committee on a Brief Contemporary Statement of Faith. In 1965 this committee, which was largely guided by the theology of Karl Barth, offered the church a ten-page confession intended to augment the Westminster Confession of Faith by presenting contemporary theological themes that included reconciliation, the mission of the church, and a more nuanced view of the inspiration of the Scriptures. Conservatives were probably most interested in the latter. According to the new Confession of 1967, the Scriptures, though inspired by the Holy Spirit, "are nevertheless the words of men, conditioned by the language, thought forms, and literary fashions of the places and times at which they were written."[40] Bailey and Dale Milligan belonged to a group called Presbyterians United for Biblical Confession and served on its advisory board. The group was originally established to be a forum for conservatives in the church to express their opinions on the revisions then being undertaken for the church's newest confession. Once the Confession of 1967 was on its way to acceptance in the church, some of the group wanted to continue meeting, perhaps to form a pressure group on the right that would work outside the structures of the denomination to seek reforms favoring a

---

39. The main speakers at the conference were Elton Trueblood and Charlie W. Shedd. Trueblood wrote thirty-three books in his lifetime, and Shedd was a popular Presbyterian minister who authored over forty books, the best-known among them being *Letters to Karen: A Father's Advice on Keeping Love in a Marriage* (Nashville: Abingdon Press, 1965). Ken enjoyed being with them and was inspired by their example.

40. "The Confession of 1967," in *Book of Confessions: Study Edition*, 325, 9:29.

conservative perspective. Bailey opposed this effort, believing that such a group would be considered a threat to church leaders and therefore be self-defeating. He wrote a seven-page paper on the subject, outlining his reasons for this decision. Dale agreed with the paper, and so he and Bailey polished it together and placed both their names at the bottom.[41] Unfortunately, the document has not been preserved among the Bailey Papers. When the church ratified the Confession of 1967, Presbyterians United for Biblical Confession continued under a new name, Presbyterians United for Biblical Concerns.

It was not until sometime early in the new year of 1967 that the Baileys learned that the Lebanese government had granted them visas and Ken a work permit. By this time a new semester at NEST was already underway and Bailey had accepted numerous speaking engagements in the United States leading up to Easter, March 26, 1967. Therefore, the New York office extended the Baileys' furloughs again and agreed that they would leave for Beirut immediately after Easter. In the meantime, Bailey's job description had become clearer. He would teach classes on the Arabic Bible at NEST, provide classes to pastors in a program of continuing education, write for various church committees, and write scripts that would be broadcast on the Radio Voice of the Gospel. The only major issue that remained unresolved was where the Baileys would reside. Ken and Mickey were more relieved than excited about finally completing their furlough and beginning a new mission assignment. After eighteen months of waiting and uncertainty, Ken explained, "We are like a man who has been straining in a starting block in a crouched position for so long that he is stiff and wonders if he will be able to race at all when the gun finally goes off. The longer he crouches there, the more his mind inevitably turns from the race to the cramps and stiffness in his legs."[42]

On the night of Tuesday, March 28, the Baileys drove to the airport in New York. The airline stewardesses allowed them to board ahead of the other passengers because they had small children—seven-year-old Sara and fourteen-month-old David. There were six seats for the four of them. Once they were seated, the enormity of what was happening suddenly struck Sara. Mickey recalled Sara's anguished words: "I didn't know it would be like this. I thought it would be happy. I like America. I don't want to wait til I'm eleven to see it again. Why can't Uncle Dale and

---

41. Ken to Mother and Dad, September 16, 1966, Black Volume, 281.

42. Ken and Mickey, Christmas 1966 [probably written in early 1967], Black Volume, 20.

Expulsion from Egypt and Furlough in Pittsburgh

Aunt Doris come with us? Why do we have to leave?" After a half an hour of this, the storm passed and Sara calmed down for the flight. When the lights in the passenger compartment were turned off at 11:00 p.m., Ken laid down on the floor between the seats to sleep for a few hours. After a stop in Geneva, the Baileys arrived in Beirut on March 29, ready for a new mission.[43]

43. Mickey to family, April 26, 1967, Black Volume, 237–39. Although Mickey wrote that Sara referred to her relatives as Dale and Doris, Sara recalls she only ever referred to them as Uncle and Aunt; hence, I have altered Mickey's account accordingly.

8

At Home in the Paris of the Middle East
1967–70

> I will take my stand to watch,
> and station myself on the tower,
> and look forth to see what he will say to me...
>
> —Habakkuk 2:1

THE BAILEYS WOULD COME to love the city of Beirut, the capital city of Lebanon, which sits on a peninsula that juts into the Mediterranean Sea. As Lebanon was a former French colony, Beirut was a modern city influenced as much by European as Middle Eastern culture. During the 1960s and seventies, it was generally known as the Paris of the Middle East, a city of culture, art, and fashion. Cosmopolitan and with a Christian government, Beirut held many possibilities for pleasure. During the Baileys' first two months in Lebanon, April and May 1967, Ken worked out his own assignment and housing arrangements. The Baileys would live in Beirut, taking over the home of Bill Davies. The apartment was ideally located, being close to the American University of Beirut, one block from the American embassy, and about a ten-minute drive from NEST—then located in downtown Beirut. The apartment was in the section of the city called Ras Beirut (*Ras* is Arabic for "top" or "tip"), a reference to its geographical location on the city's peninsula. A generally affluent area with a mixed Muslim-Christian population with a Muslim majority, Ras Beirut lay in the western part of the city.[1]

Bailey's job description was slowly being defined at this time and in the first week of May was made official by the personnel committee of the National Evangelical Synod of Syria and Lebanon (NESSL), commonly called the Synod. He would have a twofold job. First, Bailey would work at NEST where he would teach one course in the Arabic Bible and also be in charge of the field work of the Arabic-speaking students at the seminary. Bailey observed that, with only ten students who were part of the Synod, this would not be a full-time job. NEST apparently wanted to put Bailey on the teaching staff but chose to hold off for a while because doing so would only confirm the complaint that the Synod institutions in Beirut tended to snap up the newly arrived missionaries rather than allowing them to work in the churches. So, Bailey would have to bide his time before he could become a seminary professor. Second, the committee asked Bailey to develop study groups for pastors and laypeople. Bailey accepted this work but saw it as unrealistic because of the small size of the church. The Synod had only 2,000 to 3,000 members. Yet the congregations were top-heavy with leadership, with seventeen pastors and nine evangelists. Because of the large geographical areas that they covered and their distances from one another, holding regular meetings for Bible study and prayer was not a realistic possibility. On the other hand, working with interested laypeople seemed feasible.[2] In addition to the official responsibilities given by the Synod, Bailey would also pursue work as the Literature Secretary of the Near East Council of Churches (NECC) and write radio scripts for the radio program of the NECC. However, the radio project was disorganized and the leadership divided; so again, he would have wait and keep an eye out for opportunities. In fact, given his experience in Egypt, Bailey would try to make his entire first year a period of discernment. "I am looking around," he wrote his family, "for a nice high 'Hakakkukian tower' [Hab 2:1] to climb for my first year to sniff the breeze, discover the Synod pecking order, find where the Spirit is working, keep my mouth shut (if possible), and see if I can get this place 'wired' as the surfers say."[3]

---

1. Ken to Mother and Dad, April 15, 1967; and Mickey to family, April 26, 1967, Black Volume, 158–61, and 237–39.
2. Ken to Mother and Dad, April 15, 1967, Black Volume, 158–61.
3. Mickey/Ken to family, May 16, 1965, Black Volume, 252–53.

Bailey quickly learned that the church in Lebanon consisted of three elements that vied with each other for influence: (1) American missionaries, who had introduced Western Protestant ideas in theology, the Bible, culture, and scientific worldview; (2) the Arabs, who were Arabic-speaking and part of the broader pan-Arab, Middle Eastern culture; and (3) the Armenian Church, which had a long tradition stretching back to the early fourth century and was conservative and traditional. Each of these groups represented a different culture, language, and race.

Bailey of course was most directly concerned with the Western Protestant tradition introduced by American missionaries. The American Board of Commissioners for Foreign Missions (commonly known as the American Board), a nondenominational organization but generally a mission board of the Congregational Church, sent the first American missionaries into the region in 1821. The Presbyterian Church in the USA (or PCUSA, the northern branch of Presbyterianism in the United States) first sent missionaries under the American Board in 1823, and in 1837, these Presbyterians formed their own Board of Foreign Missions to support missionaries abroad. In 1870, the American Mission and the Presbyterian Board of Foreign Missions decided in an early comity agreement to divide their labors in the region. The American Board would work in Turkey, and the Presbyterians would work in Ottoman Syria, which includes present-day Lebanon. In 1920 the National Evangelical Synod of Syria and Lebanon (the Synod) was founded and became more or less independent of the American Mission. A federation of Arabic-speaking congregations, it adopted Reformed theology and Presbyterian polity. The Church of Beirut, however declined to join this federation. While cooperating with the Synod on many levels, it remained an independent church that eventually called itself the National Evangelical Church of Beirut (NECB). In the period 1957–58, when American Presbyterians (now the UPCUSA, the union of the PCUSA and UPC) sought to integrate the mission and the church in Lebanon, they formally transferred their property in the country to the Synod. At this time, the Synod and the NECB considered the possibility of a union, but nothing came of this. The failure of the two churches to form a single church meant that the NECB remained the majority Protestant church in the city of Beirut while the Synod had the merest toehold in the city. In fact, Bailey later explained to his parents, "all the Synod has to show for itself is one '*da'eef* ['weak'] church out in Ras Beirut."[4]

To these inherent differences in the Lebanese Protestant churches, the missionaries added their own. Being dispersed throughout the country in different institutions and no longer having a mission organization because of the recent integration of church and mission, they lacked unity and coherence. Moreover, there were deep theological divisions among them, which made fellowship through prayer and Bible study problematic and often uncomfortable. The result was that the missionaries had no prayer meetings. Bailey very much wanted to belong to a mission fellowship group, but he recognized that this was not possible with the Presbyterian fraternal workers[5] because he was a theological conservative while they tended to be theologically liberal. Therefore, he decided to seek out missionary colleagues who had been sent from other denominations but were similar in theological outlook.[6] Later, Bailey would invite a small number of "the more spiritually minded" Presbyterians to his home for prayer meetings. His house was well situated for this, being within easy walking distance of both the seminary and the mission offices.[7]

One clear difference from Bailey's experience in Egypt was the abundance of speaking opportunities in important centers of the church. During his ten years in Egypt, Bailey was never once asked to speak at a synod meeting, where speaking opportunities came slowly and through seniority. In contrast, speaking opportunities in Beirut were extensive. During his first week, he was asked to speak to a women's society and a group of college-aged young people meeting at the Synod church in Beirut. At their request, he spoke in English on these occasions. He soon learned that, of the twenty-eight Presbyterian fraternal workers then serving in Lebanon, a small number were able to converse fluently in Arabic and one gave brief devotionals, but he was the only one capable and sufficiently confident to teach and preach in Arabic. Therefore, he anticipated numerous teaching and preaching invitations despite the smallness of the church. By the end of May, he wrote to his parents that he had already received five requests to teach the Bible at summer conferences.[8]

---

4. Ken to Mother and Dad, August 13, 1967, Black Volume, 234.

5. This was the Presbyterian Church's newly minted term for *missionary*, which was meant to convey a relationship based on partnership rather than paternalism.

6. Ken to Mother and Dad, April 15, 1967, Black Volume, 259.

7. Ken to Mother, December 1, 1974, Bailey Papers, box 29, folder 2.

8. Ken to Mother and Dad, May 30, 1967, Black Volume, 250.

Since Ken and Mickey had had to leave Egypt so quickly, they left much of their personal property behind in Assiut. At this time the Egyptian authorities granted Bailey a visa so that he could return and retrieve his things, but then he learned that other missionaries had already packed some of his possessions and shipped them to Beirut. Since these items were scheduled to arrive on April 22, he decided to delay his trip in order to see that they were cleared by customs in Beirut, which might take two or three weeks. But when the ship from Egypt was delayed until the end of April, Bailey decided to fly to Egypt to collect his belongings, hoping to be back in ten days.[9] He did not actually fly to Egypt until the second week of May, but he only needed to be there three and a half days. He wrote to his parents that the most important possessions he wanted to recover were his books, and he returned to Beirut with a hundred pounds of personal items, which were probably nearly all books. While he was in Cairo, he learned that Dar el-Thaqafa had printed his book on Amos, and he had the pleasure of returning to Beirut with a few copies to show Mickey.[10]

After Bailey returned home, he set to work to have the family's personal effects cleared by customs. To expedite the process, he hired a "clearer" to work with him, as the process required the acquisition of forty-three signatures before everything would be released, and anyone of the forty-three officials could demand that all the boxes be opened for inspection, which would further delay the process. Fortunately, they were able to get the family car out of customs right away, but the battery was dry and the gas was missing. Also, Bailey had not yet acquired a Lebanese driver's license. It would be several more weeks before all of the customs work was complete, and the Baileys could not move into their apartment until it became available at the end of June.

The Near East School of Theology (NEST), the venue of Bailey's principal work in Lebanon, had been established through the merger of two institutions: the School for Religious Workers in Beirut and the School of Athens in Greece.[11] The earliest predecessor institution of the School for Religious Workers in Beirut had been established there in 1835; it later moved and merged with other institutions, but in 1923 had returned to

---

9. Mickey to family, April 26, 1967, Black Volume, 238.
10. Ken to Mother and Dad, May 30, 1967, Black Volume, 250–51.
11. For a general history of NEST see Sabra, *Truth and Service*.

Beirut. The School of Athens had been located in various places in Turkey, and it also merged with other seminaries in the region. But following the Turkish massacre of the Armenians in 1915, the school moved to Athens, Greece. Both of these institutions were established by the American Board of Commissioners for Foreign Missions. In 1870, when the American Board limited its work in the region to Turkey and the Presbyterian Board of Foreign Missions limited its work to Syria-Lebanon, the American Board retained the seminary that eventually moved to Athens, while the Presbyterians acquired the one in Beirut. With the budget constraints of the Great Depression in the 1930s, the two mission boards decided to merge their seminaries, forming NEST in 1932.

NEST was originally located in Colton Hall, a building that was part of the American Mission Compound in downtown Beirut. Constructed in 1912, Colton Hall accommodated the seminary's offices, classrooms, a library, and a dormitory for twenty-one students. During its first twenty-five years, NEST's principals and, with one exception, faculty members were entirely expatriates. The exception was the Lebanese Armenian Hovhannes Aharonian, who first lectured at NEST in 1944, became a full-time professor in 1949, and principal (a title later changed to president) in 1957. The two major supporting bodies of the seminary continued to be the Presbyterian Church and the American Board, which provided most of its operating budget. As late as 1972, 88 percent of NEST's budget came from these foreign sources in the form of appropriations, scholarships, and the salaries of foreign faculty members.[12] In 1969, two years after Bailey's arrival in Beirut, NEST moved to its new home in Ras Beirut, about a mile and a half away. The new building included three basement floors, two of which were for parking while the lowest level was designed as a bomb shelter. The above-ground portion of the building was a large rectangular block that consisted of a ground floor and two upper floors. The ground floor was for the administrative offices and classrooms. The first floor housed the library and faculty offices while the second floor was allotted for the kitchen and dining room. In later years, additional floors would be added for a student dormitory and faculty apartments.

Relocating to Ras Beirut meant that the new NEST was also close to the American University of Beirut, which it had already been serving as its department of religion in which students at each institution were able to take courses at the other. NEST was now also within walking

---

12. Sabra, *Truth and Service*, 181.

distance of three other institutions: Beirut College for Women (BCW), the University Christian Center, and Haigazian College (an Armenian Protestant institution). NEST established ties with all of them, but it was Haigazian College where most NEST students obtained their BA degrees. Despite its institutional connections, the number of students at NEST remained small, averaging seventeen to eighteen in its first twenty-five years. In the 1966–67 academic year, however, this number rose to forty, and in the 1972–73 academic year NEST enjoyed its highest enrollment to date with sixty-two students.[13] Although students came to NEST from all over the Middle East region and occasionally Europe and the United States, the seminary primarily served four local churches: the National Evangelical Synod of Syria and Lebanon, the Union of the Armenian Evangelical Churches in the Near East, the Diocese of Jerusalem of the Episcopal Church, and the Evangelical Lutheran Church in Jordan. When Bailey arrived in 1967, the basic course of study at NEST was the bachelor of divinity degree, which in 1970 became the master of divinity.

Bailey was sitting in his office at NEST on the morning of Monday, June 5, 1967, when another professor rushed in and asked him to translate a speech by Egypt's President Nasser that was being broadcast over Cairo radio.[14] This was the first day of the Six-Day War, launched by Israel in a preemptive strike on the Arab forces (primarily Egypt, Syria, and Jordan) massing on its borders. Nasser announced that war was in progress and that the total destruction of Israel was at hand. Though much of the Middle East was in an uproar, things remained calm in Beirut. Ken and Mickey, therefore, decided to remain where they were. When the rest of their belongings from Alexandria finally arrived in Beirut on Tuesday, June 6, Bailey began the process of having them cleared by customs authorities, which required that he leave his passport with them. That afternoon, Nasser falsely announced that the United States had intervened on the Israeli side of the conflict. As the war had not been won and Israel was putting up a stiff defense, Nasser's accusation of American involvement was calculated to rally forces in the streets throughout the Arab world, and it had that effect in Beirut. A mob attacked the American embassy

---

13. Sabra, *Truth and Service*, 124, 169.

14. Ken told the story of his evacuation from Beirut in a letter to his family, June 10, 1967, Black Volume, 243–44.

but failed to get inside, though a number of people were killed and several cars were set on fire. Another mob attacked the American University of Beirut but did not succeed in entering the campus. A third mob attacked the British Embassy and succeeded in burning the first floor.

Bailey drove home that afternoon, passing by the American embassy just thirty minutes before it was attacked. Had he driven by during the attack, his car might have been burned with the others. He and Mickey packed quickly in preparation for being evacuated. They also moved a number of their things across the street to the home of Ben Weir. That night at 9:00 Bailey drove down to the assembly point for Americans being evacuated to ascertain what was happening and where they would be sent. He saw some 2,000 people sitting with their baggage or milling around, but no one had any helpful information except a rumor that a ship would be arriving that night to evacuate them. Bailey returned home through what he described as "dark deserted streets," which he found eerie and perhaps a little frightening. If he were to be evacuated, he would have to retrieve his passport before returning to the assembly point.

The next morning, Wednesday, June 7, Bailey went to the customs house with the clearer and spent several hours cajoling and arguing with customs officials that his passport should be returned so that he could leave the country with his family. He eventually convinced a customs official to return his passport if he produced photocopies of his work permit, identification card, and two other documents. But when after some effort he returned with the required photocopies, the official needed certification that the copies were of the original documents, and he had other questions about documents and travel that could not be easily answered. Finally, the man simply refused to take responsibility and passed the matter on to his superior. It was 10:30 a.m. before Bailey returned home with his passport and 1:00 p.m. before he and the family arrived at the assembly point. But they made it with time to spare. At 2:00 they were taken to waiting buses and driven to an airfield. The Pan American plane that would evacuate them was a half a mile away across an open field, and they walked the distance, staggering under the weight of as much luggage as they had dared to bring with them. It was not until they were on the plane that they learned it would take them to Frankfort, Germany.

Though the Lebanese government had closed the airport, it granted the American Embassy permission to use it until 4:00 p.m. After the deadline, it was not certain if the government would bow to Arab political pressure to sever its diplomatic ties to the United States. If this happened, it would be unlikely to extend the deadline. Fortunately, diplomacy was not strained as the plane departed from Beirut at 3:30 and landed at 7:30 in Frankfort. When the passengers deplaned, they passed through a double line of US Marines before they reached waiting buses. The German press was present with video cameras and microphones to record the event of the arrival of the first American evacuees from Beirut. The Baileys spent the night in a room in US Army barracks and the following day, Thursday, June 8, were driven to Frutigen, Switzerland, where they remained for the duration of their evacuation. Frutigen is a small municipality in the Bernese Oberland region of the canton of Bern. At an elevation of 2,600 feet, it is a ski resort in the shadow of the Bernese Alps. The Hilgendorfs and Stelling families, Lutheran missionaries in Lebanon and soon-to-become close friends, joined the Baileys in Frutigen as fellow evacuees.

Bailey was uneasy about the evacuation, writing to his family, "I had a terrible feeling of running away from the church that I was sent to serve just as it needs all the spiritual help it can get. But with a family it seems the only choice to make."[15] The Six-Day War ended on Saturday, June 10, with victory for the Israelis and utter humiliation for Nasser, who immediately offered to resign as Egypt's president. Bailey thought that this was just a ploy to gain sympathy in the streets. In the event, Nasser allowed himself to be persuaded to remain in power. The Baileys took the opportunity of their evacuation to tour much of Switzerland, returning to Beirut on August 2.[16] They had been out of the country for seven weeks and four days.

In a letter home, Bailey raised the difficult issue of the recent Six-Day War. Americans at this time, anguished by the horror of the Holocaust and caught up in the romance of Zionism and the courage of an embattled Jewish minority surrounded by hostile Arabs, generally supported Israel. Bailey told a different story. He recounted the firsthand reports of unbiased outsiders who were present in Israel during the war and its immediate aftermath. Rather than relating stories of Israeli heroism, they recounted Israeli atrocities: the looting, dynamiting, and bulldozing of buildings in conquered territory in Jordon; French and Spanish consulate officials in Jerusalem being pushed against walls and held at gunpoint while their property was loaded onto trucks and

---

15. Ken to family, June 10, 1967, Black Volume, 244.
16. Ken to family, July 30 1967, Black Volume, 232.

hauled away; a YMCA director and staff watching their hotel looted and the stolen property being loaded onto open trucks and driven through jeering crowds; Israeli soldiers confiscating UN cars after hostilities had ended; the abuse of Christian and Muslim holy sites; and the demolition of Arab houses as reprisals against any who dared offer resistance. Since the press was not reporting the full story, Bailey believed that the West was being badly misled. Equally misinformed and deluded, in his mind, were the Christian churches of the Middle East who had turned a blind eye to Israeli misdeeds, acting like elks "who join the thundering herd and ask no questions."[17] Though this blistering jeremiad might be seen in retrospect as a powerful prophetic letter, the pro-Israeli sentiments of most Americans at the time meant that Bailey risked being dismissed as an antisemite and crank. There is no record in the Bailey Papers of any reaction to this letter, but at least some of Bailey's supporters must have blanched at his broadside in defiance of conventional wisdom.

The Baileys' main task on returning to Beirut in August was to settle into their new apartment. With the furniture allotment they received from the Presbyterian Church, they purchased a new stove, a Westinghouse refrigerator, and an automatic washing machine, which, as David was still in diapers, was a huge help for Mickey. They also bought used furniture and painted many of the rooms. But the Baileys were reluctant to spend much money on their new home because their visas and Ken's work permit would expire in May, and they were not certain that they would be renewed. Bailey learned that the work permits of six American professors at Haigazian College had recently been rejected, and he feared his would be too.[18]

Though distracted and disturbed by politics and war, Bailey still had a job to do. The academic year at NEST began in early October and ended in late May. In the first semester, Bailey planned to teach only one course, the Arabic Bible, for his ten Arabic students. About a week before the semester began, however, he was also asked to teach a course in homiletics, both courses to be taught in Arabic. Before he knew about the second course, and believing that he had plenty of time on his hands, he had also agreed to teach a survey course on the Bible at the Beirut College for Women (BCW). The course, which was a requirement for

17. Ken and Mickey to friends, September 23, 1967, Black Volume, 21–22.

18. Ken to Mother and Dad, August 13, 1967, Black Volume, 233. The detail about the automatic washing machine and David being in diapers is a later comment made by Sara.

all students, would be three hours a week and taught in English. BCW was a college of 650 women who hailed from a variety of denominations, and some of the students came from the West Bank in Jordan and had been stranded in Lebanon when Israel acquired their territory in the Six-Day War. Bailey found this to be a demanding course to teach. Not only was he learning the Old Testament, he was also learning about Arab culture and sensibilities as he taught Arabic-speaking students. His class in homiletics at NEST provided a wide window into Middle Eastern thought, as it was an advanced course intended for pastors who already had ten years of experience in preaching.[19]

In the spring semester at NEST, which began on February 19, 1968, the seminary's Professor of New Testament announced that he would be leaving in March, and Bailey was asked to prepare himself to assume his introductory course on the New Testament. He was "thrilled to be asked," he informed his parents in February, though it would take up much of his time to prepare for it.[20] A week later he further explained that he might be able to angle a full-time position as NEST's professor of New Testament.[21] Prior to this semester, perhaps in the fall of 1967, the director of the Lebanese Bible Institute, a Mr. Whitehouse, had asked Bailey to teach the Koine Greek of the New Testament for students at the institute, with Arabic as the language of instruction. Bailey began preparing for the class in mid-December, using it as an opportunity "to learn the fine points of the grammar once and for all," which apparently had not happened at Pittsburgh Theological Seminary in 1965–66, despite good intentions.[22] He confessed to his parents that he had not studied Greek since he had been a seminary student seventeen years before.[23] He began by devoting two hours a day to the task, but at the end of March it had become an all-consuming project. He had to master not only Greek grammar but also Arabic grammar in order to teach Greek using Arabic. After having devoted much of his semester to Koine Greek and the New Testament, Bailey at the age of thirty-seven was now beginning to imagine himself as a professor of the New Testament.[24]

19. Ken to Mother and Dad, November 1, 1967, Black Volume, 224.
20. Ken to Mother and Dad, February 4, 1968, Black Volume, 218.
21. Ken to Mother and Dad, February 11, 1968, Black Volume, 221.
22. Ken to Mother and Dad, February 4, 1968, Black Volume, 218.
23. Ken to Mother and Dad, March 18, 1968, Black Volume, 202.
24. Ken to Mother and Dad, March 24, 1968, Black Volume, 217.

During his first year at NEST, Bailey became increasingly engaged in work in the churches. As it became widely known that he could preach in Arabic, he soon found that he was in high demand to preach in churches and for church conferences. By the end of November, he could boast to his parents that he was preaching in churches every Sunday. By the end of March, he wrote to Dale and Doris Milligan, he had preached or given lessons to over a hundred groups in a variety of churches all over the country.[25] Aside from the satisfaction of making a contribution to the churches, he found this work personally profitable because it allowed him to be in touch with local congregations, which he felt was important for a teacher of pastors who would soon be preaching from such pulpits every Sunday.[26] Not limiting himself to speaking exclusively in Presbyterian churches, he wrote to his parents that he was receiving many invitations to teach from schools and churches of other denominations, especially those associated with the Southern Baptists, who he felt were committed to an evangelism that most others had forsaken.[27] This same affinity for evangelical ministries, regardless of denomination, was also evident in his attitude toward the Lebanese Bible Institute.[28] Though an independent mission, Bailey wrote, "They are such fine people and in many ways a lot closer to me in spirit than some of the fraternal workers" of the Presbyterian Church.[29] Bailey's growing popularity was certainly due in part to his ability to communicate in Arabic, but the evangelical content of his messages was also important.

While Bailey was flattered by the numerous invitations to speak and obviously enjoyed talking to a variety of groups, he recognized that being the only Western missionary available to preach and teach in Arabic was not a healthy situation. He found pleasure in associating with the fourteen other professorial colleagues at NEST, but he observed that they were isolated from the church at large. Lacking the ability to speak Arabic fluently, they had little or no contact with the churches. And being highly academic and theologically liberal in their understanding of Christianity

25. Ken to Dale and Doris [Milligan], March 24, 1968, Black Volume, 215.

26. Ken to Mother and Dad, November 24, 1967, Black Volume, unnumbered page between 222 and 223.

27. Ken to Mother and Dad, February 4, 1968, Black Volume, 218.

28. Ken to Mother and Dad November 24, 1967, Black Volume, unnumbered page between 222 and 223. The Lebanese Bible Institute was formerly known as the Shimlan Bible Institute and was then often referred to as the Whitehouse Mission after its director.

29. Ken to Mother and Dad, November 1, 1967, Black Volume, 224.

and prizing the "demythologizing" approach to the New Testament of Rudolf Bultmann and the existentialist theology of Paul Tillich, they shared little common ground with the conservative congregants that made up the bulk of the Christian community in Lebanon. The NEST professors were also divided. Being composed of five nationalities, they had little social contact among themselves. As an academic, who was theologically conservative and fluent in Arabic, Bailey found that he was in a unique position in that he was in touch and on good terms with all these diverse groups.[30]

Figure 19. Mickey Bailey, Christmas, in Beirut, Lebanon, 1968.

But there was a downside to his favorable repute. During the 1968–69 academic year, Bailey was serving on at least nine faculty committees at once. At the end of May 1969, he complained to Bruce and Barbara Bailey: Of the fifteen faculty members at NEST, "I am the only one who can function professionally in Arabic; thus, all kinds of things get dumped on me, and I am pressured into membership on nearly every committee..."[31]

30. Ken to Dale and Doris, March 24, 1968, Black Volume, 215.
31. Ken to Bruce and Barbara [Bailey], May 28, 1969, Black Volume, 150.

In the spring of 1968, the Evaluation and Planning Committee at NEST decided to offer Bailey the full-time position of New Testament professor who would also teach homiletics, and a formal offer was extended in the last week of May, being confirmed by both the president of NEST, Dr. Hovhanness Aharonian, and the executive secretary of the Synod, the Reverend Ibrahim Dagher. As a full-time faculty member, Bailey would of course have to earn a PhD in his chosen field of interest. He had been thinking about this possibility since the previous winter, the idea having slowly formed in his mind until it became a definite goal. As he explained to his parents, he had gone to Egypt in 1955 believing that he would be spending his entire career there, but since that career had come to an abrupt and unanticipated halt after only ten years, he felt keenly the need for job security. Having a PhD in the New Testament, he concluded, would broaden his career options should his time in Beirut also end prematurely.[32]

By September 1969, Bailey decided on Concordia Seminary in St. Louis, Missouri, as the place to pursue his doctorate. An immediate appeal of the seminary was its location halfway between Des Moine, Iowa, where Mickey's parents lived, and Waverly, Ohio, where Bailey's parents had retired. It also offered a program in which he could finish a PhD in just two years. Most important, however, it was an institution of the conservative Lutheran Church-Missouri Synod. Ken explained to Mickey, "As Missouri-Synod Lutherans, they are openminded modern conservatives, and that is the climate that I would enjoy."[33] The seminary had seven professors of New Testament, which had the advantage of providing specialists in a wide range of fields whom Bailey might consult. Once he became more familiar with the seminary's professors, Bailey selected Dr. Martin Scharlemann to be his advisor.

Bailey now needed to find ways to finance his education. At the recommendation of Beirut Lutheran missionaries John Stelling and Dennis Hilgendorf, the Lutheran Church-Missouri Synod agreed, in lieu of Bailey's future contribution to their mission in Beirut, to provide $1,000 of the $1,500 tuition charged by Concordia; and Concordia agreed to provide a scholarship to Bailey of $500 if he would catalog a number of Arabic books that its library had recently acquired. And the Synod

---

32. Ken to Mother and Dad, May 25, 1968, Black Volume, 203–4.

33. Ken to Mickey, October 1, 1969, Black Volume, 100; and Ken to Charles Arbuthnot (Program Agency), December 1, 1969, RG 424, Presbyterian Historical Society.

officially requested that COEMAR give Bailey a paid study leave and provide a housing allowance.[34]

In December 1969, Bailey sent a five-page single-spaced letter to Charles Arbuthnot of the Presbyterian Church's Program Agency, making the case for the church to grant him two years of study leave to obtain his PhD. Among the practical arguments he presented was the need for a "union card"—that is, he would not be taken seriously as a scholar unless he had an advanced degree. More important, however, he had a message burning within that he very much needed to express. "I think," he wrote to Arbuthnot, "that we in the West have for literally centuries seen the text of the Bible through Western eyes and missed much of its richness." The Jewish community that Jesus addressed in the first century was generally destroyed in the Jewish-Roman War of AD 66–70, and in subsequent centuries, Christian scholars looked at the biblical text through the lens of a Greek worldview. "Thus," Bailey concluded, "we have never really looked at the text, particularly of the teachings of Jesus, through the eyes of a Middle Eastern peasant community. To do so gives insights lost for centuries."[35] This was his great mission, the burden of his scholarship, the passion of his life.

In anticipation of the language requirements at Concordia, in October Bailey signed up for a class in German given at the German Institute in Beirut. He attended six hours of classes a week and studied an additional fourteen hours. His intention was to complete the German requirement for the PhD at Concordia before he arrived. He wanted to master German so that he would be able to read the German scholarly journals and commentaries necessary to complete his dissertation. Studying an entirely new language as he was approaching the age of forty was grueling and sometimes humiliating work, but he succeeded. Between studying German and continuing to teach a full load at NEST, Bailey's days were full.

Sometime in January of 1970 Bailey made a trip to the south of Lebanon to a village about 2,000 feet from the Israeli border. The area, which was located in a region that in biblical times was called Galilee, had many traditional homes that were built in the same way as 2,000 years ago. He visited a number of these homes and discovered that nearly all of them

---

34. Ken to Mickey, September 26, 1969; and Ken to Mickey, October 1, 1969, Black Volume, 100, 72.

35. Ken to Charles Arbuthnot (Program Agency), December 1, 1969, Box RG424, Presbyterian Historical Society.

were divided into three sections: an area for the family, a guestroom, and a small area for barn animals, which was five steps lower than the rest of the house. Mangers were built into the floor of the family section that bordered on the section for animals, which allowed the animals to eat from the mangers but not enter the area intended for human habitation. Later, Bailey learned that the Greek word *kataluma*, traditionally translated as *inn* in the birth narrative of Luke's Gospel, could also be rendered as *guestroom* (Luke 2:7). Extrapolating from these discoveries, Bailey would completely rewrite the Christmas story. Joseph did not seek lodging in an inn but in a traditional Palestinian home. Because the guestroom in the home was already occupied, Joseph and the pregnant Mary were given space in the living room, the main area occupied by the family, and Mary placed her newborn baby in the traditional built-in manger in this room.[36] In a number of articles, a chapter in a book, and in an entire play, Bailey would expound this new interpretation of the Christmas story over the next four decades.

As Bailey prepared to travel to the United States, he knew that he was returning a changed man. Writing to Dale Milligan just before the New Year's celebration of 1970, he confessed that his experience abroad had de-nationalized and de-churched him. In 1955 when he set out with Mickey to begin their missionary career in Egypt, he felt at one with his nation: "I was an American in every sense of the word. I was an enthusiast for American political goals and a spokesman for the 'American view.'" But over the years he slowly became a stranger to the American worldview. Curiously, in these days of domestic tumult in America, there are only a few mentions in the Bailey Papers of American politics and social unrest. Bailey's estrangement, it seems, was not due to the contemporary political ferment in America but rather to his experience of and immersion in Middle Eastern culture and, perhaps most important, his recognition of America's blindness regarding Israel's unjust and aggressive policies toward the Palestinians. Also important was that Bailey was increasingly at odds with the theological liberalness of his own denomination and saw himself as part of a "theological resistance movement." Aside from issues of theology, he felt that his denomination and the churches he served abroad had unfairly marginalized him as a missionary. The Presbyterian Church, he believed, did not value him as a spokesman or representative

---

36. Mickey to family, January 28, 1970, Black Volume, 85–87; and there is a duplicate in the Bailey Papers, box 27, folder 3. See too Bailey, "The Story of Jesus' Birth: Luke 2:1–20," in *Jesus through Middle Eastern Eyes*, 25–47.

in that the "flying executives," as he called them, would never designate him to represent the denomination at any international meeting. In the same way, the National Evangelical Synod of Syria and Lebanon would not select him as a delegate to an international conference because its leaders would naturally prefer one of their own for this task. Bailey was a man betwixt and between.[37]

In late January 1970, COEMAR informed Bailey that his request for a study leave had been approved. The commission had been uncertain about the quality of education offered at Concordia Seminary but upon investigation learned that the seminary had one of the best New Testament programs in the United States. Bailey sniffed paternalism and commented to Mickey, "Don't you think I did a little investigating too before?" The commission also agreed to keep Bailey on full salary and provide a grant of $160 per month as a housing allowance and $750 as a study allowance for the year. With the latter grant, Bailey would not need to accept Concordia's scholarship, which required the time-consuming work of cataloging Arabic books.[38] Taking the Cunard line flagship, *Queen Elizabeth 2*, from France to New York, the Baileys arrived home on June 24, and Bailey began his doctoral studies at Concordia two weeks later.[39]

---

37. Ken to Dale [Milligan], December 30, 1969, Black Volume, 131–32.
38. Mickey to family, January 28, 1970, Black Volume, 86.
39. Ken to Dale and Doris [Milligan], April 10, 1970, Black Volume, 114.

— **9** —

Doctorate from Concordia and *The Cross and the Prodigal*

1970–73

The son has not broken the law. Instead, he has broken his father's heart.
—Kenneth E. Bailey, *The Cross and the Prodigal*

BAILEY TOOK CLASSES AT Concordia Seminary in the summer and fall quarters of 1970 and in the winter quarter of 1971. When he was auditing courses at Pittsburgh Theological Seminary in 1965–66, he was not contemplating earning a PhD, but those courses came in handy now. He applied to have his audited courses accepted for his doctoral program, which would give him enough credit to complete the course work required for the PhD. Mickey later explained that the seminary added extra questions to Bailey's comprehensive exams to test how much he had learned at Pittsburgh, suggesting that Concordia had accepted his earlier work. According to Bailey's Condordia transcript, he took nine classes: Parables of the Kingdom, New Testament Canonization, Modern Theology, Theology of Preaching, Glory of God and [Human] Security, Current Problems in New Testament, Classics of the Reformation Era, Biblical Poetry, and a readings course. Naturally, he received As in all of these subjects, as is typical for doctoral students. Bailey took meticulous notes in all of his classes, which remain among the Bailey Papers today.[1] With his class work behind him, Bailey took comprehensive exams in five fields and a separate exam to test his German in the spring of 1971. When he passed these, he only had to take two additional required courses and write his dissertation, for which he had a year.[2]

In April 1971, Mickey wrote to Bruce and Pat Milligan to say that the house was quiet as Bailey was silently and intensively studying for his qualifying exams. Yet despite the impending exams, he was usually found in a pulpit on Sunday mornings. He also took on other speaking assignments in this period: a lecture series at Princeton Theological Seminary,[3] Bible presentations at the New Wilmington Missionary Conference, a talk at a major conference in Chicago, and others.

"Re-entry is a real shock in a number of ways." Bailey wrote toward the end of his two-year furlough. Surely having come of age in the late 1940s and early 1950s and then having lived abroad for almost fifteen years, to return to live in America during the period of 1970–72—a time of anti-war protests on college campuses, ongoing racial conflict, a tumultuous presidential election year, the beginnings of the Watergate scandal, the first phase of the feminist movement, and a mounting concern for the environment—must have been disconcerting for the Baileys. Yet, curiously, there is almost nothing in the Bailey Papers to suggest that Bailey was interested or had strong opinions about any of the issues that were at the center of American political discourse in this period. In one letter in 1968 he expressed, almost as an aside, the hope that Richard Nixon would win the presidential election in which the Democratic nominee was Hubert Humphrey.[4] In these years there was also a confrontation between the fundamentalists of the Lutheran Church-Missouri Synod and the majority of the moderate conservatives of Concordia Seminary that was playing out on Concordia campus, but he never mentioned it in his letters.[5] What provoked a strong political comment from Bailey

1. Ken's transcript from Concordia Seminary is in the Bailey Papers, box 4, folder 1. His notes for his classes are in a bound volume, Bailey Papers, box 1, folder 2.

2. Mickey to Bruce and Pat [Milligan], February 9, 1971, Bailey Papers, box 27, folder 3.

3. David Dawson recalls that Ken occasionally said that Presbyterian seminaries tended to ask him to speak on the situation in the Middle East rather than on his interpretation of the New Testament.

4. Ken to Mother and Dad, September 21, 1968, Black Volume, 183.

5. For a general introduction to the seminary see Engfehr and Thomas, *Proclaim His Salvation*. For more on the fundamentalist-evangelical confrontation between the

Doctorate from Concordia and The Cross and the Prodigal

in this period was the "Munich massacre" in which eight members of the Palestinian terrorist group Black September killed two Israeli athletes and took nine others hostage at the 1972 Summer Olympics in Munich, Germany, resulting in the death of five of the Palestinians and all nine of the Israelis. Bailey observed that the world was "rightly horrified" at this slaughter, but he was appalled that it took no notice of Israel's subsequent revenge killing of sixty-nine innocent people in Lebanon and that a village with a population of 10,000 was "totally destroyed." He found this shocking and remarked, "The political air all around us has that old familiar painful electric feeling."[6] Yet, what really seemed to bother him were the distractions of having to engage with the practical affairs of an educational institution rather than focus on strictly theology concerns.[7] Though it is possible that Bailey was simply politically obtuse, a more charitable interpretation of his comments—or lack of them—at this time would be that he was too focused on writing his dissertation from the summer of 1970 through the following June to have anything important to say on the pressing issues of the day.

By early April 1972 Bailey had completed the first draft of his dissertation, *A Study of Some Lucan Parables in the Light of Oriental Life and Poetic Style* and then set about revising it, anticipating his defense in June. In the event, he successfully defended his 479-page labor of love. Mickey wrote to family and friends on July 6—and one can almost hear the pride in her voice as well as a sigh of relief—"the long struggle is over. After years of grinding, a great deal of fear, and even a few tears, we finally made it. Ken is now Dr. Kenneth Bailey" and would be returning to Beirut as a professor of the New Testament. That Mickey wrote "*We* finally made it" (italics mine) echoes the sentiment of many that a successful dissertation is generally the accomplishment not only of the doctoral candidate but also his or her spouse.[8]

Though Bailey had completed his dissertation, many more years of additional research, reflection, and revision lay ahead before it would be published. But now having his PhD in hand, he could again approach

---

Lutherans see Adams, *Preus of Missouri*.

6. Ken to Bruce [Milligan], September 27, 1972, Bailey Papers, box 27, folder 3.
7. Ken to Bruce [Milligan], September 27, 1971, Bailey Papers, box 27, folder 3.
8. Mickey to family and friends, July 6, 1972, box 27, folder 3.

publishers about his previous work on Luke 15, which he had completed in 1966. No doubt with the endorsement of his advisor, Dr. Martin Scharlemann, *The Cross and the Prodigal: The 15th Chapter of Luke Seen through the Eyes of Middle Eastern Peasants* was accepted by Concordia Publishing House, the publishing arm of Concordia Seminary and the Lutheran Church-Missouri Synod, and the book was published in 1973.

While working in Egypt, Bailey wrote three books in English and had them translated into Arabic and published by Dar el-Thaqafa, a Protestant publisher in Cairo. He could easily have published *The Cross and the Prodigal* with this same Egyptian publisher, but he chose not to do so. These earlier books were not original works in the sense that they made a unique scholarly contribution. Rather, they were summations of the scholarship of the period that he was making available to Arabic speakers. In contrast, *The Cross and the Prodigal* was an original contribution to scholarship and contained many of the themes and ideas that he would continue to develop throughout his long career. He realized that he had produced something special and that he should bide his time until he found the right publisher who would produce his work in English for the broadest possible audience. His long patient wait came to an end at this time.[9]

The preface to his book presents an intriguing problem. The parable of the prodigal son has long been seen, in the words of R. C. Trench, as the *Evangelium in Evangelio*, the gospel in the gospel, yet the story seems to suggest that a loving divine father is able to offer salvation to his wayward children without the inconvenience of either the incarnation or the cross. The father in the parable simply forgives the prodigal son and receives him back into the family fold. If the cross and incarnation are central to the message of the gospel, why are they missing from this key story in Luke's Gospel? For centuries, Bailey explains, Muslims have used their absence to argue that Christians have corrupted the Gospels and that the Christian belief in the incarnation and the need for a propitiatory sacrifice for the forgiveness of sins are later and unnecessary inventions. In this view, Islam, which asserts Jesus' status as a prophet but denies his divinity, had it right all along. "Serving in the Middle East,"

---

9. As noted in chapter 7, Ken had started on a version of the book in 1966 that he intended to be translated into Arabic, but nothing seems to have come of this effort. I believe that on reflection he decided to drop it in favor of finding a publisher for an English version of his book.

Bailey writes, "I have wrestled with these questions for ten years. This book is the result."[10]

To find answers to his questions, Bailey informs the reader, he "talked endlessly with pastors, elders, and illiterate farmers across Egypt and Jordan about Luke 15 and what it means in a village context." This was necessary, he explains, because the Bible is a Middle Eastern book. Seeing it "through the colored glasses of Western culture," the typical Western reader is apt to "miss the subtleties of humor and many of the underlying assumptions." Therefore, to capture the true meaning of Jesus' stories one must understand the underlying cultural assumptions—what "everybody knows." Though two thousand years have passed since Jesus walked the dusty roads of Judea, the culture of the peasant people who first heard him has remained unchanged. "In isolated villages I have found young girls making clay dolls that are easily traceable to the fertility goddesses of Old Testament times. Patterns of speech, dress, and family structure remain stubbornly the same," Bailey assures his readers. He quotes Fr. Henry Habib Ayrout's *The Fellaheen* to show that the peasant farmers of Egypt use the same farming tools and follow many of the same bodily, marriage, and funerary customs as their ancient ancestors.[11] Historians from Herodotus to Volney, he avers, attest to the same "granite-like conservatism of the peasantry." "As a result," Bailey concludes, "village attitudes are often older than Abraham."[12] In future books, Bailey's romantic rhetoric will fade and be replaced with words of greater precision as his knowledge and authority as an exegete grow. His essential point, however, remains unchanged.

Each section and chapter of the book is introduced by Arabic calligraphy that is artfully rendered "to represent symbolically something of" the meaning intended in the section or chapter. The renderings are accompanied by a translation and commentary by Bailey. Though the 1973 paperback copy of the book that is generally available today is printed in black and white with some of the calligraphy fading into grey, the original 1973 edition of Bailey's commentary used the symbolic colors of black, green, and red. In chapter one, for example, the Pharisees are represented by "towering black lines," which are meant to represent

---

10. Bailey, *Cross and the Prodigal* (1973), 9.

11. Ayrout, *Fellaheen*, 19–20, cited in Bailey, *Cross and the Prodigal* (1973), 10. Ayrout's book was first published in French in 1938.

12. Bailey, *Cross and the Prodigal* (1973), 9, 10.

them as the pillars of Judaism. A shepherd calls out, "Rejoice with me," with the text in green, expressive perhaps of a fresh joy.

Bailey's book is concerned with all three parables in Luke 15—the lost sheep, the lost coin, and the climatic story of the prodigal son. The evangelist Luke introduces these stories by noting that Jesus told them a parable, not parables (Luke 15:3). In other words, the three stories are connected. Bailey informs his readers that "it is standard Oriental logic to build a series of similar illustrations" to make an argument.[13] The first story Jesus tells is that of a shepherd who, having lost a sheep, leaves a flock of ninety-nine sheep to search for the lost one. The second story that Jesus tells is of a village woman who has lost a coin in her house. These two stories can be seen as a prologue to the final story, the parable of the prodigal son. Though the title commonly given to this parable suggests the singular importance of the younger son, Bailey insists that from the beginning both sons are mentioned and that "in many ways the older son is the key figure." He suggests that the story might be better named "The Lost Sons."

This is an improbable story because a younger son, in the Arab world, would never dare to ask his father for his share of the family estate while the father was still alive. Bailey writes, "With endless village groups all across the Middle East, I have tested this. The answer has always been the same." Villagers agree that if a son made this request, his father would beat him because in effect he was wishing his father's death. Since in the story the father represents God and the prodigal wayward humanity, Jesus is saying that rebellious human beings really long "for the death of God."[14]

While the elder son might be seen as a neutral observer of these events, he is in fact not an innocent bystander. In a dispute between a father and a younger son, the elder son should naturally intervene as a mediator. Bailey also tested this part of his interpretation of the story. "In the village, when I come to this point in a sermon, I always ask, 'Who must be the reconciler?'" The answer is always the elder son.[15] That the elder son does not play this role suggests his relationships with both his father and brother are strained.

While the father might have been expected to beat his son or disown him, instead he quietly divides his estate between his two sons. English versions do not always mention this. They say that he gave a third

---

13. Bailey, *Cross and the Prodigal* (1973), 20–21, 24.
14. Bailey, *Cross and the Prodigal* (1973), 30, 31.
15. Bailey, *Cross and the Prodigal* (1973), 33, 34.

of the estate to the younger son when, in fact, he gave both of his sons his property. The younger son received both the rights of possession and disposition. The elder son presumably received only the right of possession while his father retained control of the property.[16]

When the prodigal son's money is gone and a famine strikes the land, the prodigal does not immediately decide to return home because he fears the "taunting" of the village and his elder brother's scorn. So, he attaches himself to a "citizen" of the land, who was presumably a Greek. Bailey says the word *attached* could be more literally translated as *glued*.[17] And he compares the prodigal to the street people in the Middle East who try to gain money by cleaning automobile windshields or the unsolicited helpers in a store who cannot be shaken. When the prodigal is assigned the lowest and most disagreeable task imaginable for a Jew, tending pigs, and is still starving, he finally comes to himself. Bailey argues that his repentance is at best shallow. He decides to return home not to reestablish his relationship with his father but to gain a job as a hired servant. He does not want the responsibilities of sonship. He will be satisfied with a job on the chance that "he can yet redeem himself through honorable labor."[18]

The father performs a series of acts designed to fully restore his son. Rather than preserve his honor by punishing his disgraced son, the father "raced" through the village, for an older man an undignified and disgraceful action. Yet by doing so, he prevents his son from having to run the gauntlet of the village upon returning home. The father's willingness to humiliate himself suggests the incarnation, wherein "in Christ God was reconciling the world to Himself" (2 Cor 5:19). The father kisses his son, orders that a ring, sandals, and a robe be brought for him, and calls for the killing of the fatted calf, "the highest honor that can be shown to any guest." All of these are signs of the prodigal's acceptance back into sonship. Moreover, the father performs these acts publicly and orders that the servants dress the prodigal, hence forcing them to acknowledge the prodigal's renewed status as a son. With this great material demonstration of his father's love, the prodigal is overcome. He does not give his rehearsed speech asking to be accepted as a hired servant. Rather, he silently and humbly accepts the grace offered by his father

---

16. Bailey, *Cross and the Prodigal* (1973), 36.

17. Bailey was probably influenced by the use of the word *iltasaqa* (glued) that is used in Luke 15:5 in the popular Van Dyck Arabic Bible.

18. Bailey, *Cross and the Prodigal* (1973), 42, 44, 49.

and is reconciled. Bailey notes that while Muslims would say that the story shows that a merciful God need not have undergone Golgotha to pardon sinful humanity and reconcile it to himself, he insists that the father's outward demonstration of sacrificial love was needed to melt the prodigal's heart and show him the true love of the father.[19]

The story then shifts to the elder son. Being an elder son, a *presbuteros*, suggests that he represents the "elders of the people," the Scribes and Pharisees. Hearing the sound of music and dancing, the elder son learns that a banquet is in progress for his returned younger brother. But rather than join the party, he remains outside, refusing to participate in a restoration of his brother that does not involve some form of punishment. This rudeness on the part of the elder son is a form of rebelliousness, suggesting that he is as alienated from his father as his younger brother was. Showing "the same self-emptying sacrificial love" that he had earlier shown to the prodigal, the father humbles himself by leaving the party to speak with his obstinate son.[20] In the elder son's response to his father, he reveals the envy he has for his younger brother and his deep resentment of his dutiful service to his father over the years. The elder son is arrogant and self-deceived, cold and deeply unloving.

Bailey observes that the climax of Jesus' trilogy of parables occurs in the courtyard of the father's home, but the story does not end. Jesus leaves his listeners hanging. It is not yet clear if the elder son is going to repent of his pride and self-satisfaction and enter the party, or perhaps take some other action. Similarly, it was not yet clear at that time if the Scribes and Pharisees would accept that Jesus is doing God's work by reconciling Israel's outcasts—sinners, tax collectors, and prostitutes—and join him. Given that Israel's elders would in a short time seek Jesus' judicial murder on a cross, Bailey suggests that the story should end in this way: "then the older son in great anger took his stick and beat his father"—an interpretation to which he gave dramatic illustration in the play that follows the formal exegesis of the parable, *Two Sons Have I Not*.[21]

Due to Bailey's careful exegesis of the story based on his knowledge of Middle Eastern village culture, this is a brilliant book. Though short at 134 pages and somewhat quirky with its colored Arabic calligraphy, which for an English-speaking audience would have been indecipherable, Bailey offers a fresh and compelling interpretation of an ancient

---

19. Bailey, *Cross and the Prodigal* (1973), 56–57.
20. Bailey, *Cross and the Prodigal* (1973), 66, 67.
21. Bailey, *Cross and the Prodigal* (1973), 73.

story. Seminary professors ignored it, and it was only reviewed by *Concordia Theological Monthly*.[22] No other scholarly journal bothered. Yet pastors embraced it, repeating its insights in their Sunday sermons, and over the course of the next decade, the book became a sleeper hit.[23]

∽

The Bailey family departed from St. Louis to return to Beirut in early October 1972. Upon entering their apartment in Beirut, they found things in great disarray due to the tenants to whom they had sublet their apartment for two years—much to Mickey's consternation. "What a mess," she wrote. "It seems everything they touched they managed to damage or break in some way from lite switches, lamps, clocks, mirrors, doorbell, coffee pot—you name it." While Mickey was preoccupied with repairing or replacing appliances, Bailey set about constructing bookshelves to accommodate the "five footlockers of new books" he brought with him from America. The family also had to adjust to living again in the Middle East. Since the water to the apartment was periodically cut off, they joined the local YMCA so that they could be assured of a shower in the evenings. After one weekend when the entire family became sick because of the contaminated water supply, Mickey began to boil water for their daily use. Due to a twelve-day garbage strike that occurred soon after they returned, garbage was piled high in the streets, a situation both unsightly and odoriferous. The apartment being located on Corniche Beirut, the tree-lined promenade along the city's riverfront, there was much traffic noise, and in the case of weddings or national holidays the clangorous din could not have been easily borne. They were also subject to the roar of planes passing overhead on their way to or from Beirut Airport. But whatever disagreeable aspects there were to living in the Central District of Beirut, there were also things the Baileys enjoyed about their location, such as a full view of the Mediterranean Sea and the fishing fleet docked just across the street. The family purchased binoculars to enhance their enjoyment of the local sights and to scan the horizon for ships at sea.[24]

Bailey began teaching classes once more at NEST on October 9, 1972. For the opening communion service in the seminary chapel, he

22. Danker, Review of *Cross and the Prodigal*, 312.

23. My evidence for this success is entirely anecdotal as Concordia Press declined to provide sales figures.

24. Mickey to family, October 9, 1972, Bailey Papers, box 27 folder 3.

proudly wore his newly acquired robe, one with three stripes on the arms, indicating that he had earned his doctorate. Because he continued to be a highly valued colleague in much demand due to his mastery of Arabic, he was asked regularly to take on additional assignments by well-meaning colleagues and associates. Being increasingly pressed for time, Bailey tried to stay home in the mornings to do his research and writing but was often called away. In order to guard his time for his own interests, he typed out a personal priority list and kept it on hand to show anyone who questioned why he had declined a request. Bailey also shared the list in a letter to his family:

1. Classes (all courses now being rewritten)
2. Research and Publication
3. Radio Broadcasting (52 Arabic presentations a year)[25]
4. Greek-Arabic Lexicon (40 working days still needed)
5. Synod Preaching (to be kept within 100 per year)
6. NEST Committee work:
    a. Academic counselor for Bachelor of Theology students
    b. Spiritual life counselor for Arab students
    c. Curriculum committee
    d. Chapel committee
    e. Theological Education by Extension committee
7. Private lessons in Syriac from Yousif Matti

---

25. The weekly Arabic-language Christian broadcast that Ken wrote was for a program titled "Conversations with Brother Amos," which was broadcast for Radio Voice of the Gospel. This gave Ken a format to discuss the Bible, theology, and issues of contemporary thought. Listeners wrote in to ask what Brother Amos thought about Teilhard de Chardin's view of evolution and what he might say about the existentialist idea that human beings create their own values apart from God. It is not clear how long this program remained on the air. In May 1974 Ken reported that his "Brother Amos" program "is still heard morning and evening twice a week in short wave and once a week from Cyprus on commercial broadcast time." See Bailey, Personal Report Outline [a missionary's report to the Program Office], August 1973, RG 424, Presbyterian Historical Society, and Bailey, Personal Report for Ken Bailey, June 1, 1973 to May 31, 1974, RG 424, Presbyterian Historical Society.

In a jocular but perhaps also pointed spirit, Mickey asked him why the family was not on the list, to which Bailey responded that the family was far too important to be included on a work list.[26]

Most of the items on his list were concerned with regular activities and were meant to impress interlopers with his busyness. However, the first two items on the list merit some elaboration. The first item was to rewrite his lectures. After his intensive doctorate work, Bailey found that his lectures were inadequate in that they no longer expressed the most up-to-date ideas or his best thoughts on biblical subjects. Hence, they became his highest priority. His second priority was research and publication. Though he had finished his dissertation, it had yet to be published. He sent it first to Oxford University Press, where it was rejected. He then sent it to Matthew Black, the professor of divinity and biblical criticism at St. Andrews University, Scotland, to obtain his evaluation and comments. As he explained to Bruce Milligan, "If Black doesn't like it, I'm in real trouble. It tramps on too many toes and this almost automatically evokes criticism."[27] In fact, it would require several more years of continuing research and revision before it would be accepted by a publisher.

His other research concern on his return to Beirut was the study of a passage in the apostle Paul's first letter to the Corinthians, 1:17—2:2. Bailey had discovered that in these verses Paul had employed a heretofore unseen poetic form. When he had written up his discovery as a forty-page article, he sent it to Matthew Black for his evaluation. In February 1973, he wrote to Bruce that he was "waiting on pins and needles to see what he thinks of it." Adding excitedly of the Pauline passage, "it is one of the most sophisticated pieces [of poetry] I have ever found. It gets so precise it ends up with exactly seven syllables per line in the center of the poem."[28] He wrote to his family that Paul's poetry in 1 Corinthians "established Paul as a poet of equal ability with 2 Isaiah, the great poet of the Old Testament." Moreover, he believed that it was "from the pen of Paul himself." Bailey had discovered that Paul's letter, usually seen as an occasional letter written in response to current difficulties in a new and highly volatile church, was actually a carefully prepared theological composition that employed, behind its use of Greek, traditional Hebrew forms of poetry.[29] Bailey would continue to explore this discovery over

26. Mickey/Ken to family October 22, 1972, Bailey Papers, box 27, folder 3.
27. Ken to Bruce [Milligan], February 18, 1973, Bailey Papers, box 27, folder 3.
28. Ken to Bruce [Milligan], February 2, 1973, Bailey Papers, box 27, folder 3.
29. Mickey/Ken to family, January 3, 1973, Bailey Papers, box 27, folder 3.

many years, not publishing it in book form until almost four decades later as *Paul through Mediterranean Eyes* (2011).

Bailey may have been prepared to whip out a typed card containing his ongoing work as a way of defending his decisions to say no to the endless stream of demands on his time, yet he did say yes to a number of new undertakings—those at least that interested him or, perhaps, that he simply enjoyed. Often these involved teaching new classes. In the winter semester of 1973, for example, he agreed to write lectures for two new courses to be taught at NEST. The first was "Major Concepts in the Qur'an and the Arabic Bible," an interdisciplinary course to be taught with the professor of Islamics. His course preparation would require reviewing 209 Arabic and Syriac versions of the New Testament that had been published from the second century to the present. He wanted to see how the understanding of important words and concepts evolved over time. Writing to his family of this new project in February 1973, he remarked tantalizingly, "We have already turned up some major surprises that I won't bore you with."[30] These ideas would later appear in his seminal articles and books. In March 1973, he took on another teaching responsibility in addition to his teaching load at NEST, agreeing to conduct a three-week Bible study for the women of the Community Church and an eight-week course for the faculty of the local girls' school. As a missionary, he may have felt that teaching such courses, while not advancing his scholarship, was fulfilling an important part of his calling.

Amid the crush of these multiple commitments, Mickey found a way to make sure that Ken upheld the family commitment to writing regular letters to relations and friends in the States. She began writing the first page and a quarter of a letter and then leaving the unfinished missive in the typewriter, with its multiple layers of alternating carbon and onionskin paper. Ken found that it was necessary to complete the letter before being able to do his own work on the typewriter. Far from being perturbed by this, he admired his wife's cleverness, seeing it as a bit of harmless and transparent manipulation—and much more effective than nagging.[31]

Though Ken and Mickey were devoted and diligent missionaries, they took time to ensure that their children would have normal childhoods that reflected American values and traditions. In 1972 on the

---

30. Mickey/Ken to family, February 28, 1973, Bailey Papers, box 27, folder 3.
31. Mickey/Ken to family, November 1, 1972, Bailey Papers, box 27, folder 3.

evening before Halloween, Ken, Mickey, and the two children carved two pumpkins, with each child designing and carving a face. On the morning of Halloween, the children ate their breakfasts on Halloween placemats on a table lit with Halloween candles. That year Sara made her own costume, and Mickey helped David to dress up as a devil, complete with tail, horns, and a red cape that flowed behind him. Mickey and family friend Katie Stelling took the children trick-or-treating, driving all over the city for two hours to visit American homes that would be supplied with candy.[32]

Ken and Mickey were dedicated parents, who loved their children and took an interest in their activities and pride in their accomplishments. When Sara was only seven years old, Ken commented to his parents that her spelling and handwriting "are excellent, very neat, and quite correct. She is already talking about when she will start teaching Daddy to spell." Though meant humorously it was a prescient remark. During the Christmas break, Ken and Mickey worked on the children's rooms, bringing in new furniture and installing new electrical sockets. Just after New Year's, the family traveled up to a forested spot outside the city that they loved and returned to often. They dubbed it Bailey's Hollow, though Mickey remarked sarcastically that it might just as easily have been named Bailey's Bog. The stream there had dried up during the winter, allowing the family to enjoy climbing the large stones and boulders normally in the stream's path. That day a goatherder with a herd of 400 came by looking for a lost goat. Ken sat with him a long while, asking about the customs of his work. Perhaps he was thinking of Jesus' parable of the shepherd seeking for a lost sheep.[33]

---

32. Mickey to family, November 1, 1972, Bailey Papers, box 27, folder 3.
33. Mickey to family, January 3, 1973, Bailey Papers, box 27, folder 3.

— 10 —

A Fourth Arab-Israeli War, and Civil War Comes to Lebanon

1973–76

> Then our volcano erupted
> and for a series of numbing days
>   all human voices silenced
>   amid the roar of the heavy guns,
>   the harsh clank of tank tracks,
>   the bone-jarring shudder of sonic booms,
>   as gladiators with million-dollar swords
>   killed each other high in the sky.
>
> —Kenneth E. Kailey, "Resurrection"

From October 6 to 25, 1973, the Arab nations and Israel fought their fourth war, commonly known as the Yom Kippur War or October War. That month the Baileys, while sitting on their balcony, could observe dog fights between Syrian and Israeli fighter jets over the Mediterranean Sea. Bailey reflected on this latest Arab-Israeli war with a poem, "Resurrection (Ode on a Burning Tank: The Holy Lands, October 1973)," which he later included in *Through Peasant Eyes* (1980).[1] The poem reports that the war on the ground took place "amid the roar of heavy guns," the clanking sound of tanks, and sonic booms from the aerial combat overhead "as gladiators with million-dollar swords/killed each other high in the sky."[2] During this conflict, members of the Nasserite Party in Lebanon—a Sunni faction—set up speakers in front of the Baileys' apartment building on October 12 in order to direct hate propaganda toward the American embassy ten to twelve hours a day, ending at 9:00 at night. The Baileys naturally found this exhausting. They turned the volume up on their radio and listened to music in order to block out at least some of the obnoxious noise.[3] All of this turmoil in Lebanon resulted in a cost-of-living increase of 25 percent during the last three months of the year, and in response, there were the inevitable strikes and threats of strikes.

As Christmas approached in 1973, Bailey picked up a carton of groceries that resulted in straining his back. He had difficulty walking and was soon in so much pain that he went to see a doctor who informed him that he had slipped a disc in his spine. He spent most of the next two months in bed.[4] During his recuperation in the spring semester of 1974, Bailey held his seminary classes in his apartment. While wearing a back brace and rocking gently in his rocker, which he found soothing, he taught the students who sat gathered around him in the living room.[5] At this time, Concordia Press asked him to write a follow-up book to *The Cross and the Prodigal*. Instead, Bailey decided to write a sequel to his dissertation, though it had not yet been published.[6] The Program Agency granted him a three-month home leave to work on the book, and he soon made plans to return to the United States for the summer, tentatively from June 15 to September 15, and stay in Des Moines in order to use Concordia Seminary's library.[7] By mid-March, his back was feeling much better, but Bailey still anticipated that he would need another three months before he enjoyed a complete recovery.[8] Then sometime in April, while doing his regular exercises in bed, he pulled a muscle in his back

---

1. Bailey, *Through Peasant Eyes*, 71–73.
2. Bailey, *Through Peasant Eyes*, 71–73.
3. Mickey to family, October 14, 1973, Bailey Papers, box 27, folder 3.
4. Mickey to family, December 29, 1973, Bailey Papers, box 27, folder 3.
5. Mickey to family, March 6, 1974, Bailey Papers, box 27, folder 3.
6. Mickey to family, February 4, 1974, Bailey Papers, box 27, folder 3.
7. Ken to family, February 18, 1974, Bailey Papers, box 27, folder 3.
8. Ken to family, March 17, 1974, Bailey Papers, box 27, folder 3.

just below his neck. He was forced to stay in bed for the day, resting with a heating pad. For the rest of the week his back remained stiff and painful. Later, fearing that he had developed another cyst on his tail bone, he saw a doctor who informed him that he had simply bruised his tail bone from the way he had been leaning back in his rocking chair and from spending so much time in a sitting position. Mickey wrote to her family that "in utter desperation he said to me, 'What is the Lord trying to teach me?!'"[9] Though frustrated at his slow recovery, he nevertheless improved over the next week.

Bailey's time in bed recovering from his back injury was not wasted. He wrote to his family in mid-March to describe an article he was writing on Luke 2:7, a verse that is part of Luke's narrative of Jesus' birth, and he also noted that he had made an interesting discovery about the parable of the good Samaritan.[10] Between roughly April 10 and 24, Mickey typed three of Bailey's articles for publication.[11] The articles on Luke's birth narrative and on the parable of the good Samaritan would later appear in scholarly journals and also in his book *Jesus through Middle Eastern Eyes* (2008). In November 1974, Bailey learned that two of his articles had been accepted for publication: one by *Novum Testamentum*, a prestigious New Testament journal; and another by the *Bible Society Publications*. In the meantime, he had completed two more articles, which he would send off shortly for journals to consider.[12]

Over the years Bailey had found that ancient manuscripts of both Bibles and biblical commentaries were helpful in his studies because they provided a Middle Eastern perspective unaffected by later European scholarship. As he gathered these materials, he decided that they should become part of a permanent collection and be made available to scholars. In the early spring of 1974, he decided to establish what he grandly named the Institute for Middle Eastern New Testament Studies, a research institute at NEST for the study of the New Testament from the perspective of Middle Eastern culture.[13] He would serve as the direc-

9. Mickey to family, April 24, 11974, Bailey Papers, box 27, folder 3.
10. Ken to family, March 17, 1974, Bailey Papers, box 27, folder, 3.
11. Mickey to family, April 24, 1974, Bailey Papers, box 27, folder 3.
12. Mickey to family, November 17, 1974, Bailey Papers, box 27, folder 3. Ken published articles for *Novum Testamentum* and consulted with the *Bible Society Publications,* but the specific articles he had in mind here are not certain. However, one of the articles was probably Bailey, "Recovering the Poetic Structure of 1 Corinthians," 265–96.
13. Mickey to family, April 24, 1974, Bailey Papers, box 27, folder 3.

tor of the institute and hoped that eventually it would be funded by a foundation. While awaiting a benefactor, he would operate a low-budget one-person organization and save his growing collection of documents on microfilm.[14]

The thirteenth century in Egypt was a great era of Coptic scholarship launched by Abu al-Mufaddal ibn al-'Assal, who was honored with the title Fakhr al-Dawlah ("Pride of the State"). His four sons, known as Awlad al-'Assal ("the Sons of Assal"), carried on their father's scholarly legacy by producing compilations of canon law, works of doctrine and apologetics, a theological summa, histories, and a translation of the Gospels. Though their work was part of what became known as the Coptic Renaissance of the thirteenth century, this is a misnomer as it was not so much a rebirth as a last flowering. As such, the era might be better labeled the Indian Summer of Copto-Arabic literature, for when this great century of Arabic scholarship ended, the Coptic Church fell silent and was not heard from again for over 600 years.[15] Preserving Arab Christian scholarship from the period of the early church through the Middle Ages became one of Bailey's great dreams, which he would pursue to the end of his life. Three years later (sometime in 1977) he wrote a paper entitled "A Vision is Born," probably for his own benefit, detailing the origins and intentions of his new institute. The institute would complete the work by gathering, editing, interpreting, and publishing the writings of the Arabic fathers of the church.[16]

At NEST's board meeting in May 1974 Bailey was made a full professor, an honor that meant that he would be given an office in the seminary, which occurred in the fall. Until then, largely working from home, he was busy revising his dissertation, *Poet & Peasant*, which would be published by William B. Eerdmans Publishing Company two years later in 1976; and he was working on its sequel, *Through Peasant Eyes*, which

---

14. Later, of course, he would switch to computer discs.

15. Partrick, *Traditional Egyptian Christianity*, 87–88.

16. Personal Papers, VI, 1974–1977, Bailey Papers, box 4, folder 1. Bailey's interest in historical documents extended to more recent concerns. Early in February Bailey learned that the original manuscript of the Van Dyck Arabic Bible had been discovered in the mission office in Beirut, where it had remained in four metal boxes for over a century. Ben Weir loaned it to the Bible Society, but when Bailey learned of its existence, he convinced the COEMAR office and the Bible Society that it should be kept permanently at the NEST library. It is now in the archives room of the seminary. See Ken to Mother, February 16, 1975; March 2, 1975; and March 9, 1975, Bailey Papers, box 29, folder 2. The author learned of the current location of the Van Dyck Bible manuscript when he visited NEST in 2015.

he hoped would be published by Concordia in 1980. Rather than reducing the size of his dissertation, Bailey seems to have worked on clarifying and polishing his prose.[17]

The Baileys departed from Beirut in early June 1974 to spend the summer in the States. They flew to Chicago, but then planned to separate. Mickey would travel with the children to Des Moines to stay with her parents, while Ken would travel to St. Louis to study at Concordia Seminary. These plans, however, were not followed. When Ken's backpain worsened, he checked into a hospital in Des Moines to deal with his slipped disc. The doctors injected a milligram of dye into his spinal cord so that it could be x-rayed. Bailey had to lie flat for eight hours to perform this procedure. In the end, the doctors assured him that his disc was now in good shape and that surgery would not be necessary. His muscle spasms, they concluded, were probably due to pinched nerves in his spine. They recommended that he be treated with traction.[18] Writing again to his parents on June 16, he reported that he had spent most of the past week in traction. As he lay in bed, weights were attached to his legs and hung over the edge of the end of the bed. He had three sessions a day of this, totaling about eight hours of traction per day. He also had daily physical therapy, followed by a half hour of hot packs placed on his back and then a massage. By the end of the week, Bailey felt much better. But he would still need to wear a back brace for a month and avoid strenuous activity.[19]

During the month of July, Bailey was back at Concordia Seminary in St. Louis working on the revision of his dissertation for Eerdmans and the follow-up book for Concordia Press. During this time, Mickey's father, Leslie Milligan, died on the morning of July 6, 1974, at the age of eighty-five.[20] Two and a half weeks later Ken's father, Ewing Bailey, died on July 24, 1974, at the age of seventy-eight. Ken drove to his father's memorial service in Ohio presided over by the Reverend Bob Gibson. Mickey noted that it was a memorial service and not a funeral because Ewing Bailey had given his body to the "Research Center." Consequently, Ken did not see his father's body, which she thought was difficult for him. Ken felt that his mother was failing and would die during the summer.[21] Yet she lived for another six years.

17. Ken to Mother and Dad, July 6, 1974, Bailey Papers, box 29, folder 2.
18. Ken to Mother and Dad, June 10, 1974, Bailey Papers, box 29, bolder 2.
19. Ken to Mother and Dad, June 10, 1974, Bailey Papers, box 29, folder 2.
20. Ken to Mother and Dad, July 6, 1974, Bailey Papers, box 29, folder 2.
21. Mickey to Bruce and Pat, July 25, 1974, Bailey Papers, box 27, folder 3.

A Fourth Arab-Israeli War, and Civil War Comes to Lebanon

The first week of August saw Bailey back at the New Wilmington Missionary Conference. In March, when he thought that his back was nearly healed, he had agreed to be the main speaker at the conference. He must have begged off from this commitment when his back continued to trouble him, but he was still busy at conference activities.[22] On Tuesday, during the conference, Bailey drove to Pittsburgh to spend the afternoon with Dr. William Smalley of the Bible Society to discuss the structural analysis of the New Testament parables as presented in his dissertation with an eye to producing a book for the society. Though Bailey did not believe that the meeting had gone well, he would have an article by the Society published in the fall.[23] On Thursday, August 8, he recorded some biblical material for THESIS cassettes. He said that he recorded three more tapes, efforts that contributed to a larger collection. He also hoped to do four more tapes in Beirut before the end of the year.[24]

In early September, the Baileys flew back to Beirut.[25] The new semester started in late September, and in the second week of September Bailey began to prepare to move 1,000 of his theological books to the seminary. Not only did he now have an office at the seminary in which to keep them, but the president wanted him to do his work there, which Bailey considered only right.[26] He had his books moved to the seminary with the help of several children, including Sara and David, and Dr. Vernon Fletcher's microbus.[27]

With an office in the seminary, Bailey soon discovered that he was much too easily available to students and faculty. Complaining to his family, he wrote, "When any one wants to try out anything on a faculty member, they know that they can always find Bailey. I think I am going to have to escape to get blocks of time to break the back of some writing that needs to be done."[28] Nevertheless, Bailey was soon back at his various tasks in Beirut. In the first week of October, he began broadcasting his Bible studies for the radio program again. An Assemblies of God Bible

22. Ken to Edward Fairman, March 12, 1974, Bailey Papers, box 27, folder 2.

23. Ken to Mother, August 9, 1974, Bailey Papers, box 29, folder 2. This article has not yet been found.

24. Ken to Mother, August 9, 1974, Bailey Papers, box 29, folder 2.

25. Ken to family, September 15, 1974, Bailey Papers, box 27, folder 3.

26. Ken to Mother, September 15, 1974, Bailey Papers, box 29, folder 2.

27. Ken to Mother September 22, 1974, Bailey Papers, box 29, folder 2. See too Mickey to family, September 24, 1974, Bailey Papers, box 27, folder 3.

28. Mickey/Ken to family, March 1, 1975, Bailey Papers, box 27, folder 2.

school in Beirut started sending students to NEST one day a week so that Bailey could give them lectures on the New Testament, which he did in Arabic. He also worked on recording his lessons on the parables for THESIS cassettes, which were supposed to be completed by the end of November.[29] His output was greatly increased with the use of a Dictaphone and the assistance of a volunteer secretary, Linda Bassett, from Dale Milligan's church. Bailey wrote to his mother that with Linda's help he completed a final copy of his play *When the Wind Is Right*.

Intended to be performed in churches, the theme of this fourteen-page play was mission. In the early 1970s, the concept of Western mission was under attack, and there was even a movement to put a moratorium on sending missionaries.[30] Bailey begins his play by having three performers give voice to the typical objections raised by mission detractors: American missionaries are not in a position to preach peace, justice, and reconciliation with the enormous problems of racism and poverty in their own country; the heart of the gospel message is really political and economic liberation not a spiritual message of redemption; and since the United States has so many social problems, US missionaries should return home to take care of their own country before dealing with problems existing abroad. Having established the contemporary critiques of mission, the play then moves to the first century for a discussion among three New Testament figures: Paul, Luke, and Silas. Paul has just had a dream in which a Macedonian has said, "Come over and help us" (Acts 16:6–10). The three men then discuss the call, facing the same objections to mission as the contemporary church. Is Paul, being a citizen of the oppressive Roman Empire, really in a position to preach peace, justice, and reconciliation? Luke as a Greek and Silas as a Hebrew face the same question, as each of their countries had at times also engaged in oppression. Human beings, Paul argues, will always face times of confusion because socio-political winds blow in many directions. He believes, however, that the gospel he preaches rises above such concerns. After all, he does not preach a Roman gospel but rather a gospel from outside human society, and his ultimate argument is that he must respond to the vision that God has given him. As the play draws to an end, Paul learns that the wind is now favorable to sail to Macedonia. Therefore, they must sail as "the wind is right." This is a simple but very effective short play, one that if

29. Ken to Mother September 29, 1974, Bailey Papers, box 29, folder 2.
30. Coggins, "What's Behind the Idea?," 7–9.

performed in churches at the time would have certainly sparked lively debate. Bailey submitted the play for publication to Arthur Meriwether Inc. in the fall of 1974, and it was published in 1976.[31]

Reflecting on the death of his father in July, Bailey decided in the fall to gather a number of the letters that he and Mickey had written between 1955 and about 1972 in order to create a family record for posterity. He took them to a bookbinder in Beirut, returning home in mid-November with a freshly bound volume.[32] He also had a collection of his sermons from 1950 to 1965 bound as well as two volumes of his father's sermons. Hence in short order he had four volumes of bound Bailey Papers. Later, before January 19, 1975, he had a fifth volume of family letters bound, which included family letters from as early as the 1940s but otherwise were mostly from the early 1960s. Bailey decided to give the two volumes of his father's sermons "a prominent place" on his desk.[33] Later in 1975, he would write to his mother of the memorial fund he had established in the States centered at Dale Milligan's church, First Presbyterian Church, Oklahoma City. They decided to use the funds to purchase books for NEST's library, with each book including a commemorative plate:

> This book has been placed in this library
> by the friends of
> Ewing M. Bailey, D. Ed. (1896–1974)[34]

In February 1975 the Bailey family was planning to enjoy a picnic in the valley situated in the hills behind Beirut that they called Bailey's Hollow, but in March the political situation suddenly changed. There were explosions in the hills. Soon the roads into the city were blocked by barricades, some official and some decidedly unofficial.[35] Later, letter bombs in the mails slowed down the postal system by as much as four weeks as the government screened for explosive devices. The two largest political parties in the country, the Commandos (Palestinian fighters) and the Phalangists (a Christian party), were battling for supremacy. Things continued in this way for weeks, creating fear and uncertainty. Yet some

31. Bailey, *When the Wind Is Right*. One copy is in *Personal Papers*, a bound volume in the Bailey Papers, box 12, folder 2, 110–14.

32. Mickey to family, November 17, 1974, Bailey Papers, box 27, folder 3.

33. Ken to Mother, December 1, 1974, Bailey Papers, box 29, folder 2. For Annette Bailey's account see a Biographical Memoire [of Annette Bailey], Bailey Papers, box 29, folder 3.

34. Ken to Mother, September 12, 1975, Bailey Papers, box 29, folder 2.

35. Mickey/Ken to ____, March 1, 1975, Bailey Papers, box 27, folder 2.

normalcy was maintained as Bailey continued to attend meetings at the seminary, but because his back had not yet entirely healed, he was compelled to stretch out on the floor where he managed to participate fully.[36]

In the spring semester of 1975, Bailey served as an advisor to students at the seminary, many of whom were registering for classes for the first time. Mickey quoted him as saying, "Every student there is an exception to the rule, so it takes a great deal of time" to give them good advice as to the classes they should take. Two of the students were from Sudan who arrived with substandard English. Bailey anguished over them. If they took regular classes, they would not easily be able to follow the lectures, and they might slow down the progress of their fellow students. On the other hand, if they took a year to take courses in basic English, it would add a year to their program, which would be a hardship for many of them. One student, for example, had seven children whom he had left behind who needed his care. Bailey had to balance accommodating the students' needs and maintaining the academic standards of the seminary.[37]

On June 16, Bailey flew to the States for a number of summer speaking engagements that he had planned long in advance, including one at Dale Milligan's First Presbyterian Church in Oklahoma City. It was probably at this time that he gave Dale a revised copy of his master's thesis, THE DOCTRINE OF GOD for Village People (1961), which Dale would be instrumental in having republished by the Youth Club Program in the next year as *God Is . . . Dialogues on the Nature of God for Young People* (1976).[38] Dale, who was then president of the Youth Club Program, wrote a foreword to the book, noting that the organization served over 200,000 youths in 2,500 churches across the denominational spectrum. Bailey revised the book, originally written for Egyptian villagers, so that it would be relevant and accessible to American youth.

Civil War in Lebanon broke out in 1975, but it was years in the making.[39] Lebanon had been part of the Ottoman Empire for four centuries before

---

36. Ken to Dale [Milligan], April 15, 1975, Bailey Papers, box 27, folder 2.
37. Mickey to Mother, February 20, 1975, Bailey Papers, box 27, folder 2.
38. Bailey, *God Is . . . Dialogues* (1976).
39. For a detailed account of the civil war, see Fisk, *Pity the Nation*. For a more journalistic and impressionistic account, one that Ken enjoyed and that won the National Book Award in 1989, see Friedman, *From Beirut to Jerusalem*.

A Fourth Arab-Israeli War, and Civil War Comes to Lebanon

World War I. With the collapse of the empire during the war, Lebanon would become a League of Nations mandate state under the authority of France, and in 1943 it became an independent country. The new nation, however, suffered from deep sectarian divisions. Maronite Christians were the largest group, totaling about 51 percent of the population. The rest were various Islamic groups, with the exception of the Druze, who are an Islamic splinter group. The largest of the Islamic groups were the Sunnis, but the Shiites were a significant minority. The so-called National Pact of 1943, an agreement between the Maronites and Sunnis, distributed power among the various factions. According to its terms, the nation's president would always be a Maronite Christian, the prime minister a Sunni Muslim, and the speaker of the Chamber of Deputies a Shi'a Muslim. The ratio of six to five, Christians to Muslims, parliamentary seats was also fixed. Having been cobbled together in a fragile agreement, the nation of Lebanon quickly unraveled in the mid-1970s when the Maronite population declined to about 30 percent of the total population. At that point, Islamic groups insisted on a redistribution of power, which the Christians refused to countenance. Adding to this toxic cocktail of sectarianism was the introduction of Palestinians under the authority of the Palestine Liberation Organization (PLO). The PLO began to enter the country as early as the 1960s, but it did not appear in large numbers until its expulsion from Jordan in early 1971. When PLO forces began clashing with the Lebanese Army, various Muslim groups formed their own militias and were armed by the PLO. Soon each of the sectarian groups, convinced of their own integrity and the others' malfeasance, formed militias, which were poised to seize control of territory where their groups were most populous.

On Saturday night, June 28, 1975, while Ken was away in America, Mickey wrote, "everything seemed to break loose" in Beirut. With two young children in the apartment, Mickey listened to mortar, rocket, and machine gun fire that continued until morning. Lebanon had descended into a long night of civil war. Ken phoned on the morning of June 29 to speak to Mickey, who choked up a little and was apparently not reassuring. On Sunday morning, she decided to keep the children home from church because of safety issues. They had prayer in the living room together in lieu of church. Sara and David each contributed a prayer, and Mickey's prayer was so long that one of the children, Mickey did not say which one, remarked, "Gosh, Mom, that was as long as Daddy's." Many years later, Sara recalled that in stressful times her mother often quoted one of her favorite Bible verses: "The eternal God is thy refuge, and underneath are the everlasting arms" (Deut 33:27 KJV).[40]

When mortar fire began again that afternoon at 2:00, Mickey and the children shuttered the windows and retreated to the interior hallway for safety, where they stayed until the firing died down in the evening. After speaking with Mickey earlier that day, Ken immediately decided to cancel the rest of his speaking engagements and return home. Departing from Chicago, his plane landed three hours late in London, leaving him only fifteen minutes to make his connecting flight to Beirut. He succeeded, but his luggage did not. After a thirty-six-hour sleepless journey, he phoned Mickey from Beirut International Airport on Monday, June 30, at 8:00 p.m. This surprised Mickey, who thought he was calling from the States. Because the streets continued to be unsafe, the apartment doorman kindly agreed to retrieve Ken from the airport, borrowing the family car.

On July 3, Mickey came down with what she thought was the flu. Over the course of the next week, she continued to be ill and had a fervor that abated but then returned. Finally, her doctor put her in the hospital where it was discovered that she had infectious hepatitis, more commonly known as jaundice. She was in the hospital for at least the rest of the month. In the meantime, Ken relied on the woman who cleaned for the family to provide meals, with young Sara helping out as best she could. Ken wrote of Sara, "She is doing some cooking and does the wash, orders her brother around, and sometimes her father" and "the "meals are a bit 'batchlorish,' but that's about what you would expect given the quality of the kitchen staff. We have been invited out for a number of evening meals, and I can fry eggs—so we manage."[41] When Mickey returned home around the end of July after fifteen days in the hospital, it was expected that she would need six months before she fully recovered. During this time, Bailey wrote, the political situation stabilized, though the country remained in the grip of armed parties, roadblocks all over the city hampered traffic, and tanks rumbled down its main streets. Bailey reported that the "uneasy truce" that existed between the competing parties was expected to last until October.[42]

---

40. Mickey to family, June 29, 1975, Bailey Papers, box 27, folder 2. Sara Bailey Makari quoted this passage from Deuteronomy at her mother's funeral service on February 4, 2023.

41. Ken to family, July 4, 1975, Bailey Papers, box 29, folder 2.

42. Ken to family, July 24, 1975, Bailey Papers, box 27, folder 3.

A Fourth Arab-Israeli War, and Civil War Comes to Lebanon

Despite the violence and fighting in and around Beirut, life went on. Shops stayed open, and schools opened in late September for the new academic year. In late September when the new semester began at NEST, Bailey was there every morning. However, the number of students had dropped to two or three. The nation's troubles, Mickey explained to her mother, were due to internal conflicts not external threats posed by Syria or Israel. Since elections were scheduled for the late spring of 1976, the Baileys anticipated difficulties at least until then.[43]

On September 7, 1975, Ken and Mickey celebrated their twentieth anniversary as career missionaries, which they counted from their landing in Alexandria, Egypt, in 1955. They went out to lunch together that day to mark the occasion, which became seared in their memories when at 11:35 that night a bomb exploded in the basement of the building next to the seminary, blowing out all the windows and starting a fire. The explosion also damaged surrounding buildings. The seminary building shook badly from the explosion, which shattered four plate glass windows and a dozen smaller windows, bent doorframes, and cracked the plaster in some of the rooms.[44]

Writing to the family on October 8, Ken reported that Mickey had returned to the hospital. The enzyme level in her blood had risen rapidly, though there was no apparent liver damage. Friends delivered food to the Baileys, but Ken and Sara did most of the cooking for the family. Ken worried that, should they have to evacuate, Mickey would have to be taken to the airport on a stretcher.[45] In this letter, Ken also described the worsening situation in Beirut. They were no longer living day to day, but hour to hour. Registration had opened that day for the students at the seminary, but no one had shown up. The seminary would keep the registration period open for another week, but since students had difficulty traveling to and from Beirut, Bailey doubted that it would be possible to open the seminary that year. Streets that were usually snarled in traffic were now deserted, as were sidewalks where foot traffic had disappeared. Garbage had not been removed for twenty days, leaving huge mounds of trash in the streets that were an eye sore and raised a terrible stench. As many set fire to the garbage in front of their apartments, smoke filled the air on numerous blocks. There were long bread lines and vegetables were hard to come by. At night bombs were often heard exploding followed

43. Mickey to Mother, September 27, 1975, Bailey Papers, box 27, folder 2.
44. Ken to Mother, September 8, 1975, Bailey Papers, box 29, folder 2.
45. Ken to Dale [Milligan], October 8, 1975, Bailey Papers, box 27, folder 2.

by a peal of gunfire in the immediate neighborhood. Bailey learned that gunfire meant that the faction that controlled his part of the city was simply warning other factions that they were alert and prepared should any seek to overtake them. Knowing this allowed him to sleep a little easier at night. Bailey also counted his blessings. Unlike his Lebanese neighbors, he had an uninterrupted foreign salary, the possibility of evacuation should it be necessary, and a place to stay in the United States.[46]

By mid-October Mickey was back at home, though she had to remain in bed. Bailey had planned a trip to Germany, but he cancelled it due to the uncertain situation in Beirut. He wanted to be with his family in case of further violence or the need for a quick evacuation. NEST had managed to open and the children remained in school, but Bailey did not believe that this would continue long. He occupied himself with writing another academic article and book reviews for the NEST journal, *Theological Review of the Near East School of Theology*. The government imposed a curfew from 8:00 p.m. to 5:00 a.m. and, Bailey commented, "no one breaks it. Only tanks move on the streets at night."[47]

Though Bailey had cancelled his planned trip to Germany, he decided that he could not cancel on his brother-in-law Dale Milligan, who had planned for Bailey to speak at his church in Oklahoma that October. While there, Bailey's worst fears were realized when, on October 24, what has come to be known as the Battle of the Hotels broke out in the hotel district a mile and a half from the Baileys' apartment in Ras Beirut and then spread to other areas of the city. Low-level armed conflict between the various militias in the city had begun in April, but this escalated in late October as various groups engaged in rocket and artillery exchanges, firing from hotel rooms and rooftops, as they sought to control the hotel area near the Corniche. Bailey flew back to Beirut to retrieve his family. Many at this time were fleeing the city, and some Presbyterian missionaries were evacuating. The Baileys flew to London along with their close friends the Stellings and Hilgendorfs. From there the Baileys proceeded to Oklahoma City and the home of Dale and Doris Milligan, where they hunkered down to consider their options.[48]

---

46. Ken to Dale [Milligan], October 8, 1975, Bailey Papers, box 27, folder 2.

47. Ken to family, October 17, 1975, Bailey Papers, box 27, folder 3.

48. The Bailey Papers include very little information about the evacuation other than that it occurred. This paragraph is a reconstruction of events based on the well-known events of the period. Sara recalls that the entire Bailey family, including her father, flew back to the States together. Therefore, I have written that Bailey returned to

A Fourth Arab-Israeli War, and Civil War Comes to Lebanon

Bailey anticipated that the family would remain in the States for ten months but that they might be able to return earlier than that. The American Community School, where Sara and David were attending, had closed, but if it started again in the spring semester, the family might be able to return to Beirut as early as the end of January in order for the children to begin classes on time. Another possibility would be for Bailey to return alone at the end of January. He commented to his family, "Dad stuck it out for three years alone during wartime. I guess I should be able to make it for four months."[49] While awaiting developments, Bailey wanted to find good schools where he could place Sara and David that would also be close to a university so that he could use its library for the research he would need to do for his next book. In the event, Fuller Theological Seminary's School of World Mission, located in Pasadena, California, was in the midst of a year of graduate study for mission leaders from around the world that would emphasize Islam. When school administrators learned that Dr. Kenneth Bailey of Beirut had just been evacuated to Oklahoma City, they called to offer him a position as an adjunct faculty member.

The Program Agency in New York informed Bailey that he had been granted a three-month furlough and that at the end of January he should be back in Beirut to teach at NEST. Bailey considered this unrealistic because Beirut would continue to be unsettled at least until the elections in the spring. Therefore, he felt he should take the position at Fuller, where he could teach for one semester and then return to Beirut if things had become calm. The Program Agency refused to commit itself, leaving Bailey hanging.[50] He decided to go to Fuller anyway, but he was not able to take up the teaching position in the second quarter that began in January 1976. Because of the New York Office's unwillingness to give him a long-term commitment on his furlough, he could not be employed by Fuller, which understandably needed to finalize its schedule for the winter and spring quarters of 1976. However, the seminary did grant Bailey "faculty privileges" so that he could use the library and continue the research for his next book.

Ken wrote to Dale in early December to describe his frustration with the Program Agency of the Presbyterian Church, whose heads he refers to as "the Barons of 475"—an allusion to the nineteen-story building on

---

Beirut from Oklahoma.

49. Ken to Mother, Bruce and Barbara, November 2, 1975, box 27, folder 4.
50. Ken to Dale [Milligan], November 20, 1975, Bailey Papers, box 27, folder 4.

475 Riverside Drive in New York that was known as the God Box because of the many church organizations located there. He was angry that he was considered to be on furlough while other evacuated missionaries from Beirut were still considered to be on the field. He was also concerned that he was responsible to President Hovhanness Aharonian of NEST because he had promised him that he would be returning in January. But then he considered that there would be few if any students at that time.[51] Moreover, Bailey was loath to leave his family, and he was especially solicitous of Sara, who was experiencing "reentry" problems that are typical of the children of missionaries—known as MKs (Missionary Kids).

By December, however, Sara's reentry issues soon became "serious signs of abnormal stress," as Bailey described it. Writing of Sara's difficulties he remarked to Dale, "I had only four wolves to shoot last evening, and they were shot rather easily. The terrifying packs of big wolves that do not go away, or stay dead, might appear if I left. Mickey doesn't think they will. I hope she is right."[52] Sara imagined that the police were coming to arrest her, that she would be imprisoned for tripping over someone at school, that people were coming to attack her in the night. After a month of staying up every night for three hours to calm their daughter, the Baileys finally sought professional help from a highly renowned psychologist in Oklahoma City known to Dale Milligan. The doctor discovered that Sara had an excellent memory and an IQ of 142, but she suffered from an auditory dyslexia that made it difficult for her to deal well with new situations, which she could find confusing and even terrifying. Sara, however, found no difficulty in negotiating situations that she knew well such as home, school, and the immediate community. What she needed to thrive was a calm, structured, predictable environment. As Bailey considered his options as a missionary, he must have realized that Ras Beirut was among the last places in the world suitable for his daughter.[53]

The Program Agency did not direct Bailey to return to Beirut in the early months of 1976 but, instead, extended his furlough through March. Bailey, therefore, became an adjunct professor at Fuller Theological Seminary after all.[54] Following some initial confusion, Fuller's Board

---

51. Ken to Dale [Milligan], December 9, 1975, box 27, folder 4.

52. Ken to Dale [Milligan], January 7, 1976, box 27, folder 4.

53. Ken to Robert Lodwick, March 16, 1976, RG 424, Presbyterian Historical Society. In this paragraph, I have closely followed Bailey's description of Sara's fears and apparent needs.

54. For a history of Fuller Seminary see Marsden, *Reforming Fundamentalism*, 187.

of Trustees officially made him an adjunct faculty member on January 19, and Bailey was then given full credit as the professor responsible for a seminar in Islamics in the winter quarter.[55] He also taught a course on Jesus' parables that soon attracted seventy-five students, which was more than any adjunct professor at Fuller had yet drawn.[56] Although the class was limited to seventy-five, the ninety chairs in the class were filled for each class, suggesting a wide interest in his lectures.[57]

By March the executives in the Program Agency relented, acknowledging that they were in no position to decide in New York about the circumstances on the ground in Lebanon. Therefore, they concluded that Bailey should return to Beirut at the end of March and stay through Easter, April 18, 1976, in order to evaluate the situation for himself. If a reliable political settlement were in place by then, he should return with his family to the city. Otherwise, he could continue his work in California. The Program Agency also relayed the information that NEST currently had forty-one students and was "pressing" for Bailey's return.[58]

Bailey traveled to New York for a meeting with his bosses on April 1. Though they wanted to consult with Bailey to learn about the situation in Beirut, he saw this as a useless *pro forma* exercise. After all, he had been away from Beirut for months and his information was now stale. Bailey felt vindicated since so much of what he had told them about the unsettled nature of the city had come true. "They are running scared," he wrote to Dale, "and the pawn (Bailey) is suddenly looking like a castle or a bishop?" Dale had written to the Program Agency leaders in January to question their decision to regard the Baileys' time in the States as a furlough rather than an evacuation. His letter was well-mannered but pointed as words and phrases such as "unilateral designation," "profound mistake in judgment," "insensitive," "punitive," and "penalized for being evacuated" seemed to fly off the pages.[59] Later Dale exchanged angry words over the phone with Syngman Rhee, the Coordinator for the

---

55. Ken to Dale [Milligan], January 19, 1976, Bailey Papers, box 27, folder 4.
56. Ken to Mother, March 12, 1976, Bailey Papers, box 27, folder, 4.
57. Ken to Dale [Milligan], April 29, 1976, Bailey Papers, box 27, folder 4.
58. Ken to Mother, March 12, 1976, Bailey Papers, box 27, folder 4.
59. Dale K. Milligan to Hazel J. McGeary (and copied to Robert Lodwick, Syngman Ree and Ken Bailey), January 28, 1976, RG 424, Presbyterian Historical Society. Both McGeary and Rhee responded cordially, assuring Dale that the Program Agency was not acting unilaterally or out of step with established policies. Syngman Rhee to Dale K. Milligan, February 12, 1976; and Hazel J. McGeary to Dale K. Milligan, February 13, 1976, RG 424, Presbyterian Historical Society.

Middle East for COEMAR, accusing him of sending people to Beirut as prophets when he should be bringing them home to safety.[60] On returning from his trip to New York, Bailey described the church leaders in scathing terms, seeing the current directors of Presbyterian missions as "a long way downhill from Robert E. Speer and John Coventry Smith"— revered leaders in recent Presbyterian mission history.[61]

Having met with the mission executives in early April, later that month, Bailey traveled to Dhahran, Saudi Arabia, where there was a growing international community associated with the oil industry and five Protestant congregations had already been established. Bailey toured many of the sites and preached seven times in three venues. He found the nation fascinating and his efforts there highly rewarding. In the years to come he would return many times.[62] On the way home, he stopped for five days in Beirut to secure his belongings and, as directed, evaluate the situation in the city. He was greeted warmly by his colleagues and enjoyed being "wined and dined" while he was there. To his relief, he found the family's apartment still standing and intact. Mickey had given him a list of things to retrieve, and Bailey spent two days assembling them. The things he considered the most precious he would take with him on the return flight as carry-on items, including the family's much-loved Siamese cat, Duchess, who traveled in the cabin with him. The rest of what he wanted to save would have to be air-freighted out.[63]

While in Beirut, Bailey stayed at the seminary, making it his base. He soon learned that the figure of forty-one students that NEST claimed to have was misleading. There were actually only ten full-time students, but there were twenty-five part-time students who were each taking one class in order to meet the minimum requirement to retain housing in the building. There were also five additional students on the rolls who were not attending any classes as they were living abroad in various places around the world. The current professor of New Testament was teaching two courses but had had only two students in one class and four in the other. As Bailey moved around Beirut, he found conditions in the

---

60. Ken to Dale [Milligan], March 26, 1976, Bailey Papers, box 27, folder 4.

61. Ken to Dale [Milligan], April 5, 1976, Bailey Papers, box 27, folder 4. For these church leaders, see Piper, *Robert E. Speer*, and Smith, *From Colonialism to World Community*.

62. Ken to Mother, April 26, 1976, and Ken to Dale, April 29, 1976, Bailey Papers, box 27, folder 4.

63. Ken to Mother, April 26, 1976, Bailey Papers, box 29, folder 2.

A Fourth Arab-Israeli War, and Civil War Comes to Lebanon

city appalling. There was garbage strewn everywhere and armed men roaming the streets. People did not dare go outside between 1:00 p.m. and 9:00 a.m. When the sun had set and he was safely back at NEST, he witnessed "a nightly artillery duel" between different sections of the city, with shells passing over the seminary.[64] The staff and students of NEST as well as Bailey slept in the inner hall of the seminary while rocket fire "wounded seven and killed one in the street just outside our building." On the morning that Bailey was scheduled to leave the city, the airport was shelled. But Bailey's flight on an Air France plane took off safely, the last plane to depart before the airport was closed.[65] Bailey had arranged for his things to be flown to the United States from Beirut, but when airline flights were discontinued, his trunks were sent to the seminary—and there they would stay until he retrieved them later. Though the Baileys were scheduled to return to Beirut in August, Mickey speculated that a more realistic date would be October.[66] When Sara and David finished school in June that year, the Baileys left Pasadena to drive across the country, enjoying some sightseeing on the way, and visiting family in the Midwest.[67]

---

64. Ken to Mother, April 26, 1976, Bailey Papers, box 27, folder 4.
65. Ken to Mother, May 6, 1976, Bailey Papers, box 27, folder 4.
66. Mickey to family, May 19, 1976, Bailey Papers, box 27, folder 4.
67. Mickey to family, May 19, 1976, Bailey Papers, box 29, folder 2.

11

Discerning the Poet in the Peasant
1976–77

> No one would crucify a teacher who told pleasant stories to enforce prudential morality.
>
> —C. W. F. Smith cited in Joachim Jeremias, *The Parables of Jesus*

AFTER A CROSS-COUNTRY TRIP in June and July and numerous speaking engagements along the way, Bailey arrived with his family in New Wilmington where they were given the New Wilmington mission house for furloughed Presbyterian mission personnel on Waugh Avenue for one year.[1] Bailey estimated that the old house was probably built in 1900 and knew that it would need many repairs. But its high ceilings and hardwood floors were appealing.[2] Since the house lacked a shower, Bailey did much of the work to install one in the basement, though he had to call a

---

1. Mickey to Floyd and Marg [Milligan], May 10, 1976, Bailey Papers, box 27, folder 4.
2. Ken to Floyd and Marg [Milligan], August 20, 1976, Bailey Papers, box 27, folder 4.

plumber to complete the job.³ Needing a space to work, he made an office for himself on the third floor.⁴

Uncertain about whether he would be able to return to Beirut, Bailey began to look about for other mission opportunities. One came to him from the Schutz School in Alexandria, Egypt, where he was offered a job as the school's chaplain and teacher of religion. But he quickly rejected this idea because it would mean pulling his children out of schools just when they were settling in and making friends. A more attractive offer came from Albert Isteero, who asked if Bailey would be interested in participating in the development of an Arabic-language Bible commentary to be published in Cairo. In the thousand years that Arabic had been one of Christianity's major languages there had been only one set of Bible commentaries in Arabic produced. Written and published in the nineteenth century, the commentaries were out of date even at the time. Isteero's proposal was to produce an Arabic commentary series that would be similar to the *Interpreter's Bible*. Bailey's primary contribution would be to assemble material for writers of Arabic to produce a modern commentary. He proposed to do this at the Pittsburgh Theological Seminary library.⁵ He thought that this task, in addition to preaching and writing, would be a productive use of the winter he would spend in the States.⁶ The Program Agency agreed and, in September, approved this use of his time.⁷ The Agency also extended his furlough until August 1977.⁸ Unfortunately, this project was unsuccessful, and the proposed commentary was never produced.⁹ Instead, Bailey's major writing undertaking for the fall and winter would be his new book promised to Concordia Press, *Through Peasant Eyes*. To work on these two tasks simultaneously, he obtained the use of an office at Pittsburgh Theological Seminary.

On September 23, Bailey drove to the seminary to use the library, returning with a stack of books for his research. Prior to this, he had

---

3. Ken to Mother, September 14, 1976, Bailey Papers, box 27, folder 4.
4. Ken to Mother, September 8, 1976, Bailey Papers, box 27, folder 4.
5. Bailey "Initial Reflections on the Torch Library Plan to Produce an 'Interpreter's Bible' for the Arab World." Box RG 424, Presbyterian Historical Society.
6. Ken to Mother, September 8, 1976, Bailey Papers, box 27, folder 4.
7. Mickey to Mother, September 14, Bailey Papers, box 27, folder 4.
8. Mickey to family, October 8, 1976, Bailey Papers, box 27, folder 4.
9. Albert Isteero's wife, Jean, recalled that he did not follow through on the project and soon became engaged in producing an Arabic-Greek Bible dictionary for which he was never able to find a publisher.

developed some pain in at least one of his legs and had been using crutches. On that day he forgot his crutches, and going up and down three flights of stairs in the library multiple times to find each of the books he needed took a toll. He was in considerable pain for at least a few days afterwards.[10] In early October, he went to see a specialist in Pittsburgh to have his legs x-rayed to determine if he had phlebitis. The Bailey Papers do not reveal if he had this condition, which often causes a painful swelling of the legs.[11] If he had a mild case, he could have treated it himself with homecare remedies such as applying warm compresses to the affected area and taking anti-inflammatory drugs. If he were in danger of developing blood clots, the doctor may have recommended a blood-thinning medication.

During the summer of 1976 two of Bailey's books were published. The first was an English version of *God is. . .Dialogues on the Nature of God for Young People*, described in the previous chapter.[12] The other book, at long last, was his dissertation, published by Eerdmans as *Poet & Peasant: A Literary-Cultural Approach to the Parables of Luke*. He was surprised, he told his mother, Annette, that on the back cover were endorsements from Dr. Markus Barth and his former colleague Dr. William Holliday, a professor at NEST "whose work in Old Testament poetry," Bailey wrote in the book's acknowledgments, "first opened my eyes to the new possibilities in the New Testament." Apparently, Eerdmans had contacted them without informing Bailey.[13]

Bailey's dissertation-*cum*-book *Poet & Peasant* claimed to offer a reinterpretation of Jesus' parables. But how is it possible that after nineteen centuries anyone could find in Jesus' parables something new to say, let alone present a radical new interpretation? The answer requires a brief

---

10. Mickey to Mother, September 24, 1976, Bailey Papers, box 27, folder 4.

11. Mickey to family, October 8, 1976, Bailey Papers, box 27, folder 4. See too John D. Frame, MD, "Supplement to Health Report of June 15, 1976," November 8, 1976. In checking for phlebitis, he wrote, "Venography revealed old venous occlusion of the distal third of the calf veins." He recommended "active rehabilitation" through physiotherapy. After a week, Ken believed that he had shown "dramatic" improvement and no longer needed crutches. Box RG 424, Presbyterian Historical Society.

12. Mickey to family, October 8, 1976, Bailey Papers, box 27, folder 4.

13. Ken to Mother, September 8, 1976, Bailey Papers, box 29, folder 2. Bailey, *Poet & Peasant and Through Peasant Eyes*, 6.

historical survey. Though the parables of Jesus seem to be simple stories with easily discernable messages, this is not the case. For most of the church's history, it has consistently misinterpreted the parables because it has treated them as allegories such as John Bunyan's *The Pilgrim's Progress* in which each detail has a symbolic meaning. This history is noted by Bailey in the opening interpretive chapter of *Peasant & Poet*, citing an article by Archibald M. Hunter. To some extent, Hunter had explained, the allegorical interpretive tradition was justifiable in that the church was following the example of the evangelists who gave allegorical meanings to some of the parables, such as Jesus' parable of the Sower (Matt 13; Mark 4:1–12; and Luke 8:4–10). The technique of allegorical interpretation was most highly developed by Origen of Alexandria in the third century.[14] The results, however, were generally fanciful interpretations that simply restated the interpreter's convictions. Even as perceptive a scholar as Augustine of Hippo, in *Quaestiones Evangeliorum* ("*Questions of the Gospels*"), was misled and misleading in adopting this approach. For example, in his interpretation of the parable of the good Samaritan, as summarized by Hunter,

> the wounded traveler is fallen man, half alive in his knowledge of God and half dead in his slavery to sin; the binding up of his wounds signifies Christ's restraint of sin; the pouring in of oil and wine the comfort of good hope and the exhortation to spirited work. The innkeeper, dropping in incognito is revealed as the Apostle Paul; and the two pence turn out to be the two commandments of love.[15]

Reformation scholars, no longer tethered to church tradition, attempted a clean break from the allegorical method. Martin Luther insisted that the Scriptures be interpreted literally and on their own terms. Yet Luther fell short of his own dictum, often indulging in allegorical interpretations that taught his theology of justification by grace alone. John Calvin did better, letting Scripture speak for itself and seeking a single meaning to the parables, but Protestant interpreters in the seventeenth century fell back into allegorical excesses.

---

14. Origen assigned each parable three levels of meaning: literal, moral, and spiritual; and Medieval scholars expanded this to four: literal, moral, allegorical, and anagogical.

15. Hunter, *Interpreting the Parables*, 26. Chapters 2 and 3 of this short book give a history of the interpretation of the parable. These chapters are an expansion of the article that Bailey read: Hunter, "Interpreter and the Parables," 70–84.

It was not until the late nineteenth century that German scholar Adolf Jülicher broke the spell that had enchanted nineteen centuries of earnest scholars. Writing in *Die Gleichnisreden Jesu* ("*The Parables of Jesus*"),[16] Jülicher argued that the parables of Jesus should not be interpreted allegorically with each element having a symbolic meaning. Rather, they should be interpreted as true parables—that is, as stories meant to argue a single point. Jülicher, however, came up short because he followed Aristotle's understanding of parables as simple moral stories. In other words, he used a Western understanding of parables to interpret a Hebraic literary form. In effect, he interpreted Jesus' parables as one would Aesop's Fables—as stories meant to teach a simple moral truth.

C. H. Dodd, writing in the *Parables of the Kingdom* (1935), corrected Jülicher, arguing that the parables were not told in support of a religious or moral "commonplace." Rather, seen in their time and place, they conveyed differing points that all related to the kingdom of God. Following the form-critical school of interpretation developed by German scholars after World War I,[17] he argued that the points conveyed could only be discerned by first understanding their *Sitz im Leben* ("setting in life"). Dodd believed that the setting of Jesus' parables as they appear in the Gospels was the early church, not Jesus' own lifetime. Jesus intended them for purposes that suited his situation, but the early church reinterpreted them so that they would convey messages relevant to the church. For example, Jesus' parable of the light hidden under a bushel (Matt 5:16; Mark 11:33; and Luke 8:16) was, in his historical setting, intended as an indictment of the Jewish leaders for their failure to reach the common people. The evangelists, however, changed the meaning to apply to Christians in general.[18]

Joachim Jeremias next took up the challenge of interpreting Jesus' stories in *The Parables of Jesus* (1947).[19] He agreed with Dodd's conclusion that parables were not simple moral tales, citing approvingly C. W.

---

16. Jülicher, *Gleichnisreden Jesu*.

17. Form criticism of the Gospel was first developed in Schmidt, *Rahmen der Geschichte Jesu*; Dibelius, *From Tradition to Gospel*; and Bultmann, *History of the Synoptic Tradition*. For a brief introduction to form criticism, see Bauckham, *Jesus and the Eyewitnesses*, 241–49.

18. Dodd, *Parables of the Kingdom*, 145.

19. The first edition of Jeremias' book appeared in German in 1947, and it was first translated into English in 1954. When Jeremias revised the original German version, the revision was given a fresh translation into English in 1963, which is the book that Bailey read, Jeremias, *Parables of Jesus*.

F. Smith's conclusion, "No one would crucify a teacher who told pleasant stories to enforce prudential morality."[20] But Jeremias went beyond Dodd in attempting to understand the nature of Hebrew parables by examining them in the light of the variety of ways they are put to figurative use in Hebrew literature, and he attempted to go behind the resetting of the parables in the Gospels in the time of the early church to reach back to their original setting in Jesus' life.

Bailey accepted the Dodd-Jeremias reinterpretation of the parables, but he would take this tradition several steps beyond where these scholars had gone. He believed that they lacked the cultural knowledge of the first-century Middle Eastern setting of Jesus' parables to correctly and precisely interpret them. In addition, they had not discerned the artistic dimension of the parables that reveal an underlying literary unity and integrity that pointed to Jesus as their author. Instead, following form-critical methods, they attributed too much of the parables to the early church. Other scholars, he observed, had detected the timeless quality of the parables as great works of art, but their interpretations were not anchored to the history of first-century Palestine. Consequently, in their hands the parables became "like floating balloons, ready to follow the prevailing winds."[21] Bailey would be careful to address all of these concerns while repackaging Jesus as the masterful poet-peasant of the New Testament.

Most of Bailey's books are intended for popular as well as scholarly audiences, but *Poet & Peasant* is clearly aimed at scholars in the field of biblical studies. Part one of this two-part work explains his intended contribution to biblical studies in terms of theory and methodology, which may seem to lay readers as overly dry and technical. As a dissertation, however, it was essential that Bailey conduct a literature review, showing what previous scholars had done in the field, where he differed from them, and what contribution he would make to the field. First, he considers theory. All agree, Bailey begins, that scholars should reject the allegorical method of interpreting the parables, leaving three alternative interpretive methods then available: the historical-eschatological method of C. H. Dodd and Joachim Jeremias; the parables as timeless art, a view presented by G. V. Jones; and the existential perspective of Eta Linnemann and Dan O. Via. Bailey believes that each of these has merit as well as limitations, but he prefers a theory that accepts the parables as

---

20. Jeremias, *Parables of Jesus*, 21.
21. Bailey, *Poet & Peasant*, 24.

art while insisting that they must be interpreted according to the literary conventions and cultural assumptions of first-century Palestine.

Next, he considers methodology. Bailey briefly reviews the five ways that the church has approached the problem in the past. It has "allegorized, indigenized, universalized, existentialized, and, on occasion, given up in despair."[22] Origen allegorized, but this resulted in unreliable interpretations that Jülicher corrected by insisting on a historical basis for all textual analysis. The approach of indigenization assumed that first-century people thought like people today—that, for example, a person knocking on a neighbor's door in the middle of the night in the current age would receive the same reaction as 2,000 years ago. The universalist approach assumed that these are universal stories that can be interpreted by any culture because the characters are universally recognized—e.g., a father and his sons. This and the previous approach did not take seriously how much culture affects people. The existentialist approach skipped the need to understand the problem historically and, instead, went right to the hermeneutical question, the broader meaning of the text. But this cannot be known without first examining the meaning in its specific culture and time. Finally, some have given up, recognizing that parables embedded in a culture 2,000 years ago have an original meaning that is "irrecoverably lost"—a postmodern view, though Bailey does not use this term.[23]

Bailey rejects all of these approaches, believing that the original meaning of the parables can be recovered using the tools of what he calls "Oriental exegesis."[24] One can consult contemporary peasants to ascertain what they make of the parables, examine ancient Eastern translations of the Gospels for hints about their meaning, and turn to ancient literature where it offers clues on how best to interpret cultural forms in the Scriptures. Bailey is also content to employ the tools of Western critical scholarship as long this is done in combination with these other approaches.

Bailey recognizes that some may reject the idea that contemporary Middle Eastern peasants would have anything to contribute. But he argues that the isolation of Middle Eastern villages and the quality of "changelessness" in the conservative traditional cultures of the Middle East means that peasant culture today is very similar to that of the first century. Moreover, such villagers have preserved their ancient cultures

---

22. Bailey, *Poet & Peasant*, 28.
23. Bailey, *Poet & Peasant*, 29.
24. Bailey, *Poet & Peasant*, 29.

by reciting old poems and retelling old stories. Bailey personally experienced such cultures and drew lessons from them. He writes,

> As a part of a village literacy team [in Upper Egypt] for five years, I was privileged to live in Oriental villages for long periods of time. Naturally, the villages themselves were among the most isolated and primitive, because they were the villages where the highest rates of illiteracy were to be found. Living in the village, I was able to become a part of the scenery and could interact with the village people not as a guest or stranger, researcher or scholar, but as an ordinary resident. With no camera or notebook, I could watch people interacting with each other. Over a period of years, I gradually came to the realization that a new layer of perception is available when we ask a fresh set of questions of the biblical text.[25]

Bailey took this a step beyond observation when he posed questions to villagers about the interpretation of biblical stories. "Now," he asks, "if this had happened in your village in the days of your grandfather, what would it have meant?" He was careful to employ a set of methodological controls to ensure that the responses he received were likely correct. Each man to be used as a resource, he writes, "must have spent at least the first twenty years of his life in a conservative, basically illiterate, isolated peasant community." The information must be collected orally as the subject under observation is part of an oral culture. He must have known the person for at least five years, which he hopes will guard "against receiving the stylized answers of the Easterner responding to the foreigner." Finally, the person must have sufficient knowledge of the Bible to be able to give apposite answers to Bailey's questions. Eventually over a period of some years he assembled a collection of twenty-five primary informants from Middle Eastern countries, including Egypt, Sudan, Lebanon, Palestine, and Iran.[26]

In addition to informants, Bailey also settles on eighteen versions of the Bible in Arabic and Syriac for the study. Gathered over many years from monasteries and libraries in Egypt, Mount Sinai, Lebanon, and many other places, these are texts that in general were produced by Medieval Middle Easterners and used by churches in the region. As translations of the Bible, they reflect the Middle Eastern cultural context of the time. Again, Bailey assumes that this is a highly conservative and

---

25. Bailey, *Poet & Peasant*, 34–35.
26. Bailey, *Poet & Peasant*, 35–36.

unchanging culture so that first-century cultural assumptions were still in place hundreds of years later when these translations were produced.

This aspect of Bailey's methodology was open to scholarly criticism. How did he know that contemporary villages in the Middle East retain the same culture as that of the first century? How could he be sure that Middle Eastern scholars of the Middle Ages reflected the cultural norms of Jesus' time? Because Bailey's informants were all Christian ministers, was it possible that they were unconsciously telling him exactly what he wanted to hear, caught in a circular hermeneutical trap? There are no clear answers to these objections, and Bailey would return to the problem at several different points in his career. For now, he admits that this is not a science because it can never really be known if or how much Middle Eastern peasant culture has changed over time. Yet any exegesis of the Scriptures requires that the exegete rely on cultural interpretations. The only question, he observes, is "*Whose* culture shall we allow to inform the text for us?" For him, it clearly makes more sense to allow modern Middle Eastern peasant culture to inform the scholar's analysis rather than modern Western culture.[27]

Bailey is also concerned with the nature of the Hebrew forms of parables. Western scholars are quick to assume a Western understanding of parables as comparisons made for the purpose of illustration and to convey a single point. In Hebrew literature, however, they can be employed in a variety of figurative uses and are often used not simply as illustrations, as in the West, but as carefully nuanced aspects of an argument. Parables, Bailey argues, can employ multiple symbols, but they are not allegories that present "cryptograms that must be decoded." He believes that Hebrew parables have three elements: referents or symbols for things in the real world of the listener; the single response that the parable teller seeks to evoke from his listeners; and a "theological cluster" of ideas—such as the kingdom, grace, fruit bearing, and hope—that are presented or assumed in the story to make the point.[28]

While the nature of parables is crucial to Bailey's argument, the most controversial of his ideas concerns his detection of the use of parallel structures, or chiasms, as a literary device employed in the New Testament and their significance for the interpretation of parables. Bailey, of course, was not the first scholar to observe such structures in the New

---

27. Bailey, *Poet & Peasant*, 37.
28. Bailey, *Poet & Peasant*, 38.

Testament. In chapter three he briefly reviews the history of the literary analyses of Scripture that focus on the use of chiasms. He begins in the eighteenth century and moves quickly to his own time. His most important predecessor in this tradition is Nils Wilhelm Lund, who wrote *Chiasmus in the New Testament* (1942). Though Lund made a compelling case for the use of chiasms in the New Testament, many scholars concluded that he was so convinced of their widespread existence in the Scriptures that he often saw them where they did not exist. New Testament scholar Burton B. Thurston recalled that when Lund was studying the use of chiasms in the book of Revelation, "He saw chiasmus everywhere and his fellow students and professors named him 'Chiasmus' Lund."[29] In time, Bailey too would be accused of seeing chiasms in the Scriptures whose existence were doubtful or at least apparent only to one predisposed to find them. In this book, Bailey restricts himself to applying Lund's analysis to the parables of Jesus.

Bailey finds four types of chiastic structures in the Bible: standard parallelism, an AA' BB' CC' DD' pattern; step parallelism, an ABC—A'B'C' pattern; inverted parallelism, an ABCD-D'C'B'A' pattern; and chiasms proper, two lines of poetry or prose in which the key words or themes of the first line are repeated in reverse order in the second line, following an ABBA pattern. All of these forms might be called poetry, but Bailey prefers to call them "patterned semantic relationships" as some of these structures are intended to be poetry while others are not.[30] The term *chiasm* is from the Greek letter χ (chi) because the ABB'A' pattern it denotes can easily be turned into the letter *chi* by drawing lines between the repeating letters. The chiasm (or in Latin *chiasmus*) is the form of parallelism with which English-speakers are probably most familiar, and it is one that appears throughout the Bible. The example that Bailey gives is Mark 2:27:

    A   B
The sabbath was made for man,
    B   A
not man for the sabbath.

These four types of parallel literary structures in the New Testament can be used in prose, poetry, a carefully arranged prose section that has poetic structure at its center, and what Bailey calls a parabolic ballad—a

---

29. Thurston, Review of *Poet & Peasant*, 392.
30. Bailey, *Poet & Peasant*, 47–49.

song that tells a story. It is not clear if the use of these structures was always deliberate. It seems that it often was, but sometimes it may have been merely unconscious. In the Old Testament such structured literature is frequently designated and formatted as poetry, and Bailey thinks that this should also be true of the New Testament. These structures, in addition to their aesthetic beauty, often give clues to the deeper meaning of the poem or parable. In inverted parallelism, for example, the climax is located in the center, and this is where the meaning of the passage can be found; and just after the center often comes a twist or turning in the story that at times can be startling. Bailey finds that the parables in Luke generally use the parabolic ballad structure.

When English-speakers consider such rhetorical devices as parallelism and chiasms, it is usually with reference to a single sentence or a few lines. It is perhaps startling to imagine that they could also be imposed on an entire poem, paragraph, or extended parable in the New Testament. Bailey in fact saw this technique as giving structure to the entire Travel Narrative of Luke 9:51—19:48 in which Jesus, who is in Galilee, sets out for Jerusalem to complete his earthly mission. Scholars have long pondered over how Luke organized this section of his narrative, which does not seem to be historical, theological, or geographical. Bailey argues that "90 percent of the material in the Travel Narrative of Luke follows a carefully constructed inverted outline."[31] M. D. Goulder first saw a "chiastic structure" in this section of Luke, an insight that Bailey revises and extends. Where Goulder sees six sections, Bailey sees ten, which he carefully outlines for the reader.[32] Since some of this narrative section is not concerned with travel, Bailey writes that the title *Travel Narrative* is a misnomer. He prefers *Jerusalem Document*. Bailey thinks that the original arrangement of this material was made by a Jewish-Christian theologian and that Luke inherited this document. The 10 percent that does not fit the inverted parallel structure, Bailey suggests, is due to Luke's editing of the original material: "Luke, we conjecture, had this document available to him. He did some cautious editing, moved in some new material, and shifted two pericopes out of their original position. He then incorporated the edited document into his Gospel."[33]

Having dealt with methodology, theory, and the inverted parallel structure of the Jerusalem Document, Bailey devotes the rest of *Poet &*

---

31. Bailey, *Poet & Peasant*, 79.
32. Bailey, *Poet & Peasant*, 80–82.
33. Bailey, *Poet & Peasant*, 82–83.

Peasant, chs. 5–7, to three chapters within the Jerusalem Document, Luke chapters 11, 15, and 16. These include the parable of the unjust steward (Luke 16:1–8); the poem on mammon and God (Luke 16:9–13); the parable of the friend at midnight (Luke 11:5–8); the parable or poem on a father's gifts (Luke 11:9–13); the parable of the lost sheep and the lost coin (Luke 15:4–10); and the parable of the father and the two lost sons (Luke 15:11–32). Bailey presents the underlying parallel structures of each of these parables. For example, the parable of the unjust steward (Luke 16:1–8),[34] Bailey explains, is organized in the parabolic ballad form with seven stanzas, each with three lines, following the pattern of ABBCB'B'A'. Bailey also explores the meaning of each parable by viewing them through the lens of Middle Eastern village culture.

There were at least nine English-language reviews of *Poet & Peasant* in the scholarly journals. All were genuinely admiring of the cultural data that Bailey brought to his interpretations of the text, but without exception they were also at least to some extent critical and wary of his discovery of an underlying literary structure of the parables. Several used the word *forced* to describe some of the literary structures that Bailey purports to detect in Luke's Gospel.

The most hostile of the reviewers was John Dominic Crossan, a well-known liberal Catholic biblical scholar of De Paul University. Though he found Bailey's discovery of the literary structures in the parables to be plausible and the cultural details offered often helpful, he found much of the book disappointing. He noted the "circularity" in Bailey's method of questioning Middle Eastern resource persons who were also, in his opinion, knowledgeable of the Bible. He asserted that Bailey's belief that each parable aimed at a single response from its audience while at the same time containing a cluster of theological themes treats the parables as though they were sermons or lectures rather than stories within a narrative format. He cavils that Bailey refers to the parables as ballads. "Did Jesus sing his parables?" Though Crossan found Bailey's detection of the structure of the Jerusalem Document to be "quite plausible," he faulted him for not using this knowledge to exegete the individual passages of the general narrative, which Bailey had said was "crucial for exegesis."[35] Crossan was particularly nettled that Bailey did not engage in form criticism or redaction criticism[36] when some of the passages he examined

---

34. Bailey, *Poet & Peasant*, 95–110.
35. Bailey, *Poet & Peasant*, 174.
36. Form criticism, which emerged just after World War I, was concerned primarily

in Luke were similar to those in Matthew and Mark. Finally, Crossan observed that Bailey's interpretations of the parables "never manage to challenge his theology but only to reflect and confirm it."[37]

Some of Crossan's criticisms were merely niggling while others, such as his questioning of Bailey's methodology in using Middle Eastern sources and failure to use the methods and insights of form criticism and redaction criticism, were to be expected from exacting scholars encountering previously unused sources to interpret the New Testament while presenting a radically new understanding of the material. As for his criticism that Bailey tended to affirm traditionally Protestant interpretations of the parables, it might have been too much to expect a favorable review from a scholar who was ideologically so distant from him.[38] On the other hand, his criticism that Bailey did not make better exegetical use of his analysis of the literary structures found in Luke's Gospel is unfair on two levels. First, Bailey noted in several instances where the parallel structures of the parables confirm the theological message that he concludes is being taught. Second, readers should not generally expect underlying literary structures to be the key to yielding up heretofore undetected treasures of knowledge. This is a category mistake akin to saying that the number five is yellow. In the same way, readers do not expect to be better interpreters of Shakespeare because they know that he wrote in iambic pentameter or of Pope because they know that he had a preference for heroic couplets. Yet imagine reading either poet in a foreign language in which their writing appears as prose and in which every hint of its

---

with the literary structure of individual units of the Jesus Tradition, and it tended to see the evangelists as collectors of these units or pericopes. In contrast, redaction criticism, which emerged in the 1950s and sixties, was concerned with the Gospels as literary compositions, and it tended to see the evangelists as editors, interpreters, and authors of the tradition in their own right. See footnote 17 above for form criticism, and for a concise description of redaction criticism see Martin, *New Testament Foundations*, 136–38.

37. Crossan, Review of *Poet & Peasant*, 606–8.

38. Curiously, Crossan in this same year wrote *Raid on the Articulate: Comic Eschatology in Jesus and Borges*. In reviewing Crossan's and Bailey's books together, Neil J. McEleney found Crossan's "exegesis . . . and reconstructions [of passages in the New Testament] . . . if not arbitrary, at least without sufficient justification in the present work." Moreover, while Crossan was apt to see where later tradition had modified the New Testament to suit its needs, he "places remarkable confidence in the [apocryphal] *Gospel of Thomas*." See McEleney, Review of *Poet & Peasant* and *Raid on the Articulate*, 565–67. Crossan makes some fair comments about Bailey, but in some cases, he may have been guilty of projection. For a review of Bailey's book by one at the Evangelical end of the theological spectrum, Hagner, "New Aids for Biblical Scholarship," 28–29.

original poetic nature has been erased. According to Bailey, this is what has happened to the parables of Jesus, which were spoken in Aramaic, given to the world as prose in Greek, and are now read in vernacular languages around the world—a literature twice removed from the original. Our appreciation of these stories can only be enhanced if, like Dante's *Divine Comedy* or Milton's *Paradise Lost*, they are seen as carefully crafted literary gems. At the very least, New Testaments in the future should present the parables (and other pericopes that were originally presented in verse form) as poetry in the same way that the Psalms and much of the writings of the prophets are today.

In the fall of 1976 Bailey began to think of acquiring a permanent home in the United States, and he and Mickey eventually settled on New Wilmington, Pennsylvania. He wrote to his mother on October 28 that he had come to like New Wilmington: "I can't think of any community where we have more potential friends with a friendly open community." The city of Pittsburgh was only about an hour and twenty-minute drive away, where Bailey could use the library at Pittsburgh Theological Seminary and Mickey could enjoy shopping and other urban activities. New Wilmington was a small community that had none of the problems of a large city, and that it was a college town was also appealing. Perhaps, he thought, he and Mickey could eventually retire there.[39]

Two months later on January 31, 1977, Bailey reported to his family that he and Mickey had purchased a house in New Wilmington. He wrote, "After three generations of wandering, the Bailey family . . . is finally driving in some long tent stakes deep into the ground." He had been saving money for twenty years, but it was not sufficient to buy the house outright. He needed $53,500 to buy the property but apparently had only $41,500 at his disposal, most of which was savings but some of it he anticipated receiving from his speaking engagements that year. Fortunately, his mother agreed to loan him $12,000 at 6 percent interest to meet the difference.[40] She had already discussed with Bailey her desire

---

39. Ken to Mother, October 28, 1976, Bailey Papers, box 29, folder 2, and a second copy in box 27, folder 4.

40. The amount in the Bailey letters is uncertain. In some instances, he wrote $12,000 and in others $13,000. This may be because of a rounding difference or because the amount needed was in flux.

to give much of her money away before her death.[41] In a letter to his family, Bailey pointed out all the disadvantages of the old house, but then he concluded, "so as you can see, we really have a dumpy piece of property about which WE ARE DELIRIOUSLY EXCITED!" This sentence was followed by thirty-one exclamation points.[42] He planned to renovate the house over the summer and rent it while he continued in mission service to help pay the mortgage. A local realtor, a Mr. Haines, would manage the property for him. His real estate purchase also included a substantial parcel of land comprising some fifty-six acres. He hoped to find a worthy use for it, imagining that it might become the location of the headquarters of Dale Milligan's Youth Club or that perhaps the site could be used to construct retirement cottages, such as the ones at Bristol Village in Waverly, Ohio, where his mother lived.[43]

Amid these proceedings, Bailey was trying to finish *Through Peasant Eyes* for Concordia, which had given him a deadline of February 15, 1977. By February 1 he had finished nine of the planned ten chapters, but he recognized that he would need more time to complete the tenth chapter and asked Concordia to either accept the book with nine chapters or give him an extra week to complete the tenth chapter. He went to St. Louis in the first week of February to discuss the matter with the editors at Concordia Press, who agreed to his request for more time. In the second week of February, he wrote to his mother, "we have been hard at it day and night trying to get the manuscript finished." To complete this project, he continued to depend on his wife to type the final version of the text. Sara, who was then enjoying a break from school, agreed to type his letters for 50 cents a letter. Bailey was delighted that she proved to be an excellent typist and determined to make good use of her services in the future. This was the beginning of a collaboration between them that would continue for the rest of Bailey's life and evolve from Sara being a mere typist to being his copy editor.[44]

In February, while Bailey was striving to finish his book, Sara began experiencing severe headaches. Also, she had a great many fights with David, suggesting that she was easily irritated and upset. Her behavior became so erratic that Ken and Mickey took her to see a doctor, who

---

41. Ken to Mother, October 28, 1976, Bailey Papers, box 27, folder 4.

42. Ken to family, January 31, 1977, and Ken to Mother, February 1, 1977, Bailey Papers, box 29, folder 2.

43. Ken to Mother, February 20, 1977, Bailey Papers, box 29, folder 2.

44. Ken to Mother, February 1, 1977, Bailey Papers, box 29, folder 2.

ordered a CAT scan (Computed Axial Tomography scan).[45] Fearing she might have a tumor, she underwent further tests in Cleveland in early March, but nothing was revealed. At this time, she also had a spinal tap.[46] Finally, by mid-April doctors determined that she had hypoglycemia—low blood sugar due to the body producing too much insulin and the liver responding by removing too much sugar. Fortunately, the condition could be controlled by diet. As Bailey explained to his mother, the body needs a steady supply of sugar to function normally. Because sugar deprivation was producing Sara's headaches and irritability, she was put on a very strict low-carbohydrate, non-fat protein diet, with lots of vegetables.[47] By May 1, Bailey noted a marked improvement. Sara's headaches had nearly stopped and as a result she was no longer snappish. He also reported that Mickey was cooking all the family meals without sugar or fat, which Bailey thought would benefit them all.[48]

Bailey signed the mortgage for his new house in early March, and after Easter, April 10, began working to fix it up so that it could be rented, hoping to have a renter by the end of April. Dennis and Ellen Hilgendorf and their four children visited in April to help him get the property in shape. They painted the entire house and put in new carpeting in the living room, kitchen, and two of the three bedrooms. In the detached garage, Bailey created a storage area where he could keep the family belongings while continuing to serve abroad. He also repaired broken windows and did other odd jobs around the house. He and Dennis spent an entire day cutting down a patch of 150 crabapple trees that he estimated had been growing wild for thirty years. He imagined replacing them with evergreens and some cedars of Lebanon. Bailey and David worked on an old spring house—a one-room structure built over a spring to keep the water clean and, before the advent of electricity, used to keep foods cool. The roof of the building had burned and collapsed into the interior. When father and son removed the debris, they discovered large stones that would need to be moved with the aid of rope and tackle.[49] At the end of April, the work was sufficiently complete that the Baileys and three other families enjoyed a picnic on the grounds. Bailey made a

---

45. Ken to Mother, February 20, 1977, Bailey Papers, box 29, folder 2.
46. Ken to Mother, March 4, 1977, and March 21, 1977, Bailey Papers, box 29, folder 2.
47. Ken to Mother, April 19, 1977, Bailey Papers, box 29, folder 2.
48. Ken to Mother, May 1, 1977, Bailey Papers, box 29, folder 2.
49. Ken to Mother, April 19, 1977, Bailey Papers, box 29, folder 2.

short speech dedicating the house to the glory of God, and Joe Hopkins, a professor of religion at Westminster College, offered a prayer. Bailey continued to go out to the property in the following weeks to work on clearing the debris from the spring house and also to cut a new channel through a silted-up section of the creek running through the property in order to restore a defunct waterfall. They hoped to have all the work completed in early June.[50]

Ken and Mickey celebrated their twenty-fifth wedding anniversary that June by visiting Williamsburg, Virginia.[51] In July Bailey completed the construction of the storage room in the garage. He stored many of the family things there, but the more valuable items he took to Floyd and Margaret Milligan's house in Des Moines, Iowa, for safekeeping. Writing to his mother on July 10, he noted that Sara's health had improved markedly. "She really started to come alive," he said, "and was once again enjoying the company of friends."[52] Bailey continued to speak in churches on Sundays, and during July he spoke at two summer conferences. In early September, the Baileys returned to Beirut.

---

50. Ken to Mother, April 26, 1977, and May 31, 1977, Bailey Papers, box 29, folder 2.

51. Mickey to family, June 5, 1977, Bailey Papers, box 29, folder 2.

52. Ken to Mother, July 10, 1977, Bailey Papers, box 29, folder 2.

12

Seeing through the Eyes of Peasants
1977–80

> The theme of the costly demonstration of unexpected love surfaces again and again [in the parables of Jesus].
>
> —Kenneth E. Bailey, *Through Peasant Eyes*

When the Baileys moved back into their apartment in Beirut in September 1977, they discovered that, once again, the family that had sublet from them had left many things damaged. Their first two months at home, therefore, were spent repairing broken appliances, while other repairs would take longer. It took them nearly three weeks to get their phone service operable again and several more weeks before their Volkswagen was repaired.[1] In addition to putting right these minor concerns, the Baileys had to adjust to a land where war persisted and where public services could not be taken for granted. Mickey was careful to boil drinking water and soak and wash fruit and vegetables because cholera was a known threat at this time in Beirut. Listening to the BBC, the Baileys were aware that the war continued in the south, which the local news sources were not reporting. There seemed to be a conspiracy of silence so that a feeling of normalcy would prevail. Despite the official taciturnity,

---

1. Mickey to family, October 9, 1977, Bailey Papers, box 29, folder 1.

Bailey heard many atrocity stories from people at this time, which bothered him.² He grumbled that many people had apparently "looked death in the face." Whether he was incredulous or merely irritated by endless repetition, surely many of the horrific stories he heard were true.³ What could not be denied was that the city had taken a terrible beating and would not soon be restored. Bailey commented on a section of the city near his home: "the ghastly ten block strip down the center of the city remains a destroyed, abandoned abode of rats and garbage pickers. I get a renewed feeling of shock and horror each time I have to drive through the area."⁴

In November Bailey received word from Concordia Publishing house that his book *Through Peasant Eyes* had been rejected for publication. Though there were strong voices at Concordia that spoke in its favor, the publisher's "theological reviewer" did not believe that it was acceptable. As Bailey explained to his mother, "he decided that I was a heretic or something and wouldn't let them" publish it. There was, of course, nothing in the theology of Bailey's conclusions that could be interpreted as even remotely heretical, but his interpretation of the underlying literary structures found in the writing of the parables was new and not yet widely peer-reviewed, and his Middle Eastern insights into Jesus' teachings might have been seen as threatening to more traditional, Western-oriented scholars. Also, his implicit rejection of the general insights of form and redaction criticism put him well outside the mainstream thinking of his time.⁵ But Bailey decided that Concordia's rejection of his book was actually a blessing in disguise. Since he had submitted his book to Concordia, he had developed new material that he believed "significantly strengthened" the case he was making. Therefore, Concordia's rejection would give him time to insert the new material into his argument before submitting the revised manuscript to another publisher. The other publisher he had in mind was William B. Eerdmans Publishing Company. Bailey was genuinely pleased with the high quality of the publication of his book *Poet & Peasant* by Eerdmans, and he very

2. Ken/Mickey to family, September 14, 1977, Bailey Papers, box 29, folder 2.

3. Ken/Mickey to Bruce and Pat [Milligan], October 2, 1977, Bailey Papers, box 27, folder 5.

4. Ken to Mother, November 27, 1977, Bailey Papers, box 29, folder 1.

5. Richard Bauckham points out that, though the specific contentions of the form critical approach to the New Testament have been refuted by scholars, its general insights regarding the oral transmission of the gospel message remain the conventional wisdom. See Bauckham, *Jesus and the Eyewitnesses*, 242.

much wanted Eerdmans to accept his next book as well. He might have added that Concordia was a Lutheran publisher while Eerdmans cast a wider net by appealing to evangelicals across the Protestant denominational spectrum.[6] Because of his class load in the first semester of the year, Bailey had little time then to revise his book. However, in the next semester he would be teaching only one class, which he hoped would give him plenty of time for the task.

In November, NEST's board of trustees finally decided to replace an aging and increasingly out of touch President Hovhannes Aharonian with a younger man, Dr. Vernon Fletcher. When Fletcher was elected president, there seems to have been a collective sigh of relief from the professors and staff of the seminary who could now look optimistically to the future. Having previously worked in Indonesia and also being a fluent French speaker, Fletcher had come to NEST eight years before to serve as the Professor of Systematic Theology. Well-respected and forward-looking, Fletcher would be a breath of fresh air for his beleaguered colleagues. Fletcher, however, was not scheduled to take office for another seven months and was recognized in the meantime only as the president-elect. He would not succeed Aharonian, who had served at NEST for forty years, until July. Irascible and obdurate, Aharonian would be a difficult man to work with in his last year in office. It rankled him to be forced into retirement. Despite his lame-duck status, in January 1978 he attempted a series of maneuvers that would commit the seminary to his policies for the next decade. Neither Fletcher nor others would stand for this, and the belligerent old man was successfully confronted and held in check.

Though the Board of Trustees had considered Bailey for the presidency, he would not allow his name to be put forward; and when the board offered him the position of vice president, he turned them down. Sara and David let their father know that they were disappointed and even put out by his decision, but Bailey knew that his calling was to be a professor, not an administrator. He took pride in having always successfully resisted the temptation to be anything other than a dedicated teacher and scholar. Fletcher and Bailey were good friends who saw eye-to-eye on how things at NEST should be run. During the academic year of 1977–78, he and Bailey were often together, planning and dreaming as they patiently awaited their turn at the wheel.

6. Ken to Mother, December 11, 1977, Bailey Papers, box 29, folder 1.

Soon after the board's decision, Bailey and Fletcher began planning a two-week trip they would take together to Egypt and Sudan—and, time permitting, Kenya—the following March in order to advertise the existence of NEST and recruit potential students. They saw Sudan and Egypt as the countries of the Arab-Muslim world with the largest Christian populations, and NEST, if it was to fulfill its potential as the principal Protestant theological seminary of the region, needed to reach out to them. They had a list of twenty-five Sudanese who had already applied to NEST, and they hoped on the trip to explore what the needs of these students were and how the seminary might best meet them. This excursion would also give Bailey the opportunity to see if he would finally be permitted to enter Egypt again, where he was in effect expelled in 1965.

Political tensions continued to run high in Beirut at this time, and violence was an ever-present possibility. When on November 20, 1977, Egyptian President Anwar Sadat made his dramatic appearance before Israel's Knesset to propose a new era of peace, most Westerners hailed him as a courageous and visionary leader, but in the Middle East reactions to his historic overture were mixed. In November, Bailey observed, the reaction of the Lebanese in Beirut was to put up new posters nearly every day on the city's walls to denounce Sadat. This quickly escalated to violence as the Egyptian Embassy was blown up and, subsequently, explosions were heard in the city.[7]

Striking closer to home, on an afternoon in January 1978 Sara and her friend Denell Hilgendorf were walking up a long flight of steps from the American Community School at 4:00 in the afternoon to a main street when they were suddenly accosted by a man who was following them. He grabbed Sara and then Denell, but Denell, who was taller and stronger than Sara, was able to beat him off with her umbrella. Apparently, it was no longer safe for young women to walk unescorted in broad daylight on the streets of Beirut. Sara felt it was safe enough to walk in the city alone during the day, but she would now need to be escorted to and from school.[8] In May, Mickey wrote that she and Ken were no longer allowing Sara to walk alone even in the city and that they required David to be home by a designated time each day from school. Mickey shouldered the responsibility for chauffeuring her children, sometimes spending three hours a day in the car due to Beirut's heavy traffic.[9]

7. Ken to Mother, November 27, 1977, Bailey Papers, box 29, folder 1.
8. Mickey to family, January 18, 1978, Bailey Papers, box 29, folder 1.
9. Mickey to family, May 28, 1978, Bailey Papers, box 29, folder 1.

Seeing through the Eyes of Peasants

As the time approached for Bailey and Fletcher's trip to Egypt and Sudan, Bailey learned that Samuel Habib in Egypt had attempted to obtain a visa for him, but failed—at least initially. Therefore, Fletcher would travel alone to Cairo, and Bailey would meet him in Khartoum, Sudan, before the two men would spend six days in Malakal and four in Juba, two of Sudan's major cities, from March 7 to 17, abandoning the idea of visiting Kenya and leaving the trip to Egypt for a later time.[10] Bailey had overused his legs before the trip, and his leg problems—possibly phlebitis—had returned, so he boarded the plane to Sudan on crutches.[11] He met Fletcher in Malakal as planned, but from then their trip quickly unraveled, as of course should have been predictable in a country devastated by civil war and governmental neglect. They were trapped in the city for five days, unable to find a plane to take them to Juba and dealing with officials that evoked for Bailey the disreputable characters in Joseph Conrad's novel *Lord Jim* (1899). Failing to succeed in booking a flight, the two professors were stuck in the airport without food and with temperatures reaching 110 degrees Fahrenheit. When Bailey later described the trip, the words of Shakespeare's Sonnet 29 once again came to mind: "When in disgrace with fortune and men's eyes." But then he noticed a misshapen beggar with "corn-stock sized legs tucked up under his chin." As the man approached them, "he moved along the ground using his arms as crutches, swinging his torso ahead a few inches at a time." It was his job to sweep up leaves in the mornings and evenings. As Bailey and Fletcher conversed together in increasingly despairing terms about the likelihood of completing their work in Sudan, the sound of singing crept into their consciousnesses. They looked in the direction of the sound and saw the pitiable sight of the crippled airport worker, but he did not seem to be distressed or dejected because of his condition; rather, just the opposite. He was singing a song with verses that alternated between Arabic and English:

> *Allah ku-way-yis! Allah ku-way-yis*[12]
> God is go-o-od! God is go-o-od!

---

10. Mickey to family, May 28, 1978, Bailey Papers, box 29, folder 1.
11. Mickey to family, March 5, 1978, Bailey Papers, box 27, folder 5.
12. The Arabic word for "good" in some colloquial dialects is spelled *kwayis*. Bailey's spelling here is meant to reproduce the actual sound that he heard, as is his spelling of "go-o-od."

Bailey took heart from his example and later wrote up the incident as a story, "The singer of Malakal." Despite the mishaps and discomforts of the trip as well as returning home to Beirut a week late, Bailey remained enthusiastic about Sudan. Moreover, the trip was a success. Bailey and Fletcher established relationships with some Sudanese church leaders, became reacquainted with friends and made some new ones, interviewed a number of students, administered English exams, learned much about the church in Sudan, and succeeded in advertising their seminary.[13]

When Bailey returned home after his time in Sudan, he learned that in his absence the Israelis had invaded southern Lebanon, sending 260,000 refugees into Beirut.[14] His leg still bothered him and he was using one crutch. Mickey at this time was responsible for typing NEST's scholarly journal, *Theological Review of the Near East School of Theology*, a task that kept her at the seminary throughout the mornings. Ken and Mickey enjoyed lunch together at the seminary so that Ken did not have to hobble home for a noontime meal.[15] In late March, he learned from Samuel Habib that he was no longer blacklisted in Egypt and could return whenever the government issued a visa.

Traveling to Egypt for five days during the first week of June, Bailey saw old friends such as Jack Lorimer and Samuel Habib, and he was present at a hotel for the formal dinner honoring Martha Roy on her retirement from mission service. He preached in the well-known Faggala Church and in the English service at St. Andrews in Cairo and was also honored at a reception in the offices of CEOSS. Bailey was well-pleased with the experience, which probably helped to ease his anguish over the ignominy of his expulsion thirteen years before. More important, he knew that he was now free to travel to Egypt as his ban had been lifted.

When the pastor of a house church in Riyadh, Saudi Arabia, decided to return to the United States for the month of July in 1978, Bailey replaced him for the period of his absence. The congregation was genuinely appreciative of Bailey's preaching and teaching. Attendance for his Bible studies on Sundays steadily grew, and in the end seventy people ordered copies of *The Cross and the Prodigal* and *Poet & Peasant*. Ken, accompanied by the family, took the opportunity to travel in the country,

---

13. Mickey/Ken to family, March 20, 1978, Bailey Papers, box 27, folder 5; and box 29, folder 1.
14. Ken and Mickey, Christmas letter 1978, Bailey Papers, box 29, folder 1.
15. Mickey to family, April 10, 1978, Bailey Papers, box 27, folder 5.

visiting groups in the south near the border of Yemen.[16] While the Baileys were in Saudi Arabia, violence among the various factions in Beirut intensified. Before the family's return, the American Embassy issued a warning to Americans to leave for their own protection. Knowing that Dr. Fletcher was expecting Ken back at the seminary, they decided to return if the airport was open. On landing in Beirut, the Baileys found that the danger had been exaggerated and determined to remain, though Mickey observed shops closing and many businessmen and their families leaving the city. Also, the US embassy, she wrote home, had stopped assigning staff with families to serve in Beirut and was transferring staff who had families. The Baileys found these reactions excessive even while they wrote to their family of hearing heavy shelling through the night.[17]

In August, ten months after receiving Bailey's manuscript, the editors at Eerdmans finally informed him that they were interested in publishing his new book but would make no definitive commitment until they had seen the final version. Ken and Mickey skipped their vacation that year to begin immediately to prepare the final revision of the book. They spent the first half of every day, from 8:00 a.m. to 1:00 p.m., at the seminary where it was quiet and their work could proceed apace without interruption. The editors at Eerdmans were pleased that, unlike *Poet & Peasant*, this newest book would be relatively non-technical and thereby appeal to a broader audience. The Baileys finished the book in September.

In the second half of September, before the new semester began, Bailey returned alone to the States. He had agreed with Dale Milligan to be present in his church in Oklahoma City for an annual, week-long conference in which he would teach morning and evening classes for a total of fifteen sessions on the theme of "A Biblical Foundation for Mission."[18] Though anxious about leaving his family alone in Beirut where violence might break out at any moment, he assuaged whatever misgivings he may have had by assuring himself that in the event of trouble the family could always retreat to the seminary, where they would be relatively safe and all their needs would be met.

That violence might in fact break out was not an idle speculation. Mickey explained to her family in August that Israeli fighter jets had been

---

16. This trip is summed up in the following letters: Ken to special friends and related churches, July 12, 1978; Mickey to family, July 18, 1978; and Ken to Mother, July 29, 1978, all in Bailey Papers, box 29, folder 1.

17. Mickey to family, August 11, 1978, Bailey Papers, box 27, folder 5.

18. Ken to special friends, Christmas 1978, Bailey Papers, box 2, folder 1.

engaging in raids on Lebanon that summer. Sweeping in from the sea just before dawn, their presence was presaged for the sleeping population by deafening sonic booms before they swooped low over the city. This was met with the roar of the city's antiaircraft guns, a psychologically reassuring but militarily ineffective response. Fortunately, the Israeli targets were usually south of the city, which meant that the denizens of Beirut suffered the loss of sleep but were otherwise physically unaffected.[19] Of more immediate concern was that the city also suffered bombardment by Syrian missiles and artillery from the hills and tall buildings in the east.[20]

On August 8 a White House spokesman formally announced a summit meeting to be held September 5–17 between Israeli Prime Minister Menachem Begin and Egyptian President Anwar Sadat at Camp David, the presidential retreat in Maryland. Though intended to advance the Arab-Israeli peace process, tensions remained high. On October 1, the night before Ken arrived home from the States, Mickey stayed up to watch the spectacle of flares lighting up the night sky to illuminate targets to the south. Writing to her mother, she reported that things had generally been calm in the city until the weekend before Bailey was scheduled to arrive. On the previous Wednesday, she explained, Syrians shelled the Beirut harbor, chasing ten ships out to sea where they anchored far out on the horizon. Over the weekend the shelling increased. Following a particularly loud explosion at 3:00 a.m. on the night before Ken arrived, Mickey recalled distinctly hearing a US Marine at the embassy across the street shout, "Timber-r-r!"[21]

Ten days after his arrival in Beirut, Bailey wrote to his mother a description of life in a city under war conditions. There were shortages of gasoline for cars and gas for heating and cooking. Shops were closed, and the shelves of the grocery stores were often empty, though locally grown fresh fruits and vegetables remained plentiful. The electricity came and went, and the water supply was limited.[22] At the end of October, Bailey wrote her again saying that electricity was on for only half the day and that water was available for only a half an hour about every five days. The family was learning to conserve water by reusing water from the rinse

---

19. Benjamin Weir, "Lebanon Update, August 9, 1978," Bailey Papers, box 29, folder 1.

20. Benjamin Weir, "Lebanon Update, August 9, 1978," Bailey Papers, box 29, folder 1.

21. Mickey to Mother, October 2, 1978, Bailey Papers, box 29, folder1.

22. Ken to Mother, October 10, 1978, Bailey Papers, box 29, folder 1.

cycle of the washing machine, using the wash water to flush the toilets, and bathing with a single pitcher of water.[23] Ken saved cooking gas by crafting a wooden frame to fit over a kerosene lamp so that the family could set the tea kettle on it to heat water for showers. And life went on.

Writing to Floyd and Marg, Mickey admitted that she was not fully truthful to her mother about conditions in the city because she did not want to worry her. "I'm sure it is hard for the family to understand how a war can be four blocks away to five miles and still go on living somewhat normally. But such is our crazy world now." Then she wrote of staying up with Ken and the children until 3:00 in the morning to watch phosphorus flares light up the sky and listen to the explosion of enormous bombs, one following close upon another like machine-gun fire. Though the children's school was closed the next day, school authorities had been uncertain about whether to close it when Mickey drove Sara and David over that morning. But she was told that a bullet had just whizzed through the trees, which helped them to make the decision to close.[24] When the new semester started at the seminary in the second week of October, each professor had only one class to teach, and the number of students per class was only three to five. Bailey put a good face on this. Writing to his mother, he said that this would give him time to work on his next book.[25]

In the winter semester of 1979, which began that year in February, Bailey taught a new class that he had developed in the previous months, "Women in the New Testament." Given the paucity of students at NEST in these years of intermittent conflict, he wanted to expand the student body by appealing to a largely untapped female demographic. He would also offer the course in Arabic so that there would be no language impediment.[26] The study of the Bible from a feminist perspective was a relatively new development of the period. Beginning in the late 1960s and early seventies, feminist scholars brought a fresh perspective to biblical studies, reinterpreting traditional teaching about women in the Bible in ways that often astonished and sometimes offended conservative Christians but that were clearly respectful of Scripture. The scholars in the field were generally women but Paul K. Jewett, author of *MAN as Male and Female* (1975), was a distinguished exception. Jewett's book was all

23. Ken to Mother, October 29, 1978, Bailey Papers, box 29, folder 1.
24. Mickey to family, February 27, 1979, Bailey Papers, box 27, folder 5.
25. Ken to Mother, October 15, 1978, Bailey Papers, box 29, folder 1.
26. Ken to Mother, January 29,1979, Bailey Papers, box 29, folder 1.

the rage at Fuller Seminary when Bailey was there in 1976 teaching as an adjunct professor, and it is impossible to believe that he would have been indifferent to its biblical insights or oblivious to its cultural importance. Bailey soon found the response that he desired: "a core of very bright, mature Lebanese women from various denominations" who were captivated by a message of female equality and the importance of women in the New Testament that was clear and incontrovertible once seen and understood.[27] A woman in the office of Women's Concerns of the Middle East Council of Churches learned of Bailey's class and approached him about writing a book on this subject that would be based on his class and published in Arabic. They agreed that the book would be 400 pages and intended for all the churches of the Middle East. He imagined that it would be a two-year project.[28]

Figure 20. Mickey and Ken Bailey in the living room of their apartment in Beirut, Lebanon, 1979.

27. Ken to Special Friends and Related Churches, May 3, 1979, Bailey Papers, box 29, folder 1.

28. Mickey to family, April 23, 1979; and Ken to friends, May 3, 1979, Bailey Papers, box 29, folder 1.

Seeing through the Eyes of Peasants

On April 2 two men driving past the US Embassy fired two hand grenades at the complex. No one was hurt and the police stopped traffic in front of the embassy for only about fifteen minutes, but then life went on as if nothing had happened. In a letter to his mother, Bailey linked the attack to the Camp David Accords, which tied the United States in a new way to the destinies of Israel and Egypt. Despite the efforts of some groups in Lebanon to arouse a strong public reaction to Egypt's recognition of Israel, Bailey believed that most Lebanese were entirely resigned to Sadat's decision, seeing it as both reasonable and inevitable.[29]

Bailey attached to his letter a two-page article, "Who Is a 'World Christian'?" Though many Christians from rich countries such as the United States would tend to view Christians from poorer countries as inferior, Bailey found that this view was inadequate as a Christian interpretation of the world. The World Christian, he explained, "has a different yard stick with which to measure what he sees when he looks out on the world beyond his own shores. He has no need to prove that he is better than others, for he/she kneels as a broken sinner at the cross and there finds himself as just that—a sinner in need of grace." World Christians understand, with Jesus, that "it is more blessed to give than to receive" (Acts 20:35) but also that "it is much easier." They know that the rich giving to the poor can often be a way for the rich to assert their dominance while undermining the self-worth and self-reliance of the people they are ostensibly seeking to help. World Christians know that they will often be hated by the world, but they are sustained by God's love not by the way the world receives them. World Christians have a critical perspective on the political and economic arrangements of the world. They understand, for example, that Americans were then only 6 percent of the world's population but used 40 percent of its resources—often with callous indifference to the ways they are able to enrich themselves while further impoverishing others. Finally, World Christians recognize that the Spirit often speaks through poorer Christians—those in Palestine, South Sudan, Ethiopia, and China—of whom the world generally takes little note.[30]

Amid the violence and despair of life in Beirut, Bailey received a huge psychological boost in March when Eerdmans informed him that it had decided to publish *Through Peasant Eyes*. Bailey replied to the

---

29. Ken to Mother, April 3, 1979, Bailey Papers, box 29, folder 1.
30. Bailey, "Who Is a 'World Christian?,'" Bailey Papers, box 29, folder 1.

publisher that he wanted to make some minor revisions to the book over the summer before submitting the final version. He had become aware of a hefty new commentary just published on Luke's Gospel that he thought would become the definitive work on the subject for the next generation. Therefore, he wanted to review his work to include references to it so that his book would be as up to date as possible.[31] On receiving the news from Eerdmans, he wrote to his mother, "I am really excited that it has been accepted because I think it means that I can continue to write and have real hope of publishers [accepting my material]."[32] Though this would be his third published book in English, it was this book more than any other that confirmed for him that he would have a writing career. Bailey revised the book between June 1 and July 15, and Mickey typed the new version. Then it was hand-carried by a traveler to the States and mailed to the publisher.

Sara graduated from high school on June 15, 1979, and planned to attend Grove City College the next fall. On August 24 Ken and Sara flew together to Chicago before renting a car and driving to Columbus, Ohio, to see his mother and pick up some things from her to take to their home in new Wilmington. This was the last time that Ken saw his mother as she died about six weeks later at the age of eighty-six on October 6, 1979. She was buried at Woodland Cemetery in Xenia, Ohio, where her memorial stone included her husband, Ewing. Engraved beneath their names was a Pauline verse: "His grace to them was not in vain" (1 Cor 15:10).

Although the fighting and shelling in Beirut was usually distant from the Baileys' apartment, in the first week of September before Bailey arrived home, violence came to the street where they lived. Two political factions vying for control of the neighborhood opened fire on one another, using machine guns and some larger weapons—perhaps mortars. Three men were killed before the Syrians intervened and put a stop to it. This was followed by a funeral for those killed, which included a military parade of armed men marching down the street. Mickey commented, "The amount of ammunition that went past the house that day was chilling—partly because of the youth of those carrying it." During this week, violence also broke out in the alley behind the Baileys' apartment below their bedrooms. When one group began

---

31. Mickey to Mother, June 20, 1979, Bailey Papers, box 29, folder 1. Reviewing the bibliography in *Through Peasant Eyes*, the most recent commentary on Luke that Bailey includes is Marshall, *Gospel of Luke*.

32. Ken to Mother, March 19, 1979, Bailey Papers, box 29, folder 1.

arguing with another, shooting soon erupted. Mickey and David stayed in the hallway until the shooting stopped.³³

Despite the war conditions of Beirut, the seminary opened again in the fall, and Bailey taught his usual classes. But life was difficult. Mickey wrote in late October that they had run out of cooking gas and had to use an electric skillet to cook their food for a time. Also, the water supply in the city continued to be periodically interrupted, often for days at a time; and there was another garbage strike, leaving huge mounds of festering trash on the city streets, a perfect breeding ground for flies and rats. When the rains started in October, the Baileys' family car was flooded and they were unable to dry it out because they did not dare leave the windows down. And of course, sporadic violence continued in the city, making life precarious.³⁴

In the fall of 1979 Bailey read an article by NEST's former professor of mission, Paul Löffler, a German.³⁵ In a letter to his family Bailey described the article "Mission in the Context of the Struggle for Justice," published in the *Theological Review of the Near East School of Theology*, as having drawn "a bead on the nineteenth-century missionary enterprise and blasted it as laboring hand in glove with Western imperialism and labeled the result as disastrous. I take him on and take him apart. It was a very painful exercise because he is a good friend. I urged that his article not be published and was told to write a 'Rejoinder.'"³⁶ In his "Rejoinder," Bailey selected three aspects of Löffler's article to attack.³⁷ First, Löffler wrote that the educational work of missions was aimed at the elite of society and tended to reinforce class divisions and to alienate students from their culture. Bailey very rightly pointed out that in Syria/Lebanon and Egypt missionaries established hundreds of schools for poor villagers not the urban elite and that these schools taught in Arabic, thus reinforcing traditional culture, not undermining it. There were elite Western universities, such as the American University of Beirut and the American University in Cairo, that taught a curriculum inspired by the Enlightenment that often resulted in alienating students from their culture. Though these universities began as mission institutions, they were quicky taken over by secular interests. Therefore, their faults cannot be

33. Mickey to Mother, September 15, 1979, Bailey Papers, box 27, folder 5.
34. Mickey to family, October 29, 1979, Bailey Papers, box 27, folder 5.
35. Löffler, "Mission in the Context," 13–20.
36. Mickey/Ken to family, December 10, 1979, Bailey Papers, box 27, folder 5.
37. Bailey, "Rejoinder," 21–25.

laid at the feet of missionaries. Moreover, all education results in new ideas that can be potentially alienating. The only alternative is following the Amish strategy of providing only eight years of formal education for children. But would anyone seriously advocate this approach for mission schools around the world? Second, Löffler argued that colonial and mission interests were aligned. Missionaries for example used colonial ships and trade routes to reach their destinations. In response, Bailey pointed out that the missionaries who worked in the Middle East were largely Americans who were not interested in supporting European colonialism. Moreover, they began their work in the region a generation before the colonists arrived, and they made no attempt to establish church institutions that would support imperialism. It is certainly true that they benefited from European communication and transportation infrastructures, but this did not make them complicit in colonialism. One would not, for example, accuse the apostle Paul of being complicit in Roman imperialism because he benefited from the Pax Romana. Finally, Löffler argued that the Bible's preference for the poor means that modern missions should be remodeled to work for justice. Bailey observed that the supposed preference for the poor in the Bible quickly fades when one looks closely at the biblical literature. Löffler, he believed, was simply wrong to assert that Jesus accepted the rich into the kingdom only on condition that they give their wealth to the poor, though he did make this demand of one man, the Rich Young Ruler.[38] On the contrary, Jesus appealed not only to the common people who heard him gladly but also to the well to do—boat owners such as Peter, wealthy tax collectors such as Zacchaeus, wealthy women who funded his movement such as Joanna and Susanna, and rulers such as Joseph of Arimathea and Nicodemus. Because Bailey was not a vindictive person, the article must have been a "painful exercise" because he liked Löffler. But once entered into combat, he was a spirited opponent, and it is difficult to imagine on reading the article that at some level he did not enjoy dismantling his friend's arguments.

The Baileys were scheduled for a six-month furlough for the period roughly from June to December 1980, and their home base would be New Wilmington. Bailey, however, spent the second week of June in Egypt, where he continued to find opportunities to speak, before he returned to Beirut for the graduation ceremony at NEST held on June 15. This was followed by a two-week conference for Lebanese pastors. He

---

38. Matt 19:16–22; Mark 10:17–27; and Luke 18:18–23.

then proceeded to Cyprus in July to meet his commitment to speak at the Ayia Napa Conference Center. Mickey typed two new articles for him in June before departing for the United States with David on June 28. Ken met them in New Wilmington around July 23. Mickey wrote that Ken was booked every Sunday in churches while the family was on furlough. They returned to Beirut in mid-January 1981. During this furlough period, Eerdmans published *Through Peasant Eyes*.

While *Poet & Peasant* was a scholarly book intended for fellow academics, Bailey writes in the introduction to *Through Peasant Eyes* that this newest of his books would be less technical. Writing for both a specialist and nonspecialist audience, it would have less documentation and references to previous scholarly works. Rather, it would be more concerned with "the pay-offs." The goal of his study is to recover "the original Palestinian setting, along with the timeless theological content" of the material. To achieve these aims, he examines the text from the perspective of Middle Eastern culture using the methodology and literary theories he had developed in his previous book and further develops and applies here.[39]

Jesus' parables, he insists once again, are "Palestinian stories" whose cultural context and assumptions have not been sufficiently examined by previous scholars. The modern Westerner's situation today, he explains, is like an Englishman telling the story of King Arthur to a group of Eskimos. The known pattern of life from the days of King Arthur is the "grand piano on which the storyteller plays," and much of the meaning will be conveyed by slight alterations in received tradition. In reading the parables of Jesus, "*We are the Eskimos.*" We in the West are separated from the literature of the first century by 2,000 years and an entirely different culture. To recapture this lost world, he will use four tools: consultations with Middle Eastern informants to recover the cultural aspects of the parables; an examination of twenty-four Syriac and Arabic translations of the Bible; a search for literary parallels to the New Testament that are roughly contemporaneous with Jesus; and a careful study of the literary settings and the structure of the parables—that is, the various forms of

---

39. Bailey, *Through Peasant Eyes*, x, xiii.

Hebrew parallelism that are employed.[40] Bailey will then apply this methodology to ten parables in Luke's Gospel.

In the conclusion of his book, Bailey writes that the character of Jesus becomes clearer upon studying the parables. Jesus attacks Israel's racism implicitly by making a Samaritan the hero of one of his parables. He also often offered two paired parables, one with a man and the other with a woman as the protagonists, to implicitly undercut the sexism of the time. Though Jesus could "use words like naked steel," he was "courteous and compassionate."[41] For example, he criticizes Simon the Pharisee for being a poor host, but he did not expect him to wash his feet. Most important, in a critical examination of the parables Jesus inevitably emerges as a true theologian, not just one who ushers in the kingdom and sets ethical standards. Form and redaction critics might attribute much of the artistry to be found in the parables to later writers who shaped the Gospel narratives for their own ends, but Bailey believes that Jesus was the true author whose own Aramaic words stand directly behind the Greek of the Gospels.

There were at least ten scholarly reviews of *Through Peasant Eyes*. John Trimmer, writing for *Calvin*, wrote for many in concluding that the book was "full of exegetical surprises and will be of great homiletical value to many preachers."[42] Some critics, however, continued to complain that Bailey's use of seminary students and Arabic-writing commentators from various historical periods lacked methodological control.[43] Here again was the problem of circularity mentioned previously by Crossan. Some complained that Bailey's approach to the parables did not produce new insights into their meaning, while others gave examples of fresh insights that his focus on Middle Eastern culture alone provided.[44] Those who approached the parables as form and redaction critics were probably the most hostile. Gary M. Burge, then of King College, Bristol, Tennessee, put his finger on the problem. The most controversial aspect of Bailey's work, Burge observed, is that he argues "for the essential unity and coherence of the text in contrast to the current over-emphasis on redaction

40. Bailey, *Through Peasant Eyes*, xiv.
41. Bailey, *Through Peasant Eyes*, 171.
42. Timmer, Review of *Through Peasant Eyes*, 80–81.
43. For an example of this critique, see Perkins, Review of *Through Peasant Eyes*, 139–40.
44. For examples of the contrasting views see Johnson, Review of *Through Peasant Eyes*, 102–3, and Hultgren, Review of *Through Peasant Eyes*, 401–2.

criticism." He disagreed, however, with those who argued that Bailey was not concerned with the issues of form and redaction criticism. Bailey understood, he wrote, that the parables were not "floating unit[s] of tradition" and so strove to place them into the historical setting that Luke provides. Burge probably hit upon the crux of the problem in remarking that Bailey's work required New Testament scholars who embraced form and redaction criticism to question their premises. Unwilling to do this, they concluded that Bailey's work was ultimately inadequate.[45]

Clearly the jury is still out on the value of Bailey's scholarly contribution to the understanding of the parables. But it is also clear that, even from this brief review of the reaction to *Through Peasant Eyes*, scholars often responded to him based on their own preconceived understanding of the standards of biblical interpretation. In other words, they were pleased to welcome his cultural insights into the parables as long as he did not challenge the premises of form and redaction criticism or their preconceived theological convictions. Whether Bailey offered significant new interpretations of the parables is, perhaps, a matter of judgment. At a minimum, one might argue that Bailey's cultural insights, while not leading to fundamental departures from the way the parables have been traditionally understood, have sharpened the focus and added color that would otherwise have been lacking.

---

45. Burge, Review of *Through Peasant Eyes*, 341–42.

13

The Israeli Invasion of Lebanon
1981–84

> I came to think of Beirut as a huge abyss, the darkest corner of human behavior, an urban jungle where not even the law of the jungle applied.
> —THOMAS L. FRIEDMAN, *FROM BEIRUT TO JERUSALEM*

KEN, MICKEY, AND DAVID returned to Beirut in mid-January 1981, while Sara continued her studies at Grove City College in Pennsylvania. At this time the Syrian army, which had occupied much of Lebanon since 1976, was still in place in the country, and other outside powers—Israel, the Palestine Liberation Army (PLA), Hezbollah, Libya, Iraq, the United States, and the Soviet Union—continued to support militia groups in the land, resulting in an ongoing brutal civil war that would continue until October 1990. The chaos in the country meant that there was little order and efficiency in public services. The streetlights in Beirut were dark, the Baileys' phone did not work because it was said a new cable was being installed, and the traffic was worse than ever. People now triple parked on the streets, further impeding the already snarled traffic. Writing to her family in April, Mickey observed that the fighting in the city was ongoing and that they all were wary of stray shells and machine gun fire. For ten days they had very little water and no hot water at all. Exaggerated news from war-afflicted places like Beirut can often make life seem untenable even as most of the locals are going about their normal activities. Nevertheless, on reading the Baileys' letters from this period, the image of the proverbial frog in the boiling beaker comes easily to mind.

Working in his office at the seminary, Bailey found that people often stopped by to seek his advice or help with some project, encumbering his work. To carve out more time for his own projects, he began taking a study day at home once a week. When the president and other administrators of NEST briefly left the city and found their return temporarily impeded, Bailey became the acting president for the last week of April. But in general, the extra activities that impinged on his schedule were mostly speaking engagements. In addition to his regular classes, he was preparing a conference in March for pastors in Aleppo, Syria, one in the same month for a congregation in Jeddah, Saudi Arabia, one in July at the Ayia Napa Conference Center in Cyprus, and one in September in Egypt. While at home, he was the worship leader at the American Community Church in Beirut, where he also preached occasionally.[1] When the pastor left the church, Bailey organized a roster of people to preach on Sundays, but in the month of June they all reneged and Bailey was forced to preach through the month himself. In summarizing the year 1981 for friends, Mickey said that Ken spoke "117 times all across the Middle East." Bailey attributed his growing demand as a speaker to his new book, *Through Peasant Eyes*. He felt, however, that he had reached a fork in the road. Either he must become a "circuit rider" in order to respond to all the invitations to speak, or he must learn to respond with a "gentle no" to those requests so that he could concentrate on writing for a broader audience.[2] Despite this wise perception, Bailey never seems to have made any such resolution, or at least not one that he long held. Rather, he continued to speak as often as he could.

In early 1982 NEST professors and the Synod began to maneuver over the selection of a new seminary president as Vernon Fletcher's term was to end at the close of the academic year. Bailey wanted his friend Verne to be given a second five-year term, but the Synod had other ideas. It nominated NEST professor Wanis Seman, who Bailey believed had demonstrated his incompetence as a professor over the previous ten years and would be a disaster as president. He privately told five or six professors that, if Wanis were elected, he would resign; and it later

---

1. Mickey to family, March 6, 1981, and April 19, 1981, Bailey Papers, box 27, folder 5,

2. Mickey to friends, January 12, 1982, Bailey Papers, box 27, folder 5.

became apparent that he unadvisedly wrote letters to some of his colleagues opposing Wanis's election. Getting wind of his dissension, the head of the Synod asked to see him in his office. Bailey went and explained his reasoning. When the head asked Bailey why he had not spoken up sooner, he responded that he had not been asked and because the man was a colleague. The election was held in May and Wanis won. It was then decided that Fletcher would be terminated at the end of the following academic year—that is, in June 1983.[3]

Having failed to back the Synod candidate and because he had, presumably due to his private conversations with other professors and letters to his colleagues, "caused dissension among the church," the Synod voted to ask the Presbyterian Program Agency in New York to withdraw Bailey from mission service in Lebanon. This issue arose in the Synod without church leaders informing Bailey, without giving him a chance to explain or defend himself, without any semblance of due process.[4] Presbyterian representatives Ben Weir and Ed Hanna were at the Synod meeting for the vote, but they made no objections. Weir informed Bailey of the decision and then cabled the New York office with the news. In Mickey's view—and she was almost certainly reflecting Ken's thoughts—it was the church and not Weir who should have done this. They feared that the Program Agency might take precipitous action before anything had been decided definitively. About ten days later Bailey had a meeting with Synod leaders, who indicated that he would not be asked to leave his ministry after all. However, they did not say that there would be a formal Synod vote to rescind its previous decision, leaving a sword suspended above Bailey's head that could fall at any time.[5]

On June 6, 1982, while Bailey was considering what other employment options he had, the Israeli Defense Forces (IDF) invaded southern Lebanon with approximately 60,000 troops supported by tanks, aircraft, missile boats, and submarines. Called "Operation Peace for Galilee," it was an attempt to neutralize the Palestine Liberation Organization (PLO), which was occupying the region and using it as a base from which to launch attacks on Israel. The Israeli forces advanced rapidly up the coast, reaching the outskirts of Beirut on June 11 and by June 14 had

---

3. Mickey to family, May 24, 1982, Bailey Papers, box 27, folder 5.

4. Kenneth E. Bailey to Robert Lodwick (Associate for Middle East Concerns, PCUSA), December 1, 1984, Box RG 424, Presbyterian Historical Society, Philadelphia, PA.

5. Mickey to family, May 24, 1982, Bailey Papers, box 27, folder 5.

The Israeli Invasion of Lebanon

encircled the city by land and imposed a blockade by sea. The Israelis put the city under siege, bombarding selected targets, but declined to invade, which would have resulted in an unacceptable number of civilian casualties. Before the end of June, Yasser Arafat was forced to move the PLO headquarters from Beirut to Tripoli, in northern Lebanon. The Israeli siege continued until August, when the PLO agreed to withdraw its forces from Lebanon altogether, relocating them in surrounding countries. That August the United States and France established the Multinational Force (MNF) to be peacekeepers in Lebanon, sending troops to Beirut and other places in the country.

Bailey wrote to his family on June 13 of the tense situation in the city. In the following week, the streets were filled with roaming bands of men with automatic weapons often looking for places to stay—empty buildings, schools, and apartments. Ken, Mickey, Sara (who was home again for the summer), and David did not dare go to church on Sunday, June 13, because they feared that their apartment would be occupied by fighters when they returned. Bailey continued with lines that merit quotation in full:

> The streets are empty except for undisciplined irregular fighters aged 12 to 40 with all types of weapons. A large anti-tank gun and anti-aircraft battery are set up in the parking lot outside our front door each night. Five jeeps of communists (armed to the teeth) tried to force the occupation of a building next to us two days ago, [but] our party talked them out of it. We have groups of armed men in the seminary demanding this or that every hour. One leading Palestinian pastor [Fuad Bahnan] has proved himself a man of great personal courage and in effect moved in to support us, meet the armed men, [and] save the school and its students from harm—what a man. This week in one incident four armed men with attack rifles and machine guns tried to take over the building and one of them, in a very dramatic gesture, inserted a clip into his machine gun and switched off the safety. Reverend Fouad told him to put his gun down while giving him a shove. Fouad won the face down and we are still in business. The tensest time was on Wednesday and Thursday when there were five Israeli gunboats off our coast directly in front of our building. With each other city [that] the Israelis [have attacked in the past they have first] landed troops beyond the city and fought their way in from both sides. If they had chosen to do the same with Beirut, it would have been another Stalingrad.[6]

---

6. Ken to family, June 13, 1982, Bailey Papers, box 27, folder 5.

As Bailey wrote these lines an Israeli air raid was in progress, and the anti-aircraft guns just outside his apartment building were making a deafening roar. Perhaps the most frightening moment came when five Israeli gunboats positioned themselves on the sea directly in front of the Baileys' apartment with the apparent intention of opening fire. Fortunately, this did not occur.[7] The Israeli attack resulted in 15,000 dead or wounded and 600,000 homeless and displaced Lebanese, many of whom fled from the south of the country north to Beirut. Since the Syrians had withdrawn from the city, there was no longer any order provided by a disciplined, central force. More likely than civilians being hit by an Israeli shell was the possibility of being accosted in their apartments or on the street by an armed gang. Two days later, despite the heroic stand of people like Fouad Bahnan, the Palestinian Liberation Organization (PLO) took over the two lower floors of the seminary building to use as a makeshift hospital. Bailey could still work in his office, but he was not sure how much longer this would be allowed. Moreover, he had to abandon his planned book on women in the New Testament. Under war conditions, the most that he would be able to manage would be a small collection of articles on the subject.

Bailey resolved to remain in the city. He felt it was important to show solidarity with the thirty international students at NEST who had nowhere to go and to the Lebanese in their time of crisis. How could he later preach trust or "be a healing presence among them" if he fled and returned only when he was physically safe? "Suffering," he wrote, "is like capital in the bank of effective ministry. So, our account is getting deposits daily and, if we can make it, it will be like the widow's cruse of oil that never runs out [1 Kgs 17:8–16] as long as we remain in Lebanon." The family seemed to agree. Ken wrote, "The kids are doing well. Mickey is holding up magnificently. We are delighted that we are living through it together."[8]

By mid-June the seminary had been able to see all of its students safely out of the country. David's school ended around mid-June, but there was no graduation or prom that year, and the students generally left without having the opportunity to say their goodbyes. On June 19 David and four of his friends were arrested by one of the militias. They were taken to two different offices, were interrogated, and had their identity

---

7. Ken to friends, September 25, 1982, Bailey Papers, box 27, folder 5.
8. Ken to family, June 13, 1982, Bailey Papers, box 27, folder 5.

papers taken from them. One of the interrogators slapped David before he and his friends were released. This was the last straw for the Baileys, who then moved temporarily to East Beirut, the Christian section of the city. A few days later they evacuated to Cyprus on a ship of the US Sixth Fleet.[9] In the fall, David would begin his last two years of high school at Black Forest Academy, a conservative Christian school in Germany.

The family spent at least part of the month of July at the mission campgrounds in Troodos, Cyprus, where for a few weeks they enjoyed the beauty and serenity of their mountain top retreat. About August 4, Ken and Sara traveled back to Beirut and stayed for a little more than three weeks with mission friends at the Baptist seminary in the mountains in Mansouriyeh. Sara wanted to finish a readings course in church history she had started with a professor at NEST, which would allow her to graduate from Grove City College in May 1983. And Bailey wanted to be present in the city to show solidarity with the Christian community there. While in East Beirut, they watched the ongoing Israeli bombardment of Ras Beirut, the invaders pounding the city with their heavy artillery in an attempt to drive the PLO out. The assault reached a crescendo on August 12 when Israeli planes bombed West Beirut for eleven uninterrupted hours. Appalled at the cost of civilian lives, President Ronald Reagan spoke with Prime Minister Menachem Begin on the phone to urge him to cease the bombing. "Menachem," he said in a rare show of emotion, "this is a holocaust." Begin replied with words one listener described as "dripping with sarcasm." "Mr. President," Begin said, "I think I know what a holocaust is." Reagan, however, continued to press the Israeli leader, concluding, "It has gone too far. You must stop it." Begin called back twenty minutes later to say that he had ordered a halt to the bombing.[10]

As an uncertain peace settled on Beirut, Ken and Sara drove through the rubble of the ruined city to Ras Beirut where, Ken related to his supporters, they found their quarter of the city "relatively unscathed and most of our friends still alive." The Baileys' apartment was also spared except for some of the windows that had shattered. Ken and Sara had ventured back to their apartment to retrieve clothing and bedding. While Sara finished her readings course, Ken visited church leaders and various Christian friends. By this time, Ken reported, Beirut had sustained 17,000

---

9. Ken to friends, September 25, 1982, Bailey Papers, box 27, folder 5.
10. Canon, *President Reagan*, 349–50.

dead and 33,000 wounded. He was outraged by the Israeli brutality. After three weeks Ken and Sara were back in Cyprus. In the last week of August, the family moved to Larnaca, on the coast, where they stayed in a mission apartment and had many friends with whom to pass the time.

A few weeks later, Bailey flew to Pittsburgh to begin a two-week lecture series at Beulah Presbyterian Church, teaching pastors the first week and lay people the second. While in the States, he encountered Fundamentalists who expressed their delight at what was happening in the Middle East. Bailey, who also took a conservative view of the Scriptures but not one that was dispensationalist, reminded them that the prophets had opposed the injustice in the land committed by Israel's kings. To those who insisted that Christians must support the Jews at this time, he asked them which Jews, those committing atrocities or those who stood in opposition to the government's brutality? To those who appealed to the apocalyptic texts in which Jesus predicted "wars and rumors of wars" during the end times, Bailey argued that of course there would be violence in the end but that Christians should not support evil forces in the world in the name of ushering in the kingdom of God.[11]

Before the end of September Bailey was back in Cyprus to complete a new set of video recordings. When this was done, he and Mickey took the boat from Cyprus to Beirut, now empty nesters.[12] They drove back to their apartment through a devastated city but were encouraged that people were cleaning up the mess and bulldozers had already pushed much of the rubble off of the streets to make them passable. At NEST, they found that the Red Crescent had taken over the makeshift hospital set up by the PLO in the seminary's lower floors. The PLO left behind a generator, which the seminary restored in order to use when electricity was cut off in the city.[13] The Israelis at this time were still occupying Beirut and had commandeered the airport, disrupting the usual mail service. Many of the buildings were badly damaged during the Israeli bombardment in July and August. The Baileys' found their own apartment disheveled but intact. They immediately set about cleaning it, repairing two shattered windows and painting all the woodwork, a task that would not be completed until early December. Since the water lines had been broken, water was being trucked into the neighborhood. The telephone also went

---

11. Ken to family, September 25, 1982, Bailey Papers, box 27, folder 5.
12. Mickey to family, September 23, 1982, Bailey Papers, box 27, folder 5.
13. Mickey to David, October 20, 1982, Bailey Papers, box 28, folder 16. See too Sabra, *Truth and Service*, 188.

off from time to time. One day Israeli soldiers came to the door demanding to search the apartment. They looked all through it, even opening cupboards. Sometime later, they came again while Ken and Mickey were eating lunch. Mickey offered them a meal, but they only smiled, took a quick look around, and left.[14]

Bailey's relationship with the Synod continued to be strained. That year Paul Hopkins from the Program Agency in New York visited Beirut to meet with Synod leaders. Only after he had conferred with them did he see Bailey. Hopkins then gave him three options: withdraw from Beirut, make an official appeal to the Synod, or resign immediately with his resignation to go into effect at the end of the academic year. Bailey concluded that the Program Agency was willing to sacrifice him for the sake of its relationship with the Synod. He also noted that his position and opinions were not consulted before a decision had been made. He was simply given options.[15] Writing of this experience to Bruce and Pat Milligan, Bailey explained that Hopkins had come to Beirut and re-inflamed tempers just when passions seemed to be cooling down. But despite what may have been a clumsy intervention by Hopkins, cooler heads must have prevailed as Bailey was not forced to accept any of the three options Hopkins had proposed.

In January of 1983 Bailey had a doctor's visit and was informed that he needed to cut down on the number of his activities. He did not explain the reason for the doctor's order, but exhaustion, tension, or heart trouble are likely. On hearing this news, Sara and David urged their father to take it seriously and stop being everyone's "donkey." Bailey seems to have taken this to heart—at least for a time. In one week in January, Mickey reported, he declined eight speaking invitations, adding, "Sara cheers him each time he does."[16] Freed from his speaking engagements, he spent more time developing lectures he intended to give in the United States.

Despite the small number of students at NEST, classes opened on time in the new year of 1983 while Bailey's status at the seminary remained uncertain. Fearing that he was still in trouble with the church, he went to see the head of the Synod, who suggested that he let the matter "die away," but Bailey knew that others might not be so forgiving. Nevertheless, he soldiered on. In the last week of January, a Beirut pastor whom Bailey held in high regard flew to New York to discuss the Baileys with

14. Mickey to family, October 7, 1982, Bailey Papers, box 27, folder 5.
15. Mickey to family, October 26, 1982, Bailey Papers, box 28, folder 3.
16. Mickey to family, January 15, 1983, Bailey Papers, box 27, folder 5.

the Program Agency. Though Bailey did not record the outcome of this meeting in any of his letters, apparently this pastor worked things out so that he could continue in his position at least for the time being.[17]

Mickey flew in early April to Pittsburgh to spend time with Sara and attend her graduation from college.[18] Sara wrote a handwritten note to her father on April 5, addressed to "Dear Baba" ("Daddy" in Arabic). She confessed to having trouble with depression. She found herself, she wrote, at times to be in a deep well and had trouble climbing out. Nevertheless, her spirits were lifted that April because of the visit of her mother.[19] A few weeks later, Sara wrote again to her father to say that she was having nightmares of being in Beirut and being pursued by Israeli jets and hit men. "Perhaps," she suggested, "the cumulative effects of war since I was thirteen have in some ways taken their toll." At such times she would awaken in a cold sweat, with soaked sheets, wishing she could have a long comforting talk with her father. But she was quick to add, "Yet, I do not regret what we have undergone as a family."[20] Though the term did not yet exist, Mickey later said that she was experiencing post-traumatic stress disorder (PTSD). The effects had appeared gradually over the course of her college years and perhaps even earlier. Sara would continue to experience these night terrors for years to come.

At the same time, David was enjoying high school at Black Forest Academy in Germany. A handsome youth, who resembled his mother, he was intelligent, thoughtful, and artistic. He also enjoyed being the center of attention. At school he formed a rock band and wrote the music and lyrics for the group himself. He often sought his father's advice, sending him poetry but never music. Bailey praised one set of lyrics but said that the "discipline of the stresses and long and short syllables needs some work, but great potential there."[21] He also commented on David's occasional use of vulgarities, of which he unfailingly disapproved, finding their use offensive as well as intellectually lazy. In general, however, he approved of his son's efforts and encouraged his ambitions to be a

17. Ken to Bruce and Pat [Milligan], January 31, 1983, Bailey Papers, box 28, folder 3.

18. Mickey to Mother, May 12, 1983, Bailey Papers, box 27, folder 5; Ken to Sara, David, and Ethel, April 20, 1983; and Mickey to Ken, ca. April 1983, Bailey Papers, box 27, folder 6; Ken to Bruce and Pat, January 31, 1983, Bailey Papers, box 28, folder 3.

19. Sara to Baba [Ken], April 5, 1983, Bailey Papers, box 27, folder 5.

20. Sara to Baba [Ken], April 22, 1983, Bailey Papers, box 27, folder 6.

21. Ken to Dave, April 24, 1984, Bailey Papers, box 27, folder 6.

musician. David also raised theological questions. Black Forest Academy was a Fundamentalist school, and David wrote to his father for advice on how to consider such matters as biblical inerrancy, Christian ethics, and infant baptism.[22]

Bailey wrote to his wife and children on April 20 to explain that a truck bomb had exploded in front of the American Embassy, and since it was just three buildings away from the Bailey's home, all the windows in their apartment and the front door had been blown in. Fortunately, he was at the seminary at the time. With the help of students and friends, he cleaned up the mess and over the next day made provisional repairs on the shattered windows and broken door. It was obviously a harrowing experience.[23] By early May, carpenters had repaired the windows, door, and other broken things in the apartment so that, when Mickey returned, she would find it in good working order.[24] Mickey was back in Beirut on May 18 after being away for nearly two months.

Wanis Seman's presidency at NEST continued for one year but by June 1983 the seminary had a new president-elect, Ray H. Kiely, the pastor of the Grosse Pointe Presbyterian Church in Grosse Pointe, Michigan. President Kiely arrived with his wife, Martha, in Beirut that month, and in mid-June the seminary's board, faculty, and students held a dinner to welcome them. Mickey thought that attendance was sparse and that the event seemed strained but that, nonetheless, those present seemed to like the new man.[25] The Kielys returned to the States for the summer to prepare for a long stay in Beirut.

On September 30, 1983, when Beirut International Airport opened after over a month of being closed, Mickey reported that people stood on their balconies and cheered as the first plane came in for a landing.[26] But this turned out not to be an augury for better times. In mid-September at 11:00 in the morning three rockets fell on the city in the Baileys' neighborhood.[27] The new fall semester at NEST opened on October 24, which was several weeks late. This was because President Kiely had difficulty

22. Mickey/Ken to David, November 7, 1983, Bailey Papers, box 27, folder 6.
23. Ken to Sara, David, and Ethel, April 20, 1983, Bailey Papers, box 27, folder 6.
24. Ken to Sara, May 4, 1983, Bailey Papers, box 27, folder 6.
25. Mickey to David, June 8, 1982 and June 19, 1983, Bailey Papers, box 28, folder 16.
26. Mickey to Floyd and Marg, October 1, 1983, Bailey Papers, box 27, folder 5. See too Friedman, "Lebanese Reopen Beiruts [sic] Airport," A8.
27. Mickey to David, September 11, 1983, Bailey Papers, box 28, folder 16.

reentering Lebanon. The political situation in the country remained tense, and both sides seemed to be using the lull in the conflict to rearm themselves and prepare for the next phase of the war.[28]

On October 23, two suicide bombers set off a truck bomb outside of the barracks of the Multinational Force (MNF) located in Beirut that resulted in the deaths of 307 people, including 241 US Marines and 58 French troops. Bailey wrote of this incident, "The bombing of the Marines has really left people doubly discouraged with a kind of hopelessness hanging over everything."[29] Political talks continued, but few had expectations of their success anytime soon. Many Lebanese were asking themselves if a unified country were any longer possible, or should they simply opt for a partition that would bring immediate peace? The economy was in poor shape and Lebanese were fleeing the country in large numbers. The Baileys had always enjoyed entertaining, but with an 8:00 p.m. curfew in place, this was difficult. They began entertaining instead at lunch time but, of course, this meant that the visits of friends must be short as all had to return to work.[30]

In the new semester at NEST there were only twenty-five students, but the small number of students did not diminish Bailey's workload. He taught more than a full load of classes. In fact, he believed that he had the heaviest load of all the professors and thought of himself as the seminary's "work horse."[31] This could not be helped because there were few other professors teaching that semester—just the new president, the professor of church history, and two local adjuncts. There were many Sudanese students that year, which Bailey and former president Fletcher had worked hard to bring about. But now that they were students in the seminary, Bailey had second thoughts about their presence. While greatly enjoying and admiring them as people, Bailey found it stressful to teach them because their English skills and educational levels were quite low, making it difficult to convey complex information to them. He felt compelled to accommodate them, but this meant allowing things to slow to a crawl in the classroom and lowering the academic level of his classes.

In anticipation of his furlough at the end of the academic year, Bailey was preparing lectures to be given at the universities of Oxford and Cambridge in England in the first two weeks of June, lecture opportunities

28. Mickey to Floyd and Marg, October 2, 1983, Bailey Papers, box 27, folder 5.
29. Ken to Dave, October 26, 1983, Bailey Papers, box 27, folder 6.
30. Mickey to family, October 31, 1983, Bailey Papers, box 27, folder 5.
31. Ken to Dave, October 26, 1983, Bailey Papers, box 27, folder 6.

arranged by his friend Colin Chapman, who had given him a copy of his newest book, *Whose Promised Land?* (1983).[32] He would also be delivering the Don McClure Memorial Lectures on Mission and Evangelism at Pittsburgh Theological Seminary as well as lectures at McCormick Theological Seminary in Chicago. These lectureships would have to be prepared entirely in advance as each institution expected to publish them.[33]

Mickey wrote to the family in early December that her husband was unwilling to continue in Beirut under the current circumstances of his relationship to the Synod and seminary. The Synod had voted nearly two years before that Bailey should withdraw from Lebanon and had never reversed the decision; and the situation at the seminary, she wrote, was untenable as "life there is grimmer and grimmer" and as the level of the students continued to sink.[34] In May 1983, Paul Hopkins of the Program Agency met with Salim Sahyouni of the Synod and Wanis Seman of the seminary to discuss the ongoing antipathy between Bailey and the Synod. He also arranged a meeting between Wanis and Bailey to try to reach an accord. During their two-hour discussion, both agreed to try to work together to put the matter behind them. Hopkins then met with Bailey alone to impress upon him that the letters he had written had put him in a compromised position. "At this point," he recalled, "I tried to help him see how he was seen by his colleagues in Lebanon and by many of us in New York—as a loner who did not want or need collegial fellowship." Bailey expressed his feeling that he had been rejected by the Program Agency, which should have supported him.[35] The frank airing of grievances and perceptions helped to clear the air, but subsequent events made it uncertain that the Synod was dealing in good faith.

Missionaries in the post-colonial era often found themselves in difficult, even painful, situations. The churches in Lebanon and Egypt in this time took an ambivalent attitude toward missionaries. On the one hand, they were valued for the service they provided, but on the other, they were a living, breathing reminder of the church's Western origins in the colonial era and its ongoing inadequacies—at least to the extent that it needed foreign missionaries to undertake jobs that local people were not yet able to perform or for which the church was not yet able to

32. Ken to Mickey, April 22, 1983, Bailey Papers, box 27, folder 6.

33. Mickey to Mother, December 14, 1983, Bailey Papers, box 27, folder 5.

34. Mickey to family, December 2, 1983, Bailey Papers, box 28, folder 3.

35. Paul A. Hopkins to William H. Miller (The Program Agency), UPCUSA), May 13, 1983, box RG 424, Presbyterian Historical Society.

pay. Bailey may have been largely oblivious to this reality, both in Egypt and in Lebanon. Missionaries such as Bailey, who learned the language and customs of the people he served, might come to think of themselves as valuable members of the local church, insiders whose opinions and ideas should be welcomed or at least respected. However, missionaries in this period would always be seen as outsiders and treated cordially as guests as long as they operated appropriately. If they became disruptive, expressing ideas contrary to those of the church leaders, then they would have to be put in their place, even expelled.

Missionaries could also have an equally awkward relationship with the mission agencies that had sent them. The executives of foreign mission boards may have come to think of themselves as chess grandmasters, who moved missionaries about the board according to the needs of global strategy. They generally had direct relations with the leaders of the partner churches that they served, and it was to these partnerships that they were primarily loyal. As Bailey had experienced, they might fly into a city, meet with their church counterparts, make important decisions, and only then—if at all—meet with missionaries to present a fait accompli.[36] To have met with the missionaries first would have suggested that they were in need of counsel and advice, that they were not in fact grandmasters but rather people with a limited knowledge and experience of the local scene. In any conflict between a local church and missionary, the sending agency would likely take the side of the church partner, without whom they would be out of business. The only leverage the missionaries had was the home churches that supported them. Mission-sending agencies could not deal too cavalierly with missionaries on the field for fear of offending the donors on whom mission was entirely dependent. Therefore, when well-supported missionaries developed strained relationships with a local church, the easiest solution for the sending agency was simply to move the obstreperous pawn to another square. For both the local church and the Presbyterian Program Agency, missionaries were expendable and easily replaced. This was the situation in which Baily found himself.

Having been told that all would be forgiven if he apologized, Bailey dutifully apologized to the Synod leaders three times in writing and twice in person. The apologies were always formally accepted, but the

---

36. Mickey to family, October 26, 1982, Bailey Papers, box 28, folder 3.

Synod never actually reinstated him.[37] In January 1984, President Kiely of NEST wrote to the Program Agency to formally request that Bailey continue to work at the seminary.[38] The Program Agency, however, already seems to have decided to accept the position of the Synod, not the seminary.

Given this situation, at the beginning of the new year, 1984, Bailey began to entertain other work possibilities. In a letter written about a year later, he listed five job offers he had received from institutions in East Beirut. As the situation in Ras Beirut was becoming intolerable, he seriously considered these positions.[39] He also pondered settling elsewhere in the Middle East, perhaps in Cyprus. But being an independent missionary in Beirut seems to have been especially appealing to Bailey at this time. It would allow him to continue to use his Arabic language skills and preach in churches in and around Beirut while not being subject to either the Synod or the seminary. Being independent would mean relying on the current thirty or so Presbyterian churches that were providing his financial needs. Dale Milligan did some checking at this time and was able to inform Bailey early in the new year that his supporting churches would be willing to continue their financial backing outside the denominational structure.[40] Curiously, nothing came of any of these ideas. For all of his ambivalence about the Presbyterian Church, Bailey might not have been able to give up this relationship. He also remained conflicted for other reasons as to what his future should be. Mickey wrote to the family that given the instability of Lebanon, the seminary, the Synod, and even the Presbyterian Program Agency, she and Ken intended to wait until they were in the States during the coming summer to make a final decision.[41]

The year 1984 started tragically for Beirut. On January 19, Bailey wrote home that the president of the American University of Beirut (AUB), Malcolm Kerr, had been assassinated two days before. He and Bailey had been friends, and they shared the same learning disability, dyslexia, though Bailey thought that Kerr's case was more severe. In the

---

37. Kenneth E. Bailey to Robert Lodwick (Associate for Middle East Concerns, PCUSA), December 1, 1984, box RG 424, Presbyterian Historical Society.

38. Ray H. Kiely to Haydn White (Program Agency—UPCUSA), box RG 424, Presbyterian Historical Society.

39. Kenneth E. Bailey to Robert Lodwick (Associate for Middle East Concerns, PCUSA), December 1, 1984, box RG 424, Presbyterian Historical Society.

40. Ken to David, March 11, 1984, Bailey Papers, box 27, folder 6.

41. Mickey to family, February 3, 1984, Bailey Papers, box 28, folder 3.

wake of this event, the two deans of AUB were given bodyguards.[42] On February 6, the Lebanese army broke into two parts, and local Muslim militias and underground groups began seizing foreigners on the streets to hold for ransom. Bailey spent the next four months under self-imposed house arrest in order to complete the semester at NEST before returning to the States. In mid-February Bailey wrote to David that an American professor at AUB had been kidnaped right off the street—and this just two blocks away. Then he added, "Fifty percent of the foreign faculty at AUB [had already] left."[43] Bailey feared being kidnaped in this way and took precautions to prevent it, but despite the dangers, he chose to remain. He reasoned that since he was teaching 50 percent of the classes at NEST, if he left the seminary would have to close. Also, the many African students who had come to NEST would have nowhere to go, and Bailey felt that this would be a betrayal. Therefore, he decided to stay and "accept self-imposed house arrest." He no longer appeared on the streets. He wrote to his family in the States that he stayed at the seminary four days a week to teach his classes, and Mickey and Sara, who had finished college and was teaching history part-time at the American Community School, drove him the short distance to the seminary while he crouched out of sight in the back of the car. Four days later they returned and took him home in the same way.[44] Given the current political conditions and his problems with the Synod, Bailey felt increasingly that it was time for him to move on. But where should he go?

While Ken considered his options, Sara and Mickey continued to drive him to NEST as needed and also took care of the shopping since women were safe on the streets due to Middle Eastern chivalry. Bailey had earlier explained in *Through Peasant Eyes* (1980) the special consideration extended to women in the Middle East. In relating the story of the parable of the judge and the widow (Luke 18:1–8), he observed that "Men can be mistreated in public, but not women. Women can scream at a public figure and nothing will happen to them." But if men behave in such a manner, they would be killed instantly.[45] Ken and Mickey planned

---

42. Ken to Dave, January 22, 1984, Bailey Papers, box 27, folder 6.
43. Ken to David, February 14, 1984, Bailey Papers, box 27, folder 6.
44. Ken to family, March 3, 1984, Bailey Papers, box 27, folder 6.
45. Ken to family, March 3, 1984, Bailey Papers, box 27, folder 5. For the quotation see Bailey, *Through Peasant Eyes*, 135. For another account of Middle Eastern chivalry at this time see Bailey, *Jesus through Middle Eastern Eyes*, 265.

to return to New Wilmington for their furlough that summer and to stay at the missionary house that they had occupied before.[46]

At this time, Bailey continued to express frustration at the heavy class load he was carrying at NEST. Amid the violence and uncertainty of the moment, he would spend much of his time in the first half of the year preparing to give the McClure Lectures at Pittsburgh Theological Seminary. At the same time, he was also working on a study of Paul's First Letter to the Corinthians and, by mid-February, had completed a thirty-three-page-single-spaced study. He wrote to David, "It is actually a rhetorical analysis of the text, and if I am right then all the current commentaries will have to be redone.[47] This was the precursor to his book *Paul through Mediterranean Eyes*, which was not to be published for another twenty-six years. Yet this was not the first time he had written on the subject. The previous May (1983) he wrote to Mary Milligan, Mickey's niece, that he had written an article for the Dutch journal *Novum Testamentus* on the structure of 1 Corinthians.[48]

In March, interim President Kiely announced his resignation. The Baileys and Keilys had become close friends, and Ray and Martha would be much missed. Mickey commented that he did not want to recruit professors to work at NEST only to see them treated as Ken had been.[49] Perhaps, too, he simply saw the situation in Beirut as hopelessly dangerous and chaotic and, therefore, chose to withdraw. The Baileys were coming to the same conclusion. The violence in the streets, the threat of being kidnapped, and the chaos within the seminary presented compelling reasons to leave NEST as well as Beirut. Toward the end of March, someone threw a grenade into the outside door of NEST, breaking the glass in two sets of doors.[50] In early April another American reporter was kidnapped off the streets.[51] Throughout the semester, Bailey continued to ride in the back of the car out of sight as Mickey drove him to and from the seminary.

---

46. Ken to Bruce and Barbara [Bailey], February 3, 1984, Bailey Papers, box 27, folder 6.

47. Ken to Dave, February 26, 1984, Bailey Papers, box 27, folder 6.

48. Ken to Mary [Milligan], May 28, 1983, Bailey Papers, box 27, folder 6. For the article see Bailey, "Structure of 1 Corinthians," 152–81.

49. Mickey to family, March 7, 1984, Bailey Papers, box 27, folder 5.

50. Ken to David, March 25, 1984, Bailey Papers, box 27, folder 6.

51. Ken to David, April 9, 1984, Bailey Papers, box 27, folder 6.

By April 1 Bailey had become resigned about the fate of NEST. A three-day conference was planned in May on "the future of the seminary," but he chose not to attend. On April 3 he learned that a Synod meeting held in Cyprus the previous week had concluded that it would not reinstate Bailey but that it would not stand in the way of the seminary if it wanted to retain him. Since the Synod had formally stated its antipathy towards him, Bailey concluded that the Program Agency in New York would insist on his withdrawal. This confirmed his conclusion that it was time to leave Lebanon, and he submitted his resignation letter on April 10, setting the date for his formal resignation on December 31, 1984. On May 31, he wrote to his friends and supporting churches of his decision, explaining that the reason for his resignation was the political problems in the country, including the numerous kidnaping of Americans.[52] The point was underscored that very month by the kidnapping of Ben Weir, a Presbyterian missionary and Bailey's colleague. Seized on a Beirut street by Muslim extremists, Weir would spend the next sixteen months as a hostage.[53] The Baileys left Beirut shortly after graduation that year in mid-June.

Though the Baileys' life in Beirut had been difficult because of the civil war and Ken's *contretemps* with the Synod, the family would remember Beirut fondly. Sara later reflected that they enjoyed their time there and came to love the city.[54] Ken's decision to leave Beirut made perfect sense and was probably overdue, but he too would later come to realize that, despite the hardships of life in the city, the Bailey family had benefitted from its time there in an unexpected way. Ken wrote to David about five years later that the wartime-enforced confinement of the family meant that they spent their evenings together becoming "truly great friends." He wrote, "Those were great days," though understandably they were not appreciated as such at the time.[55]

---

52. Ken to Dave, April 8, 1984, Bailey Papers, box 27, folder 6. Ken and Ethel to special friends and related churches, May 31, 1984, Bailey Papers, box 28, folder 3.

53. See Weir and Weir, *Hostage Bound, Hostage Free*.

54. Based on a telephone interview with Sara on September 9, 2023.

55. Ken to Leslie and David, April 15, 1990, Bailey Papers, Box 28, folder 1.

14

The Antiochian Missionary
1984–86

> Antiochians are a lonely breed. After a life-time of service in a country other than our own we are, on the deepest levels, strangers both in Jerusalem and in Philippi. We are Antiochians...
>
> —KENNETH E. BAILEY, *CROSS-CULTURAL MISSION: A TALE OF THREE CITIES*

IN JUNE 1984 THE Baileys flew to Britain, where Ken lectured at Cambridge and Oxford. They were back in the United States in July so that Ken could deliver lectures at McCormick Theological Seminary in Chicago in July. This was the beginning of a busy summer of lecturing and preaching for Ken, which took him from Hanover, Illinois, to Des Moines, Iowa, to Washington state.[1] The summer ended with him giving the Don McClure Memorial Lectures on Mission and Evangelism at Pittsburgh Theological Seminary, September 23–27, 1984, for which he had been preparing for a year.

Of the various lectures that Bailey gave in the summer of 1984, the McClure Lectures are the only ones preserved, having been published

---

1. Ken to Floyd and Bruce [Milligan], November 28, 1983, Bailey Papers, box 28, bolder 3.

as *A Tale of Three Cities*.² Using the New Testament imagery of three cities—Jerusalem, Antioch, and Philippi—Bailey argues that modern Protestant missions involve three elements: the missionary-sending church (Jerusalem), the missionaries (Antioch), and the newly formed churches (Philippi). Pioneer missionaries established new churches and generally retained power for subsequent missionaries to direct their own work and control their own funds. In the 1950s, Presbyterians rightly saw this arrangement as colonial in nature, and at the famous Lake Mohonk Conference in New York in 1957, the church agreed to take power from the missionaries and transfer it to local churches in an effort at decolonization.

This effort was led by John Coventry Smith, whose recent autobiography, *From Colonialism to World Community: The Church's Pilgrimages* (1982), Bailey had no doubt read. He avers that "Smith saw clearly the need to strike power out of the hands of the missionaries; he failed to see the need to strike power out of his own hands." Smith, a representative of Jerusalem, allowed the Presbyterian executives in the United States to retain power, directing missionaries and the use of funds. In effect, he decolonized the missionaries but not the home mission office. Bailey writes, Smith did not give power to the local church. Rather, he concentrated it in the hands of the mission executives in New York and Atlanta, inadvertently creating "the most powerful mission executive staff in the history of the modern missionary movement." These mission executives could now talk smugly to missionaries of the need for "partnership" in mission while ironically and hypocritically retaining power for themselves and denying it to the missionaries.³

Having succeeded in disempowering the missionaries, decisions would henceforth be made at meetings between Jerusalem and Philippi at which Antioch would not be invited. Yet, Bailey argues, it is missionaries who learn the local language, work directly with the church on a daily basis, and spend years developing a hard-won understanding of the local context. In contrast, mission executives fly in once a year, make decisions, and return home. Moreover, the missionaries are generally robbed of any significant self-determination, being assigned to whatever

---

2. Bailey's lecture *A Tale of Three Cities* was published as a thirty-two-page double-columned book. There is a copy of the manuscript in the Bailey Papers, box 42, folder 2. The Pittsburgh Theological Seminary library also has three cassette recordings archived of Ken's lectures. See Bailey, *Cross-Cultural Mission*.

3. Bailey, *Tale of Three Cities*, 12.

the local church desires. By the way of comparison, he noted, the apostle Paul, once he had established the church at Philippi, was free to move on to new work as the Spirit guided him. He was not required to teach Sunday school in the local congregation, if the church so ordered.

Bailey asserts that a new missional structure was needed in which executives and missionaries share power, one in which missionaries are given greater power over their own lives and direction of the mission work. He offers, as a model, the Middle East Christian Outreach (MECO), an organization of churches engaging in mission in which the mission decisions are made by a council established in Cyprus where church executives and missionaries participate as equals. But this approach was hardly realistic about the prospects for change. Since the northern and southern branches of the Presbyterian Church were reunited in 1983 for the first time since the Civil War as the Presbyterian Church (U.S.A.), Bailey may have hoped that in a newly reunified Presbyterian Church new thinking might be expected, but he also understood that people with power rarely give it up without a struggle and that this was unlikely to happen given the way the church was then structured.

Bailey writes in summary: "Antiochians are a lonely breed. After a lifetime of service in a country other than our own we are, on the deepest levels, strangers both in Jerusalem and in Philippi. We are Antiochians..." He continues, "Ecclesiologically we do not exist. Twenty-five years ago, we were erased from the ecclesiological memory bank. Structurally we were eliminated. We are Antiochians. Our city was torn down and nothing was rebuilt in its place."[4] Prevented from exercising any real freedom, Bailey believes that many Antiochians had simply stepped out of the system and sought to serve in independent mission organizations.

Bailey of course was speaking from personal experience. Frustrated at being ignored and marginalized by his church's Program Agency and by the Synod he had served in Lebanon, he sought to help the Presbyterian Church to see that new mission structures were needed so that missionaries would have a voice in church councils where decisions were made. It was a valid point, but it seems to have been ignored. In the near future, Bailey would find creative ways to remain formally within the church and yet enjoy the freedom and recognition that he craved.

---

4. Bailey, *Tale of Three Cities*, 18, 20.

For the Baileys' 1984–85 furlough, they again settled temporarily in the mission home in New Wilmington, which for Ken became a base from which to preach in churches, synods, presbyteries, and various other venues across the United States. He also taught pastors' seminars and gave a lecture series at Princeton Theological Seminary. In the fall of 1984, David began his freshman year at Grove City College, while Sara remained with her parents studying for a master's degree in education at Westminster College in New Wilmington. In December of 1984, Bailey made arrangements to acquire an electronic typewriter that could be attached to a home computer and printer. Sometime early in 1985 Bailey entered the computer age.[5]

In the summer of 1984, Bailey applied for and was granted an extension of his furlough assignment in the United States so that he could continue research on his new book, *Jesus Interprets His Own Cross*. While he never published this as an independent book, some of its chapters may be included in *Jesus through Middle Eastern Eyes* (2008). In a letter to his supporters in July 1985, he described what he had in mind: "It is generally assumed that Jesus announced his coming cross but never explained its meaning. We are trying to demonstrate that the deepest level of understanding of the cross is available in the dramatic actions and teachings of Jesus, and that Paul's theology comes then as an enriching supplement, not as a first-time explanation of an unknown mystery." He adds that his initial draft was then complete.[6]

During this furlough, Bailey was offered a position at the Tantur Ecumenical Institute for Theological Research in Jerusalem, Israel-Palestine. Bailey's title would be "Research professor of Middle Eastern New Testament Studies" and his assignment threefold: to teach seminars and colloquiums for visitors, record audio and video cassettes in New Testament studies for distribution in the Arab world and around the world, and continue his research and writing. Owned by the Vatican and run by the University of Notre Dame in South Bend, Indiana, Tantur is a Catholic institution open to Catholic and Protestant scholars to meet, discuss, and do research. It had a library of 50,000 books and holdings of 400 journals. Bailey soon discovered the nearby Dominican library in Jerusalem, which he also found helpful. These libraries would enable him to continue his research outside of the United States. Despite Tantur

---

5. Ken to Jud Allen (Overseas Treasury Service, PCUSA), December 11, 1984, vertical files, RG 424, Presbyterian Historical Society.

6. Bailey family to friends, July 1985, Bailey Papers, box 28, folder 3.

being a Catholic institution, he would continue to work as a Presbyterian missionary under the auspices of the PCUSA. The church's headquarters had been in New York, but after the northern and southern branches of the Presbyterians Church were reunited in 1983, the denomination's headquarters was moved to Louisville, Kentucky, in 1988. Though Bailey was given an initial three-year assignment in Jerusalem, he would spend the next five years of his mission service at Tantur.

Bailey initially enjoyed lecturing at Tantur. Catholic students came from all over the world to spend time at the institute and take classes or listen to lectures. From Notre Dame came American undergraduates, but otherwise the students were priests, nuns, or Catholic lay people from around the world. The Institute for Middle Eastern New Testament Studies that Bailey had started at NEST would continue, though the team of scholars he had assembled there was now dispersed. Bailey shipped the books and various materials that he had collected in his offices at NEST to his new address at Tantur. As Ken and Mickey set out for Jerusalem on September 1, 1985, Ken contemplated the work that he hoped to accomplish at Tantur and considered the move to be "a new and exciting adventure."[7]

In June 1985, Mickey and Sara flew back to Beirut to retrieve the family's possessions at their old apartment and, as Ken put it, "rescue my library and papers."[8] While it was prudent for Mickey and Sara to travel alone to Beirut because Middle Eastern chivalry meant that women were safe on the streets while men were not, it is also possible that Bailey did not accompany them because he had hurt his foot and would spend at least the next ten months on crutches. The exact nature of this most recent of his physical ailments is not revealed in his letters.[9] Given Sara's ongoing struggle with depression, she decided to settle with her parents in Jerusalem. As Mickey wrote, she felt "she needed her family for stability and that they could find a good doctor" in Israel.[10]

The Tantur Ecumenical Institute in the 1980s was a thirty-four-acre campus at the top of a hill about six miles from Jerusalem and two

---

7. Ken to Ny Lea Vorhoff, March 5, 1986, Bailey Papers, box 27, folder 8. Bailey further described the center in a letter to his family, October 3, 1985, Bailey Papers, box 28, folder 3.

8. Ken and Ethel to family and friends, November 7, 1985, Bailey Papers, box 28, folder 15. Ken to family and friends, July 1985, Bailey Papers, box 28, folder 3.

9. Ken to Ethel, March 30, 1986, Bailey Papers, box 27, folder 8.

10. Mickey to family, October 29, 1985, Bailey Papers, box 28, folder 3.

miles from Bethlehem. Today it is a much smaller campus due to Israeli road expansion. The Baileys were given a small apartment on the Tantur grounds that had a balcony from which they could look out upon Bethlehem, other villages in the area, and the Judean hills that rose above them. They enjoyed having breakfast on the balcony to take in the sights. The rector of the institute from 1985 to 1988 was a man named Landrum Bolling, a well-respected leader in international ecumenical circles. Bailey, however, believed that he would be a poor administrator. At seventy-two years of age, Bailey concluded that, though an amiable and gentle man, he took a lackadaisical attitude toward administration. Moreover, there was no dean to organize the teaching calendar and no academic program to follow. Consequently, Bailey anticipated that a great deal of "muddling through" would be required. Having been chastened for his outspokenness at NEST, he resolved to do things differently at Tantur. "My current strategy," he wrote to his family, "is to keep my head down, my nose clean, my powder dry, my mouth shut, and myself busy at my writing."[11] He had said something similar at the outset of his career in Lebanon.

In addition to lecturing to visitors at Tantur, as early as December 1985 Bailey began to hold classes for the Sisters of Zion, a group of Catholic nuns in the convent located on the Via Dolorosa in the Old City of Jerusalem named Ecce Homo (Latin for "Behold the man"), the words that Pilate spoke to a crowd while displaying the scourged Christ.[12] The convent is appropriately named because it is located on the supposed site of Pilate's judgment hall. In the coming years, Bailey would often express irritation, boredom, and discouragement regarding his teaching of the transient groups passing through Tantur, but he always wrote positively of his experience teaching the nuns of Ecce Homo, whom he found to be intelligent and highly engaged.[13]

While Ken was enjoying lecturing and much free time for writing and research and Mickey was settling into new routines at the institute, Sara continued to struggle with depression. In late August, David wrote to commend his father for the "endless hours in patient love" that he had devoted to his daughter, but he also recognized that her neediness was sapping his father of emotional energy, limiting the productivity of

---

11. Ken to family, October 3, 1985, Bailey Papers, box 27, folder 7.

12. Ken and Ethel to friends and family, November 7, 1985, Bailey Papers, box 28, folder 15.

13. Ken and Ethel to special friends, July 10, 1986, Bailey Papers, box 28, folder 15.

his ministry, and probably contributing "many moments of despair."[14] In his response, Bailey did not deny these adverse effects of his daughter's condition on his life and ministry, but he was determined to "mirror to her the love of God as best we can."[15] Sara's dreams were still haunted by the violence that the family had experienced in Beirut, which led to panic attacks, depression, anorexia, emotional outbursts, and suicidal ideation. The Baileys decided that Sara and Micky should return together to New Wilmington and stay at the mission house so that Sara could seek better treatment in the United States.[16] They left on November 7 and would remain through May 1986, a period of about seven months.

Sara was fully aware of the anxiety she was causing her parents and was deeply grateful for their care. She wrote a card to her father on November 7, possibly sending it from the Larnaca Airport in Cyprus, thanking him for all the love he had shown her over her twenty-four years and especially for the last two, difficult months.[17] Ken was deeply moved and wrote back immediately:

> I came home and read your card. It was so beautiful that I wept. I will cherish it always. I am very proud of you and there was only one part of your letter that is not accurate. You write "I am so sorry that once again I am the cause for unhappiness." That is not true. You have never been the cause for unhappiness. When any member of the family is in pain, we all hurt—but that is not unhappiness, it is just a way of saying that we also hurt when you are hurting.

He urged her not to be distracted by secondary things such as finding a job, obtaining further education, seeking housing, or becoming self-supporting. Rather, she should focus on the top priority of becoming well again.[18]

That winter and spring Sara saw a doctor twice a week. Bailey, meanwhile, traveled to the United States in mid-February to address a week-long Presbyterian conference for senior pastors held in Orlando, Florida. Having been granted emergency home leave by the Presbyterian Church, he traveled to New Wilmington, where he stayed until March 15

---

14. David to dear buddy [Ken], August 29, 1985, Bailey Papers, box 27, folder 7.
15. Ken to dear buddy [David], September 2, 1985, Bailey Papers, box 27, folder 7.
16. Ken to Dave, October 7, 1985, and October 13, 1985, Bailey Papers, box 27, folder 7.
17. Sara to Baba [Ken], November 7, 1985, Bailey Papers, box 27, folder 7.
18. Ken to Sara, November 8, 1985, Bailey Papers, box 27, folder 7.

before returning to Jerusalem.[19] During this time, he observed that Sara seemed to be improving. That spring the doctors discovered, as Bailey later described it, "the right combination of medications" so that Sara could begin to improve. Feeling much better, she applied to resume her graduate studies at Kent State University in the summer for a master's degree in library science with the goal of becoming a children's librarian. When Ken arrived back in Jerusalem in March, lonely and missing his family, he set up a chart with seventy days, titling it "Babylonian Captivity II" on which he checked off the days until Mickey's return.[20]

Figure 21. Ken Bailey at the Tantur Ecumenical Institute, Jerusalem, Israel, circa 1985–90.

Before Bailey returned to Jerusalem, he wrote to David at Grove City College, asking him to telephone Sara and Mickey twice a week, making collect calls for ten minutes at a time. Each of the women, he advised him, would benefit in different ways from his effort.[21] Two weeks later, David reported to his father his observations of Mickey and Sara's interactions. Mickey genuinely tried to help her daughter, offering sage

19. Ken and Ethel to special friends, July 100, 1986, Bailey Papers, box 28, folder 15; and Ken to Bruce and Barbara [Bailey], March 23, 1986, Bailey Papers, box 28, folder 8.

20. Ken to Ethel, March 23, 1986, Bailey Papers, box 28, folder 8.

21. Ken to Dave, March 16, 1986, Bailey Papers, box 27, folder 8.

advice and showing enormous patience in the face of Sara's mood swings. But Sara continued at times to lash out.[22] Bailey wrote back to David to explain, at least in part, Mickey and Sara's then strained relationship. He believed that Mickey as a child had never received much encouragement from her parents and therefore was now incapable of giving this to Sara. Yet a steady stream of encouragement was exactly what Sara then needed.[23] January and February were difficult months for Sara, but she showed much improvement in March and April. In May, however, she had a relapse, fasting for forty-eight hours. Mickey said that she was terrified of her parents leaving, about beginning her studies at Kent State, and about her living arrangements.[24] Mickey's spirits sank, but Sara's relapse proved to be temporary and by the end of the month she had improved enough that Mickey decided to return to Jerusalem, leaving Sara to begin the master's program in library science at Kent State.

Figure 22. Kenneth E. Bailey promotional photo, circa 1985.

22. Dave to Dad, March 27, 1986, Bailey Papers, box 27, folder 8.
23. Ken to dear buddy [David], May 2, 1986, Bailey Papers, box 27, folder 8.
24. Mickey to Ken, May 4, 1986, Bailey Papers, box 27, folder 8.

Though the past year had been a difficult one for Bailey because of Sara's health, it was one in which he forged a deeper relationship with his son, David, who was in his sophomore year at Grove City College. In September 1985, he wrote a beautiful, thoughtful letter to his son about spiritual gifts, avoiding pride, and being authentic. But it was not simply a letter of fatherly advice as he also opened his heart to his son, writing of his anger toward his superiors in the Presbyterian Church and his deep concern for Sara's well-being.[25] In subsequent letters, he wrote of his work and family news in ways completely transparent and disarming. In this year and for some time to come, Ken and David began to address each other as "Buddy," which in practice did not signify a false attempt at equality but a real yearning for comradery. David, for his part, seemed to completely trust his father and was able to pour out his heart to him, sharing his concerns, his youthful passions, his ideas and hopes for a career in music.

In December, David flew to Israel-Palestine to spend the Christmas of 1985 with his father. Ken and David, while traveling with another family, devoted a number of days to touring Holy Land sites. It was a good chance for Ken to speak seriously with his son, whom he found to be "drifting." Ken advised him that in addition to pursuing his music he should also develop the skills needed for a "functional profession," but he found that he made little impression on his son. He was especially concerned that David seemed to be straying from the Christian faith. His music, Ken observed, was often secular and "at times anti-Christian, and at times barroom ballads boarding on the vulgar." Perhaps, he speculated, this was just a little "theological rebellion." Was not this to be expected since, after all, he was only a sophomore in college? At the beach at Caesarea, he and David stood together watching the waves break over the rocks on the shore, staring out at the Mediterranean Sea. Ken thought back to the period in Beirut before the war "when we were together and Sara was well and the seminary [NEST] was bright with hope, and we had a beautiful settled home." Contemplating the dashed hopes of just a few short years before, he began to weep. "Maybe," he wrote to Mickey, "there are some bright days yet to come—we must believe that it is so."[26]

As early as the 1985 holiday season, just a few months after beginning at Tantur, Bailey was already discouraged not simply because of past

---

25. Ken to dear Buddy [David], September 2, 1985, Bailey Papers, box 27, folder 7.
26. Ken to Ethel, ca. New Year's 1986, Bailey Papers, box 27, folder 7.

frustrations or ongoing family concerns but because of his current situation at the Tantur Institute itself. He wrote to Mickey,

> I can't figure out if it is because Sara is sick, or that we are apart, or that I can't get out stuff [scholarly articles], or that the community keeps changing here and that I am really spending my time teaching Americans rather than Arabs or all of the above plus my unresolved anger at the PA [Program Agency]. Anyway, I guess I am really discouraged about Tantur but don't dare say so because I don't want to reflect badly on all of Landrum's efforts—and right now I have no place to go.[27]

In these long months away from his wife, one thing that offered a ray of hope was contemplating the land that they owned in New Wilmington. He told David that as a missionary kid (or MK) in the United States, he had felt that there was no place that he could call home. Owning land in western Pennsylvania gave him a sense of deep rootedness that he had always lacked. Naturally, he hoped that David would come to identify with the land as he had.[28] To Mickey he wrote that he was now counting the years before he could retire and return to his own land where "we will have our own house in the woods, or at the edge of the woods."[29] Writing again to David in March 1986, he introduced the subject of working together with him on the family property while he was on furlough in 1988. Though Bailey had never spent much time in western Pennsylvania, he had come to consider this part to the United States as his homeland.[30]

As Bailey experimented with his new electronic typewriter and home computer in 1985, his writing became noticeably better, with fewer spelling and grammatical errors. Also, this was a very productive period in his life. Though he was lonely without his family around him, he was also isolated and with few responsibilities and few classes to teach. He wrote David in October 1985 that he had finished his first short article since arriving at Tantur and that he was then loading a longer one into the computer so that he could revise and complete it.[31] In the new year of 1986, he was writing short articles for the *Oxford Companion to the Bible*, edited by Bruce M. Metzger and Michael D. Coogan, which he hoped

---

27. Ken to Mickey, ca. just after Christmas 1985, Bailey Papers, box 27, folder 7.
28. Ken to David, March 16, 1986, Bailey Papers, box 27, folder 8.
29. Ken to Ethel, March 19, 1986, Bailey Papers, box 27, folder 8.
30. Ken to Ethel, March 23, 1986, Bailey Papers, box 27, folder 8.
31. Ken to David, October 16, 1985, Bailey Papers, box 27, folder 7.

to complete by late June.³² In April he wrote to Mickey that he had also completed four editorials for the *Presbyterian Outlook*.

During the first three months of 1986, Bailey considered what the origins were of the chiasmic structures he had found in the Gospels and especially in Paul's First Letter to the Corinthians. Examining the writings of the major and minor prophets of the Old Testament, he soon settled on 2 Isaiah (Isa 44–66) as a promising venue. He wrote excitedly to Mickey about 2 Isaiah, "it is really a goldmine. I am coming up with so much stuff I can't believe it." Chapters 44–66 of Isaiah, he discovered, contained the same underlying chiasmic structures that he had first seen in the Gospels and later detected in 1 Corinthians. He concluded that this "clinches my case" that Paul had learned this technique from 2 Isaiah, and he wondered if he might be able to produce a commentary on 1 Corinthians that would clarify this point. He sometimes regretted having to teach classes at this time because they took him away from this study, which fascinated him. But then he remembered that the classes gave him a venue to test his ideas. Above all, he enjoyed "working up some new ideas and new texts."³³ He wrote again to Mickey that he had "been working flat out trying to finish my analysis of 2 Isaiah." He completed a first draft of an article by the end of the April, writing that 1 Corinthians had thirty-two "plates"—that is, independent poetic structures that used the chiasmic form—while 2 Isaiah had sixty-seven plates. This made sense to him because 1 Corinthians had only fifteen chapters while 2 Isaiah had twenty-six. He believed now that New Testament writers often quoted the Old Testament in a way that followed this rhetorical structure and that this would have been easily recognized by Jewish readers who lived in biblical times. Such discoveries were what Bailey lived for. He wrote to Mickey, "For the first time in goodness [knows] how long I am starting to really produce some new material rather than just grind the crank with the old stuff that I have done over and over and over."³⁴ By August 1987, he anticipated completing a book of 400 pages by the end of the coming winter. Bailey would continue to examine both 2 Isaiah and 1 Corinthians for years to come, not publishing his study on the subject, *Paul through Mediterranean Eyes*, until 2011.

---

32. Ken to Ethel, March 23, 1986, Bailey Papers, box 27, folder 8.
33. Ken to Ethel, April 8, 1986, and April 15, 1986, Bailey Papers, box 27, folder 8.
34. Ken to Ethel, April 31, 1986, Bailey Papers, box 27, folder 8.

In this same letter he reflected that his loneliness and isolation at Tantur were the price he was paying for the extensive time he now had for original research. He had learned recently from professor Mark Swanson at the Evangelical Theological Seminary in Cairo (ETSC) that he had a heavy teaching load of fifteen hours a week and had to spend many hours on the road because of Cairo's traffic. "Now that Egyptians run the place [ETSC]," Ken wrote to Mickey, "they load the hours onto their staff and of course there is no assumption of anyone doing any writing or anything like that." Then again if he were at an institution such as Pittsburgh Theological Seminary (PTS), he reasoned that the situation would be equally frustrating. At PTS he would be expected to constantly develop new courses, attend endless meetings, and regularly preach in local churches. "So, here I can really put in the hours. If I just had my girlfriend [Mickey] here, maybe then I could be happy."[35]

Though Tantur was a place that offered Bailey something of an Arcadian retreat from the world, allowing him to concentrate on his scholarship, life at the center could nevertheless be a trial for him. The lack of careful administration was annoying. Sometimes he would not be informed that he was to teach a seminar or colloquium until a few weeks before it began.[36] Another concern was the transient nature of the Tantur community. People came for a few weeks and left, never to be seen again. The hope of having a scholarly community in which to participate did not materialize, as there were few scholars present who were actually living in the community. When scholars were at hand, Bailey often felt out of place. He said that he had always worked within Christian institutions but that Tantur "is on the fringes of the faith and is kind of in that never, never land between the three communities [Jewish, Christian, and Muslim]."[37] In effect, it had an interreligious ethos that did not appeal to one of Bailey's conservative evangelical orientation. Ken suggested to Mickey that they would have to look to the Arab Episcopal community in the city to find friends and fellowship.

Of more prosaic concern in these months were family finances. Bailey was then supporting David at Grove City College and paying for Sara's ongoing medical expenses, and in January and again in February Mickey had overdrawn their bank account. In March he wrote to her about trying to contain their burgeoning expenses. The previous summer

35. Ken to Ethel, April 31, 1986, Bailey Papers, box 27, folder 8.
36. Ken to Ethel, April 13, 1986, Bailey Papers, box 27, folder 8.
37. Ken to Ethel, April 10, 1986, Bailey Papers, box 27, folder 8.

he had paid for David to enjoy an $800 youth mission experience with the church in Korea and later a $200 camping trip. David also enjoyed an expensive trip to Europe. Bailey concluded, "So, last year we spent $2,000 for him to travel around and have fun." He worried that David needed to become more financially responsible. "He is asking for money," Bailey continued, "for books, to join a fraternity, for a new guitar; and no doubt he will soon be asking for a car." Bailey felt that he should be paying for his son's college tuition, room and board, and occasional trips home, but other expenses—especially travel, entertainment, and pocket money—should be on him. Bailey also wanted to purchase a car so that he and Mickey could do errands and travel more easily in Israel-Palestine—an expense he saw as essential. Yet cars were expensive there. He estimated that a six-year-old Volkswagen with 50,000 miles would cost $5,000, while a similar car in the United States would cost $900.[38] Fortunately, in addition to his salary as a missionary, Bailey had also earned money from his speaking engagements in 1984 and 1985, though these funds had already been spent. He concluded, "If Sara doesn't work next year that will mean $10,000 more to get her master's [at Kent State University]. And we must buy a car here if we are going to function. I know that it is hard for you to get strict with David, but we must for his sake and for ours."[39]

Bailey filed a claim with the Presbyterian Board of Pensions to cover the major part of Sara's medical expenses for the period February 1, 1985, to January 31, 1986. During this period, he had already paid a 2 percent deductible.[40] Looking carefully at the sources of his income, he calculated that his thirty or so supporting churches were contributing $44,000 a year but he was receiving only about $33,000 of this in salary, social security payments, pension payments, and housing allowance. The Program Agency, he reasoned, collected about $11,000 a year above what it actually spent on him. He knew that the church had to pay its own overhead expenses as well as pay the expenses of missionaries who were not as successful as he was in raising support. Nevertheless, it was galling to him that the Program Agency was taking about a quarter of the money he was raising at a time when his own finances were so tight.[41]

38. Ken to ___, ca. October 1985, Bailey Papers, box 27, folder 7. David's youth mission experience is mentioned in Ken and Ethel to family and friends, November 7, 1985, Bailey Papers, box 28, folder 15.
39. Ken to Ethel, March 20, 1986, Bailey Papers, box 27, folder 8.
40. Ken to Ethel, March 30, 1986, Bailey Papers, box 27, folder 8.
41. Ken to Ethel, April 1, 1986, Bailey Papers, box 27, folder 8.

The Antiochian Missionary

Bailey, however, found a way to meet some of his expenses in a way that worked around the Program Agency's auspices. He found a group of possible supporters in California who were willing to contribute money to pay for some of the specific needs of his ministry such as his travel expenditures to the United States for speaking engagements, his outlays for producing audio and video tapes, and the price of an automobile. Regarding his transportation needs, he suggested that acquiring a serviceable car would require about $7,000 plus ongoing costs. If this group could contribute $4,000, the Program Agency $2,500, and he $3,000, then a fine used car could be had. He called this group of Californians the "Cowboys," alluding to the posters that depicted President Ronald Reagan, who owned a ranch in Santa Barbara, California, as a cowboy. He also referred to Reagan at this time as "the cowboy." In the event, these generous Californians, the cowboys, were offering to raise $25,000 for his ministry expenses—a welcome contribution to meet his financial needs at the time.[42]

Whatever had happened to Bailey's foot the previous June requiring him to use crutches was still a problem through at least April and May of 1986. Not only did he continue to walk with the aid of crutches but his foot was still so badly swollen that he taught his classes while standing with crutches and also had to keep his foot elevated when home. By the spring he was seeing a British physiotherapist three times a week, but she did not improve his condition. Bailey's lack of mobility meant that his home, as he confessed to David, was "really getting grimy—don't tell Mom. I don't know what to do. I really can't hobble around and clear it all up. And then I am moving out anyway."[43] To Sara he confessed that he had the same thing for breakfast and lunch every day, day after day. For breakfast he had "za'tir, bread, honey, jam, grapefruit juice, coffee, yogurt." And for lunch he had "bread, butter, olives, cheese, tomato, apple, tea and one of Ethel's special cookies."[44] For dinner, he probably had a meal from the Tantur dining room. Clearly, the man needed his wife.

Bailey flew to the United States in May to deliver four lectures to the alumni at Princeton Theological Seminary. He enjoyed a good turnout of 250 in attendance and commented, "I was treated royally and put up in the 'Presidential suite.' It was very plush, and I had a good time."[45] With

---

42. Ken to Ethel, April 1, 1986, Bailey Papers, box 27, folder 8.
43. Ken to David, April 12,1986, Bailey Papers, box 27, folder 8.
44. Ken to Sara, April 7, 1986, Bailey Papers, box 27, folder 8.
45. Ken to Habib, September 24, 1986, Baily Papers, box 27, folder 8.

these lectures behind him, Ken and Mickey returned together to Jerusalem in June, bringing to an end Ken's *annus horribilis*. He had written to David on April 2 that there is an Arabic expression that he had taken to heart, "God has no right to count this year as one of the years of my life." In other words, if God had given him a certain number of years to live, he should not count this one because it had been too harrowing to consider including it with the rest. He was thinking of his conflict with the Synod in Beirut, having to leave the city, Sara's health issues, and finally having to live apart from Mickey.[46]

Things then began to look up for the Bailey family. Sara had sufficiently improved that in mid-June she recommenced her studies at Kent State University, and sometime that month Bailey learned that the "cowboys out in California" had managed to raise $8,500 for the various projects he had recommended. His first thought seems to have been to set aside $3,000 to purchase a car so that he and Mickey could get around more easily in Israel-Palestine.[47] Bailey was also glad to be reunited with his wife in their apartment. Mickey wrote to David soon after her arrival, "Dad is tickled pink that I am here of course and acts as tho it were a second honeymoon." They began to make long overdue improvements on their apartment, though Mickey confessed that her slowness in decision-making was retarding their progress. Still, she wrote to David, "He [Ken] feels as though he has a home again, and I haven't seen him look so happy for a long, long time. He loves being on the balcony and looking out over Bethlehem and Beit Jala and seeing the hills above both of them."[48] Ken and Mickey slipped back into a comfortable routine, which ended every day with a chapel service at Tantur and an evening meal in the Tantur dining room together with other members of the community.[49]

46. Ken to David, April 2, 1986, Bailey Papers, box 27, folder 8.
47. Ken to David, June 20, 1986, Bailey Papers, box 27, folder 8.
48. Mickey to David, July 7, 1986, Bailey Papers, box 27, folder 8.
49. Ken to David, June 27, 1986, Bailey Papers, box 27, folder 8.

— 15 —

O Jerusalem, Jerusalem
1986–90

> The stories of Jesus that circulated in the first generation [of the church] are in principle to be taken as just that: stories of Jesus.
>
> —N. T. Wright, *Jesus and the Victory of God*

THE YEARS THAT KEN and Mickey lived in Jerusalem were a time of growing frustration over the annoyances and discomforts of life in general in Israel-Palestine. This was the period of the First Intifada in Israel, which both endangered and complicated the Baileys' lives. The Tantur Institute was an island of peace, but Ken and Mickey grew increasingly restive under the management styles of the two directors it had in these years. At the same time, Ken and Sara suffered from debilitating physical ailments while, back in the United States, David was taking uncertain steps toward independence and adulthood. Through all of this, Ken was making remarkable scholarly breakthroughs in his exegesis of 1 Corinthians and the development of a theory for the reliability of the oral tradition behind the Gospels.

Ken remarked to David in October that he was disturbed by the shabby conditions of the grounds of the Tantur campus. He estimated that for the previous hundred years people passing by had treated the campus as a dumping ground for their garbage and various discards. He and Mickey, therefore, organized three teams of Tantur residents and staff members in a community-wide effort to rid the thirty-four-acre campus of the unsightly accumulation. In one day, they collected ninety-six large garbage bags of rubbish that they burned. They also gathered two tons of metal discards that had to be hauled away. Ken then set about designing walking and jogging paths around the property for people to enjoy. Ken and Mickey also organized a second community activity: the collection on the grounds of pine nuts and pine cones that contained nuts. These were a local Palestinian delicacy, which needed only to be cracked and shelled.[1]

In the last week of May, Ken and Mickey flew to Cairo and then took a seven-hour taxi ride to Sharm El Sheikh, a city on the southern end of the Sinai Peninsula, in order to participate in a conference for Mennonite mission personnel in the region. Since their expulsion from Egypt in 1965, Ken had visited the country numerous times, usually for conferences in Alexandria. For Mickey, however, it would be her first trip back in twenty-two years. She enjoyed seeing some old friends in Cairo, but driving through the city, she was dismayed by the new slums that had emerged since her departure. She and Ken stopped at the American Cemetery to lay flowers at the graves of two of Sara's friends, Ann Weir and Kathy Lorimer, both of whom had died in Cairo in a tragic train accident in the fall of 1985.[2] Ken thought that the conference center at Sharm El Sheikh was "okay but nothing extraordinary." Sometime during the three-day conference, they went out on a boat to do some snorkeling, but the high winds and rough sea made swimming unpleasant. They spent four days traveling for a three-day conference and returned home at 2:00 a.m. exhausted and disappointed. Mickey probably expressed their mutual feeling when she commented, "I really don't care tho if I never go back."[3]

Bailey completed his last class for the spring season at Tantur on May 2 and continued teaching his class at Ecce Homo through May. On June 24, he and Mickey flew to Cyprus for their annual vacation, and then on July 11 flew to Pittsburgh and drove on to New Wilmington,

---

1. Mickey to ____, November 6, 1986, and Ken to David, October 30, 1986, Bailey Papers, box 27, folder 8.

2. Ken and Ethel to family and friends, November 7, 1985, box 28, folder 15.

3. Mickey to Marsha and Bob [Pitts] (former residents at Tantur), April 25 1987; Mickey to Marsha and Bob Pitts, May 8, 1987; Mickey to Leslie, May 12, 1987; Mickey and Ken to David, May 14, Bailey Papers, box 27, folder 9.

where they would spend the summer.[4] They had the pleasure that August of seeing their son, David, marry Leslie McGarvey, whom Mickey described as "a good Scotch Presbyterian lassie."[5] The marriage ceremony, which occurred on August 15, 1987, was performed by Pastor Darrell D. Knopp at the Presbyterian Church of Emlenton, Pennsylvania, which was Leslie's family's church and the one that she and David frequented while college students. The ceremony was well attended by both families, and there were also friends from Beirut and college present. The ceremony was memorable for the several songs performed that were written by David,[6] and there was a reception at the nearby Wolf's Den Restaurant, which was a favorite place of the bride and groom.[7] Later that summer, David and Lelise moved into the Bailey home in New Wilmington where it was agreed that they would live during David's senior year at Grove City College.

There were many aspects to living in the Holy Land that Ken and Mickey enjoyed. For example, they discovered a pleasant picnic area in a valley that lay "beyond the Herodium," the palace-fortress built on a hilltop by King Herod in the first century BC, about seven miles from Jerusalem. Snaking around the hill was a wadi, a river bed in which the water dries up in the spring. It was there that Ken and Mickey went to relax. During one of their hikes in the area, Ken discovered a cave where shepherds kept their flocks. Standing in the cave and looking across the valley, he saw shepherds leading their flocks. In other parts of the world, shepherds drive their flocks before them, often using dogs. But it is a peculiarity of Israel-Palestine that sheep follow their shepherds, who often call them by name and sing a tune to which they respond.[8] Such experiences informed Ken's understanding of the parable of the lost sheep in Luke 15 and later of the entire thousand-year shepherd-king tradition in the Bible, which he would write about in his last book, *The Good Shepherd* (2014).

---

4. Mickey to family, May 4, 1987, Bailey Papers, box 27, folder 9.

5. Mickey to Floyd and Marg [Milligan], October 21, 1986, Bailey Papers, box 27, folder 8.

6. The wedding bulletin is among the Bailey Papers, box 28, folder 15.

7. The description of the wedding was provided by Leslie Bailey, interviewed February 19, 2023.

8. Mickey to Leslie and David, January 24, 1988, and Mickey to Sara, January 25, 1988, Bailey Papers, box 27, folder 9.

Although Ken and Mickey initially found Tantur an enjoyable place to live and work, a number of aspects of community life there became increasingly irksome to them. Writing to David, Mickey summed up their concerns in three points. First, there was little true community life at the center as people came and went so often that there was little opportunity to form lasting friendships. Second, some of the children at the center were ill-disciplined. In a previous letter Mickey noted in particular five children in apartments at the center that were causing havoc, running around and screaming all the time. Third, Rector Landrum Bolling continued to be a poor administrator, which meant that the scheduling of programs and the handling of personnel problems were often neglected, producing "chaos and confusion." Another issue, mentioned in a previous letter, was that some of the visitors to the ecumenical center differed culturally and perhaps morally from American evangelicals. One group, called the Foundation for the Realization of Love, Peace, and Simplicity, held a chapel service one evening that Mickey found simply "weird." It was led by a woman in a see-through blouse, whom Mickey dismissively referred to as the "guru woman." Some members of the same group engaged in inappropriate "necking and petting" in the main building's reception area and under trees where they could be seen by the community's children. Ken handled the confusion and irritations of the community by immersing himself further in his work and doing his best to ignore his surroundings.[9]

While some of the worship services at Tantur were experimental by design, others followed traditional Roman Catholic patterns. When they were conducted by Roman Catholic priests, Holy Communion was restricted to members of the Catholic Church in good standing even though they were billed as ecumenical in nature. Mickey was offended enough by this that she wrote a formal complaint to the rector that this was against the spirit of ecumenism and that if Communion was not open to all it should not be part of the service.[10] One of the last worship events at Tantur that they attended was a Good Friday service that featured the "seven last words" of Jesus on the cross. In Ken's opinion, the nun who presided in the service had a tortured interpretation of Jesus' words, "'Woman, behold, your son!' Then he said to the disciple, 'Behold, your mother!'" (John 19:26–27). Ken commented that she neglected to

9. Mickey to David, May 14, 1987; and Mickey to Marsha and Bob (former residents at the center), Bailey Papers, box 27, folder 9.

10. Mickey to Landrum [Bolling], March 14, 1988, Bailey Papers, box 27, folder 9.

note Jesus' self-possession and courage on the cross, which enabled him to express care for his mother. She also missed the bravery of John who was the only disciple to remain. Instead, he observed, "We got the most revolting medieval Catholic piety dumped on us that climaxed with a call on Mary to 'Please pray for us.'"[11] Though Bailey generally enjoyed teaching Roman Catholics, whom he typically found to be friendly and engaging, incidents such as these were probably not isolated but recurrent events in the Baileys' experiences at the center, which in time inevitably began to grate. It is no wonder, then, that they attended services at St. George's Cathedral, an Anglican congregation in Jerusalem. The cathedral became for them a spiritual home, and they forged close friendships there with members of the congregation.[12]

During the first half of 1988, Bailey continued to teach classes at Tantur, Ecce Homo, and an organization called Educational Opportunities that organized study tours of the Holy Land. Otherwise, he was devoting all of his time to his new book, a comparative study of 2 Isaiah and 1 Corinthians. Mickey noted that he seemed to be spending ten hours a day on it.[13] Every day when he came home for lunch, she observed, Ken seemed to be more and more excited about new discoveries he was making. Mickey looked forward to doing the proofreading for it, but she could not get started because Ken was continuously revising it.[14] Bailey gained more time to work on his book when he declined to teach a module in the spring. He had been teaching every module at Tantur until Mickey pointed out that no other members of the teaching staff were doing this. He also found himself with more time that spring when two groups that had planned to be at Tantur in March and April decided to cancel, leaving the time open for his scholarly pursuits. He was pushing himself hard so that he could have the manuscript finished in time for a six-month furlough that would begin in late June. Mickey wrote, "we are eating, sleeping, and breathing the book."[15]

As Bailey was doggedly pursuing his study of 1 Corinthians, the situation in Israel was becoming increasingly tense until on December 9, 1987, an Israeli Defense Forces truck struck a car of Palestinian workers, killing four and sparking the First Intifada. Believing that the collision

---

11. Ken to Leslie and David, April 15, 1990, Bailey Papers, box 28, folder 1.
12. Mickey to family, November 19, 1987, Bailey Papers, box 27, folder 9.
13. Mickey to family, February 8, 1988, Bailey Papers, box 27, folder 9.
14. Mickey to David and Leslie, February 14, 1988, Bailey Papers, box 27, folder 9.
15. Mickey to Ellen, February 18, 1988, Bailey Papers, box 27, folder 9.

had been deliberate, Palestinians engaged in demonstrations, strikes, and violent rioting on the West Bank and Gaza Strip. Israeli officials responded by closing the temple area and ordering a police and army crackdown on protestors. The Baileys, of course, were largely protected from these disturbances because they were safely ensconced at Tantur. In early February, Sara returned to the States to see her doctor, who advised her not to return to Jerusalem during this time of unrest. Mickey agreed, and Sara stayed in the United States for a couple of months while they all hoped that the political situation would cool down.[16]

In the Gospel passage that begins "O Jerusalem, Jerusalem," Jesus famously lamented the unfaithfulness and murderous history of Israel's capital and predicted its destruction (Luke 13:34; Matt 23:37). The situation of the modern state of Israel, with its ongoing injustice and brutality, evokes similar anguish. The Israel that Ken and Mickey relocated to in September 1985 was a deeply troubled land—financially, morally, and politically. In that year, Israel suffered an annual inflation rate of 480 percent, but the government took emergency measures to meet the crisis, imposing price controls, slashing government expenses, and creating a new currency, which soon brought inflation under control.

More important in the long run was the state of the Israeli-Palestinian conflict. The Six-Day War of 1967, in which Israel had gained the territories of the West Bank, Gaza Strip, Golan Heights, and Sinai Peninsula, posed existential questions that the nation was unwilling to face fully and honestly. The territory acquired in the war was the land held by ancient Israel—that is, land largely in the hills of Judea, not the plains and coastal areas that included the modern cities of Tel Aviv and Haifa, which had been the land of the Philistines. The West Bank included Jerusalem, Jericho, Hebron, and other cities and towns named in the Bible, where the ancient history of the nation had been played out. It was the land that had been trod by Abraham, Joshua, David, Solomon, and Isaiah. The Israelis were neither willing to give up the land, which would mean sacrificing their deepest Zionist dreams, nor were they willing to incorporate the Palestinians into their society, which would mean sacrificing the Jewish identity of the nation. They were also unwilling

---

16. Mickey to Ellen, February 18, 1988, Bailey Papers, box 27, folder 9.

simply to displace the Palestinians, which would be a violation of their deepest democratic impulses. Bereft of good choices, Israeli politicians waffled and prevaricated. They allowed the settlement movement in the West Bank but always considered these outpost communities to be provisional, whose fate could safely be deferred until the final status of the entire West Bank was decided.

The Labor Party, which had ruled the country from its inception through its first three decades, was ousted from power in 1977 and replaced by Menachem Begin's Likud Party, which called unequivocally for the annexation of the West Bank. Yet despite Likud's bold rhetoric, it continued Labor's policy of allowing the establishment of "facts on the ground" while deferring a final settlement. Begin even signed the Camp David Accords in 1979, ceding the Sinai Peninsula for the sake of peace with Egypt. Labor and Likud, the nation's two leading parties, had little difficulty forming a national coalition government in 1984 as their differences were more a matter of emphasis and rhetoric than of policy and principle.

Israel's feckless leadership and immoral policies of displacement, repression, and reprisals could not continue forever without provoking a response from the Palestinians. The Palestinians began to protest in earnest following Israel's invasion of Lebanon in 1982. Palestinian resentments simmered for the next five years and finally exploded in December 1987 with the First Intifada, an Arabic word that means "tremor," "shaking," or "shuddering" but whose practical meaning is "uprising" or "rebellion." It was in fact a violent protest movement that claimed some 2,000 lives and did not fully come to an end until the Oslo Accords of 1993 were accepted by the PLO and Israel.

Bailey was sympathetic to the Palestinian cause, which he reimagined in the essay "'Terrorism' and the Year 3001." How might European Americans respond, he wondered, if a thousand years from now Native Americans gained the upper hand and drove out those who had long ago taken their land? How would they feel about being relegated to the "East Bank" of the Mississippi and labeled as terrorists for asserting their property rights? It was an interesting essay, but too much a flight of fancy to find a publisher.[17]

The Baileys lived in Israel from 1985 to 1990, the period of much of the First Intifada. As they had in Beirut, they believed it was important

---

17. Bailey, "'Terrorism' and the Year 3001," April 1986, RG 424, Presbyterian Historical Society.

to show solidarity with the oppressed among whom they lived. They were committed to staying the course, but it was a trying and debilitating experience—especially since they had already endured years of war and violence in Beirut.[18]

⁓

In early March 1988, Mickey began to proofread the first parts of the text of Ken's 1 Corinthians manuscript as he continued to work on the latter parts. But his efforts were hindered on March 2 when he pulled a muscle in his back and had to spend two days in bed. He had a number of speaking engagements at this time and was able to meet them all with the help of heating pads, drugs, and a back brace.[19] Determined to finish his book, he kept repeating to Mickey, perhaps through clinched teeth, "I just can't get sick now."[20] In the first week of April, contrary to her doctor's advice, Sara returned to Tantur. Now Ken, Mickey, and Sara were all working on Ken's book. They wanted to have it finished by early May so that Mickey could attend David's graduation from college. By April 11, Mickey had finished proofreading Ken's text, and Sara, working steadily alongside her parents, was within a few days of completing the typing of the verse numbers on the 110 plates of biblical text.[21] Ken would then have a little over three weeks to complete the task of making the corrections on the text in his computer.[22] They completed the work before the end of the month, an achievement that was all the more remarkable because, with strikes and demonstrations and forced closings in Israel at this time, it was difficult to shop for even basic food needs.[23]

Mickey flew to the United States as planned in May to attend David's baccalaureate and graduation. When Ken had finished teaching all of his classes, he also traveled to the United States at the beginning of June but did not proceed to New Wilmington until June 10, leaving Mickey some

18. Ken and Ethel to special friends, Christmas 1988, Bailey Papers, box 28, folder 15.

19. Mickey to David and Leslie, March 9, 1988, Bailey Papers, box 27, folder 9.

20. Mickey to Floyd and Marg [Milligan], March 3, 1988, Bailey Papers, box 27, folder 9.

21. Mickey to Floyd and Marg [Milligan], April 11, 1988, Bailey Papers, box 27, folder 9.

22. Mickey to David and Leslie, April 11, 1988, Bailey Papers, box 27, folder 9.

23. Mickey to Floyd and Marg [Milligan], April 11, 1988, Bailey Papers, box 27, folder 9.

time alone to relax.[24] Ken and Mickey spent the rest of the year in the United States on furlough and returned to Jerusalem in January 1989. During this period in America, Bailey taught a lecture series at Georgia United Methodist Group and a class at McCormick Theological Seminary in Chicago, August 31 through September 4. The class schedule lists him as an adjunct faculty member of the seminary, and the subject of his class was his book *Poet & Peasant*.[25]

Rector Bolling, who was now seventy-three years old, had by this time largely lost interest in the affairs of Tantur and would soon be retiring. The new rector of Tantur, Fr. Thomas Stransky, who headed the center from 1988 to 1999, arrived on March 9, 1988, but he did not take up residence at the center until August, when Ken and Mickey were away on furlough. In February, Fr. Stransky had asked for the resignations of all the professors at Tantur, including Bailey's. Apparently, he wanted to have a free hand in deciding about teaching positions. However, he wrote to Bailey in advance of his trip to assure him that he wanted him to remain at the Institute. When Ken and Mickey returned to Tantur in January 1989, the new rector had things well organized. After the chaos of Bolling's hands-off approach, Bailey at first welcomed Stransky's take-charge, top-down style of leadership. At the very least, it meant that he would have to sit on fewer committees. However, over time, Bailey came to resent his approach. Stransky was distant and unapproachable, and Bailey had few opportunities to influence the direction of the center. The pendulum had swung too far in the opposite direction.

From the Baileys' view from the hilltop on which the Tantur center was perched, the situation in Israel-Palestine seemed calm and peaceful, but they knew better. They could hear the sound of distant gunfire and see the twirling smoke rising from burning tires. The Baileys' car had a yellow license plate, which was an indication that they were living in Israel, not the West Bank. Consequently, Bailey was unable to give lectures in Bethlehem, which was in Palestinian territory, without fear that his car would be stoned. They had been taking their car to a mechanic in Beit Sahour, a Palestinian town east of Bethlehem, but it was no longer safe to go there. The Baileys, therefore, began to look for a mechanic in East Jerusalem where travel would not be an issue when car repairs were

---

24. Mickey to Floyd and Marg [Milligan], April 11, 1988, Bailey Papers, box 27, folder 9.

25. ___ to ___, August 27, 1989. This letter in the Bailey Papers has the schedule of Bailey's class printed on the back. See Bailey Papers, box 27, folder 9.

necessary.[26] Mickey continued to struggle to find good times to shop for groceries. Writing in late April during the week of Passover, Mickey remarked that there were strikes of three days' duration during the week and that on the West Bank stores were only open for half a day when they were open at all.[27] In May she reported that the electricity had been switched off twenty times in one day for no apparent reason and without the government issuing any warning. Ken by this time was relying heavily on his computer. When the electricity shut off, his computer had five minutes of battery life before it shut down. He did not lose any of his work product but was frustrated by the nuisance this posed.[28]

Even with the disturbances in Israel-Palestine, Bailey remained very busy. From the last week in May to the last week in June, a period of four weeks, he planned to travel in the United States to give talks in various churches. Knowing that he would be away, he accepted a double class load in the months before his departure. In July he would be teaching at the Greek Catholic Seminary outside of Bethlehem, and on July 20 he would travel to the conference center in Cyprus to give a series of lectures.[29]

By this time, Bailey was growing increasingly disenchanted with life in Israel-Palestine in general and Tantur in particular. The new rector was making all the decisions without input from others, and Bailey's class schedule had been reduced to teaching only one morning a week. He spoke with the priest in charge of running the continuing education program at Tantur about this, proposing that if he taught his classes at Tantur for one month in the fall and one month in the spring and perhaps a few weeks in the summer, he could do all the work that he was now doing for the Institute. This would free him to move his family to Cyprus where life would be safer and less complicated.

Living in Cyprus would also allow Bailey to take advantage of the Middle East Christian Outreach in Larnaca, Cyprus, a video studio that he discovered was at least as good and possibly better than the one he had been using in Wichita, Kansas. In 1988 Bailey recorded a series of lectures at the studio in Larnaca and, over the following eighteen months, sold 1,024 sets of lectures to Arabic-speakers in the Middle East—as well as others in Europe. Mickey noted that Ken had sold over 1,000 videos for the Arab market, where people tend not to buy authorized copies of

26. Mickey to David and Leslie, April 18, 1989, Bailey Papers, box 27, folder 9.
27. Mickey to David and Leslie, April 27, 1989, Bailey Papers, box 27, folder 9.
28. Mickey to David and Leslie, May 17, 1989, Bailey Papers, box 27, folder 9.
29. Mickey to family, June 21, 1989, Bailey Papers, box 27, folder 9.

anything if cheaper pirated ones were available.³⁰ The team in Larnaca could produce videos adapted to both the American NTSC (National Television System Committee) system and the European PAL (Phase Alternating Line) system that most of the rest of the world used. The studio in Cyprus proposed that Bailey move to the island to facilitate his recording ministry. Also, they were willing to convert his past lectures that had been recorded using the NTSC system to the PAL system, making them available for distribution to the world outside of the United States. During the previous eight years, Bailey had recorded sixty-three thirty-minute lectures in English in the studios in Wichita. Making these available to the British Isles as well as the rest of the English-speaking world would be a huge bonus for moving to Cyprus. Bailey also foresaw limitless possibilities of reaching the markets of the developing world. He wrote to his supporters: "It would appear that the Lord has, through His grace, opened a unique door to us for Bible teaching to many of His children, particularly throughout the Third World. Over the past year we have gradually sensed that we cannot refuse to do our best to walk faithfully through this door."³¹

Bailey might have added, as he later did to his supporters in the United States, that it was difficult to use Israel as a base for a preaching ministry in the Middle East because he was unfailingly harassed every time he entered Israel due to living on the West Bank. He might also have been badgered in Middle East airports for living in Israel, but he avoided this difficulty by having two passports, one for Israel and one for the rest of the region. He later wrote to his supporters that he was simply exhausted by the stress involved in living in Israel: "Finally, after fifteen years of life [1975–90] in areas of very high stress we are exhausted and feel deeply that to continue to fulfill our own calling and to be effective in ministry to the churches of the Middle East and beyond we need the tranquility of some place of service away from war."³²

The program director at Tantur agreed with Bailey's plan for working at the Institute for two months of the year, and Bailey in turn wrote to Wilbur Patterson at the PCUSA headquarters in Louisville, Kentucky, to tender his proposal. The answer came back quickly. Before the end of the month of October, Dick Gibson at the Global Mission Unit at the

30. Mickey to Floyd and Marg [Milligan], October 20, 1989, Bailey Papers, box 27, folder 9.
31. Ken and Ethel to Special Friends, May 23, 1990, Bailey Papers, box 28, folder 15.
32. Ken and Ethel to Special Friends, May 23, 1990, Bailey Papers, box 28, folder 15.

Louisville office reported that he considered the idea perfectly acceptable. In the meantime, Sara moved into her own efficiency apartment at Tantur, and Ken used his carpentry skills to make modifications that made it more suitable for her.[33] But despite this investment in time and effort, the Baileys were ready for a change.

In May or June Ken and Sara contracted virulent intestinal parasites from the contaminated water at Tantur that caused continuous stomach aches and nausea. They saw a local doctor and had lab tests performed, but Israeli medical experts were unable to discover the reason for their aliment. They next met with the head of the Gastroenterology Department at Hadassah Medical Center, but even this did not result in answers or a cure.[34] By this time they decided to give up on local medicine. At the beginning of November, they flew together to London to receive medical help. Since Bailey had been assisting at the Anglican Cathedral in Jerusalem, he and Sara were given access to British medical facilities due to Bailey's connection with the Church Mission Society (CMS) and his clergy status.[35] Staying with their friends the Jabbours, Ken and Sara saw a specialist at the London School of Tropical Medicine, whose specialty was amoeba and giardia. The doctors concluded that Ken and Sara had parasites but that the chronic irritation of their intestinal tracts was probably due to the harsh regimen of medicines that they had been taking. Following a battery of further tests, they were prescribed milder medication. Ken seems to have responded quickly to the new treatment while Sara had to stop taking it because it interacted with her other medications, resulting in mood swings. Ken returned to Cyprus in the middle of November. Feeling much better, he was hopeful that the doctors had discovered the root of the problem, though he was warned that full recovery might take a few months and perhaps even a year.[36] Sara stayed on a little longer in London to find the right mix of medications before returning to Cyprus.

In the last week of December 1989 Bailey met with Tantur's rector, Fr. Tom Stransky, to discuss his plans to move to Cyprus. Stransky

---

33. Mickey to David and Leslie, October 19, 1989, Bailey Papers, box 27, folder 9.
34. Mickey to David and Leslie, October 19, 1989, Bailey Papers, box 27, folder 9.
35. Mickey to David and Leslie, October 31, 1989, Bailey Papers, box 27, folder 9.
36. Mickey to David and Leslie, November 8, 1989, and November 15, 1989, Bailey Papers, box 27, folder 9. For a summary of Ken's and Sara's medical problems see Mickey to family, November 9, 1989; and Mickey to David and Leslie, November 21 and December 4, 1989, Bailey Papers, box 27, folder 9.

approved the idea, and the two agreed that Bailey would return to Tantur in February and October each year to teach his classes and that Tantur would pay for his plane tickets and continue to provide housing at the Institute.[37] In the new year, Bailey began to rely increasingly on Sara as a typist for his correspondence. Her typing was so fast and accurate that Bailey ceased using a Dictaphone for dictation. Instead, Sara joined her father every afternoon and typed his letters as fast as he could dictate them. Soon he was entirely caught up.[38]

On January 22, 1990, Bailey traveled to Cyprus to visit the Anglican Bishop of Cyprus and the Gulf, John Brown, and the two agreed that Bailey would be named Theologian in Residence for the diocese, a position that later became formalized as Canon Theologian of the Episcopal Diocese of Cyprus and the Gulf. During this trip, Bailey looked at an apartment at Nicosia, the capital and largest city on Cyprus. On March 2, about six weeks later, he made the commitment to rent it. He was happy to report to Mickey that the apartment was twice as large as the small one at Tantur that they had had to squeeze into, and it was also largely furnished—simply but tastefully.

Around this time, Bailey wrote a thirty-five-page article on the reliability of oral tradition, "Informal Controlled Oral Tradition and the Synoptic Gospels," which was published in the *Asia Journal of Theology* in April 1991.[39] In the article he returned to a theme that he had first raised in his dissertation, the idea that oral tradition as it is preserved in a village culture is reliable. The issue was crucial for him because if the oral tradition that was the basis for the writing of the Gospels was not reliable, then the Gospels themselves were not authentic accounts of the historic Jesus. Rather, they were a modification of Jesus' life and words meant to meet the needs of the early church.

Bailey wrote that there were three positions that scholars take on this issue. The first is "Informal uncontrolled oral tradition." This was the position of New Testament scholar Rudolf Bultmann and others in

---

37. Ken to David and Leslie, January 2, 1990, Bailey Papers, box 28, folder 1.

38. Ken to Leslie and David, March 11, 1990, Bailey Papers, box 28, folder 1.

39. Ken to Leslie and David, April 1, 1990, Bailey Papers, box 28, folder 1. The article referred to is Bailey, "Informal Controlled Oral Traditional," 34–54. This can be found in the Bailey Papers, box 45, folder 3.

the form critical school who, beginning in the years immediately following World War I, held that the Gospels are not reliable accounts of the life and words of Jesus; rather the early church, lacking controls on the transmission of the Jesus tradition, changed it while continuing to attribute the Gospel stories and speeches to him.[40] The second is "formal controlled oral tradition." Bailey referred to this position as the Scandinavian school of Harald Riesenfeld and Gerger Gerhardsson, who in the early 1960s contended that Jesus is the true author of the tradition.[41] According to this school of thought, those who followed Jesus memorized and recited the words that he spoke, using mnemonic techniques (devices, summaries, notes, repeated words or phrases) of the Jewish schools that had succeeded in preserving the Oral Torah. This transmission of the tradition is formal because there is a teacher and students and a clearly prescribed way to pass on the tradition so that its integrity is maintained. The third position is that of New Testament scholar C. H. Dodd, who took a middle road, arguing that though the early church may have made some minor alterations in the material to meet its own needs, Jesus was still the originator of the sayings and stories in the Gospels. Hence the Gospels can be treated as the authentic teachings of Jesus, though some allowances must be made for minor changes that may have crept into the material while it was being transmitted orally, translated, and shaped into its final written form.

To this scholarly debate Bailey added a fourth position he named "informal controlled oral tradition," which was based on his personal experience of village life in Egypt in the period 1955–65. He held that traditional communities in the Middle East today and in the first century practiced a form of oral preservation of tradition that was informal but nevertheless controlled. The practice of preservation took place at village gatherings that were called *haflat samar*, an Arabic term that Bailey translated as "a party for preservation." During these gatherings, recitations of stories, poems, and proverbs were made by elders in the midst of the community for purposes of entertainment as well as the preservation of the tradition. Bailey wrote that this was an informal system of preservation because the elders were not formally teachers and the listeners were not formally students. The reciter had various levels of flexibility depending

---

40. For this position, Ken refers his readers to Bultmann, *Jesus and the Word*.

41. Bailey was referring to Gerhardsson, *Memory and Manuscript*; Gerhardsson, *Tradition and Transmission*; and Riesenfeld, "Gospel Tradition and Its Beginning," 1–29.

on the importance of the recitation. With parables and recollections they were given some flexibility in the relating of specific details, but the essential nature of a story must be recounted faithfully. The storyteller, for example, might change the order of some parts of a story or he could change the name of a character, but he could not change the meaning of the story or alter its proverbial conclusion. Hence flexibility had limits. Moreover, poems and proverbs were so important that no flexibility in recounting them was allowed. To illustrate his point, Bailey gave a number of specific examples of the accurate preservation of stories and then concluded that this informal oral control of tradition was in place in first-century Palestine, from the time of Jesus' life through the Jewish-Roman War (AD 66–70). The stories of Jesus, therefore, could have been accurately preserved using the techniques of village oral culture until the Gospel stories were written in the latter third of the first century.

In his article Bailey made a significant contribution to the scholarly quest for the historical Jesus and to the debate over the authenticity of the Gospel accounts. Unfortunately, as pointed out by New Testament scholar James D. G. Dunn, his theory was overlooked by many scholars because he did not publish his article in a prominent scholarly journal. Also, his presentation of the theory was largely anecdotal. Failing to apply rigorous scientific techniques to verify his theory, it had not been widely embraced, and he opened himself up to criticism by other scholars. Nonetheless, Bailey presented what Dunn regarded as a "plausible explanation" for the accurate oral transmission of the sayings and stories of Jesus by the early church, and N. T. Wright in *Jesus and the Victory of God* (1996) accepted Bailey's theory as a "working model" that New Testament scholars can employ to understand how the traditions of Jesus would have been preserved by first-century Palestinians using what were then acceptable and well-understood methods of preservation. This approach is much preferred, Wright argued, to the "strand of New Testament criticism that runs from [William] Wrede to [John Dominic] Crossan" in which it is conjectured that "the evangelists were radical innovators, who spun their tales with such art that they deceived, if possible, even the elect."[42]

42. For Dunn's endorsement of the theory see Dunn, *Christianity in the Making*, 210. For Wright's endorsement see Wright, *Jesus and the Victory of God*, 136. For the later debate between Dunn and Weeden see Weeden, "Kenneth Bailey's Theory," 3–43; and Dunn, "Kenneth Bailey's Theology," 44–62. For Bailey's unpublished response to Weeden, see Bailey, "Informal Controlled Oral Tradition Revisited," Bailey Papers, box 43, folder 2.

A different approach is taken by Richard Bauckham in *Jesus and the Eyewitnesses: The Gospels as Eyewitness Testimony* (published in 2006, with an expanded edition in 2016). Bauckham shows great appreciation for Bailey's ideas, but he observes that Bailey is inconsistent (or at least unclear) in that he insists on both the importance of eyewitnesses in conveying an authoritative testimony about Jesus and the role of the community in exercising control over the Jesus tradition. Bauckham, as the title of his book suggests, emphasizes the role of the eyewitnesses as both the source and, as long as they lived, the control of the Jesus tradition. Rather than seeing the tradition as developing in Palestinian villages, he argues that it was developed in Jerusalem among the twelve disciples and other close followers of Jesus, and these eyewitnesses and those they trained as tradents[43] would have guaranteed the authenticity of the tradition until it was finally written as gospels. Bauckham seems to imply that Bailey's insights into the oral tradition of conservative village communities provide helpful insights into how the Jesus tradition came to be formulated in Jerusalem, but Bailey—and the form critics to whom he was responding—was mistaken in seeing the Jesus tradition as the product of village communities. In Bauckham's view, New Testament writers clearly base the authenticity of the Gospels on the reliability of eyewitnesses not the preservation techniques of traditional village communities. Also, since the Gospels were written within a generation of Jesus' death, a long period of preservation in villages did not occur.[44] This fascinating scholarly debate will no doubt continue, and at this time Bailey's contribution seems to be well-regarded but in danger of being eclipsed—at least in part—by Bauckham's competing theory.

Bailey taught his last classes at Tantur and at Ecce Homo through the middle of March and then in the spring taught a final ten classes at the Greek Catholic Seminary in Beit Sahour, located south of Bethlehem. In the last week of April, he and Mickey began packing their belongings with the intention of sending their things immediately to Cyprus. At the

---

43. Those charged with the task of preserving and handing on an oral tradition.

44. Bauckham, *Jesus and the Eyewitnesses*, 262–63. For Bauckham's review of the three scholarly positions on the oral tradition, see chapter 10. For his further refinement of the transmission process, harmonizing the contributions of the eyewitnesses and the control of the community over the Jesus tradition, see chapters 11 and 12.

end of April, Bailey shipped about 3,000 books weighting some 3,400 pounds, or 1.7 tons, from the port of Haifa to Cyprus. The Baileys also shipped two tables and a chair but no other furniture.[45]

By this time, Bailey's relationship with the Catholic bishop and rector of Tantur, Thomas Stransky, had become strained. Writing to David and Leslie, Bailey explained, "I preached this last Sunday here at Tantur—people seemed to like it—all but the boss. He has not said a word, and I think he studiously avoided me that night. He is a difficult guy in a lot of ways. The Catholics refer to him as an 'old time Catholic bishop' who decides everything himself, consults no one, informs no one, includes no one, notices no one, talks to no one." Mickey had given two hours a day over the previous two years to creating floral arrangements in the chapel that, Sara recalled, were simply "stunning."[46] But Rector Stransky never bothered to thank her, either in public or private, which she took as his assessment that her efforts were not really needed and therefore unworthy of notice.[47]

During the spring, Bailey wrote to David and Leslie, asking them to be sure to date their letters and use 8½ by 11 inch paper. He explained that he selected worthy letters for preservation and had them bound, and he would like to have them properly dated for the sake of "future generations" who would be interested in accuracy. David and Leslie responded the next month by sending their letters on high-quality typing paper. Bailey thanked them and added that this would be a help to the "definitive biographer" in his or her task of chronicling his life. Naturally, this was all tongue in cheek and perfectly serious at the same time. In this letter, Bailey also included a curious Arab proverb that ostensibly counsels a rigid adherence to tradition but, in Bailey's playful translation, seems to imply the opposite: "Stick to the path even if it is the long way around, and marry the girl from the good family even if she is old."[48] As Bailey prepared to leave Israel-Palestine, he was thinking not only of his legacy but also of a Middle Eastern conservativeness that he had found to be professionally helpful but, on a personal level, often farcical and exasperating.

45. Mickey to David and Leslie, May 1, 1990; and Ken to Bruce and Barbara [Milligan], May 13, 1990, Bailey Papers, box 28, folder 1.

46. Noted in an interview with Sara on September 9, 2023.

47. Ken to Leslie and David, May 1, 1990, box 28, folder 1.

48. Ken to Leslie and David, April 1, 1990; and Ken to David and Leslie, May 19, 1990, Bailey Papers, box 28, folder 1. In this letter, Ken provided an Arabic version in Latin script of the proverb: "*Dur ma' al-tariq isa darit wa khuth bint al-aseel isa barit.*"

Various friends in the Jerusalem area invited the Baileys to private dinners to mark their departure and say goodbye. About the first of May, the person who managed the continuing education program for priests at Tantur, Fr. Steve Doyle, announced to Ken that he was planning to hold a farewell party at the Institute for the Baileys and asked him and Mickey to select twelve of their closest friends in Jerusalem to attend. On the evening before they left, the Institute also had a going-away dinner for the Baileys that Ken found heartening. The kitchen staff, he noted, "out did themselves," and even Fr. Stransky gave a generous speech, remembering to mention Mickey's contribution of daily flowers for the chapel. The next day, May 7, the vice rector took the Baileys to the airport. Sara was in a wheelchair as she was struggling with chronic fatigue syndrome, Bailey reported to David and Leslie. In an attempt to shame officials into limiting official harassment, they "had her look as sick as possible." Nevertheless, Bailey wrote, they endured "the usual thirty minutes of infuriating grilling" at the airport reserved by Israeli security for foreigners living on the West Bank.[49] By the end of Bailey's sojourn in Israel, he could think of nothing better than, as he put it, to "be out of this—£$%&'=N£$+ place."[50]

49. Ken to David and Leslie, May 9, 1990, box 28, folder 1.
50. Ken to Leslie and David, May 1, 1990; and Ken to Bruce and Barbara [Milligan], May 13, 1990, Bailey Papers, box 28, folder 1.

16

On the Island of Aphrodite
1990–95

> For if Jesus is an uneducated young man who tells stories primarily for children and simple fisher folk, then one set of perceptions apply as we examine his teachings. But if he is the first mind of the NT (Paul being the second), and if Jesus' teachings are to be considered as serious theology, offered primarily to intellectuals, then a quite different set of assumptions and perceptions come into play for the interpreter.
>
> —Kenneth E. Bailey, *Finding the Lost*

In Greek mythology, Cyprus was the island of Aphrodite, the goddess of love, who according to the Greek poet Sappho was born on the island. But despite this, the history of Cyprus has often been violent. In the three centuries before the birth of Christ, it came under Greek cultural and political influence and many Greeks settled on the island. Later Cyprus became part of the Roman Empire and during the Medieval period its people generally adhered to the Eastern Orthodox Church of Byzantium. From 1571 to 1878, it was part of the Ottoman Empire, and Christians and Muslims on the island lived together peacefully. In 1878, Cyprus became a protectorate of Great Britain, and in 1960, it became an independent republic. With a population that was 80 percent Greek

Cypriot and 20 percent Turkish Cypriot, power-sharing arrangements were made, but the two sides nevertheless clashed in armed conflict in 1964, and the United Nations sent in a peacekeeping force that imposed a settlement. In 1974, the Greek Cypriots seized the government in a coup, and Turkish forces invaded the island, capturing a northern section that in 1975 became the Turkish Republic of Northern Cyprus, an independent nation recognized only by Turkey. With its warm climate, beautiful beaches, and historic sites, Cyprus continues to enjoy its reputation as the island of Aphrodite and is sometimes known as "the island of love." In recognition of this tradition, thousands of Europeans travel every year to Cyprus to get married. Ken and Mickey would live in a spacious apartment in Nicosia, the capital of the Greek Cypriot part of the island known as the Republic of Cyprus.

Bailey appreciated Cyprus from the start. Nicosia was small enough that he rode a bicycle around the town to do errands as well as for exercise and enjoyment though he soon also bought a ten-year-old Ford sedan that he had reupholstered.[1] The language of the island was Cypriot Greek, which Ken and Mickey did not speak, and which became a source of frustration when dealing with taxi drivers, shopkeepers, and repair people. But the second language of the island was English, which was spoken by all educated people. Bailey's personal relationships also seem to have been good in Cyprus. He wrote in September, "I had a fantastic interview with Bishop John Brown. We are just about exactly the same age, and I really like him, and he has convinced me that he really wants me here not only professionally but also as a friend and personal advisor. I was honored and touched by what he said. We are really glad to be here."[2]

In November, Ken and Mickey rearranged things in their apartment to accommodate Sara, who for health reasons could not yet manage her own apartment but certainly needed her own space. The Baileys gave her two rooms in their apartment, with one to be converted into a guest room when friends and family came to visit.[3] Bailey had agreed by this time to produce a new book for Concordia Press that would be published in March or April of 1991. This was his collection of updated

---

1. Ken to David and Leslie, May 27, 1990, Bailey Papers, box 28, folder 1.
2. Ken to David and Leslie, September 16, 1990, Bailey Papers, box 28, folder 1.
3. Ken to David and Leslie, November 4, 1990, Bailey Papers, box 28, folder 1.

interpretations of the parables in Luke 15, *Finding the Lost: Cultural Keys to Luke 15* (1992). He wrote, "it must be the number one item on the agenda starting October 28 from then until I get it finished."[4]

Bailey seems to have set the date of October 28, 1990, to begin writing the book as that was when he would be back from Jerusalem. He and Mickey returned to Jerusalem and lived in their old apartment at Tantur for the month of October. During this time, Bailey taught at the Greek Catholic Seminary, at Ecce Homo in the Old City of Jerusalem, at St. George's College, and at the Jerusalem Center of the Study of Early Christianity.[5] He also taught eight hours a week at Tantur itself where he availed himself of the institute's large library to read up on all the scholarship that had been done on Luke 15 over the previous twenty years. He wanted his new book to be entirely up to date.

While the Baileys were in Jerusalem, the Persian Gulf War (1990–91) was being fought. In his letters home, Bailey acknowledged the existence of the war, but given that he was in Israel, he felt constrained about what he could write. He saw American intervention in Iraq as a "big mistake," believing that the decision about an invasion should have been made by the United Nations, not the United States. An invasion under UN auspices by forces that included the United States, the Soviet Union, and others, he thought, could then have taken place through Saudi Arabia. And he was disturbed by the "apparent delight and glee" that some of his compatriots showed on learning of America's decision to launch a new war.[6]

On October 8, 1990, known as "Black Monday," a massacre took place at the Dome of the Rock on the Temple Mount. An extremist Orthodox Jewish group called the Temple Mount Faithful attempted to lay the cornerstone of a new temple on the Temple Mount, which Muslims know as al-Haram al-Sharif ("the Noble Sanctuary"). Israelis and Palestinians clashed, though who started the violence is disputed. The Israelis, Bailey explained in two letters home, manufactured a false account of what happened. Piecing together old footage, they argued for the benefit of their own people, as well as the world, that Palestinians had rioted and that Israeli soldiers had responded in self-defense. Bailey, however, reported that the head of Israeli security forces for the Temple Mount was known to have said to his soldiers, "We are going to soak the ground

---

4. Ken to David and Leslie, September 16, 1990, Bailey Papers, box 28, folder 1.
5. Ken to David and Leslie, September 25, 1990, Bailey Papers, box 28, folder 1.
6. Ken to Bruce and Barbara, August 30, 1990, Bailey Papers, box 28, folder 1.

with blood this morning." The massacre, Bailey concluded, was entirely premeditated, but he believed that the US public was simply incapable of hearing that message. Americans preferred to embrace old myths of Israeli virtue and heroism.[7]

Bailey corresponded with his son, David, about this and other subjects. At this time, David and Leslie lived in northern Virginia, and David worked as a computer trainer for a company called Vantage Technologies, Inc. In the fall of 1990, David was writing a paper for a class he was taking about American perceptions or misperceptions of the Middle East and consulted his father about it. In a five-and-a-half-page single-spaced letter, Bailey advised his son that he had identified seven "American myths" about the Middle East. The seventh myth was particularly telling, and Bailey included as part of this myth sixteen different ways that Americans think differently than Middle Easterners. For example, Americans respect the law while Middle Easterners value relationships over law; Americans generally prefer to resolve conflict *mano a mano*, while Middle Easterners traditionally rely on third-party interventions; Americans interpret Middle Eastern business practices as often deceitful, while Middle Easterners justify cheating foreigners as a form of justice or revenge; Americans value politeness and strict honesty, while Middle Easterners often use exaggeration and violent language as a substitute for physical violence; Americans value personal integrity, while Middle Easterners see personal honor as the supreme virtue; Americans are fond of swift, decisive action, while Middle Easterners often take a long view, practicing long-suffering patience and consistently out-waiting invaders. By misunderstanding the fundamentals of Middle Eastern culture, he concluded, Americans often underestimate their competitors in the region.[8]

In the same class, David was also considering the issue of Western missionaries as cultural imperialists. Bailey suggested to his son that there were three alternative ways to understand how the West might relate to undeveloped peoples. First, anthropologists seem to want to ensure such people are isolated from Western advances, keeping them as though they were animals to be observed in a kind of "human zoo." This of course also serves the interest of the anthropologists whose purpose it is to study such groups. Second, political leaders and businessmen would destroy indigenous peoples in order to exploit their natural resources

---

7. Ken to David and Leslie, October 21, 1990; and Ken to Barbara, December 9, 1990, Bailey Papers, box 28, folder 1.

8. Ken to David, November 4, 1990, Bailey Papers, box 28, folder 1.

or bolster the interests of their nations. Third, Christian missionaries want to evangelize them, translating the Bible into their own language. This third option, he argued, was not cultural imperialism. Rather, it was enabling "them to preserve their identity, culture and language." He gave the example of his own Scottish ancestors who were evangelized by the Irish, which did not displace their culture but empowered it with a new energy. "If the anthropologists had had their way, we would still be dressed in skins dancing around a fire at dawn in the woods."

He and David also approvingly discussed an article by Lamin Sanneh that had appeared recently in *The Christian Century*, "Christian Missions and the Western Guilt Complex." Sanneh was at this time the professor of missions and world Christianity at Yale Divinity School and Professor of History at Yale University. Originally from Gambia, he had been a student at NEST in the late 1960s. Bailey was personally familiar with him, remembering him from his days at NEST, though Sanneh had never taken one of his classes. Sanneh's point, as Bailey summarized it, was that Western Christians should stop feeling guilty about Christian missions. In another letter, Bailey took up the subject again, giving a more expansive summary of Sanneh's view:

> Hey you Western Liberals—quit feeling guilty over the coming of the Christian Faith to Africa. For us it was the greatest thing that ever happened to us. It set us free deep in our own hearts, it helped us preserve our culture, it gave us the vision of freedom and the sense of our own worth that gave us the inner resources with which to fight off the negative effects of the very imperialism that you think Christianity was a part of.[9]

In this same letter to David and Leslie, Bailey wrote that he had resolved to become more serious about completing his book *Finding the Lost*, which was due at the end of April 1991. He seems to have met his deadline, and the new book was published by Concordia Press the following year, 1992.

In the preface to *Finding the Lost: Cultural Keys to Luke 15*, Bailey does not apologize for writing yet another book on the parables of Luke 15,

---

9. Ken to David and Leslie, November 1, 1990, and Ken to David, December 9, 1990, Bailey Papers, box 28, folder 1.

but he does attempt to explain himself. He notes that prior to this volume, he had already written two books on the subject, *The Cross and the Prodigal* (1973) and *Poet & Peasant* (1976).[10] He is writing this third interpretation because he believes that he had recently found something new. He explains this development in a parable of his own:

> Recently I have found myself to be like a person who for thirty years enjoys the beauty of a garden walled with plastered stone. Then in the fading light of a particular evening the person's eye is suddenly caught by what appears to be a faint blue line in the plastered wall. The patron of the garden turns aside to examine the line and to his amazement finds it to be in the shape of an arch. Digging feverishly through the plaster, a sealed doorway appears. With intense excitement he breaks through the doorway to discover a long-abandoned room, and in the room a chest—of gold![11]

After thirty years of research, the gold that he discovered was, among other findings, that the parable of the lost sheep in Luke 15 was an expansion of themes that first appeared in Psalm 23—an interpretation that Bailey would elaborate at greater length in his final book, *The Good Shepherd* (2014). He also hints that the Old Testament patriarch Jacob may be a model for the prodigal, an idea that he will develop a decade later into a full book, *Jacob & the Prodigal: How Jesus Retold Israel's Story* (2003).[12] In addition to these discoveries, Bailey further developed his ideas about the parables of Luke 15 in a variety of ways.

In his introduction, Bailey is particularly concerned to sharpen his argument that Jesus is a metaphorical theologian and one, therefore, well outside the Western tradition. Western theology, he explains, develops concepts that are connected by logic and held together by a philosophical framework. In this approach, concepts are illustrated by "simile, metaphor, proverb, parable, and dramatic action," but these rhetorical techniques are merely optional and secondary. In contrast, Middle Eastern theologians reverse this approach. They begin with an illustration such as a parable, which can then be expressed as a concept. He notes that biblical writers also do this, providing metaphors that are encased in a conceptual frame. To fully appreciate a biblical illustration, one must enter into it, examine the details and consider the implications. When

---

10. See too, Bailey, "Psalm 23 and Luke 15," 54–71.
11. Bailey, *Finding the Lost*, 10.
12. Bailey, *Finding the Lost*, 118–19.

the biblical writer reduces the illustration to a concept, he is presenting only a part of the whole. The metaphor, in contrast, speaks to the whole person, including a person's emotions. While Western thinkers might dismiss emotions as a hindrance to understanding, a Middle Eastern thinker wants his hearers and readers to feel the emotional content inherent in a story or metaphor.

Bailey admits that his Western education in philosophy and systematic theology initially hindered his appreciation of Jesus as a thinker. "I discovered," he writes, "that I had been unconsciously trained to admire everything about Jesus except his intellectual astuteness." For Bailey, Paul was a theologian because he wrote in a Greek style, while Jesus was not because he told "childlike stories." By considering the intellectual depths inherent in Jesus' stories, Bailey had to change his mind about him as a thinker, concluding that he was an incisive and thoughtful theologian, one whose "intellectual acumen is no less significant than the matchless quality of his ethics." In *Finding the Lost,* Bailey strives "to take Jesus seriously as the major theologian of the New Testament and to follow his theological thinking as that thinking is set forth in the trilogy of stories in Luke 15," especially the parable of the prodigal son, "the *Evangelium in Evangelio,*" the essential story that encapsulates Jesus' thought.[13]

Though Bailey updates and deepens his interpretation of Luke 15, he seems particularly interested, in chapter 3, in justifying Jesus' use of the metaphor *father* to signify God, which in the 1980s had become highly controversial among Christians in the United States. Bailey finds ten places in the Old Testament where *father* is used to refer to God. Yet, with Joachim Jeremias, he believes that Jesus' use of this metaphor for God is unique as he alone addresses God intimately as *Abba*, an Aramaic term that in the Greek New Testament is translated as *father* (Mark 14:36; Rom 8:15; Gal 4:6). In the discussion about this term in the West, Bailey observes that it is generally assumed that Jesus' use of *father* signifies a Middle Eastern patriarch with all the negative connotations associated with that authoritarian, patriarchal image. Seen in this way, feminists inevitably object to the term as one that leads to the restriction of women's rights and dignity. According to Bailey, however, Jesus did not have this image in mind. As a thoughtful theologian, Bailey points out, Jesus defined his terms. His definition of father was given in the parable of the prodigal son where the father is portrayed as a loving, merciful,

---

13. Bailey, *Finding the Lost*, 21, 22, 193.

compassionate man who is willing to endure terrible indignities for the sake of his children.[14]

Later in chapter 3, Bailey takes up this subject again but this time to show that God has both male and female characteristics. Bailey argues, Jesus is following the example set by the prophet Isaiah, who in Isaiah 63:16 and 64:8 used the word *father* as a metaphor for God. However, this was not intended to depict God as entirely male because in Isaiah 66:10–14 the prophet used a mother as a simile for God: "As a mother comforts her child, so I will comfort you." By using a male metaphor for God and a female simile, Isaiah was avoiding a definition of God as both father and mother, both male and female. For Isaiah, God is male, but at times he behaves like a female. In fact, he has both male and female attributes. Bailey argues that Isaiah had chosen his words carefully. In the religious milieu of the ancient Middle East, depicting God as male and female would have had sexual connotations, suggesting that the gods did not create the world *ex nihilo* but copulated to bring it into existence. Also, if God were male and female, the idol-worshipping people of the time might have concluded that there were two gods. Isaiah avoided these implications by his precision in word choice.

In telling the parable of the prodigal son, according to Bailey, Jesus follows Isaiah's lead. In this interpretation, the absence of a mother in the parable of the prodigal son does not suggest patriarchalism or a negative attitude toward women but rather a sensitivity to theological considerations. Like Isaiah, Jesus presents God as a father but one who acts like a mother. A father would not run through the village and fall on his son's neck and kiss him passionately, but a mother might. Bailey continues, "the father who acts with the tender compassion of a mother displays that compassion from the beginning of the story until its end."[15] In chapter 5, Bailey returns to the theme, noting that the Greek term that Luke employed in this passage is *kataphileo*, which "means either to 'kiss tenderly' or to 'kiss again and again.'" Bailey's interpretation here differs from that given in the first edition of *The Cross and the Prodigal* where he argued that the kisses showered on the prodigal were manly and appropriate. Here they were given tenderly. In effect, they were motherly kisses. Jesus' very modern view of women is all the more remarkable in

---

14. Bailey, *Finding the Lost*, 114–16.
15. Bailey, *Finding the Lost*, 158–59.

that it was at odds both with the Rabbinic tradition and that of the early church fathers.[16]

The reviews for this book were excellent. Paul Hollenbach, of Iowa State University, writing in *The Catholic Biblical Quarterly*, praised Bailey for showing the limitations of Western theology in interpreting Middle Eastern texts. For example, he noted that Westerners have missed Jesus' rebuke of the Pharisees as lost sheep and for their unwillingness to take responsibility for losing God's sheep due to their own prejudice and inattention. He, like Bailey, found it "amazing" that Jesus made a woman the heroine of a parable (Luke 15:8–10). Most important, he praised Bailey for lifting up Jesus as a "metaphorical theologian."[17] Writing for *Concordia Journal*, Erich H. Kiehl found the book, together with *Poet & Peasant* and *Through Peasant Eyes,* to be "must resources" for those interested in understanding the parables.[18] And John F. Brug, writing for *Wisconsin Lutheran Journal*, applauded Bailey for looking at a well-known text through the lens of neglected Middle Eastern exegetical sources to bring new insights.[19]

A gap in the Bailey Papers leaves the Baileys' activities for 1991 and some of 1992 a mystery. Fortunately, they summarized some of 1992 in their Christmas letter for that year. For eight of the twelve months of 1992 the Baileys were in the United States, and Ken traveled every weekend to preach in churches from Florida to California. During the spring semester, he delivered the Warren Lectures at the University of Dubuque Theological Seminary on "Jesus as Theologian: A Compendium of his Theology." In April, when David and Leslie announced the birth of their first child, Kelcey Tess Bailey, Mickey naturally went to help the new parents and stayed for five weeks in David and Leslie's home in Virginia while Ken remained on the road, teaching and preaching. At the completion of his semester at Dubuque Seminary, where he and Mickey had based themselves for their furlough, Ken continued to travel throughout the country teaching and preaching in various churches. He wrote, "1992 for us was a year of dislocation. It was a good year full of opportunity to

---

16. Bailey, *Finding the Lost*, 203.
17. Hollenbach, Review of *Finding the Lost*, 793–94.
18. Kiehl, Review of *Finding the Lost*, 420.
19. Brug, Review of *Finding the Lost*, 315–16.

fulfill our callings but eight months of the year were spent away from home. Seven times Ethel [Mickey] had to face an empty kitchen, stock it from scratch and then get rid of everything a few weeks or months later." They managed to spend at least two weeks at the mission house in New Wilmington, which they utilized to complete repairs on the roof of their own house where they intended to move in several years when they formally retired.[20]

Figure 23. David, Leslie, and Sara Bailey, circa 1992.

Bailey visited Ireland in March 1993 and then traveled to Oxford to present a series of lectures for a week. In April Ken and Mickey flew to Muscat, Oman, where Ken preached a series of sermons during Holy Week. In the second half of the month, he was back in Cyprus where he met with an Egyptian who had agreed to direct a movie version of his play on the parable of the prodigal son. Also present for the consultation was a representative from the Bible Society in Egypt, which would be funding the project. Bailey agreed to fly to Egypt in May to prepare a final version of the script and later return to serve as a biblical and theological consultant during the filming, which would be in October or November 1993. He was assured that he was in fact more than a consultant because

20. Ken to friends and loved ones, Christmas letter, January 1993, Bailey Papers, box 28, folder 2.

he would have the final say over the content of the film.[21] As it turned out, the director flew to Cyprus in November, and he and Bailey finalized the script at that time.[22] On May 20, Bailey traveled to Cairo where he stayed for a month to participate in the filming of the movie version of his play. Titled *Finding the Lost,* the one-hour-and-forty-minute movie was in Arabic with English subtitles and utilized well-known Egyptian actors. After his sojourn in Egypt, Bailey returned to Cyprus but then immediately set out for Jerusalem, where he taught a course for a week for ten conservative Catholic priests. And for a fortnight following that he was in the Emirates to lecture to an ecumenical group of Christians who met in one building but comprised twenty-eight separate congregations.[23]

On June 3, Mickey and Sara flew from the United States to London, where Ken met them at Heathrow Airport. All three then traveled to Lambeth Palace where they would be the houseguests of the Archbishop of Canterbury, George Carey, and his wife, Eileen. They were only there for two days and rarely saw the archbishop except at breakfast as he was busy the rest of the time with various engagements. While at home, Carey was occupied with writing his speech for the fiftieth anniversary of the D-Day landing. The Baileys had dinner twice with Elieen, who obtained tickets for them to see the musical *Les Misérables*. During this time, Carey invited Bailey to be the Bible study leader at the primates' conference in March 1995 to be held at Cumberland Lodge in the Windsor Great Park west of London. Although Bailey had stopped taking speaking engagements for 1995, he felt that he could not refuse the honor of speaking to all of the Anglican archbishops from around the world, especially as the invitation was being issued personally by the Archbishop of Canterbury in his own home.

Following the D-Day celebrations in London on June 6, 1994, Bailey left on Sunday afternoon and traveled to Cambridge where he lectured for four days. Sara and Mickey stayed at Lambeth Palace until Monday morning and then took the train to Lymington on the south coast of England where they stayed in the home of Ken's English second cousin Jill Banks. Ken arrived a few days later, and the four of them then took the ferry to the Isle of Wight to visit the sites of Annette Bailey's childhood. They also viewed the graves of Ken's grandparents and the church

21. Mickey to family, February 7, 1993, Bailey Papers, box 28, folder 3.

22. Mickey to family, Christmas 1993 [December 5, 1993], Bailey Papers, box 28, folder 3.

23. Ken to Jim Bruce and Barbara [Bailey], May 20, 1994, Bailey Papers, box 28, folder 2.

where his parents were married. They made sure, too, to see the tourist attractions, such as the Needles and the Downs, about which his mother had often spoken. They also visited Yarmouth Harbor to gaze at the pier jetting out into the sea on which the common family names of the isle are painted on the boards. The four walked along the pier until they came upon the name *Meader*.

In January 1994, David and Leslie announced the birth of their second child, Cameron James Bailey. David at this time was enjoying great success in his secular employment, but Bailey nevertheless had been concerned for his son for some time. He noticed that David had first begun to slip away from his Christian moorings in his sophomore year in college and that the trend had continued unbroken ever since. "These deep commitments," he explained to Leslie, "are all I have that matter to me that I have to give to him, and his gradual losing of them is more painful to me than I can express."[24] In September 1994, Ken wrote to David, who was then in London on an extended business trip. David took the opportunity to open up about his feelings, admitting that he felt lost and, in some respects, was in need of a fresh start. In response, Ken set forth his view that, given his son's background and upbringing, a recovery of his Christian faith was necessary "or the reintegration of your twenty-eight years of life will not be possible."[25] This conversation continued for many weeks, and in late October Bailey once again gave a gentle nudge to his son to return to the Christian fold, quoting a poem by Terry Anderson that appeared in his recent book, *Den of Lions*, about being held hostage for seven years in Beirut:

> No man can ever start anew completely
> He's everything he's ever done
> Or said or failed to do.[26]

In early December Bailey wrote to Leslie, recommending that she try to have David see the 1956 movie *The Man in the Gray Flannel Suit*, which starred Gregory Peck and was based on the 1955 book of the same title by Sloan Wilson. Though the movie was not well received at the time and the author found it unfaithful to his plot, Bailey thought that it was well done and apropos to David's situation. It is a story about a man who

---

24. Ken to Leslie, September 27, 1994, Bailey Papers, box 28, folder 2.
25. Ken to David, September 30, 1994, Bailey Papers, box 28, folder 2.
26. Anderson, *Den of Lions*, 348. Cited in Ken to David, October 28, 1994, Bailey Papers, box 28, folder 2.

returns home following World War II and is employed by a company that wants his very soul, which inevitably undermines other aspects of his life.[27] It is uncertain if David viewed the film, but by the end of the year he does seem to have taken steps to renew his fundamental spiritual commitments—a process that would be sharply accelerated about a year and a half later.

During this period in which Bailey was concerned for his son's spiritual well-being, he remained busy with teaching and writing. While he was in Jerusalem in the early fall teaching at Tantur again and accompanied by Mickey and Sara, he enjoyed seeing old friends and teaching a class of about sixty, most of whom were Roman Catholics. He was not, however, delighted about being back in Israel, which he had begun referring to as "Dixie." He admitted, "I hate Dixie with a passion." Sometime later, he read a book about Jerusalem that quoted the Muslim scholar Al-Muquddassia who in the year AD 985 described the city as "a golden bowl full of scorpions." Bailey commented, "So what's new?"[28] What he detested was the ongoing Israeli occupation of the West Bank and the way Israeli police, soldiers, and bureaucrats treated Palestinians. The Israeli indifference to Palestinian suffering was also evident in the failure of the police to work among the Palestinian population, resulting in a wave of petty thievery on the West Bank. Bailey used a money belt, never carried more money than he needed, and kept his important documents in the safe at Tantur.[29] While the Baileys were in Israel during this teaching stint, Mickey noted that the Tantur apartments had been the subject of three break-ins that had occurred in broad daylight, yet the Israeli police did nothing about it.[30]

Throughout the fall, Bailey had been preparing his lectures to be given in the new year in Finland and Britain. He was especially concerned

---

27. Ken to Leslie, November 30, 1994, Bailey Papers, box 28, folder 2. For a brief analysis of Wilson's novel, see Halliwell, *American Culture in the 1950s*, 62–65; for the broad cultural context of the novel, see Marsden, *Twilight of the American Enlightenment*, 21–42.

28. Ken to Bruce and Barbara, April 2, 1995, Bailey Papers, box 28, folder 2. Bailey was referring to a comment in Al-Muquddassi, *The Best Division for Knowledge of the Regions*, 985, that was cited in Le Strange, *Palestine under the Moslems*, 86. The book was first published in 1890, but Bailey was probably reading a modern reprint. Although Bailey referred to a "golden bowl," Le Strange translated this as a "golden basin."

29. Ken to Jim Bruce and Barbara [Bailey], November 6, 1994, Bailey Papers, box 28, folder 2.

30. Mickey to family, November 8, 1994, Bailey Papers, box 28, folder 2.

Through Middle Eastern Eyes

to have the study sheets for his lectures for the archbishops' conference to be given in March 1995 at Cumberland Lodge in Windsor ready before the end of the year. He finished them just in time, completing them at 6:00 p.m. on December 3. For each of the participants he had prepared a fifty-three-page study guide, which would be taken to London by a friend and mailed the next day.[31]

The new year of 1995 found Bailey in Helsinki, Finland, where he was to deliver lectures at two conferences that were to be translated sometimes into both Finnish and Swedish. The conference of 250 pastors, most of whom (Bailey guessed about 90 percent) were Lutherans in the Pietist tradition, generally felt that their church had become too theologically liberal and, therefore, had organized fellowship groups to support their conservative brethren in the ministry. Bailey identified with them as they reminded him of the rump of conservative UPC pastors who were now a tiny minority in the generally liberal Presbyterian Church USA. He knew in advance that the churches were having his book *Through Peasant Eyes* translated into Swedish and published, but at the start of the first of the two conferences he was pleasantly surprised to be presented with a copy. And on the second night, his one-act play of the parable of the prodigal son, *Two Sons Have I Not*, was performed to a packed sanctuary.[32]

From January 21 to 26, Bailey was invited by the clergy of the Episcopal Diocese of Cyprus and the Gulf to a meeting in a Nicosia hotel to deliver a talk on his "Reflections of Forty Years of Life and Service in the Middle East." Though Bailey had been a part of this group for five years, he had never felt that he had been warmly received by its members. Being British, he believed that they were wary of overly gregarious and superficially pleasant Americans. He recalled that his mother once explained to him that the British insist that visitors sit patiently outside of the moat for three days before they let down the drawbridge and invite one into the castle. Bailey had waited patiently for five years and now, on the eve of his retirement, felt that his talk had been "well received" and that this group of diffident British clergymen had finally opened up to him and taken him in.[33] The address he gave that day was a brilliant summary of his ideas and insights, gained over a forty-year career in the Middle East,

31. Ken to Leslie and David, January 1, 1995, Bailey Papers, box 28, folder 2.
32. Ken to Leslie and David, January 15, 1995, Bailey Papers, box 28, folder 2.
33. Ken to Leslie, February 2, 1995, Bailey Papers, box 28, folder 2.

and it is no wonder that those listening were dazzled by it and asked for a formal copy of his remarks.[34]

Ken and Mickey were back in Jerusalem again from January 26 to February 26, 1995, so that Ken could teach three classes. The problem of crime persisted at Tantur as thieves and robbers continued to enter the campus with impunity. Once when Ken and Mickey were walking on the grounds a thief accosted them. The oddly sententious robber felt the need to justify his actions by comparing himself to Jean Valjean, the protagonist of *Les Miserable,* arguing that his conduct was warranted since he was stealing only to obtain bread. Bailey, however, had the presence of mind to recall the denouement of the story, reminding the thief that Jean Valjean was imprisoned for his crime and then spent the rest of his years trying to live a worthy life. The robber laughed awkwardly and let them go on their way.[35]

From March 8–18, Bailey was in the UK for the conference of Anglican archbishops described in the prologue of this book. Following his presentation, he went to the studios of the BBC in London at 8:30 a.m. to record three ten-minute scripts, which he accomplished in a flawless reading of thirty minutes. He marveled at the efficiency of the BBC recording staff, but his own long experience in audio and video recording no doubt also contributed to the apparent effortlessness of the session. From there he hastened to be on time for a luncheon with Lesslie Newbigin, a man who had served as a missionary in India for nearly four decades and capped his career as the bishop of the Church of South India. Newbigin retired to the UK in 1974 and settled down to a second career as a prolific author on subjects ranging from Christian mission to the proper Christian response to a pluralistic society. When Bailey met him, he had written forty books and was the director of an organization studying how Christians can best engage modern Western culture. Bailey had been reading his works for years and looked forward to the encounter. Newbigin, who was then eighty-four years old and losing his

---

34. Ken to Leslie and David, April 16, 1995, Bailey Papers, Box 28, folder 2. See too Ken to Leslie, February 2, 1995, Bailey Papers, box 28, folder 2; and Bailey "1955–1995: Reflections on the Bible and the Church after 40 years of Ministry in the Middle East," Bailey Papers, box 46, folder 3. This address is a twenty-four-page manuscript in double-spaced type.

35. Mickey to family, March 5, 1995, Bailey Papers, box 28, folder 3.

sight, had also been reading Bailey's books, though the last one had been read to him.[36]

The two scholars met in an exclusive London pub that, Bailey observed, had been built in the year 1600 and had somehow survived the Great Fire of London in 1666. In later recounting the story, Bailey said of Newbigin, "I count him as the most distinguished theologian I have ever met in my entire life." In their three-hour talk that day, it was clear that Newbigin also had a high regard for Bailey, inviting him to move to London and become the director of a center for the study of the interaction of Christianity and Islam. Though flattered by the offer, Bailey politely declined, explaining that his field of study was the New Testament, not "Arabic Patristics." Patristics is a field of study for Christian historians and theologians of the early church fathers, usually Greek- and Latin-speakers, who lived during the first thousand years after Christ. Bailey sometimes referred to them as the Eastern fathers as a way of expanding the field to include Syriac- and Arabic-speakers as well. On hearing the phrase *Arabic Patristics* Newbigin was taken aback. "What on earth is Arabic Patristics?" he asked. "I have never heard of such a field!" Bailey patiently explained that roughly between the years 900 and 1300 the Arabic-speaking Christian world of the Middle East had produced a number of books, including versions of the Bible, biblical commentaries, theological treatises, histories, and Christian apologetics *vis-à-vis* Islam. These manuscripts, however, were mostly unpublished and not widely available even in the Middle East, and there were few English translations of any of them. Consequently, the Arabic fathers were generally unknown in the West. Bailey told Newbigin of three scholars who were experts in Arabic Patristics and would be competent to direct an organization dedicated to Christian-Muslim relations. Though their encounter might at points have been frustrating, the two Christian intellectuals parted friends that day. Newbigin died on January 3, 1998, and nothing seems to have come of his idea for a Christian-Islamic study center. That so renowned and influential a Christian scholar as Lesslie Newbigin should never have heard of the field of Arabic Patristics should not be wondered at, but it is nevertheless a telling commentary on the huge lacuna that currently exists in Christian historical and theological understanding.

As Bailey was concluding his formal career as a missionary, he took stock of his situation and considered the future. Writing to Leslie and

---

36. Ken to Leslie and David, March 25, 1995, Bailey Papers, box 28, folder 2.

David in April 1995, he recalled that he had often been urged at NEST to become an administrator, but he had always successfully managed to resist that pressure. His first and best calling, he averred, was to be a scholar, writer, and teacher. He then referenced C. S. Lewis's essay "The Inner Ring," which he considered "terrific." Lewis argues that we would all like to be within the "inner ring" that enjoys power and runs institutions and organizations. Most of us, however, do not have this opportunity or are excluded from it. Such people should focus on being good craftsmen in their chosen fields, knowing that other good craftsmen will recognize the quality of their contributions and provide sufficient approbation. Bailey said that he would love to give his own version of this essay as a graduation address to a private boys' school, but the opportunity had never arisen.[37] He did, however, briefly reiterate Lewis's argument in his last book, *The Good Shepherd* (2014).[38]

As Bailey considered his return to the United States, he conveyed to Dale Milligan his sadness and disappointment in observing the rapid decline of the Presbyterian Church during his lifetime. The denomination had become increasingly liberal even as it lost members, declining from 12 million in 1960 to about 5 million in 1995. The number of missionaries of the combined Northern and Southern Presbyterian Churches peaked in the year 1927 at 2,544. By the mid-1990s, however, the total number of of missionaries in the united churches (then also including the UPC) had declined to about 500.[39] Bailey also pointed to the decline in the number of Presbyterian missionaries in the Middle East who could speak fluent Arabic. When he started in 1955 there were some 300 Arabic-speaking mission personnel, but by 1995 they were down to about seven—and in a few years, given retirements, it would be down to two. He concluded:

> I think that there are now at least three times as many Western missionaries in the Middle East as there were forty years ago, but our church has opted out. My conclusion at this point is that our church is dying and can't even agree on the disease and so cannot proceed as a church on any treatment. So, are we as a denomination to be trusted to send out missionaries who will infect other churches with whatever it is that is killing us? Or, if

---

37. Ken to Leslie and David, April 9, 1995, Bailey Papers, box 28, folder 2. See Lewis, "Inner Ring," in *Weight of Glory*, 141–57.

38. Bailey, *Good Shepherd*, 196.

39. Brown, *Presbyterians in World Mission*, 41; and Jamison, *United Presbyterian Story*, 192.

such people have a hold on the essence of the gospel, they will be estranged from the leadership that has sent them?[40]

One of the great what-ifs of Bailey's career concerns why he waited until his retirement to move back to the United States. If he had returned in 1985, when he was forced out of Beirut, he might have become a professor in a well-established seminary or university in the United States. Had he taken this step, he would have enjoyed ten years in which to train graduate students to continue his legacy. At this time, he wrote to Dale that he had been offered such an opportunity in 1985 but "it didn't work out." Bailey also recognized, however, that there had been "no place for me in Presbyterian theological education," which he believed was more concerned with issues of diversity than in professors who would teach traditional evangelical faith.[41]

Bailey was clearly excited to be finally retiring and returning home. He wrote to David and Leslie, "As the monkey with his tail in the lawn mower said, 'It won't be long now!'"[42] On July 2 as Bailey considered the painful way he had had to leave Beirut in 1985, he recognized that his antagonists, as Joseph said of his brothers in Genesis, "meant it for evil, but the Lord meant it for good." He concluded, "The last ten years, [in] Jerusalem and Cyprus, have been the happiest, the most creative, the most productive years of our lives, and none of it would have happened if we had not been driven out of Lebanon."[43] During the Baileys' final week in their apartment, Ken and Mickey and Sara slept on the floor, surrounded by six packed suitcases as their beds had already been sold along with most of their other furnishings. On July 16 at 10:20 a.m., two friends loaded the Baileys' luggage into a car and drove them to the airport. The Baileys flew home to the United States, bringing to a close for Ken and Mickey forty years on the mission field.[44]

---

40. Ken to Dale [Milligan], April 30, 1995, Bailey Papers, box 28, folder 2.

41. Ken to Dale [Milligan], April 30, 1995, Bailey Papers, box 28, folder 2. To support this position, Ken referred Dale to Leith, "On Choosing a Seminary Professor," 6–7, and 11.

42. Ken to David and Leslie, April 30, 1995, Bailey Papers, box 28, folder 2.

43. Ken to David and Leslie, July 2, 1995, Bailey Papers, box 28, folder 2.

44. Ken to David and Leslie, July 15, 1995, Bailey Papers, box 28, folder 2.

17

A Tale of Two Brothers, Redux
1996–2003

> Jesus tells a new story, but the new story follows the outline of and interacts with the old story.
>
> —Kenneth E. Bailey, *Jacob & the Prodigal*

The Baileys lived at the mission house in New Wilmington while they fixed up their home from August 1 through mid-September, 1995. Ken wrote that they put in many twelve-hour days, moving walls, repairing the plumbing, patching holes in the roof, and painting. Of course, they did not do all the work themselves. Rather, they contracted with plumbers, electricians, and carpenters. Having rented the house out from the time of its purchase in 1977 until 1995, the property had suffered from the usual renters' neglect, which the Baileys had to address in just a few weeks. Once settled into their home by mid-September, Ken launched into a series of speaking engagements in churches from New England to Colorado, which he continued through November. On November 24, he turned sixty-five and officially retired. As Presbyterians put it, he and Mickey were "honorably retired." Having thrust himself back into American society after being abroad for four decades, Ken confessed that during his first five months at home he had felt some "reverse culture shock." In the Baileys' Christmas letter for 1995, he summed up his experience:

"The giant stores leave us depressed. The electronic invasion of privacy leaves us angered. The complexities of insurance and taxes leave us confused, and the moral collapse evident in many arenas leaves us alarmed."[1]

Although Bailey had returned to the United States every few years during his mission career and was never completely out of touch with his own culture, reentering American society after a general absence of forty years was trying for him, and he suffered from "reverse culture shock" for several years. Still, his concern at this time was how to engage in effective ministry in the United States. In this his model was Lesslie Newbigin who, when he retired from mission service and returned to England in 1974, began a new career as a lecturer and writer in the UK. Yet despite his decades overseas, he did not let his thoughts dwell on his past experience as a missionary. Bailey observed of him approvingly, "When he lectures or writes, India is never mentioned unless his previous experience there contributes to the new reality with which he is currently struggling—namely—to proclaim the gospel in the postmodern Western world." Inspired by Newbigin's example, Bailey would also take up a ministry in retirement of preaching, lecturing, and writing. However, unlike Newbigin, who was concerned with the gospel in a postmodern culture, Bailey would continue his work as an interpreter of the New Testament. He thought of himself accurately, albeit tritely, not as "retired" but as "refired."[2]

It is fortuitous that Bailey did not rush into a new regimen of activity because on December 23 he suffered a heart attack, which he described as "serious but not severe." When he understood that he might be experiencing heart trouble, or coronary thrombosis, Mickey drove him to the local hospital where, while under the care of doctors, the heart attack occurred. Only one artery was blocked and, after a few weeks of observation, doctors performed a thallium stress test, inserting a small amount of radioisotope into his veins, which allowed the doctors to observe how his heart muscle was performing. Doctors then performed an angioplasty—the insertion of a small balloon into the artery to widen it so that blood can flow normally. Bailey wrote to family and friends in February that he was at home and expecting a full recovery by the end of March. He concluded his message in the third person: "The fact of this event has obliged Bailey to rethink 'the game plan' for ministry in

---

1. Ken and Ethel to family and special friends, December 1995, Bailey Papers, box 28, folder 15.

2. Ken and Ethel to family and special friends, December 1995, Bailey Papers, box 28, folder 15.

the years ahead. He is contemplating less travel and lecturing and more writing and recording."[3]

While Bailey was recovering from his heart attack, his son suffered a major medical emergency in July 1996. David had had debilitating headaches throughout the month of June, but on July 1 the severity of his headache was so alarming that his wife, Leslie, phoned for an ambulance, and he was taken to the emergency room of Mary Washington Hospital in Fredericksburg, Virginia. There, while doctors were examining him, he had a seizure, and doctors soon discovered he had a tumor in his brain about the size of a baseball. He was transported by helicopter to Fairfax Hospital where, on July 4, surgeons removed the tumor. Mickey drove down from New Wilmington on July 3 to be with her son and look after her grandchildren, and Ken left at 6:00 a.m. on July 4 for Virginia, arriving in time for the surgery. While recovering in the hospital, David's doctors informed him that he had a grade four astrocytoma tumor, otherwise known as glioblastoma multiforme (GBM). Patients in his condition, he was told, are terminal, usually with a one-to-two-year life expectancy. In his case, however, all indications were good. The surgery had been successful in removing the tumor, and he was a healthy young man. After researching the medical science on his condition, David drove with Leslie to Duke University Hospital in North Carolina to place himself under the care of Dr. Henry S. Friedman. After tests were completed, Friedman put David on a chemotherapy program and a drug treatment regimen using temozolomide. He was then required to return to Duke every four months for a checkup.

For thirty-year-old David, the discovery of a cancerous brain tumor propelled his life in new directions. The integration of the faith in which he was raised with his current life, which his father had recommended nearly two years before, now became a top priority. David recommitted himself to his Christian faith and also rediscovered his music, which he had given up soon after graduation from college. Although he kept his job at Vantage Technologies, Inc., it was no longer the center of his life. He went on disability for a while and retained the job primarily for the health insurance it provided. He joined with Doug Ebert, a friend from his church, to form a duo called Not by Chance and began a Christian music ministry. Defying the dire prediction of the doctors, David would live another fourteen years. Leslie recalled that after a few years, his

---

3. Ken, Ethel, and Sara Bailey to Jim and Rachel Pollock, February 1996, Bailey Papers, box 28, folder 15.

music career was sufficiently profitable that he was able to obtain private health insurance and quit his job at Vantage Technologies. His work as a computer specialist was no longer meaningful to him, and thus he decided to focus entirely on his music. In 1997, Not by Chance performed 100 concerts in twenty-two cities across the United States. On January 13, 1998, David's story was told on the CBS television program 48 Hours, hosted by Dan Rather. By this time Not by Chance had already produced three CDs.[4]

Figure 24. David Bailey and his music partner, Doug Ebert, in Not by Chance, circa 1997.

Meanwhile, Bailey's heart attack hardly seems to have slowed him down as he continued to lecture and preach across the United States and even occasionally in Cyprus, Israel, and Egypt. He also continued to produce video lectures that he made available in the United States, and his film on the parables of Luke 15, *Finding the Lost,* which had been filmed

---

4. David M. Bailey produced the following twenty-three audio CDs: *Life* (2000); *One More Day* (2000); *Peace* (2000); *Lost and Found* (2001); *Live* (2001); *Coffee with Angels* (2002); *Rusty Brick Road* (2003); *Hope: The Anthology* (2004); *Silent Conversation* (2004); *Bitter Sweet* (2005); *Comfort* (2005); *Some Quiet Night* (2006); *Two to See* (2006); *Faith: The Anthology* (2007); *All that Matters* (2007); *Home by Another Way* (2008); *Alive and Well* (2008); *A Deep Well* (2008); *Notes* (2008); *Love the Time* (2009); *Love-Still the Greatest* (2009); *Above and Beyond* (2010); and *Watermarked* (2011). David also provided most of the music for Open Hearts in Bethlehem, a CD that accompanied his father's play by the same name (InterVarsity, 2005).

in Egypt in 1994, was released in April 1997. The actors spoke in Arabic, with English subtitles. By October, 20,000 copies had been sold in the Middle East.

The Episcopal Diocese of Pittsburgh honored Bailey on June 21, 1997, by installing him as Canon Theologian of the Diocese of Pittsburgh.[5] The event was held at Trinity Episcopal Cathedral in Pittsburgh, and the consecration was conducted by the Right Reverend Alden Moinet Hathaway, Bishop of Pittsburgh. This event was followed by a reception at the cathedral in which Ken and Mickey invited Sara and nineteen couples to celebrate with them.[6] Bailey noted in his Christmas letter that year that he would attempt to decline future lecture opportunities for the period from November 1997 through March 1998 so that he could concentrate on writing.

Early in the year 2000 Bailey was diagnosed with prostate cancer. He decided on a treatment using "isotopic seed implants and external beam radiation." When the treatment was completed at the end of April, his prognosis was good, and he slowly began to regain energy. He continued his lecturing and preaching, but he was finally forced to slow his pace. Because he was spending more time at home, he took up a number of writing tasks. One that he completed at this time was his Christmas play, *Open Hearts in Bethlehem*, which would not be published for another five years. On his desk too was a contract waiting to be signed for a new publication—possibly *Jacob & the Prodigal: How Jesus Retold Israel's Story*—and he also had other writing projects in mind. Bailey decided that he would commit the next three years to writing, a program he determined to inaugurate on June 1, 2000. His daughter, Sara, would be critical to his success as she worked as his secretary and editor.

Forced to spend more time at home, Bailey turned his attention to further developing his property. During the year 1999, he contracted to have a house built for Sara about 100 yards from his own home. When it was completed in March 2000, he and Mickey helped Sara move into her new "little yellow house." Though this was initiated entirely for Sara's benefit, Bailey would profit from the proximity of his daughter in the writing projects he undertook in coming years. At this time, he also started the construction of an open-air chapel in the woods on his property. In this

---

5. Ken and Ethel to family and friends, Christmas 1997, Bailey Papers, box 28, folder 15.

6. Ken and Mickey to Bruce and Pat [Milligan], June 11, 1997, Bailey Papers, box 28, folder 3.

he may have been inspired by Romantic-era writers such as Ralph Waldo Emerson who imagined forests to be natural cathedrals. The chapel on Bailey's property was enclosed by trees 100 feet in height. At the center was a ten-ton glacial boulder that served as a communion table, which was flanked by a "living cross"—perhaps a tree trimmed to form a cross. He prepared wooden slabs for benches made from planks that he had earlier put in his shed for curing. He had not yet decided how to fashion a natural lectern or pulpit, but he assured family and friends that it was "taking shape in our minds." The chapel could be accessed by car via a dirt road, and Bailey was also working on a footpath. All of these efforts seem to have been a mere diversion from his serious work of lecturing and writing. He wrote of his activities on the property, "It is great fun to dream and see those dreams materialize."[7]

Though Sara worked closely with her father on his writing projects, she did not participate in his outdoor activities because her health continued to be precarious. She had suffered from chronic fatigue syndrome for twenty years, and doctors in the United States had not been able to provide help. Amelioration of her condition, however, came into sight when the Baileys' close friends Jeremy and Lorna Shearman recommended the Paracelsus Clinic in Switzerland. Sara began treatments there in January 2001. Though often despairing of ever recovering, she found the detoxification protocol at the clinic to be life-changing. The intensive therapy she underwent for weeks at a time was designed to remove heavy metals and toxins from her body that were due to exposure to spent ordnance in Lebanon during the civil war. Though she never seems to have recovered fully, by late 2005 she found that she looked fine and could function far better than she had in years. Unfortunately, the Presbyterian Church's Board of Pensions would not pay for any of these medical expenses, possibly because the treatment was considered experimental in the United States. After a year when Sara was showing marked improvement, Bailey thought that the "insurance barons" at the Board of Pensions would change their minds, but they did not.[8] In June 2008 Sara underwent a final set of detoxification procedures in Switzerland, which were unavailable in the United States and that Bailey believed would be "particularly

---

7. Ken and Ethel to family and friends, Christmas 2000, Bailey Papers, box 28, folder 15.

8. Ken to John and Susan Bailey, February 8, 2007, Bailey Papers, box 28, folder 4.

effective."⁹ On the completion of that treatment, Sara began to feel that she had now largely recovered.

When Bailey returned to the United States in 1995, he created an organization that would receive funds for his ministry and to which he would be accountable. At first, he appealed to the Reverend Gordon Bean, the pastor of the Neshannock Presbyterian Church in New Wilmington, to form a Committee for New Testament Studies. This organization, which may initially have consisted only of Gordon and Bailey, officially received funds from donors who sent contributions directly to the Neshannock Presbyterian Church, where they were subject to auditing. This arrangement would have appealed to many disaffected Presbyterians who would not have wanted to send funds to the Worldwide Ministry Division of the Presbyterian Church. In the year 2000, Bailey arranged that funds would be sent to Shenango Presbytery instead and be managed by a Board of Overseers. One expenditure he soon undertook was that of a secretary. On July 1, 2002, Bailey formally hired Sara Bailey as a secretary (later designated a copy editor) for his ongoing literary projects. She would soon become the indispensable secretary-editor of Bailey's books and articles.

While traveling by train in June 2005 from Upper Egypt to Cairo, Bailey's good friend and CPA, Bill McKnight, suggested that he form a new foundation to receive and disperse funds. Bailey decided to call the organization the Foundation for Middle Eastern New Testament Studies. Later Bill suggested to Bailey the acronym FoMENTS, which Bailey readily accepted. He initially conceived of it as being at once a company, committee, and research facility. In 2006 FoMENTS was incorporated as a tax-exempt organization so that donors could receive tax deductions for their contributions. Funds continued to be sent to the Presbytery until 2013, and these funds were then disbursed to FoMENTS. Bailey began sending reports to the Board of Overseers as early as 2002, and beginning in 2006, he submitted annual reports of his ministry to FoMENTS, making possible a general understanding of his activities in subsequent years. This is important to the historian because, when Ken and Mickey retired from mission service in 1995, they also ceased to

---

9. Ken to Irene, March 4, 2008; and Ken to John and Susan, March 4, 2008, Bailey Papers, box 28, folder 4.

write their regular mission letters to family and friends in which their affairs had been recorded for posterity.

~

In the first year of the new century, the issue of homosexuality continued to be an important and divisive issue in the Presbyterian Church, USA.[10] In that year, Bailey wrote a review of Robert Gagnon's new book, *The Bible and Homosexual Practice: Texts and Hermeneutics* (2001), an exhaustive study of how homosexuality is treated in the Scriptures. Gagnon, a professor of New Testament at Pittsburgh Theological Seminary, concluded that the authors of the Scriptures, from Genesis to Revelation, spoke "unequivocally"—a word he used repeatedly—to condemn the practice of homosexuality (not the orientation) as sin. For Gagnon the controlling passage of the Scriptures dealing with marriage is Genesis 1:27—a verse to which Jesus also appealed (Matt 19:4–6 and Mark 10:6–9)—which states that marriage was made for a man and a woman. Gagnon met head-on the opposing arguments that appealed to modern science and a looser interpretation of the Scriptures, exposing their shallowness and unwarranted conclusions. Bailey was delighted. "The author's antenna," he wrote, "is finely tuned to 'baloney' and thus he is able, with clarity and precision, to spot the aspects of the contemporary discussion which are illogical, scientifically inaccurate and biblically misguided." Bailey gave the book a ringing endorsement, finding it "magisterial" and an "unmatched encyclopedic work on homosexual practice and the Bible."[11] The practical matters of the ordination of practicing homosexuals and the marriage of homosexuals would continue to vex the church for years to come.

In 2002 Bailey reported to the board of FoMENTS that he had written seven articles for denominational publications, written twenty-one reflections for *Guideposts* magazine, and given eighty-six lectures or sermons. One of his articles, "Metaphors Matter: The Confessions and a Gang of Four," is an expression of his ongoing engagement with the intramural controversies of the Presbyterian Church. The church had long before adopted the *Book of Confessions*, which included the Westminster Confession of Faith and others that were generally expressions

---

10. This section is based on Ken's reports to FoMENTS and was written in consultation with Bill McKnight.
11. Bailey, "Review of Robert Gagnon," 23.

of traditional Reformed thought from the sixteenth and seventeenth centuries—though the most recent were written in 1967 and 1991.[12] How a Presbyterian was to understand the *Book of Confessions* was an open question. Should the confessions be merely guidelines, as Hamlet observed of Denmark's customs, "more honored in the breach than the observance"? Or, were the confessions, which often employed antiquated language and took unnuanced positions, to be taken as expressions of the faith to be adhered to rigorously? Taken literally and contractually, many Presbyterians felt them to be overly constricting. They preferred to see them as guidelines and historical markers rather than precise statements to be strictly adhered to and defended. Though a conservative Evangelical, Bailey felt this way as well. In asking the question of how Presbyterians see their confessions, Bailey suggested in the article that four metaphors came to mind when thinking about the Presbyterian Church's *Book of Confessions*. First, it was a bird cage—that is, a prison that one cannot freely leave. In Islam a person leaving the faith is called *murtadd* ("those who have turned back from Islam"). Such persons must be killed. Presbyterianism does not have *murtaddin* as millions have left the church without physical consequences. Second, the confessions might be like the British crown jewels. These precious objects are truly loved by the British people, but they have no impact on the day-to-day decisions of the government. They would be missed if they were stolen, but their loss would not have any practical impact. They are in fact an "irrelevant relic from the past, and no more. Perhaps this is what our *Book of Confessions* is in danger of becoming," he mused. Third, the Confessions might be "a bird bath." Birds can bathe anywhere. The location does not matter, and using a particular bird bath requires no commitment. Fourth, the Confessions might be considered to be an ancestral home. It is where we live, but it is not a prison. The main load-bearing walls cannot be moved, but the furniture can be rearranged and new things added as long as they "blend in with the old." Moreover, a house has windows from which the world can be seen and doors that allow people to come and go. It is a place where a family lives, eats, and sleeps. The family members feel they belong there and gain a sense of personal identity from it. There can, of course, be disagreements among the members of the household, but these do not lead to members leaving. He concluded, "Metaphors matter. Meaning is shaped by them. Out of this gang of four I recommend only the last."[13]

12. See *Book of Confessions: Study Edition*.
13. Bailey, "Metaphors Matter," 5, 7, 9.

Figure 25. Ken and Mickey Bailey in New Wilmington, PA, circa 1996.

Figure 26. Kenneth E. Bailey promotional photo, June 18, 1997.

A Tale of Two Brothers, Redux

The following year, 2003, Bailey published three book reviews and twelve articles, and gave 100 lectures or sermons. Two articles in particular stand out as they concerned his ongoing discomfort with the Presbyterian Church. The first, published on January 27, 2003, in *Presbyterian Outlook,* was "Worsh-o-tainment: A Needed Neologism." Bailey worried that as the evening news over the past few decades had slowly become "info-tainment" so Christian worship was becoming "worsh-o-tainment." As a reality check on what the news should be, Bailey regularly listened on shortwave to the World Service of the BBC, which had neither ads nor infotainment. Sadly, he observed, there is no such reality check on worship.[14] The second article was "C. S. Lewis, Thomas More and Bitter Conflict," which appeared in the *Presbyterian Outlook* on April 28, 2003. The Presbyterian Church was at the time divided over such things as inclusive language, the authority of the Scriptures, and the ordination of noncelibate homosexuals, which reminded Bailey of an exchange between C. S. Lewis and the Roman Catholic Italian monk Don Giovanni Calabria. Calabria held that schism in the church was due to sin. Lewis admitted that this was sometimes true, but he refused to say that it was always so. Looking at the great disputants of the past such as Thomas More and William Tyndale, "Their disagreement," Lewis argued, "seems to me to spring not from their vices nor from their ignorance but rather from their virtues and the depths of their faith, so that the more they were at their best the more they were at variance." Thomas More at least seems to have recognized this as he, in his last words to the judges who condemned him, trusted and prayed that "we may yet hereafter in heaven merrily all meet together, to our everlasting joy." In conclusion, Bailey asked if More and others that he mentioned as examples "have things to say to our deeply troubled church?"[15] Surely, he believed, they did.

The most important publication that Bailey completed in 2002, though it would not be published until the following year, was a new book, *Jacob &*

---

14. Bailey, "Worsh-o-tainment," 10–11.

15. Bailey, "C. S. Lewis, Thomas More," 9, 16. Bailey gathered this from a comment in the book review by Reed, Review of *Jacob & the Prodigal*, 408, but he did not give a full citation. The quotation, however, is from Moynihan, *Letters*, 39. The quotation from Thomas More can be found in Marius, *Thomas More*, 510, where the last word in the quotation is not *joy*, but *salvation*.

the Prodigal: How Jesus Retold Israel's Story (2003). As noted in the previous chapter, Bailey had been thinking about the connection between the story of Jacob and Esau and Jesus' parable of the prodigal son at least as far back as his 1992 book, *Finding the Lost*. In an attempt to justify yet another book on Luke 15, Bailey writes in the preface, "Biblical exegesis is much like Middle Eastern archeology. The archeologist often returns, season after season, to the same tell, each year penetrating a deeper level of the ancient site in the hope of making a new and significant discovery. There is always the tantalizing possibility that the next dig *may* uncover a mosaic floor, a stone inscription or even a library." In fact, he did make a new discovery, which he said he was prompted to pursue by reading a footnote in N. T. Wright's *Jesus and the Victory of God* (1996) in which Wright observes that when Jacob returns to Palestine after a long exile his brother Esau runs to him and falls on his neck to kiss him. In the same way, the father in the story of the prodigal son also runs, falls on, and kisses the neck of his son. Moreover, in both stories there is a conflict between a younger and an older brother, a theme observed by several other scholars. "A gnawing hint of a connection between Luke 15 and the Jacob saga has lingered at the back of my mind for decades," writes Bailey. Though the connection between the Jacob saga in Genesis and the parable of the prodigal son in the Gospel of Luke had been hinted at by others, Bailey saw it as "uncharted territory" that scholars needed to explore.[16]

Bailey believes that Jesus was essentially a theologian who "deliberately creates a new story patterned after the Jacob saga and offers his people a revised identity story with himself at its center." In fact, Bailey finds fifty-one points of comparison between the story of Jacob and the parable of the prodigal son, which he lists in an appendix. Nonetheless, this book builds on his previous books, and for careful readers of his work, there is both much repetition and a sharpening of previous arguments. He notes again, for example, that Jesus was a metaphorical theologian, a carpenter-intellectual, one of the *haberim* (associations of "companions/friends," who studied the Jewish law and engaged in scholarly debates) versus the *am ha-arets* ("the people of the land," who did not follow the law strictly and spent their time in other ways). With eighteen years of rabbinic training, Bailey writes, "it is possible to see Jesus as the first mind of the New Testament

---

16. Bailey, *Jacob & the Prodigal*, 14, 16, 17. See also Wright, *Jesus and the Victory*, 127n10.

and Paul as the second. From Jesus we have indescribably profound theological perceptions of the faith available to us."[17]

Bailey argues that Jesus, in retelling the Jacob saga, was acting well within the rabbinical tradition of his day. In examining this tradition, he reviews the salient literature of the time that commented on the story of Jacob: the Book of Jubilees, written between 140 and 161 BC; the writings of Philo of Alexandria, a contemporary of Jesus; Josephus's *Antiquities of the Jews,* written in the latter part of the first century; and the numerous rabbis who are included in the *Genesis Rabbah,* a fourth-century commentary on Genesis. He concludes that Jewish writers in this era felt perfectly free to rewrite the Jacob saga to advance their own agendas, such as to commend Judaism to a hostile gentile audience or to champion a narrow partisan perspective within Judaism itself. Rabbis, on the other hand, did not tend to rewrite the story. Rather, they added commentary that creatively drew lessons from the story to fit contemporary needs. Bailey agrees with the Jewish scholar Jacob Neusner that the rabbis were "writing with Scripture."[18] In other words, their commentaries were not attempts to understand the original meaning of the Scriptures but to stretch their meaning in order to address their own concerns. This is especially true of the rabbis commenting in the *Genesis Rabbah,* who had few inhibitions about repurposing the text. Bailey notes that Matthew's Gospel exercised a similar freedom in creatively using Old Testament verses to show that Jesus of Nazareth had fulfilled the prophesies expected of the Messiah.[19]

Hence Jesus, operating in this tradition, would also have felt free to revise the story for his own purposes. Though Jesus chose to tell "a new story," he followed the pattern set in the Jacob saga. Jesus adopted this approach in order to present his essential message in a form that would have been culturally recognizable. Bailey observes that Andrew Walls spoke of two translations of the Gospel. First, "the word became flesh," and second, the Gospel he produced was "'translated' into other cultures."[20] Bailey suggests that there was yet another stage of translation that occurred between these two. Jesus himself, he argues, had to translate his purposes into the literary idioms of the times so that he could be understood. He accomplished this by cleverly "reshaping the

---

17. Bailey, *Jacob & the Prodigal,* 15, 23–26.
18. Neusner, *Writing with Scripture.*
19. Bailey, *Jacob & the Prodigal,* 129–31.
20. Walls, *Missionary Movement,* 28.

Old Testament stories of the Good Shepherd and the saga of Jacob into new forms with himself at their centers."[21]

Bailey argues that the story of Jacob is central to the Jewish people's self-understanding because in the Old Testament the nation is often identified as "the house of Jacob" and because it is the story that gave the nation its name, Israel. In the same way, Bailey believes that the parable of the prodigal son—the *Evangelium in Evangelio*—is for Christians a "new identity-forming story."[22] Because the parable of the prodigal son was a retelling of the story of Jacob, it would have had some appeal to the Jewish people. For Luke's Greek audience, however, the various details and nuances of the story that reflect the Jacob saga would have had no resonance. Yet for them it would have had a universal nature that transcended its roots in Jewish culture.

There were at least nine reviews of Bailey's book in scholarly journals, and they were almost all positive. Blake R. Grangaard, writing for *Interpretation,* found his work significant and accessible, one that "pastors, students, and scholars will want to read and have . . . on their shelves."[23] David A. Reed, of Wycliffe College, a graduate school at the University of Toronto, writing for *Review of Biblical Literature,* pronounced it "a monumental work [that] will set the stage for all subsequent New Testament scholars working on the 'so-called' parable of the Prodigal Son." He wrote, "Perhaps the best compliment that one can pay to Bailey is to say that once a scholar sees how Bailey uses the sources of Arab Christians to better understand the New Testament in the twenty-first century, one will wonder why Arabic was never a part of one's PhD program."[24]

Though the reviews were generally positive, several offered pointed critiques. For example, Randy Holm, writing for Διδασκαλια (*Didaskalia,* "Teaching" or "Instruction"), found that Bailey's insistence on a "Chiastic structure" for the parables and Luke's Travel Narrative to be "a stretch." Also, "the Jacob comparison with Luke 15 is sometimes more apparent to Bailey than to his reader."[25] Halvor Moxnes, writing for the *Scottish Journal of Theology,* found Bailey to be "the master storyteller providing the cultural context of NT stories," but he questioned Bailey's "master narrative," finding that interpreting the parable of the prodigal son to be

---

21. Bailey, *Jacob & the Prodigal,* 132, 134, 135.
22. Bailey, *Jacob & the Prodigal,* 194, 214–15.
23. Grangaard, Review of *Jacob & the Prodigal,* 220.
24. Reed, Review of *Jacob & the Prodigal,* 408, 411.
25. Holm, Review of *Jacob & the Prodigal,* 75.

a reworking of the Jacob sage "sometimes makes for forced readings."[26] Mark S. Krause of Puget Sound Christian College, Washington, writing for the *Journal of the Evangelical Theological Society,* wrote the most critical review. He found Bailey's argument that Jesus was "retelling" the Jacob story unconvincing. There were, he believed, simply too many "incongruities that are not adequately explained." Krause also faulted Bailey for not taking a form critical or redactionist approach to Jesus' parable. He wanted Bailey to discuss how Luke reworked Jesus' stories in order to present his own understanding of Jesus' parable. Finally, he argued that first-century Jews did not see the Jacob saga as a story of national identity. Rather, for them the story was a warning to Israel that its men should not marry foreign wives as Esau had done and as a historical explanation for the long-standing hostility that existed between the nations of Israel and Edom.[27]

Bailey would have read all these reviews, but nowhere in the Bailey Papers can he be found to comment on them. He probably shrugged over the negative comments, recognizing that his perspective and that of the hostile reviewers were too far apart to merit recriminations of any sort. He was simply prepared to go his own way, as he had for years.

---

26. Moxnes, Review of *Jacob & the Prodigal,* 355.
27. Krause, Review of *Jacob & the Prodigal,* 526–28.

18

Seeing Anew through Middle Eastern Eyes
2004–8

> It is my prayer that a more culturally sensitive and historically accurate understanding of the birth story of Jesus will help "rescue truth from familiarity."
>
> —Kenneth E. Bailey, *Open Hearts in Bethlehem: A Christmas Drama*

ONE OF THE INITIAL impetuses that Bailey had in 2005 for establishing the Foundation for Middle Eastern New Testament Studies, or FoMENTS, was to raise funds to modernize and market the large collection of video recordings he had made over the previous twenty years. The recordings that he had were on VHS tapes, and he had enlisted the aid of friends to transfer them to the DVD format. Interested churches and individuals also volunteered to distribute them. Bailey, however, was not content with simply revisiting the past. He also envisioned recording new videos as well as producing new books. To do this, he would need the help and supervision of FoMENTS to contribute to his ministry by raising funds and advising him as he engaged in new projects. For the period January 2004 through April 2005, Bailey reported to the board of overseers that he had written three new articles, would have three books published (or republished), had produced three new DVDs, and delivered 137 lectures or sermons. During this year, he also reported that the Eastminster Presbyterian Church in Wichita, Kansas, donated $4,000 so that he could begin to convert his videos into DVDs, a project that would continue for several years. The next four years would continue to be highly productive ones in Bailey's career, ones in which he would bring four major writing projects to completion.

In addition to his own work, Bailey also sought to promote the study of the New Testament from a Middle Eastern perspective by supporting a new study center in Cairo, Egypt. On May 5, 2005, Bailey flew to Cairo to participate in the inauguration of the Center for Middle Eastern Christianity (CMEC) on the campus of the Evangelical Theological Seminary in Cairo (ETSC), and Sara, who was then in Jerusalem volunteering for a few months at the Tantur Ecumenical Institute, joined her father for the occasion. The president of ETSC, Atef Gendy, had been deeply influenced by Bailey's approach to the Scriptures. Gendy obtained a PhD in New Testament studies from the University of Aberdeen in 2001 before returning to Cairo, where he was immediately promoted to be the president of the seminary. At that time, he was the only Egyptian professor at ETSC with a doctorate. In 2003 he visited Bailey in Pittsburgh, Pennsylvania, in order to discuss with him his plans for establishing the CMEC. Recognizing that his scholarly approach was the inspiration and guiding vision of the new center, Bailey became an immediate and enthusiastic supporter of the project. Gendy organized the building of a fourth story on the seminary's main building to house the center. The new facility would include three offices, a library, a lecture hall, a reception area, and an exhibit room. The architect who designed the spaces utilized traditional Egyptian motifs to underscore the center's intended purpose. Work began in 2004 and was still in progress in June 2005 when Gendy held opening ceremonies for the new institution at which he invited Bailey to present his vision for the center in an inaugural lecture. On June 1 Bailey gave a stirring speech in Arabic, which was simultaneously translated into English for the English speakers present, urging Egyptians to take seriously the task of reinterpreting the Bible in terms of Middle Eastern culture. After recalling the "heavenly vision" he had beheld in 1958 on listening to the sermon by the Reverend Adib Qaldas in the small village church of Abu Hennis in Upper Egypt (see chapter 4), Bailey laid out what he believed to be the rationale for the new center.[1]

---

1. Bailey, "Kenneth Bailey's Inaugural Lecture."

Figure 27. Ken Bailey, circa 2005.

He explained that there were four barriers that prevented Western scholars from understanding the Bible from a Middle Eastern perspective. First, the centers of biblical study in the West had enjoyed little or no access to a Middle Eastern perspective since the Council of Chalcedon (AD 451) had largely marginalized the churches of the East within the greater church. Second, this access had been almost completely blocked as the Islamic conquest of the region in the seventh century had succeeded in generally isolating Middle Eastern churches from the West. Third, this inaccessibility was reinforced by a linguistic barrier in that Western scholars learned Hebrew and Greek to study the Scriptures but did not know the common languages of the culture from which the Bible had emerged: Aramaic, Syriac, and Arabic. Fourth, Western scholars labored under two crippling misconceptions: that Jesus' parables were allegories meant to illustrate abstract truths, and that Hellenistic culture was so widely diffused in the ancient Middle East that it was unnecessary to understand the local culture to interpret the Scriptures. The erection of these barriers resulted in scholars not recognizing that Jesus himself was the founding and controlling theologian of the New Testament and that his primary means of conveying truth was through the intricacies of carefully wrought stories that were rooted in the cultural context of the Middle East.

The great challenge of reinterpreting the Scriptures in terms of Middle Eastern culture could be met, Bailey believed, by first recovering the interpretations of the Scriptures that had already been made by Arabic-speaking Christian scholars in the Middle East who lived in the period from the ninth through the thirteenth centuries. This was a period that included what scholars consider the Golden Age of Islam, when scholarship flourished in the Middle East at a time when the West was sunk in the Dark Ages. While Medieval Muslim scholars were making breakthroughs in medicine, science, and philosophy, Arabic-speaking Christians paralleled their work in the areas of Christian scholarship. Today, their interpretations of the Bible lay hidden in plain sight in the Arabic translations of the Scriptures, biblical commentaries, and theological works. "A significant part of that Arabic Christian scholarship," Bailey explained, "focused on the New Testament and those scholars . . . remain unknown, unpublished, unhonored, and unsung." Speaking to an audience of Christian scholars, pastors, seminarians, and interested lay people, Bailey referred to the parable of Jesus in Matthew's Gospel of a field in which a great treasure lay hidden (Matt 13:44). "You here in the Middle East," he said, "do not need to go out and buy the field in which the treasure lies. You already own the field! All that is required is that you dig it up and put its gold coins back into circulation."

Before the church of the Middle East—and specifically the CMEC—Bailey set forth two great tasks that evening. The first was to identify the texts of the Arabic Christian heritage, publish critical editions of these texts in Arabic, and finally translate these works into English so that they would be available to the broadest possible audience. The second great task he enunciated was for the church of the Middle East, specifically the Egyptian church, to take up the task of reinterpreting the Scriptures in the light of Middle Eastern culture. It was, he believed, uniquely situated to accomplish this work for several reasons. First, it need look no further than to its own cultural heritage to find a window into the deeper meanings contained in the biblical stories. Conservative village culture, he believed, was an excellent starting place because this culture still retained the values and many of the traditions of those who lived in the biblical age. Second, the churches of the Middle East spoke and read Arabic as a vernacular language, which gave them a familiarity with the Medieval Arabic texts unmatched by scholars from any other region in the world. Finally, he recognized and applauded the efforts of the Orthodox and Catholic Churches of the Middle East to produce biblical commentaries reflecting Middle Eastern culture, but he believed Evangelical scholars, because of their Arabic language skills, their closeness to village culture, and their high regard for the authority and inspiration of the Scriptures, should assume this task as their special burden. "In short," he declared, "this treasure is buried in the garden around your house. It is on your property. If you do not dig it up, who is going to do so?"

Immediately following the inauguration of the CMEC, Bailey and several others visited St. Catherine's Monastery at the base of Mount Sinai on the Sinai Peninsula. Bailey then traveled with a group of twelve friends to Upper Egypt. Accompanied by Emile Zaki, who had worked with him as a chaplain in the 1960s at Assiut College and who had planned the trip, Bailey visited some of the places where he had served from 1955 to 1965. This trip would have been especially meaningful to him as it marked the fiftieth anniversary of the beginning of his career in mission. One of the villages he visited was Deir el-Barsha, where he and Mickey had worked for a period of over two years. He wrote, "To my utter amazement the people of the village were recalling stories that took place from 1957–1961. I have just written to James Dunn reporting that 'informal controlled oral tradition' is still alive and well in spite of electricity and television. Some of the vignettes were about—guess who—me! And some of the older women insisted on kissing my hand."[2] During this trip, Bailey saw his old friend Baki Sadaka Girgis, who remembered him as a Bible teacher at the First Evangelical Church in Assiut and who believed, as he said in a later interview, that Bailey was a teacher "second to none."[3] Bailey, Zaki, and others walked around the property beside the Ibrahimiya Canal in Assiut where he and Mickey had lived but had since been converted into a retreat center and student residence.[4]

When Bailey returned to his home in New Wilmington, he had a minor surgery performed—possibly for his prostrate—and recovered

---

2. Ken to Gary Burge, July 7, 2005, Bailey Papers, box 28, folder 5. Hand-kissing in the Middle East is a sign of respect usually reserved for religious leaders.

3. I interviewed the Reverend Baki Sadaka Girgis on January 29, 2020, in his apartment in Assiut. Still lucid at the age of ninety-one, he remembered Bailey fondly.

4. Ken to Baki Sadaka Girgis, July 8, 2005; and Ken to Emil Zaki, July 8, 2005, Bailey Papers, box 28, folder 5.

within two weeks. He also had surgery for cataracts that year. These medical inconveniences did not prevent him in August from attending the New Wilmington Missionary Conference, which was now being ably run by Don Dawson. Bailey had been attending these conferences since 1942, and he was often asked to teach or speak at them. Being among enthusiastic young people, listening to fervent messages of faith, and swaying to the rhythms of Christian pop music always seemed to give him a spiritual lift. On the program for the first Saturday night of the week-long conference, Bailey was listed as a speaker who would make "a few appropriate remarks." Since this was supposed to be a worship service, Bailey was offended that he would not be given more time. He dismissed the worship service of another evening that week as "entertainment dressed up as worship." Writing to his son, David, about his week at the conference, he could not contain his anger:

> This last conference is the first time in in my life that I have ever experienced "entertainment" pure and simple placed in the middle of worship with no apology or attempt to pretend that it has anything to do with worship. On the other hand, if Saturday night was not meant to be worship then why were there hymns, prayer, scripture and a theologian as a speaker? . . . Friday morning, as you know, I was too mad and fed up. I walked out.[5]

Bailey had a point, and had he been criticizing the worship styles of many mega churches there would be many people to support him. But in fairness to Don Dawson, who was every bit as dedicated and warmhearted an evangelical as Bailey, it also has to be said that he was struggling to find ways to connect to Christian youths with the limited attention spans associated with the Facebook and texting generation. Did Bailey, who was now approaching seventy-five, really think that his lecture-style sermons would have held the attention of this crowd? Bailey may have sensed his growing distance from the new generation. A few years later, reading a collection of the poems of Alfred Lord Tennyson that David had given him as a gift, he wrote that he "was amazed as I read . . . how many lines I remember because my mother often quoted them." Three lines from "Morte d'Arthur" particularly moved him. He had used them before in his 1984 McClure Lectures entitled *A Tale of Three Cities,* and now perhaps he suspected that the time had come to apply them to himself:

---

5. Ken to David, August 7, 2005, Bailey Papers, box 28, folder 5.

The old order changeth, yielding place to new,
And God fulfills himself in many ways
Lest one good custom should corrupt the world.⁶

∽

Bailey's play *Open Hearts in Bethlehem: A Christmas Drama* was first performed publicly in January 2001 at the Lutheran Seminary in Kauniainen, Finland, by the faculty and students. In the first week of December 2005, Bailey had the pleasure of seeing this play, which was published by Westminster John Knox Press earlier that year, performed in a large church in Pittsburgh. David Bailey was also present in order to sing the songs he had written for the play. There would be five performances.⁷ A second edition of the play, edited by Andrew Le Peau, was published by InterVarsity Press in 2013. Both editions were accompanied by a thirty-minute CD consisting of five folk songs written and performed by David and a choir anthem using the words by the Ceylonese pastor and theologian D. T. Niles's hymn "On a Day."⁸ The music for the anthem was arranged by Lois Hopkins, professor of music at Westminster College in New Wilmington, Pennsylvania, and performed by the Westminster College Chamber Choir under the direction of Robin Lind and accompanied by Ashley Rexrode. The book is eighty-two pages, and the play, with four scenes, can be performed in twenty-five to thirty minutes or, if accompanied by music, forty-five to fifty minutes.

Bailey's hope was that this play would "rescue truth from familiarity" in the account of Jesus' birth as recorded in Luke's Gospel.⁹ His major concerns were to correct a number of misconceptions about the nativity commonly held in the West: that Joseph and Mary sought a room in an inn rather than a place in a peasant home; that Jesus was born in a stable and placed in a free-standing manger; that Joseph was an incompetent husband unable to find a place for his pregnant wife to give birth; and

---

6. Ken to David, December 16, 2008, Bailey Papers, box 28, folder 4. Bailey may have been reading Roberts, "Morte d'Arthur," 91. Tennyson wrote "Morte d'Arthur" in 1842 and incorporated it into *Idylls of the King* as "The Passing of Arthur" in 1870. The traditional citation is "The Passing of the King," 408–10. See also Tennyson, *Idylls of the King*, 299.

7. Ken to Bruce, November 16, 2005, Bailey Papers, box 28, folder 5.

8. Daniel Thambyrajah Niles (1908–70).

9. Bailey, *Open Hearts in Bethlehem*, 14.

that the villagers of Bethlehem were heartless and selfish. All of these misunderstandings have their root in the mistranslation of the Greek word *kataluma* as "inn" instead of "guest room." In the preface, Bailey makes the arch observation that "The churches of the Middle East, for two thousand years, have never seen an 'inn' in the story."[10] The mistaken Western view probably arose from Jerome's fourth-century version of Luke's Gospel in which he translated *kataluma* with the Latin word *diversorio*, which Bailey explains is a generic word for "a place to stay" but that at times might be interpreted to mean an "inn."[11]

Bailey also sought authenticity in other ways in his play. The performers in the play do not use forks, spoons, or plates to dine. Instead, they employ pita bread for these purposes as Middle Easterners traditionally do. Joseph knocks on the door with a walking stick, not his knuckles. Since he is not able to call out the names of the family to which he has come, they are initially afraid because he is a stranger. However, when he recites his lineage, he is readily welcomed into the home. The performers are meant to imagine that the window in the house is a "slit high in the wall," which a peasant home would likely have.[12] Finally, when the shepherds approach the home, they do not knock on the door but clap to announce their presence. Bailey's concern is that the West embrace his understanding of the Christmas story, which he believed is "culturally sensitive and historically accurate."[13]

In 2005 Bailey also republished *THE DOCTRINE OF GOD for Village People*, which he wrote in 1960–61 as his master's thesis in Systematic Theology at Pittsburgh Theological Seminary. It had been published in Arabic in Egypt (1964?), and Bailey had revised it in 1976 as *God Is . . . Dialogues on the Nature of God for Young People,* so that it would be appropriate for an audience of American youth (see chapters 5 and 10). The latest edition of Bailey's master's thesis appeared in 2005 as *God Is . . . Dialogues on the Nature of God*. Revised once again by Bailey and edited by his daughter, Sara Bailey,[14] this edition was intended for the English-speaking world,

---

10. Bailey, *Open Hearts in Bethlehem*, 18.
11. Bailey, *Open Hearts in Bethlehem*, 17–18.
12. Bailey, *Open Hearts in Bethlehem*, 74.
13. Bailey, *Open Hearts in Bethlehem*, 14.
14. Bailey, *God Is . . . Dialogues* (2005).

especially those among the younger churches of the developing world. By this time, he wrote in the preface, it had been translated "into more than twenty languages and used in radio ministry around the world. To my delight it has continued to be used in many places for these forty-plus years." It was produced by Vision through Vision (VTV) as a film in 1990, with the title *God Is Love*. Acted by Egyptians in Egyptian locations, it has been shown on television in Egypt, Iraq, Lebanon, and Sudan, with an estimated viewing audience of over 10 million people. Though the characters speak in Arabic, it has English subtitles, and subsequently it has appeared with subtitles in twelve other languages.[15]

Since the book was not intended for a Western audience, it was never reviewed in scholarly or popular journals. Its success can only be measured in its wide use by Christians in the developing world as it was produced for television, enacted in numerous church dramas, and published in book translations. Bailey's use of drama, his emphasis on themes important to Muslims, and his use of illustrations taken from village life make it relevant and accessible in a way that more traditional presentations are not. Though it cannot be considered great literature, it can be appreciated as a work well suited for the ends its author intended.

The third book Bailey saw republished at this time was *The Cross & the Prodigal*, which he had originally published in 1973 but had completed in 1966. Nearly forty years later, in 2005, he revised the book and republished it.[16] This was not a minor effort in revision. He revised his language throughout, often line-by-line, and he updated the book to include many of the new insights he had gleamed from four decades of scholarly study.

Bailey's writing in the 2005 edition is smoother than that in the earlier edition, but it is also less dramatic and more measured. For example, while discussing the conservative nature of Arab villages in the preface to the 1973 edition, he says with panache, "As a result village attitudes are often older than Abraham."[17] In the new edition, he writes more soberly, "As a result, in the main, village attitudes are of great antiquity."[18] The

---

15. This publishing information is given in Bailey, *God Is . . . Dialogues* (2005), 5.
16. Bailey, *Cross & the Prodigal* (2005).
17. Bailey, *Cross & the Prodigal* (1973), 10.
18. Bailey, *Cross & the Prodigal* (2005), 18.

florid prose he used in the first edition to describe Jesus' calculated insult to the Pharisees—"If you talk to a Pharisee as you would to a shepherd, you infuriate him"[19]—has been dropped. In the new edition, he simply explains as a professor would the Pharisees' attitude to the "people of the land," which includes shepherds. And he adds a qualifying detail: shepherds might also represent families of wealth.[20] Finally, in the first edition, he refers to Christ, but in the second it is always to Jesus, reflecting contemporary usage.

After the new edition of *The Cross & the Prodigal* was published, Bailey's friend and fellow New Testament scholar Gary Burge wrote to him to praise the new book. "The cover," he wrote, "looks absolutely spectacular with aspects of Middle East geometric design and of course a fabulous portrait of the prodigal son (a picture I have not seen—not the usual Rembrandt)." He continued, "Sometimes we wonder if the books we write have a lasting influence. This little book from 1973 certainly has. As I wrote in the little endorsement, your contribution has been to make people think differently about the parables as well as much of the rest of the NT. It is no small achievement." He then wrote of his two daughters, Ashleigh and Grace. Ashleigh would be twenty-three soon and would begin a master's in philosophy program in Illinois. She was doing well, and Burge was obviously proud of her. His other daughter, however, was struggling. The Burges had adopted Grace at the age of four, but when she reached eighteen the previous February, Burge reported, she "promptly announced that she was leaving for Texas." Anticipating her departure, Burge wrote, "I printed in small font all of Luke 15, laminated it, and slipped it into a zippered pouch in her backpack along with her birth certificate and high school diploma. I also gave her pictures of our family. She phones every two weeks or so and who knows but that someday she may return. A prodigal."[21]

As Bailey reported to FoMENTS at this time, *The Cross & the Prodigal* was honored in 2006 as one of the "Year's Best Book[s] for Preachers" by *Preaching* magazine.[22]

---

19. Bailey, *Cross & the Prodigal* (1973), 21.
20. Bailey, *Cross & the Prodigal* (2005), 30.
21. Gary Burges to Ken, June 15, 2005, Bailey Papers, box 28, folder 5.
22. Mohler, "Year's Best Books—2006," para. 15.

Through Middle Eastern Eyes

In July 2005, Bailey wrote to his friend Gary Burge that InterVarsity Press had accepted a collection of thirty New Testament essays he had written. Twenty-six of these were transcriptions of his video presentations, and he agreed to write six new essays for the collection. The book would be *Jesus through Middle Eastern Eyes*.[23] As Bailey spent the next year or two revising his essays and adding new ones, he continued to be in demand as a lecturer. Soon after he turned seventy-five on November 24, 2005, he wrote to his son, David, that in the coming year he would be speaking in June in Scotland, in August in Cyprus, in September in Beirut, and in November in Jerusalem. "Not bad," he chortled, "for an old broken down seventy-five-year-old!"[24] And this was just his international itinerary. In his FoMENTS report for the period May 2005 through April 2007, Bailey reported that he had written six articles, given 227 lectures or sermons, and written three study guides for his taped lectures. And in this year, he also began to report on those of his books and articles that were being translated into foreign languages. The books that would be most translated were *The Cross & the Prodigal*, and later *Jesus through Middle Eastern Eyes*, and then *Paul through Mediterranean Eyes*. He noted that the languages his books were being translated into included Latvian, Japanese, German, Italian, and Persian.

In September 2005, Sara Bailey and Victor Makari, the PCUSA's Area Coordinator for the Middle East and Europe, announced their engagement. They had met three months before at the ceremony for the launching the CMEC in Cairo in June 2005. When Victor first saw Sara, he was immediately smitten with her. He sat with her under a tent on the seminary grounds for meetings and tea breaks, where they had a long and meaningful conversation. They were married on August 14, 2006, appropriately enough, on the Island of Aphrodite, Sara's beloved Cyprus. Sara arrived a few weeks early to be with her parents where they were vacationing at the mission camp to enjoy the peace, cool, and pine-scented mountain air of Troodos. Some fifty friends and family members flew to Cyprus for the occasion while a number of friends living on the island also attended. Friends from Beirut, however, could not be present as Israel had attacked Lebanon that summer, resulting in the closing of Beirut International Airport. The service and reception were held at the Palm Beach Hotel in Larnaca, which is also where the Baileys, Victor,

---

23. Ken to Gary, July 7, 2005, Bailey Papers, box 28, folder 5.

24. Ken to David and Leslie and family, December 14, 2005, Bailey Papers, box 28, folder 5.

and the international guests were staying. Sara wrote to her parents later to thank them, saying that "it was a wedding of which I could only have dreamed."[25] After honeymooning on the island, Sara and Victor flew to Louisville, Kentucky, where Victor worked at the headquarters of the Presbyterian Church, USA. Writing to her parents in June 2007, Sara expressed her gratitude to them for standing by her throughout her years of illness. She was especially grateful for their gift of the "little yellow house," which "is a place of such happy memories and proof positive of your great love for me."[26] Some months later, in December 2007, Victor also wrote to his in-laws to thank them for help with the mortgage on their apartment in Louisville.[27] Perhaps as Ken and Mickey had been assisted by Ken's mother, Annette, in purchasing their home in New Wilmington, Pennsylvania, they wanted to repay the gift by "paying it forward" to their daughter and her new husband.

Figure 28. Sara Bailey, circa 2005.

25. Sara to Baba [Ken] and Girlie [Mickey], June 2007, Bailey Papers, box 28, folder 4.

26. Sara to Baba [Ken] and Girlie [Mickey], June 2007, Bailey Papers, box 28, folder 4.

27. Ken to Victor, November 1, 2008; and Victor to Ken, November 9, 2008, Bailey Papers, box 28, folder 4.

Figure 29. Victor Makari and Sara Bailey Makari at the Palm Beach Hotel, Larnaca, Cyprus, on their wedding day, August 14, 2006.

On May 26, 2007, Bailey sent David the first letter he had prepared on the new stationary of the organization he had formed to support his work: the Foundation for Middle Eastern New Testament Studies (FoMENTS). The Board of Overseers was listed in the left sidebar, headed by Bailey as lecturer and author. At the top of the page the stationary showcased a quotation from the fourth- and fifth-century Greek pastor and scholar John Chrysostom, but curiously—and deliberately—the quotation is in Arabic, not the original Greek. The address of the organization given at the bottom was Bailey's home in New Wilmington, Pennsylvania.[28] Later in the year, Bailey prepared a brochure to be given to potential donors and sent a copy to Bruce and Barbara Bailey for their comments. When Bruce wrote to the board to make suggestions about the brochure, Bailey responded that "all of the statements in the brochure from my friends need to focus not on 'That which Ken Bailey has done'

---

28. Ken to David, May 26, 2007, Bailey Papers, box 28, folder 4.

but on 'These are the doors that Ken Bailey has opened and others can be encouraged to move through them.'"[29]

The latter years of Bailey's life saw him continue to preach and lecture widely, generally averaging over a hundred presentations in over twenty-five venues per year. One set of lectures he gave in October 2007 was both gratifying and perplexing. The leadership team at Presbyterian World Mission, headquartered in Louisville, Kentucky, invited Bailey to present a series of lectures at a week-long mission conference sponsored by the denomination. He wrote to a friend of his experience and his feelings about the event: "After fifty years of ignoring me," he began, "I was quite amazed to find myself invited. I went with a good heart and did my best, and the 700 people around the church who were gathered together 'heard me gladly.'" Yet, strangely, the only staff person to thank him for his not inconsiderable efforts was his son-in-law, Victor Makari. Bailey expressed his appreciation and well wishes for the new director of Presbyterian World Mission, Hunter Farrell, who he hoped would "be able to build a staff that makes the 'preaching of the gospel' as important as engaging in 'social justice issues.'" But he also observed that Farrell had not attended his Bible studies that week, and he was taken aback by one staff person who led a worship service during the week who began the Lord's Prayer with the words "Our *God*, who art in heaven," pointedly declining to address God as Father, as Jesus taught.[30] Though the event might have been expected to result in Bailey being drawn more closely to his denomination, it seems to have had the opposite effect. Indeed, he felt ever more estranged and distant from the church he had faithfully served for forty years.

Bailey's latest book, *Jesus through Middle Eastern Eyes: Cultural Studies in the Gospels*, was published in early 2008 by InterVarsity Press (IVP), which informed Bailey around July that his book was selling well and was then in its fourth printing. Also, a Danish translation was underway, and IVP was aware that the Japanese had also decided to translate it as well.[31] This collection of essays on New Testament themes and passages would be one of his bestselling works. In the preface, Bailey states that some of

29. Ken to Bruce and Barbara, January 12, 2008, Bailey Papers, box 28, folder 4.
30. Ken to Sally Millison, October 15, 2007, FoMENTS Records.
31. Ken to David and Leslie, August 2, 2008, Bailey Papers, box 28, folder 4.

the chapters were originally video lectures that were transcribed by his "dear friend and colleague, Dr. Dale Bowne, professor New Testament (emeritus), Grove City College." Others were essays written three decades earlier (around 1978). The majority, however, were compositions presented to the public for the first time. Bailey thanks his daughter, Sara Bailey Makari, for serving as his copy editor, and he thanks the seven members of his "advisory committee" from the Presbytery of Shenango and the Episcopal Diocese of Pittsburgh for their support over the years. The book is dedicated in moving words to his son who had spent the past dozen years of his life in fear of a medical relapse from which there would be no hope of remission.

In the introduction Bailey laments that the Christians of the Middle East, though numbering 10 million, are the "forgotten faithful." He promises to hear their voices by consulting Syriac and Arabic literature, both from the Middle Ages and contemporary writers. From the distant past, he would pay special attention to Ibn al-Tayyib, Hibat Allah ibn al-'Assal, and Diyunisiyus Ia'qub inb al-Salibi. Among the more recent writers he pledges to consult are Ibrahim Sa'id and Matta al-Miskin—also known in English as Matthew the Poor. He says of Matta, "His six large volumes on the Gospels are stunning and unknown outside the Arabic-speaking Christian world." Finally, he promises to take counsel from Syriac, Arabic, Coptic, and Greek versions of the New Testament, for "translation is always interpretation."[32] Bailey reviews once again the literary technique of Hebrew parallelism, which he believes often appears in the New Testament and can, at times, provide helpful insights into the text. These structures, he explains, are of Hebrew origin and, when found in the New Testament, clearly show that the cultural origin of the text is Jewish, not Greek. Bailey believes that they give solid evidence for the historical authenticity of the texts he is analyzing, showing that they were the creation of Jesus himself. These texts, he believes, were produced in four distinct stages: an original Aramaic teaching by Jesus; the eyewitness testimony to Jesus by Aramaic speakers; the Greek translation of this material; and finally, the assembling and editing of the Greek material into gospels by the four evangelists. Through this involute transmission process, Bailey believes that the Holy Spirit was present at every step inspiring the original author, his witnesses, the translators, and lastly the Gospel writers. For Bailey, the Gospels are "history theologically interpreted." Far from

---

32. Bailey, *Jesus through Middle Eastern Eyes*, 11, 13.

being a dry collection of facts and dates, the Gospels seek to convey the deeper meaning of the events and words they record. Bailey arranges his book in six parts: "The Birth of Jesus," "The Beatitudes," "The Lord's Prayer," "Dramatic Actions of Jesus," "Jesus and Women," and "Parables of Jesus." His intention is not to present a comprehensive commentary of the Gospels but rather to "offer brief glimpses of some of the treasures that await us as Western isolation from Middle Eastern Christian interpretation of the Bible is slowly brought to an end."[33]

The book reviews for *Jesus through Middle Eastern Eyes* were generally positive and even at times enthusiastic. Roy B. Zuck in *Bibliotheca Sacra* wrote, it "is a brilliant addition to Bailey's other works."[34] Carol Schersten LaHurd, writing for the *Catholic Biblical Quarterly*, wrote that Bailey, "a careful reader who shares his knowledge of ancient sources, poetic conventions, and cultural background," was at his best in explaining the story of Zacchaeus.[35] Geoffrey Turner in *The Heythrop Journal* wrote that "The book is full of insights into social practices that are implicit in the texts about Jesus and so the author is able to open fresh perspectives, which are not often found in the standard commentaries."[36] John David Boman in *Brethren Life & Thought* pronounced it "eminently practical, insightful and provocative. It would be a great addition to the toolkit of any pastor or Sunday school teacher."[37] Graydon F. Snyder, writing for *Currents in Theology and Mission*, concluded that "though his arguments are not necessarily simple, his style make them easy to comprehend," and he recommended the book for college students, seminarians, congregational classes, and pastors to study.[38] Cynthia Long Westfall in *Priscilla Papers* praised Bailey for allowing non-Western voices into the scholarly conversation: "Bailey has brought some guest speakers to the table who should have been primary participants in the discussion of the interpretation of the Bible all along."[39]

Even those who were critical of Bailey at various points generally found his book to be helpful, insightful, and often a delight to read. LaHurd, cited above, commented that Bailey "pays insufficient attention

---

33. Bailey, *Jesus through Middle Eastern Eyes*, 9.
34. Zuck, Review of *Jesus through Middle Eastern Eyes*, 499.
35. LaHurd, Review of *Jesus through Middle Eastern Eyes*, 606.
36. Turner, Review of *Jesus through Middle Eastern Eyes*, 312.
37. Bowman, Review of *Jesus through Middle Eastern Eyes*, 93.
38. Snyder, Review of *Jesus through Middle Eastern Eyes*, 61.
39. Westfall, Review of *Jesus through Middle Eastern Eyes*, 30.

to redaction factors," a comment commonly made of Bailey's previous books. She also found Bailey's account of Jesus' rejection at Nazareth to contain "some inappropriately placed political intent" with his use of the terms "settler" and "settler town."[40] Bowman, cited above, gave a positive review but also offered up a criticism often directed at Bailey's work: "At times . . . the evidence supporting his rhetorical constructs was not as sufficient as one would wish."[41] Gene R. Smillie in the *Journal of the Evangelical Theological Society* offered a similar caution: "While we may recognize 'Hebrew parallelism' here and there outside the OT, Bailey's fascination with chiastic forms of composition causes him to see them everywhere. Not all readers will be persuaded by his presentations, but one has to admit that the implications are far-reaching."[42] Deborah Storie, writing for *Pacifica*, wrote the longest (fourteen pages) and most incisively critical review of Bailey's book. Perhaps her most pointed observation was that, in the parable of the pounds (Luke 19:11–27), Bailey often failed to even mention the "exploitative economic practices" of Palestine's first-century rich, especially the existence of slavery, which he ignored simply by translating the word for slaves (*douloi*) as servants. He was also insufficiently aware of the violence that was just beneath the surface of many of the parables, and he ignored the "power disparities" between rich and poor, conquerors and conquered. For example, he explained Joseph's anger on learning of Mary's pregnancy as a natural reaction to her betrayal, but Storie pointed out that, given the proximity of Roman soldiers in Sepphoris to Nazareth, he probably concluded that she had been raped.[43]

Storie made a number of valid criticisms of Bailey's interpretations, but to be fair to him, several of her criticisms were adequately addressed in Bailey's previous works. For example, his supposed tendency to see dominant figures in Jesus' parables as good even when they are bad was a point that Bailey also made in *Poet & Peasant* when he commented on the "surprising list of unsavory characters" that appear in Jesus' parables.[44] Similarly, in the parable of the good Samaritan, Bailey's failure to appreciate the danger entailed in stopping to help the wounded traveler is

---

40. LaHurd, Review of *Jesus through Middle Eastern Eyes*, 605, 606.
41. Bowman, Review of *Jesus through Middle Eastern Eyes*, 93.
42. Smillie, Review of *Jesus through Middle Eastern Eyes*, 376.
43. Storie, Review of *Jesus through Middle Eastern Eyes*, 96–109.
44. Bailey, *Poet & Peasant*, 105.

a point he made in *Through Peasant Eyes*.[45] In abbreviating his interpretations for a large collection, Bailey inadvertently—and perhaps inevitably—opened himself up to such criticisms. Storie, however, was surely on solid ground in critiquing Bailey's failure to fully account for economic and social factors in some of his accounts. Then again, perhaps he might have responded that his short interpretive essays were never intended to be taken as exhaustive treatments of the subjects they reviewed. In the preface, in fact, he declared that they were only "brief glimpses" of treasures yet to be fully explored.[46]

During a business trip to Europe in the fall of 2008, David Bailey visited the village of Freshwater on the Isle of Wight to see where his paternal grandmother, Annette Meader Bailey, had lived. While on the island, he spent time in the graveyard where his great-grandfather was buried, and he walked down the aisle of the church where Annette and Ewing were wed, imagining his grandmother whispering a blessing and words of advice to him. Reflecting on his visit to the Isle of Wight, he wrote to his father about his trip and included a poem he wrote entitled "Freshwater Bay."[47] Bailey responded two weeks later to thank him for the package he had sent, which included some reading material and at least one photograph of what David mistakenly thought was the Meader house:

> Thanks also for the poem. I loved it. I could see you walking down the aisle and only wished I was with you. Maybe I should take a trip to England and have a "walk down memory lane" myself. Anyway, nice poem. The part about my mother giving you some advice is really nice. She was some lady. I think of her almost every day. If she had not walked down that aisle, neither of us would be here.[48]

After David returned home, he reported to the hospital for his annual checkup. The doctors informed him that his brain tumor had returned

---

45. Bailey, *Through Peasant Eyes*, 43.

46. Bailey, *Jesus through Middle Eastern Eyes*, 9.

47. David Bailey, "Freshwater Bay," October 30, 2008, Bailey Papers, Box 28, folder 6.

48. Ken to David, November 14, 2008, Bailey Papers, box 28, folder 6. Ken Bailey also notes that the poem may be mistitled since the village is named Freshwater while the Freshwater Bay lies to the south.

and that it was malignant. He was forty-two years old, and he had the same GBM as he had had twelve years before at the age of thirty. Around November 22 he again underwent brain surgery, awakening eight days later in the Intensive Care Unit with a new scar on his head. During the last three months of 2008, Bailey gave lectures across the United States, probably promoting his new book. By mid-December, however, he was back home, and he and Mickey turned to attending to the needs of their son and his family.[49]

---

49. Ken to Frank Bailey, December 22, 2008, Bailey Papers, box 28, folder 4.

19

Chiasms Everywhere
2009–11

> The reason for our non-remembrance of wrongs will be the same as its cause: Our minds will be rapt in the goodness of God and in the goodness of God's new world, and the memories of wrongs will wither away like plants without water.
>
> —Miroslav Volf, *The End of Memory*

As David and Leslie struggled to meet the new medical costs that they incurred due to the expense of David's chemotherapy treatments, Ken and Mickey must have contemplated the approaching death of their son and wondered whether Leslie would be able to support herself and her two children without David. As they had with Victor and Sara, the Baileys decided to help David and Leslie pay off their mortgage so that when David passed the family home would not be in jeopardy. Leslie wrote to thank them in March 2009. "Your gifts," she said, "are assuring that we will always have a home—no matter our future. Thank you."[1] Leslie later recalled that by this time David's music career provided a sufficient income that Ken and Mickey's gift was not needed in the way it would have been in earlier years. Nonetheless, it was much appreciated.[2]

1. Leslie to Mom and Dad, March 30, 2009, Bailey Papers, box 28, folder 7.
2. Interview with Leslie Bailey, February 19, 2023.

The first three months of 2009 found Bailey traveling throughout the country lecturing. He wrote to Bruce and Barbara Bailey at the end of March to say that he had recently given presentations in Grand Rapids, Michigan; Indianapolis, Indiana; Pittsburgh, Pennsylvania; Blackburn, Virginia; and Juneau, Alaska. He planned, however, to limit his travels for the rest of the year so that he could work on his new book on 1 Corinthians. Nevertheless, he ended his letter with these parting words: "I must quit and close my suitcase. I am off to the airport again tomorrow morning."[3] If he commenced his 1 Corinthians project where he had left off in May 1988, he already had a 400-page manuscript in hand (see chapter 14).

Although David realized that he did not have long to live, he continued to write poetry and songs, and to give concerts. Sometime in the second half of May 2009 he performed a benefit concert at Churchill Downs, where the Kentucky Derby was run on May 2. Later that month he sent his father his latest poem, "Still Standing." Though Bailey knew that David's days were numbered, he did not temper his judgment to spare his son's feelings. He should not, Bailey advised once again, use vulgarity, which suggests a person lacks "intelligence and imagination." He understood of course that David was trying to appear to be a regular guy, but Bailey contended that he would lose more than he gained. He was especially bothered about the underlying philosophy behind the words "Still Standing." He thought that David was saying, or would be interpreted as saying, that in a difficult situation all a person has to do is show courage and resolve in order to win in the end. Bailey wrote that this is simply untrue as there are forces, physical and spiritual, that are beyond the power of human beings to control. Even purely secular people "will have experienced brutal evil, and mindless disease that overwhelm the most powerful will in the world. Even as a secular poet could you [not] allow for unanswered questions, mystery, forces we cannot control, and tragedy?"[4] David wrote back humbly, owning that he had been producing a "flurry" of poems but that his frame of mind was not always balanced. "I am blessed to have someone in my life who is both wise enough to see it and loving enough to speak the truth. From the bottom of my heart, thank you. I'm a better me because of you. Always have been."[5]

3. Ken to Bruce and Barbara [Bailey], March 27, 2009, Bailey Papers, box 28, folder 7.
4. Ken to David, May 23, 2009, Bailey Papers, box 28, folder 7.
5. David to Dad, May 30, 2009, Bailey Papers, box 28, folder 7.

Chiasms Everywhere

Figure 30. David and Ken Bailey, circa 2007–8.

Figure 31. Kelcey, David, Cameron, and Leslie Bailey
at Cam's confirmation, May 31, 2009.

David continued to give performances throughout the year, wanting to make the most of his remaining time. In late July he paused long enough to write once more to his parents, no doubt imagining that it would be one of his last letters to them:

> The day has yet to begin & I hate to say goodbye. But my next stage awaits, & I will mount it with a fresh spirit tonight, encouraged, refreshed, & restarted by simply being near you. "Thank you," of course, hardly begins to capture my gratitude, but somehow, I hold on to the hope that you have some idea of the depth & magnitude of my feelings & for that I am also grateful. No child, no boy, no man could ever ask for more. You remain two of the brightest stars in my sky & continue to always guide me home. I love you.[6]

During this year in which his son was often on his mind, Bailey probably traveled to at least one speaking engagement per month, and he also continued to speak locally, which he did not count in his effort to limit his speaking so that he could complete his book on 1 Corinthians. In his small home office, he had access to forty-seven commentaries on 1 Corinthians; and on the shelves behind his desk were translations of Paul's letter in Hebrew, Syriac, German, Latin, Greek, and Arabic—some dating from as early as the third and fourth centuries. He also had microfilmed copies of commentaries from the ninth and tenth centuries that he consulted. Bailey thought of his task as "more like woodcarving than writing." He explained to his son, "Like carving, the question is 'what are you going to carve away and what are you going to leave?'" Bailey was exhilarated that he was making discoveries about the text that no one had ever observed before. He felt as though he was "wandering in pure delight through a hidden valley that no one else even knows exits."[7] By the end of the year Bailey had completed a first draft of his 1 Corinthians manuscript. It was 175,000 words, which at 350 words per printed page would be 500 pages. This was the longest book he had yet written, and he did not want it to grow any larger. He planned to spend the first five months of 2010 revising and polishing it.[8] In fact, Bailey would continue working on the book well into 2011.

In May, David had to undergo another surgery to remove a new tumor that had appeared in his brain. The operation was successful but then he had to undergo further chemotherapy. Ken and Mickey were

---

6. David to Mom and Dad, July 27, 2009, Bailey Papers, box 28, folder 7.

7. Ken to David, August 15, 2009, Bailey Papers, box 28, folder 7.

8. Ken to Kelcey and Cammy [Cameron], January 8, 2010, Bailey Papers, box 28, folder 7.

present at Duke University Hospital, in Durham, North Carolina, for the initial surgery, and afterwards they took their son to a rehabilitation hospital in Charlottesville, Virginia. After a week there, David returned home to rest and recuperate. Unlike the previous procedures, however, his left leg and hand were weakened, and the chemotherapy had a debilitating effect on him.[9] He died five months later on October 2, 2010. A Service of Witness to the Resurrection was held on October 19, 2010, at Blue Ridge Presbyterian Church, Charlottesville, Virginia, David's home church where he was a charter member and elder. The reception afterwards was held in the church fellowship hall and was sponsored by Leslie, Kelcey, and Cameron Bailey and by Ken and Ethel Bailey. Memorial gifts to honor David were evenly divided between the church's building fund and several brain tumor associations. Sara participated in the service by reading a Scripture passage, but Ken was not a formal participant. At the funeral service, Eric Hilgendorf spoke movingly of the friend he had known since their youth in Beirut. He recalled that they had been interrogated by the police, an event that neither could ever forget. He said that when David learned of his tumor and that the number of days left to him was short, he decided to change the course of his life. He returned to his music, writing and producing song after song, eventually recording twenty-three CDs.[10]

When Bailey turned eighty years old on November 24, 2010, Sara visited her parents to celebrate the occasion. Victor was in Jerusalem for work at the time, and while there his father, Emmanuel Makari, died in Canada. Victor flew back for the memorial service and burial. Bailey remembered Emmanuel and sent a letter of condolence to the Makari family. He wrote that his father, Ewing Bailey, had opened an experimental school in Upper Egypt in the 1930s in the village of Edmu, which lies outside of Minia. Ewing had recruited Emmanuel, who was a pastor in the Evangelical Church, to be the headmaster of the school. Bailey was only a boy at the time, but he remembered Emmanuel fondly as he had been kind to him. When Bailey returned to Egypt in 1955 as a missionary, he soon met Victor Makari, Emmanuel's eldest son. Later in September 1956, Emmanuel brought the precocious Victor, then only fifteen years old, to Cairo to enroll him in the Evangelical Theological Seminary

---

9. Ken to Melanie, May 25, 2010, Bailey Papers, box 28, folder 7.

10. Ken to Melanie, May 25, 2010, Bailey Papers, box 28, folder 7. Eric Hilgendorf said that he had produced eighteen, but the most recent count places the number at twenty-three.

in Cairo. During Bailey's ten years in Egypt, he was often invited to speak at Emmanuel's church in Al Mahalla al-Kubra in the Nile Delta region, and he recalled always being warmly welcomed into the Makari home.[11]

Eric Hilgendorf wrote to the Baileys on November 28, enclosing a copy of his eulogy for David's memorial service, which Bailey had asked for at the close of the funeral. Bailey, however, did not respond until late the following August. Perhaps he could not bring himself yet to write about the loss of his son. By way of excuse, however, he said that he had spent "every spare minute" of most of the previous nine months working on his book, which had now grown to 600 pages. He thanked Eric for the eulogy and his reflections on his son, which he commended as "wonderful, just wonderful!" Bailey wrote that at the age of eighty he knew that he would be reunited with his son soon. His worry therefore was for Sara. She had lost not only her only sibling but also her close friends Ann Weir and Denell Hilgendorf. And, her husband was twenty years her senior. He noted too the continuing fragility of her health. He pleaded with Eric, "Please don't forget her—please! She will need a 'big brother' to talk to." He also reported that David's body had been cremated and that he intended that half of the ashes would be buried near his home in Charlottesville, Virginia, and half in New Wilmington, Pennsylvania.[12]

Bailey's newest book, *Paul through Mediterranean Eyes: Cultural Studies in 1 Corinthians*, was published by InterVarsity Press in 2011. At 508 pages of narrative text, it is Bailey's longest book and his most sustained effort at biblical commentary. In the preface, he writes, "Some forty years ago"—that is, about 1970—he first noticed that Paul's beautiful love poem, 1 Corinthians 13, was composed using the literary technique of ring composition employed in classical Hebrew literature. "A few years later I observed that this same chapter was encased within two discussions of "the spiritual gifts," 1 Cor 12 and 14:1–25, suggesting that the entire letter might have been written following a single, overarching structure. "Ever

---

11. Dr. and Mrs. Kenneth E. Bailey to Makari family, November 24, 2010, Bailey Papers, box 28, folder 7.

12. Uncle Ken to Eric and Ange Hilgendorf, August 23, 2011, Bailey Papers, box 28, folder 7. As of this writing, half of David Bailey's ashes have been interred at the Fair Oaks Cemetery in New Wilmington while the other half continue to be in the possession of his wife, Leslie.

so slowly," Bailey writes, "the composition of the other chapters in the epistle appeared like a magnificent castle emerging into bright sunlight with the gradual lifting of a dense fog (that was in my mind)."[13]

He writes that *Paul through Mediterranean Eyes* would not be a typical commentary on 1 Corinthians. Instead, it would be a "Cultural Studies" project, which is intended "to suggest a more modest enterprise." The commentary, Bailey explains, would have three areas of concern: the rhetorical styles used by Paul; his use of "metaphors and parables," which he believes are not merely illustrations but devices that Paul—like Jesus before him—used to create meaning; and the examination of twenty-three translations of 1 Corinthians in the languages of Syriac, Arabic, and Hebrew, which are representative samples of the "long and illustrious heritage" of Middle Eastern renditions of Paul's letter. Bailey did not intend to review all the literature on 1 Corinthains. Rather, he would focus on the rhetorical styles of 1 Corinthians that can be traced to the writing of the prophets of the Hebrew Scriptures and the broader culture of the Eastern Mediterranean region. Though Paul was usually a plain-spoken man who wrote "straightforward prose," 1 Corinthians, he believes, is an exception.[14]

Bailey's understanding of 1 Corinthians is of course a radical departure from the standard view of most commentors who think that Paul wrote an "occasional" letter—that is, one written to deal with the practical problems of one church in a specific time and place not one written to expound grand theological themes. Moreover, its lack of apparent artfulness suggests that it was a hasty composition, one written over time by a busy man who had no patience for logically arranging his arguments or later revising them to remove redundancies. Bailey takes the opposite view. The apostle Paul, he believes, wrote his letter not simply for the unruly members of the church at Corinth but also for "all those in every place on whom is called the name of our Lord Jesus Christ" (1 Cor 1:2, Bailey's translation). In other words, it was written as a general letter intended for the whole church, which explains the lengths to which Paul went to craft an intricate piece of literature.[15] Indeed, where others see a disjunctive composition in which Paul keeps circling back to review previously covered issues, Bailey detects the telltale signs of a carefully arranged letter employing classical Hebrew parallel structures.

13. Bailey, *Paul through Mediterranean Eyes*, 15, 16.
14. Bailey, *Paul through Mediterranean Eyes*, 19, 22.
15. Bailey, *Paul through Mediterranean Eyes*, 23.

"The entire book," writes Bailey, "has a carefully designed inner coherence that exhibits amazing precision in composition and admirable grandeur in overall theological concept."[16] It consists of five distinct essays that are arranged in an inverted parallel form, a chiasm that follows an ABCBA pattern with the theme of food offered to idols forming the rhetorical center (1 Cor 8:1—11:1). Bailey developed a unique vocabulary to analyze Paul's literary structures. Each of these essays is composed of distinct homilies (poems), and each homily is made up of cameos (couplets, or paired lines of poetry). The individual homilies are also arranged according to classical Hebraic parallel structures—ring composition (which he also calls, employing American idioms, a "double-decker sandwich" that follows a "high jump format"), inverted parallelism, a straight-line structure, and others. Having studied to become a Jewish rabbi, Paul had mastered the literature of the Old Testament, and in writing 1 Corinthians, he employs the literary techniques he had learned, perhaps utilizing the writings of Isaiah as his basic model.

The Corinthians had sent Paul some practical questions to which they wanted answers, but he does not allow them to dictate his agenda. He deals with a set of issues that were important to him, and along the way he works in answers to some of their questions. All five of Paul's essays contain a set of shorter homilies, each of which is also arranged using parallel structures common in Hebraic literature. There is repetition as when in chapter 1 Paul discusses divisions in the church—those who follow Paul, Apollos, or Cephas—and addresses this issue in chapter 4 too. Again, in chapter 8 he discusses food offered to idols and then returns to the subject in chapter 10. Similarly, in chapters 12 and 14 he discusses the nature and use of spiritual gifts. Where other commentators have seen disjointed redundancy, Bailey sees a carefully arranged essay following classical Hebrew patterns.

Bailey observes that, of the Pauline corpus of thirteen letters in the New Testament, 1 Corinthians is the only one that is arranged in the intricate patterns of Hebraic poetry. The reasons for this cannot be known with certainty, but Bailey conjectures that some of his readers in Corinth were simply confused by his style. Being Greek and of limited education, they would not have recognized, appreciated, or understood his sophisticated literary style. Consequently, he dropped it. In 2 Corinthians, Paul wrote, "I hope you will understand [this letter] fully, as

---

16. Bailey, *Paul through Mediterranean Eyes*, 25.

you have understood [my first letter] in part" (2 Cor 1:13–14). That his Greek audience would not have understood that his carefully written letter employing the rhetorical styles of the classical prophets of the Old Testament is certainly understandable. Moreover, this style, with its reliance on similes, metaphors, parables, and dramatic actions, has built-in limitations. Bailey quotes Thomas Friedman's *The World Is Flat* (2007) to explain that an author using big metaphors trades "a certain degree of academic precision for a much larger degree of explanatory power."[17] Friedman argues that modern communication techniques and business organizations have lowered the importance of towering governments, resulting in a flattening of the world. His literal-minded critics, however, responded that Friedman's metaphor overstated his case. The world, they insisted, is not flat! The apostle Paul may have encountered similar recalcitrance.

Paul, Bailey explains, uses a variation of Hebraic ring compositions for his homilies that consist of four parts. He explains Paul's technique with a metaphor of his own, borrowed from track and field sports. Paul, he writes, utilizes a "high jump format." This means that Paul usually begins with an introduction, "a short sprint." This is followed by the jumper's ascent into the air, crossing over the horizontal bar, and a descent back to the ground that reverses the process. Careful readers of Paul's homilies will note that the climax in this pattern occurs in the middle—the point when the jumper crosses the bar.[18]

Did ancient people recognize Paul's literary allusions and techniques? In a world in which at most 10 percent were literate, this is unlikely. Bailey, however, believes that at least some of them did. Otherwise, accomplished writers such as Isaiah and Paul would hardly have made the effort to employ such an intricate style. Isaiah and Paul understood that it was not necessary for readers to fully appreciate their poetic style in order to understand the general point being made. Ring composition, for example, is a kind of literary music with its careful "1–2–3–4–3–2–1" ordering of cameos. Yet, readers can understand the point of the lyrics even if the "tune" escapes them. "We modern Christians," Bailey explains, "may have the Old Testament stories in the backs of our minds, but not their literary 'tunes.'" Consequently, we can understand most of what Paul writes even if we occasionally miss a point because we are reading

---

17. Friedman, *World Is Flat*, x, cited in Bailey, *Paul through Mediterranean Eyes*, 31.
18. Bailey, *Paul through Mediterranean Eyes*, 43.

poetry as if it were prose. In the same way, Bailey suggests, as he had in *Jesus through Middle Eastern Eyes*, a person can appreciate the music of a Bach cantata even while missing his counterpoints.[19]

Nevertheless, Bailey believes that for a number of reasons it is crucial for general readers to appreciate the "tune." It is essential to understand that Paul is using an ABC-CBA structure because the ideas presented in the first three points (ABC) are completed in the second three points but in reverse order (CBA). Also, the climax—the central lesson being taught—occurs in the middle, not the end. Western readers, accustomed to thinking in a linear fashion, on encountering a letter using ring composition are liable to misunderstand the message, miss its full meaning, or conclude that the writer is hopelessly disorganized. For scholars to recognize the "tune" is also important for all these reasons but also because understanding Paul's rhetorical techniques can sometimes help textual critics to make more informed choices between variant readings of a Pauline text. Additionally, knowing the "tune" may also help scholars to appreciate how fully Paul had absorbed his Jewish literary heritage and how skillful he was in composing his poetic missives. This is in contrast to the usual view that Paul, a busy and distracted composer of occasional letters, merely dictated his epistles and that interruptions and changes in circumstances over the time of the writing often led to disjointed compositions. Paul is generally lauded as a great theologian and ethicist, but fully appreciating the literary style of 1 Corinthians may also lead scholars to commend him as a consummate Jewish poet and literary artist.[20]

Given the literary sophistication of 1 Corinthians, Paul must have smiled at the irony of beginning his epistle by insisting that he did not come to preach the gospel with "lofty words or [worldly]wisdom" (1 Cor 2:1), while in fact he was writing to the Corinthians in highly cultured and elegant Greek. Bailey explains that what Paul meant is that he was not engaged in providing literary entertainment for his readers but that his letter, nonetheless, would be well crafted. Some want to find in 1 Corinthians an excuse for anti-intellectualism, but Bailey writes that Paul does not give them one. Paul was not anti-intellectual. His polished Greek, based on ancient Jewish rhetorical techniques and allusions to

---

19. Bailey, *Paul through Mediterranean Eyes*, 47n27, 50. Counterpoints are multiple musical lines in which the melodies are independent but the harmonies interdependent.

20. Bailey, *Paul through Mediterranean Eyes*, 51, 52.

Old Testament prophets, clearly shows his intellectualism and his commitment to literary excellence.[21]

While Bailey's general approach to 1 Corinthians is detached and highly intellectual, Paul's observation that love "keeps no record of wrongs," gives him pause for more personal reflection. Despite Paul's statement, Bailey notes, he had not forgotten the suffering he experienced in his own life. In fact, he even mentioned instances of it in this letter, using language that suggests an anguish that lay just beneath the surface (1 Cor 4:9–13). Bailey reflects: "As a survivor of seven Middle Eastern wars, stretching from 1942 to 1995, suffering and injustice surrounded our family for decades, and some of that suffering reached into the depths of our own lives. Thus, for me this concern opens deep questions." He believes that "Yes, Paul had lists and remembered them." Bailey then provides a couple of pages of his reflections on suffering. He mentions genocide in Turkey, ethnic cleansing in Palestine, and civil war in Sudan. In all three cases responsible government authorities "flatly denied" that any wrong had taken place. In such cases, remembering injustices is crucial if justice is ever to be achieved, a position taken by Elie Wiesel in *Night* (1956) where the Nobel Peace Prize writer recounted the horrors he suffered in Auschwitz and Buchenwald and his resolution not to forget lest justice not be done.[22] Similarly, Miroslav Volf, writing in the *End of Memory: Remembering Rightly in a Violent World* (2006), recalled his brutal interrogation by communist security forces in Yugoslavia. Yet it was Volf's pious Christian belief that, though memories of such horrors will not be forgotten, they will eventually fade in the age to come when "the memories of wrongs will wither away like plants without water."[23] Bailey suggests that perhaps this is what Paul meant when he wrote that love "keeps no record of wrong." Paul, Bailey believes, certainly had records of the wrongs he experienced, but the "memories of his suffering did not constantly return uninvited to the screen of his mind in the form of nightmares or mind-numbing daytime recollections. They were there, but they did not control his present or his future." Presenting Paul's personal suffering in this way raises the question of whether Bailey himself had memories that continued to "return uninvited to the screen of his mind." Was he perhaps thinking of the pain he had experienced in having a distant father and a wayward son, or was he thinking, in an

---

21. Bailey, *Paul through Mediterranean Eyes*, 76.
22. Wiesel, *Night*, 53, cited in Bailey, *Paul through Mediterranean Eyes*, 373.
23. Volf, *End of Memory*, 214, cited in Bailey, *Paul through Mediterranean Eyes*, 374.

introspective moment, of the pain he may have caused to a fragile daughter by choosing to remain in an area rife with internecine conflict?[24]

There were at least eighteen scholarly reviews of *Paul through Mediterranean Eyes*. They were all positive, full of praise for Bailey's accessible writing, cultural insights, and above all, presentation of something entirely new: a rhetorical analysis of Paul's letter that found it to be a closely structured composition based on Hebrew parallelisms. Jack Barentsen, writing in *Review of Biblical Literature*, found Bailey's structural analysis "intriguing." "Did Bailey, with his Middle Eastern experience and access to oriental versions, indeed identify rhetorical patterns that have been overlooked in decades of scholarly research into rhetorical structure? This is an amazing claim."[25] Similarly, Geoffrey Turner, writing for the *Heythrop Journal*, concluded that "in the end, the rhetorical structures are so consistent in general and so all-pervasive that Bailey carries the day."[26] Michelle Lee-Barnewall, writing in the *Journal of the Evangelical Theological Society*, accepted Bailey's analysis and was ready to pursue his insights: "The issue is to what extent we should expect more clear linguistic markers to help indicate corresponding units in the large structures, especially for a document intended for what was still an essentially oral culture."[27]

Yet a number of the reviews also offered some sharp criticisms. Speaking for many, Barentsen generally praised Bailey but concluded that the jury is still out on a number of his interpretations that seem either forced or speculative. Barentsen found that "one could wish for a bit more engagement with the scholarly discussion." He felt that "sometimes Bailey pushes the parallels too far," and his "analyses of parallelisms and ring compositions are not in every case convincing." Malcolm J. Gill, writing in *Themelios*, found the results of Bailey's efforts to be mixed: "While there are times when 'ring progression' and rhetorical nuancing are evident . . . there are other times when Bailey's approach seems to override the obvious flow of the text."[28] Catherine Jones, writing for *Studies in Religion*, agreed. "The structures that Bailey suggests," she wrote, "are so complex and convoluted that such claims strain credibility."[29] Alicia J. Batten commented in *Toronto Journal of Theology* that Bailey failed

24. Bailey, *Paul through Mediterranean Eyes*, 371, 372, 374.
25. Barentsen, Review of *Paul through Mediterranean Eyes*, 365.
26. Turner, Review of *Paul through Mediterranean Eyes*, 131.
27. Lee-Barnewall, Review of *Paul through Mediterranean Eyes*, 624.
28. Gill, Review of *Paul through Mediterranean Eyes*, 61.
29. Jones, Review of *Paul through Mediterranean Eyes*, 619.

to acknowledge that other scholars have reasoned that Paul, as a writer of Greek, was following both "Greco-Roman concepts and literary patterns" as well as those of his Hebrew ancestors. Bailey's unwillingness to engage with contemporary scholars on this issue, she concluded, "constitutes a deficiency in the overall academic rigour [sic] of the book." Batten also found, as some others did, that his title was misleading. The book, she commented, is not really written from a cultural or Mediterranean perspective. Its primary contribution was the discovery of Hebrew literary structures in 1 Corinthians.[30] Others suggested that "cultural studies" denote studies drawn from the disciplines of "either cultural anthropology or critical cultural studies, both disciplines commonly referred to as 'cultural studies.'"[31] Such criticism was meant not so much to undercut the value of Bailey's work as to place it within a broader scholarly context. Another reviewer, Nicholas H. Taylor, noted that Bailey's references to contemporary scholarly works were "nearly all from the conservative evangelical end of the spectrum, and even then there are some conspicuous omissions"; consequently, and ironically, Bailey unquestioningly accepted evangelical assumptions, such as "using Acts to illuminate the life and letters of Paul."[32]

Despite these sorts of criticisms, sometimes pointed and at other times merely niggling, the book was generally well received. On January 1, 2012, the Evangelical Christian magazine *Christianity Today* recognized *Paul through Mediterranean Eyes* as the outstanding book of the year in Biblical Studies for 2011.[33] However, Bailey's discernment of chiasmic structures throughout 1 Corinthians remains controversial. His good friend David Dawson commented that "he saw them everywhere," a radical reinterpretation of Paul that many scholars decline to follow.

In Bailey's reports to FoMENTS for the years 2008 through 2011, he observed that he had continued to write five to ten articles a year and had given a little over one hundred lectures and sermons annually. He

---

30. Batten, Review of *Paul through Mediterranean Eyes*, 155–56.

31. Foster, Review of *Paul through Mediterranean Eyes*, 732; and Docherty, Review of *Paul through Mediterranean Eyes*, 314–15.

32. Taylor, Review of *Paul through Mediterranean Eyes*, 90.

33. "Book Awards," 44. *Paul through Mediterranean Eyes* was the best book in the category of "Biblical Studies."

also noted that his articles and books were being translated into Spanish, Danish, Finnish, Arabic, Chinese, Italian, and German. Though it was clear that Bailey was not slowing down, he recognized that he would not be able to maintain his current pace for many more years, and he began to dream of what FoMENTS could do to carry on his legacy.

On January 23, 2010, he met with the president of the Evangelical Theological Seminary in Cairo (ETSC), Atef Gendy, and the ETSC Professor of Theology, Darren Kennedy, at Pittsburgh Theological Seminary to discuss how FoMENTS and ETSC might work together through the Center for Middle Eastern Christianity (CMEC), which Bailey had helped to launch in 2005. The center, in fact, had been established to pursue a threefold mission: the study of Islam and Christian relations, theology, and the New Testament from a Middle Eastern perspective. Bailey naturally hoped that the organization would embrace his vision by helping to generate a Middle Eastern interpretation of the New Testament. In Bailey's subsequent report to FoMENTS about what was discussed, he imagined that ETSC would become a world center for the publication of Arabic versions of the Bible and biblical commentaries. Funds for these publication projects would be raised jointly by FoMENTS and World Mission Initiative (WMI), an organization dedicated to promoting mission that was associated with Pittsburgh Theological Seminary. The combination of FoMENTS, CMEC, ETSC, and WMI would promote the publication of the eastern fathers of the church, who were then generally forgotten or neglected.

Together, the three scholars envisioned the CMEC producing a series of books that they called "Middle Eastern Biblical Studies," which would be formally published by Dar el-Thaqafa ("The House of Culture")—a Protestant publisher in Cairo, Egypt. FoMENTS, as its name indicates, would act as a foundation, funding worthy projects that fell within its vision. It would make grants to authors for essential studies or for translations of classical works. The CMEC, in turn, would select, edit, and promote these works; and Dar el-Thaqafa would publish them. These books would include Bailey's seminal works, such as *Jesus through Middle Eastern Eyes* and *Paul through Mediterranean Eyes*. Classical Arabic books to be translated or transcribed included Ibn al-Tayyib's *Commentary on the Four Gospels*, a critical edition of Ibn al-Assal's works in English, and Moshe bar Kepha's *Commentary on Luke*. Following the meeting, Bailey wrote a letter to summarize what they had discussed and agreed upon. With Ibn al-Tayyib's Gospel commentaries in mind, Bailey anticipated that the CMEC would need a general editor, four translators (one for each of the four Gospels) working from Arabic to English, and a copy editor to correct the English texts. Excluding the Gospel texts included in Ibn al-Tayyib's commentaries, this translation would be 408 pages for Matthew, 47 for Mark, 260 for Luke, and 220 for John—a total of 935 published pages to be translated. Bailey also promised to donate his entire library to ETSC to become part of the CMEC collection. However, since he was working at that time on *Paul through Mediterranean Eyes*, he still needed his library for his ongoing scholarship. Therefore, he estimated that he would send the books to ETSC in about five years. He was then seventy-nine years old and anticipated that by age eighty-four he would no longer require his academic library because, by that time, he would have ceased to be a productive scholar.

FoMENTS faithfully proceeded apace to bring about this vision, hiring Victor Makari to translate *Jesus through Middle Eastern Eyes* into Arabic, and he would later begin work on Ibn al-Tayyib's commentaries. At the FoMENTS executive council meeting in April 2011, Victor reported on the progress he was making on translating *Jesus through Middle Eastern Eyes* and discussed plans for translating *Paul through Mediterranean Eyes*. Fully committed to this work, Victor signed a Memorandum of Understanding with FoMENTS in December 2011 in which he agreed to complete the translation of *Jesus through Middle Eastern Eyes* and serve as FoMENTS's liaison with ETSC and the CMEC in order that they might produce in tandem a series of publications. FoMENTS in turn agreed to provide him a salary of $2,000 per month for two years, beginning on January 1, 2012. Bailey wrote to congratulate Victor on the completion of *Jesus through Middle Eastern Eyes* in July 2013 and immediately inquired about his plans to begin the translation of Ibn al-Tayyib's commentary on the Gospels. In the FoMENTs executive council meeting that reviewed Bailey's work for the year 2012, Bailey announced that he would be stepping down from his position as president of FoMENTS in two years, when he reached the age of eighty-five on November 24, 2015.

Though FoMENTS was moving forward to achieve Bailey's vision, the CMEC never seems to have generated any formal plan to complete the task. The problem at the CMEC may have been that those present at the January 2010 meeting did not have direct responsibility for the goals that had been set. Darren Kennedy as a professor of theology had no role in the CMEC, and Atef Gendy as the president of the seminary had no hands-on responsibility for the center's day-to-day work. Consequently, the center's goals were allowed to drift. When the CMEC was rededicated on January 2, 2012, Bailey and Victor Makari were invited to attend, but neither were asked to speak formally, suggesting that Bailey's vision was no longer positioned front and center. The following year, Wageeh Mikhail was appointed to be the director of the center. Having just obtained a PhD in Christian-Muslim Relations in the Middle Ages, he seemed to be an ideal candidate for the position. As the director of the center from 2013 to 2019, he organized a number of interfaith gatherings, ecumenical conferences, and public lectures. He also oversaw the translation and publication of seven books on theological topics. Of the threefold vision that launched the CMEC, Wageeh had shown a strong interest in pursuing theology and to a lesser extent Muslim-Christians relations, but he had shown little interest in reinterpreting the New Testament through the lens of Middle Eastern culture. His accomplishments, though not inconsiderable, show little indication that he had bought into the vision cast in January 2010. When he resigned his position in 2019 to take up another post outside the seminary, little or nothing of Bailey's dream had been accomplished. Bailey and FoMENTS had been left in the frustrating position of observing the work of the CMEC from six thousand miles away and not being able to influence it.

At the FoMENTS executive council meeting at the beginning of 2012, Bailey raised the question as to what the future of FoMENTS should be. Should it remain a foundation that meets once a year to grant funds for worthy publication projects? Should it continue for another two years until Bailey retired and then decide what its future course would be? Should it simply disperse all its remaining funds and shut down at the end of 2015? Nothing seems to have been decided at that meeting. Instead, the members of FoMENTS continued to meet and dream of possible publications though they were impotent to forge a better relationship with the CMEC, the very organization on which they had laid their hopes to realize Bailey's vision.

20

The Shepherd King's Thousand-Year Prologue

2011–16

> At the cross the finest system of justice in the ancient world (Rome) combined with the leaders of the finest religion the world had ever known (Judaism) to destroy this good man [Jesus].
>
> —Kenneth E. Bailey, *The Good Shepherd*

IN THE LAST YEARS of Bailey's life, he looked on the slow decline of the PCUSA with the heartache commonly associated with the passing of close relatives or friends. For much of his professional life he had been at odds with his denomination, angry at its leaders who seemed to scorn or ignore him, perturbed by its steady decline in numbers since the 1960s, and alarmed at its increasingly theological liberalness. The last concern, for him, was highlighted in this period of his life by the church's changing stance toward homosexuality. When Bailey wrote or spoke out on this issue, it was without bitterness, spite, or sarcasm. His comments were measured and analytical, and one has the feeling that he wrote with a certain weary resignation.

Although the issues of homosexual ordination and marriage were ostensibly theological in nature, the church was clearly influenced by the groundswell of change in American culture that was occurring at this time. The issue of same-sex marriage in the United States had been working its way through the courts, and on June 26, 2015, the Supreme Court ruled in *Obergefell v. Hodges* that the Due Process and Equal Protection Clauses of the Fourteenth Amendment to the Constitution required that all states recognize the marriages of same-sex couples.

The issue of ordaining homosexuals had first been raised among Presbyterians in 1976 at the church's 188th General Assembly, which directed that a task force be established to study the issue. The task force issued a report in January 1978, which included a minority report.[1] The 190th General Assembly of 1978 was the first to grapple with the issue, and over the ensuing thirty-three years the debate continued, being heard at every subsequent General Assembly throughout those years. Evangelicals maintained that the Bible was univocal, from Genesis to Revelation, in its condemnation of the practice of homosexuality. In their view, those with a homosexual orientation should be welcomed into the church, but the practice of homosexuality was inconsistent with the Scriptures and must be condemned as sin.

The Presbyterian Church continued to debate the issue until the church's 219th General Assembly in Minneapolis, held in July 2010, took the decisive step of adopting Amendment 10-A in its *Book of Order*, the church's constitution, which allowed homosexuals in same-sex relationships to be ordained as ministers, elders, and deacons in the church. The amendment was then taken to the denomination's presbyteries, which voted on the issue one at a time over the ensuing ten months. In May 2011 the Twin Cities Presbytery cast the deciding vote. With the completion of this vote, 205 presbyteries had voted yes and 56 no, with 3 abstentions. The 221st General Assembly in Detroit, held in June 2014, took the next logical step, voting to change the definition of marriage as defined in the denomination's *Book of Order*. The General Assembly had clarified this issue as recently as 1997 when it adopted two amendments to the *Book of Order* that required ministers to live in "either fidelity within the covenant of marriage between a man and a woman" or "in chastity in singleness."[2] The 2014 General Assembly amended the definition of marriage from being between "a man and a woman" to being between "two people."[3] The Assembly also voted to allow ministers in the church

---

1. "Statement and Recommendations" in *The Church and Homosexuality*.
2. *Constitution of the Presbyterian Church (USA)*, G6.016.
3. *Constitution of the Presbyterian Church (USA)*, W4.9001.

to marry same-sex couples in states where this was legal, which a majority of presbyteries approved by March of 2015. Hence, the PCUSA joined the United Church of Christ, the Evangelical Lutheran Church in America, and the Episcopal Church in deciding to accept openly gay ministers and church leaders and to marry same-sex couples.

After the presbyteries voted to adopt Amendment 10-A in May 2011, Bailey addressed the issue of the ordination of homosexuals in "A Tale of Elephants and the Mouse: Presbyterians, 10-A, and the World Church," a short article he wrote for Presbyterians for Renewal that was published on its website on July 14, 2011. In the article Bailey looked at the decision of the church to change its ordination standards from the perspective of a world Christian. He observed that the Roman Catholic Church (with over a billion members), the Global South (with 60 percent of the world's Christians), the Eastern Orthodox Church (with over 300 million members), and the world of Islam (with over a billion adherents, though he does not supply a number) would reject this decision, seeing it as opposed to biblical teaching and the tradition of 2,000 years of church history.

While in the past the Western church was the "superpower" of the Christian world, this was no longer the case. Bailey observed that the Western church had become a shrinking mouse among the elephants.[4] American Presbyterians might delude themselves into thinking that their actions would provide leadership to the world church, but Bailey utterly rejected this possibility. The little mouse of American Presbyterianism, he wrote, has decided to "run down the hill away from the elephants," but the elephants will not follow the mouse's lead. Bailey also saw the church's decision as a departure from Scripture that would have missional repercussions. American missionaries went to Africa in the nineteenth century, teaching that Africans must put aside polygamy as practiced in their cultures because it was inconsistent with the Scriptures. Now Western Christians were embracing homosexuality in step with their culture but inconsistent with biblical teaching. The hypocrisy was glaring and would be seen as a betrayal.

There was also the reaction of Islam to consider. Western scholars, Bailey wrote, have called into question "the authenticity of the gospel

---

4. Mission enthusiasts would have appreciated the analogy as a clever variation on the well-known story by Miriam Adeney in which Western Christians are depicted as elephants and African Christians as mice. See Adeney, "When Elephants Dance, the Mouse May Die," in Berry, *INTO ALL THE WORLD*, 86–89. This is based on a longer paper, "When Elephants Dance: Thoughts on Short Term Missions," commissioned by the Fellowship of Short-Term Missions Agencies.

accounts of the life and teachings of Jesus," and Muslims have understood them to agree with their longstanding charge that the Gospels have been corrupted. Muslim preachers can now add to their arguments against Christianity that its own leaders decided to set aside what the Scriptures clearly teach. Finally, Bailey expressed the concern that the rejection of biblical standards on homosexuality raises the issue of whether there are any standards that the church holds to be inviolable. If homosexuality was now permissible, why not polygamy? And he might have added consensual incest and euthanasia, among others, to a list of dubious practices. Bailey then responded to liberal Presbyterians who argued, as Jack Rogers had in *Jesus, the Bible, and Homosexuality* (2009),[5] for a historical analogy between the acceptance of homosexuality now and the issues in the past of slavery and women's ordination. Bailey argued that these were false analogies. The apostle Paul recognized the reality of slavery in his culture, and he offered pastoral advice to slaves, telling them to obey their masters. Not to have done so, Bailey pointed out, would have been an offense warranting crucifixion. But Paul also urged Christian slaves to seek freedom if they could. In the same way, the Bible does not oppose women in leadership. Bailey noted the examples of female leaders in the New Testament church such as Lydia and Phoebe. It is not the Bible, he argued, but Western culture that has opposed women in leadership. In other words, there is plenty of biblical warrant for opposing slavery and favoring the ordination of women while the same cannot be said for the ordination of homosexuals or (the next issue then down the line) same-sex marriage. As Robert Gagnon had written, the Bible is "unequivocal" in its condemnation of homosexuality and in its positive teaching that marriage was intended for men and women alone.[6]

Various groups had recently arisen within the Presbyterian Church USA that opposed the church's decisions on homosexuality and implicitly threatened schism. One of these called itself the Fellowship of Presbyterians. Though conservative evangelicals in this organization felt betrayed by the PCUSA for having abandoned unambiguous biblical teachings, the Fellowship studiously avoided denouncing its opponents as apostates. Instead, it sought a way to remain in communion with the PCUSA while organizing a fellowship of like-minded evangelicals within the church. On August 25–26, 2011, the Fellowship of Presbyterians met

---

5. Rogers, *Bible, and Homosexuality*.
6. Bailey, "Tale of Elephants."

The Shepherd King's Thousand-Year Prologue

in Minneapolis to consider what to do in light of the of the church's decision on homosexual ordination.

Bailey was invited to address the meeting during the morning worship service on Friday, August 26. The title of his address was "Reprocessing Anger into Grace." Bailey was a well-known figure to this group of conservatives in the church and was warmly applauded when introduced to the plenary session. Like many of those present, he was angry with the Presbyterian Church, which seemed to be more responsive to developments in American culture than to the timeless—and often countercultural—teachings of Scripture. What was one to do with the anger resulting from feelings of abandonment and betrayal? Bailey avoided such blunt language that day. Instead, he diplomatically referred to the anger Presbyterians felt as a "diminished sense of belonging in our own spiritual home." He then marshaled a number of biblical stories in which anger might have led to reprisals, revenge, or destructive behavior. In the parable of the great feast (Luke 14:15–24), a nobleman might have struck out against the invited guests to his banquet who gave insulting excuses for declining to attend at the last moment. Instead of retaliating, however, he chose to become missional, sending his servant into the streets to invite the poor, blind, and lame to his feast. Hence, he reprocessed anger into grace. Similarly, in the parable of the vineyard (Luke 20:9–18), a nobleman's tenants refused to pay their rent and even assailed his servants when they went to collect it. Though the nobleman might have sent armed men to take back what was his, instead he sent his beloved son, seeking to shame the tenants into right behavior. By choosing an option that left his son vulnerable, he reprocessed anger into grace. Finally, in the parable of the prodigal son (Luke 15:11–32), a father who had been disgraced by a feckless son might have rejected the son who had scornfully rejected him. Instead, he waited patiently and, when he saw his disheveled son returning home, ran to meet him, welcomed him affectionately, and restored him completely to the family. This, however, was a costly love on several levels, not the least being the shame he brought upon himself in his village. Yet in assuming this shame, he reprocessed anger into grace, restoring a lost and broken son.

That these were not simply idealistic biblical stories for Bailey is apparent in that he had learned to apply the lesson in his own life many times. When his parents left him in his junior year in high school and did not reappear until he graduated from college, he committed himself to being a more attentive father if ever given the chance. When the government of Egypt denied him a visa, he did not shake the dust of the country from his feet but waited patiently for the government to reverse itself. And when the Synod of Syria and Lebanon abandoned him, Bailey did not retaliate. Instead, he maintained some connection with the Synod as best he could until eventually the relationship was entirely mended. Bailey had long felt that as a missionary he had been ignored and marginalized by the PCUSA, and that sense of betrayal was compounded by the church's recent decision on the issue of the ordination of homosexuals. In short, the lesson of "Reprocessing Anger into Grace," which Bailey had learned in his study of the Scriptures and had applied at key moments in his personal life, was one he now commended to the church.

The Fellowship, for its part, seeking to avoid schism and remain in the PCUSA, proposed various ways that it might remain within the denomination. For example, the church might become congregational in nature so that individual congregations within the larger body could maintain their own convictions while not separating from the main body, or the congregations associated with the Fellowship might form a separate presbytery within the PCUSA, hence establishing a differentiation while avoiding complete separation. The PCUSA, however, ignored these overtures. More from exhaustion than conviction, it simply allowed many of the Fellowship churches to drift away. Bailey was in great sympathy with the Fellowship of Presbyterians, but he never abandoned the Presbyterian Church and died within its fold.

To celebrate their sixtieth wedding anniversary on June 12, 2012, Ken and Mickey invited a few family members and close friends to join them to mark the occasion. The family members were Pat Milligan, Frank Bailey, John and Susan Bailey, and Sara Bailey Makari. The friends were Bill and Karen Crooks, Tim and Elizabeth Daigle, Dave and Joani Dawson, Mary Louise Ireland, and Bill and Carole McKnight. The group of sixteen had dinner in a private room at the Tuscany Square Ristorante in New Castle and then retired to the Dawsons' home to watch the documentary *The Shot Felt 'Round the World*, which told the story of the Salk Vaccine for polio and included several on-camera interviews with Mickey. Ken noted in the invitation, "It has taken us five years to acquire a copy, and seeing it (at last) we would like to share it with you, our dear family and friends."[7]

Sara was understandably concerned, as she had been for some years, about her parents' health. In February and March of 2011 Mickey had had back surgery and Ken had another minor surgical procedure. When he continued to give lectures and accept new speaking engagements in 2012, Sara pleaded with her father to slow down. "Please, please," she wrote, "be wise about the speaking engagements you decide to accept in the next year as you and I have to make *The Good Shepherd* your finest monograph yet."[8] As it was, it was not until late November that Bailey had sufficiently completed his various self-imposed tasks so that he could begin to work seriously on his newest project.[9] His good friend David Dawson recalls that Bailey would consider this his finest book.

Bailey's last book, *The Good Shepherd: A Thousand-Year Journey from Psalm 23 to the New Testament* (2014), is the culminating achievement of his long fascination with the theme of Jesus as the good shepherd, having by this time written four books on the parables in Luke 15, which begin with Jesus' story of the shepherd who goes in search of a lost sheep. The book looks at nine key biblical texts concerning the good shepherd. These include four from the Old Testament (Ps 23; Jer 23:1–8; Ezek 34; and Zech 10:2–12) and five from the New Testament (Luke 15:1–19; Mark 6:7–52; Matt 18:10–14; John 10:1–18; and 1 Pet 5:1–4). Though there are hundreds of verses in the Bible that concern sheep and shepherds, Bailey chooses these nine texts because they are connected by a common theme. They are, he writes, "like notes in a tune that is known to the various singers of the biblical song of the good shepherd."[10]

After years of promoting the use of Middle Eastern sources for the interpretation of the Scriptures, Bailey, in the preface to his final book, cites the extensive Middle Eastern texts that he consulted in the course of his research. He begins with a list of monographs written by Middle

---

7. Ken and Mickey to Frank Bailey et al., May 7, 2012, Bailey Papers, box 28, folder 8.

8. Sara to Baba [Ken], June 17, 2012, Bailey Papers, box 28, folder 8.

9. Ken to Bruce and Barbara [Bailey], November 28, 2011, Bailey Papers, box 28, folder 8.

10. Bailey, *Good Shepherd*, 22, 32.

Easterners or men who spent time in the region, all of whom had personal experience in shepherding. These include M. P. Krikorian, Faddoul Moghabghab, George M. Lamsa, Stephen A. Haboush, Abraham Mitrie Rihbany, William Thompson, and Eric F. F. Bishop. He also states that he used several Arabic-language commentaries, including works by the eleventh-century scholar Ibn al-Tayyib, the twelfth-century scholar Ibn al-Salibi, the twentieth-century Coptic Orthodox scholar Matta al-Miskin, and the twentieth-century Protestant scholar Ibrahim Sa'id. In addition, he utilized four Arabic versions of the Old Testament, twenty Arabic versions of the New Testament, and one twelfth-century Armenian commentary on the Psalms. He pays tribute too to his Middle Eastern students at NEST who, over a twenty-year period, provided him with valuable insights into shepherding. Finally, he informs his readers that he spoke personally and at length with a number of shepherds about the management of sheep during his decades in the Middle East.

When he had worked through the Old Testament and the Synoptic Gospels, Bailey came to John 10:1–18, arguably the fullest development of the good shepherd theme in all of Scripture. He assumes that the passage here was originally crafted by Jesus but then "shaped" by John and/or his disciples. In the first part of this parable, John 10:1–10, Bailey imagines that the scene takes place early in the morning in a small Middle Eastern village. If a family had only a few sheep, they could be kept in the house during the night. But if it had ten or more, they would need to be kept in a village sheepfold with six-foot-high walls. The shepherd calls the sheep and they come into the street. New sheep need to learn the shepherd's unique call because in the street there will be sheep from other flocks as well as people and various kinds of traffic. The flocks mingle, but the shepherds' calls soon separate them. Out in the wilderness, the shepherd will construct a makeshift sheepfold from stones in the field, and he will lie across the entrance during the night, becoming in effect the door of the sheepfold. This is the practice behind Jesus' odd metaphor, "I am the gate for the sheep" (John 10:7).

Jesus warns his listeners that the sheep are threatened by thieves and robbers. In the three hundred years before Jesus, Bailey observes, Israel was endangered by many such men: Judas the Galilean and Theudas (Acts 5:36–37), the Hasidu, the Maccabees, and the gods of Hellenism. The same can be said for the modern age. "With the information technology that surrounds us," Bailey explains, "never in human history have there been as many divergent, strident voices calling loudly for the attention and loyalty of 'the flock.' Daily the sheep must consciously seek to ignore those noises and listen for the voice of their good shepherd and follow it."[11]

The shepherd leads the sheep out from the sheepfold, through the village, and into the wilderness. He calls them as a flock, but he has a few favorite sheep, whom he calls by name. From the wilderness sheepfold, "the sheep will go in and out and find pasture" (John 10:9)—in other words, the shepherd has found a good green valley in which to pasture the flock. The sheep come and go at will while the Shepherd, Jesus, watches over them. Theologically, this is "life abundant" (John 10:10).

The next part of the parable, John 10:11–18, has three major sections that are made up of shorter poetic units, or strophes as Bailey refers to them. In the third section, strophe A has seven cameos (paired lines) in the inverted parallel pattern. It concerns the good shepherd who lays down his life for the sheep. This section is the first place where the shepherd is described explicitly as "the good shepherd." He is good in the sense of being "morally good," "noble," or "beautiful." This strophe alludes to a great battle between the good shepherd and a wolf. The hired servants will run away rather than face such danger. But the good shepherd is known by the Father and knows the sheep and "lays down his life for his sheep" (John 10:11). Bailey notes that the word "to know" means to know intimately. "This much is clear. When anyone pays a huge price to save me, that savior thereby creates a special relationship with me." The reference to a "hired hand" in Jesus' parable is code for the Jewish "priestly establishment." The wolf is code for the Roman Empire. Curiously, the scene of the fight between the good shepherd and the wolf is missing. Why does Jesus leave out this crucial scene? "The modern film industry," Bailey explains, "would make this scene the central focus of the story. Not so the authors of the New Testament, who in describing the cross, refuse to participate in the 'pornography of suffering.'" He continues, "In the New Testament the brutality of the cross is never described."[12] It is difficult to imagine that in this passage Bailey is not thinking of Mel Gibson's 2004 film, *The Passion of the Christ*, which many critics found objectionable for its prolonged depiction of the savage violence of scourging and crucifixion.

---

11. Bailey, *Good Shepherd*, 219, 222–23.
12. Bailey, *Good Shepherd*, 227, 232, 235.

In John 10:16, the third and final strophe in this series, there are three cameos. Here Jesus says that he has other sheep besides Israel but that in the end there will be one flock and one shepherd. Bailey notes that the last cameo in this strophe "affirms 'one flock' but not 'one sheepfold.'" From this he draws an ecumenical inference:

> Our differing languages, cultures, styles of worship and theological heritages all deserve to be preserved and nourished. Let the Coptic Orthodox rejoice in Athanasius, the Lutherans in Luther, the Latin Catholics in Thomas Aquinas, the Syrian Orthodox in Ephrem the Syrian, the Orthodox in Chrysostom and the Reformed tradition in Calvin and Barth.[13]

In his postscript, Bailey summarizes his scholarship. The Western mind, he explains, naturally turns to statements like the Nicene Creed to declare Christian belief. In contrast, Jesus in Luke 15 turned to metaphorical language to explain his self-understanding. Bailey avers, "In the inevitable coming theological interface with Islam, surely this Christology from the mouth of Jesus has the potential to bypass centuries-old roadblocks to understanding and authentically communicate afresh." He concludes, Jesus' "parables and dramatic actions studied here, edited as they are by the Gospel authors, present Jesus as a thinker, not merely as a doer; a theologian as well as an ethicist."[14] With this statement, Bailey recapitulates the key insights of his life's scholarly work and brings to a close his career as an interpreter of the New Testament, which he had begun over fifty years before.

There were at least ten scholarly reviews of Bailey's book, all of them generally positive. They especially appreciated his use of Arabic, Armenian, and Syriac Middle Eastern sources. Sherif Gendy, writing for *Westminster Theological Journal*, summed up the general reaction well: "In spite of . . . occasional weaknesses, this worthwhile book is lucidly written, accessible, and comprehensive. Bailey's astute insights, enriched by his unique access to ancient commentaries and familiarity with Middle Eastern culture, bring new light to our understanding of this biblical theme and reveal a sophisticated amalgam of theological and pastoral threads related to the good shepherd motif."[15] John Willis, writing for the *Catholic Biblical Quarterly*, was even more effusive: Bailey's "sensitive,

---

13. Bailey, *Good Shepherd*, 238.
14. Bailey, *Good Shepherd*, 273.
15. Gendy, Review of *Good Shepherd*, 402.

penetrating, profound, perceptive, unexpected, unique insights and comprehension of the functions and roles of shepherds and sheep motivate thinkers to gain fresh understandings of the good shepherd and his flock."[16] Others agreed and recommended the book for scholars, pastors, and laypeople.

The criticisms of the book, issued amid general praise, were mostly mild and pointed to specific faults, not to systemic weaknesses. Several noted that Bailey's work was not exhaustive on the subject of the good shepherd in the Old Testament. Gendy observed that Bailey neglected a number of Israel's leaders who were seen as shepherds of their people: Moses, the judges, and the kings.[17] Some gave the by-now-common complaint that Bailey had failed to engage in sufficient form and redaction criticism of the Gospel writers.[18] Andrew Sargent, writing for *Criswell Theological Review*, thought that Bailey was uncertain about the identity of his audience. He concluded that the rhetorical analysis was suited for an academic audience and the "light commentary" for laypeople. The "audience confusion," he felt, probably limited the audience to "reasonably educated pastors."[19] Alan Le Grys's concluding comments, in a review for the *Journal for the Study of the New Testament*, were the most scathing and dismissive. He thought that the book lacked sufficient "critical analysis" for a scholarly audience: "This book will certainly appeal to readers who share the author's conservative evangelical presuppositions, which are simply read back into the text, alongside a certain amount of romantic glossing, speculative exegesis, and reading of the historical Jesus which many scholars would regard as naïve. There is certainly some thoughtful reflection; but this book is more likely, perhaps, to be a resource for conservative church groups rather than a wider academic audience."[20] Silviu Tatu, writing for *Themelios*, concluded on an equally condescending note: "The volume will prove to be stimulating devotional reading and a useful tool for preaching."[21] Bailey was not entirely inured to such frosty or patronizing comments but rarely commented on them outside the family, seeing them perhaps as the inevitable flotsam and jetsam to be

---

16. Willis, Review of *Good Shepherd*, 515.
17. Gendy, Review of *Good Shepherd*, 402.
18. For example, see Weaver, Review of *Good Shepherd*, 103.
19. Sargent, Review of *Good Shepherd*, 143.
20. Le Grys, Review of *Good Shepherd*, 12.
21. Tatu, Review of *Good Shepherd*, 269.

expected from reviewers holding widely divergent theological perspectives from his own.[22]

⁓

After the completion of Bailey's last book in 2014, the Baileys slowed down considerably. Mickey had suffered from rheumatoid arthritis over the previous dozen years, and in January 2015, she experienced a health crisis and was hospitalized at Sharon Regional Medical Center. "We almost lost her," Bailey wrote, and "We are still struggling to recover." Mickey, in fact, could now move about only with the aid of a walker. Given the Baileys' failing health and ages, Mickey being now eighty-five and Ken eighty-four, they decided to leave their beloved home on the hill in New Wilmington and move to Shenango on the Green, a Presbyterian retirement home in New Wilmington, which was only a few miles away and just across the street from the New Wilmington Presbyterian Church and Westminster College, where the New Wilmington Mission Conference[23] was held every summer. They would have their own apartment in the retirement complex in the Independent Living section of the community.[24]

Bailey grew progressively more fatigued in the last six years of his life, though he was not aware of any specific health problem. However, in February 2016 he was diagnosed as having an aggressive form of leukemia, a cancer of the blood. Though it had probably been developing in his body for a long time, his battle with cancer would be short-lived, only about ten weeks. In early May a visitor dropped in on Bailey in the hospital and found him lost in thought and asked what was distracting him. Bailey said that at age eighty-five it was time for him to review his life and write a memoir. As he lay in bed that day, he was organizing chapters in his mind for this final work.[25]

---

22. In reviewing this section of the manuscript, his daughter, Sara, commented that "my father took some of these criticisms very hard indeed."

23. Under Don Dawson's leadership in 2006, the name of the conference was changed from the New Wilmington Missionary Conference to the New Wilmington Mission Conference.

24. Uncle Ken and Aunt Mickey to Bruce, Allen Bailey, August 20, 2015, Bailey Papers, box 28, folder 9.

25. This story was told by his pastor, William D. Crooks at Ken's memorial service. See online, "Dr. Kenneth E. Bailey, Memorial Service."

In mid-May, Bailey occupied a bed in the last of four hospitals in Pittsburgh in which he had sought treatment. When it was apparent that there was little more that doctors could do, he decided that he wanted to return home. Shenango on the Green, however, did not have any nursing home beds available at that time. Therefore, on May 20, he was transferred to Grove Manor, a healthcare facility in Grove City that provides inpatient nursing care and is only a twenty-three-minute drive from New Wilmington. Naturally, this was a great disappointment to Mickey, who would have preferred to have had her husband close to her and in the same building. Cameron Bailey, now in his last year at Westminster College, visited his grandfather on May 22 at Grove Manor.[26] The next day, one of the last people to speak with him was his good friend David Dawson, the former executive presbyter of Shenango Presbytery. Bailey had recently seen the seventeen-minute video *Blessed Be Egypt My People* about the murder of twenty Egyptian Coptic Christians and one Ghanan Christian by an ISIL-affiliated militia in Libya, which identified itself as the Tripoli Province of ISIL.[27] The men were construction workers who had been kidnapped in the city of Sirte, Libya. On February 15, 2015, they were beheaded on the beach near the Al Mahary Hotel in Sirte. In the video Bailey watched, one of the people who spoke about the meaning of this event was Anne Zaki, professor of homiletics at the Evangelical Theological Seminary in Cairo (ETSC). Bailey knew her as the daughter of Emile Zaki, his old friend who had been the chaplain for the pre-seminary program at Assiut College in the 1960s. He also knew Anne from the time in January 2012 when he had traveled to Cairo for the rededication ceremony of the Center for Middle Eastern Christianity (CMEC) at ETSC and from the two times that he had spoken at the Calvin Worship Symposium, at Calvin College in Grand Rapids, Michigan—one as recently as 2014. Recognizing her talent and potential as a leader, he said to Dawson that the church must continue to encourage women leaders in the Middle East and urged him to invite her to participate in the work of FoMENTS. Also, in the nursing home room that day were Victor and Sara Makari, and John and Susan Bailey. Dawson briefly attended to them before looking back at Ken. In the interval, without the least warning, his friend had quietly slipped away. Bailey died on May 23, 2016.

---

26. Leslie Bailey interview, February 19, 2023.

27. ISIL is an acronym for the Islamic State of Iraq and the Levant. It is also known as ISIS, the Islamic State of Iraq and Syria. The video is Kim, *Blessed Be Egypt My People.*

Two days after Bailey's death an obituary appeared in *Christianity Today*, the leading evangelical journal in the United States. Though it briefly reviewed Bailey's life, its title captured the significance of his life in a few words: "The Scholar Who Made Jesus Middle Eastern Again."[28] The most impressive and insightful tribute to Bailey was an article by his former student and long-time friend and colleague Gary M. Burge, then professor of New Testament at Wheaton College and Graduate School, that appeared in the *International Bulletin of Mission Research*. For Burge, Bailey was not only a missionary to the Middle East but also "an academic missionary" to the scholars of the West. Burge explained that Bailey had called upon Western scholars to understand the Scriptures through the lens of first-century Middle Eastern culture, which can be recovered through "a judicious use of anthropology, archaeology, ancient literature, and the cultural echoes still found in villages of the non-Westernized Middle East."[29]

Bailey's memorial service was held on June 2, 2016, at 1:00 in the afternoon at Trinity Presbyterian Church in the town of Mercer, Pennsylvania. David Dawson, who offered his reflections on the life of his friend during the service, observed that Bailey would not have wanted eulogies. Bailey's pastor, the Reverend Dr. William Crooks, appropriately titled the event in the bulletin a "Service of Witness to the Resurrection and Thanksgiving for the Life and Ministry of Kenneth E. Bailey." The church was full that day with Bailey's family, friends, and admirers—the latter including many pastors whom he had influenced over the years. His daughter, Sara, and her husband, Victor, who worked in Bethlehem, Israel-Palestine, were among the mourners. Victor, the first speaker that day, read the 23rd Psalm in Arabic, which he said was a "compass and creed" for Bailey, who kept an Arabic copy on a piece of papyrus that he had framed and placed on the wall of his office so that he could see it every day. Another speaker was Dr. Atef Gendy, the president of ETSC who had flown from Egypt to be present for the occasion. Gendy referred to Bailey as his scholarly mentor whom he greatly admired as an interpreter of the parables of Jesus. When David Dawson spoke, he was careful to remind listeners of Bailey's importance as a biblical scholar but also of the reality that the scholarly world had not yet fully taken the measure of the man. He observed that in 2001 James A. Walther,

---

28. Shellnutt, "Died: Kenneth E. Bailey."
29. Burge, "Kenneth E. Bailey: An Ambassador," 152–59.

professor of New Testament at Pittsburgh Theological Seminary, the founder and first author of the Kerygma Bible Series and a coauthor of *1 Corinthians* in the Anchor Bible commentary series, said, "Bailey's work will be discovered and become widely influential fifty years from now." Current Western scholars, he implied, were simply not yet equipped to appreciate or evaluate Bailey's contribution. Dawson also cited Dale E. Allison, formerly professor of New Testament at Pittsburgh Theological Seminary and currently professor of New Testament at Princeton Theological Seminary, to enlarge on this point. He paraphrased Allison's comments on Bailey in this way: "It is beyond him to evaluate Bailey's work because he, like virtually all biblical scholars in the Western church, is not fluent in Arabic nor can he read the ancient Aramaic and Syriac as Ken did." Bailey was laid to rest next to his son, David Bailey, at Fair Oaks Cemetery in New Wilmington. His tombstone, which was elegantly designed by Leslie Bailey, includes the opening phrase of Psalm 23: "The Lord is my shepherd." It also has engraved upon it the Jerusalem Cross, one large cross surrounded by four smaller crosses meant to be suggestive of the four corners of the earth and, therefore, the worldwide cause of Christian mission.[30]

A second memorial service was held on Sunday, October 9, 2016, at the Near East School of Theology (NEST). The service at the seminary had been postponed until the beginning of the new academic year so that many of Bailey's former students and the leaders of the church could attend. Sara and Victor, in nearby Bethlehem, were invited and in attendance that day too. George Sabra, the president of NEST, was the first of six speakers to pay tribute to Bailey in the service. Sabra noted that NEST is now often identified in the West and around the world as the school where Ken Bailey taught; hence, he helped to make NEST known. Sabra said that he planned to ask that the seminary's chapel be renamed in his honor.[31]

Sabra was successful, and the Kenneth E. Bailey Chapel was formally dedicated on November 24, 2021—when Bailey would have been ninety-one years old. Speakers that day included the general secretaries of the National Evangelical Synod of Syria and Lebanon (NESSL) and the Fellowship of Middle East Evangelical Churches. Speaking for the NESSL, the Reverend Joseph Kassab observed that Bailey had left Lebanon in

---

30. The service can be viewed online at "Dr. Kenneth E. Bailey, Memorial Service."
31. The service can be viewed online at "Near East School of Theology—Memorial."

1985 not only because of the violence and danger to Westerners at that time but because of the poor relations he had with the Synod. In 2005 he wrote a letter of reconciliation to Bailey on behalf of the Synod and invited him to Lebanon the next year, a trip not then possible because of ongoing violence in the country. However, Bailey did travel to Beirut in 2007 on the occasion of the seventy-fifth anniversary of the founding of NEST and was the main speaker for the event. He returned to NEST again in 2011 to lead the Continuing Education Seminar on a study of 1 Corinthians based on his book *Paul through Mediterranean Eyes*. Kassab was pleased that, long before his death, Bailey had reconciled with NEST, an institution he had served for twenty years.[32] Bailey's forbearance, a character trait so often on display in his long life, had in this instance been warmly rewarded.

Figure 32. Ken relaxing in the living room of the Baileys'
New Wilmington home, February 2004.

---

32. The dedication of the Kenneth E. Bailey Chapel at NEST can be viewed online at "Bailey Chapel—Dedication."

Author's Note and Acknowledgments

BAILEY ESTABLISHED THE FOUNDATION for Middle Eastern New Testament Studies, or FoMENTS, to support his work, and after his death, the men and women of this organization have faithfully sought to advance his vision by supporting scholars in the United States and Egypt. I owe them a debt of gratitude for making possible my investigation of the life of Ken Bailey by providing a generous grant to cover the entire cost of renting an apartment in New Haven, Connecticut, for a year so that I could conduct research at the Special Collections section of the Yale Divinity School library, where the Bailey Papers are held. I would especially like to thank the chairperson of FoMENTS, the Reverend Dr. David Dawson, for recommending me to FoMENTS as a biographer. The Dawsons, David and his wife, Joani, also graciously opened their home to me in New Wilmington, Pennsylvania, as I regularly made the fourteen-hour drive back and forth between my home in Louisville, Kentucky, and my newly acquired apartment in New Haven. Fortunately, this is generally an enjoyable trip because of the beautiful countryside, though it sometimes became wearying due to traffic or inclement weather. But whether pleasing or unpleasant, I always knew that in New Wilmington, roughly at the halfway point of my journey, I could look forward to a warm welcome, a nourishing meal, and engaging conversation at the "pleasant Arbour" that is the Dawson home. David Dawson, it should also be noted, is a close friend of the Bailey family, who undertook the mammoth tasking of preparing the Bailey Papers to be shipped to Yale, gave many hours over the period of a year to cataloging and packing boxes of Bailey's extensive theological library to send to ETSC in Egypt, and introduced me to Mickey Bailey.

I am, as well, grateful to others who helped to make my study successful. Since the bulk of the research for this book was conducted at the Special Collections section of the Yale Divinity School library, I owe a special thanks to Scott Libson, Martha Smalley, Joan Duffy, and Abigail Kromminga whose professionalism and friendliness made researching the Bailey Papers a rewarding as well as a pleasurable experience. I would also like to thank Charlene Peacock and Jennifer Barr of the Presbyterian Historical Society in Philadelphia for making accessible to me the papers of the American Mission in Egypt as well as the official files kept by the Presbyterian Church on Ewing M. Bailey, Kenneth E. Bailey, and Ethel Jean Bailey, and for patiently and graciously guiding me through their archival system. Finally, some of my secondary research was conducted at the libraries of Louisville Presbyterian Theological Seminary and Pittsburgh Theological Seminary, whose librarians are reliably professional and courteous.

This biography has been based, to a large extent, on the letters contained in the Kenneth E. Bailey Papers at the Yale Divinity School library. I am fortunate that the Baileys were inveterate and dedicated letter writers, producing in general during their years in mission service at least one letter a month, often two, and sometimes more. The letters of Ken and Mickey, which I have relied on the most heavily, were usually each two pages of single-spaced type. They always made six or seven carbon copies of their letters and sent them to family members, retaining one for their records. Often these copies were made on onion skin paper or on the back of previously used paper. Sometimes the copy was so faint that it was difficult to read. On one particularly crucial letter the typing appeared inverted on the page, like Leonardo da Vinci's mirror writing, but I found I could read it if I held the onion skin paper up to the light and read it from the reverse side. But whatever the condition of the letters, I relied so much on them to create the narrative of this book that it would be inconceivable to have produced it in its present form without them. In fact, if Ken and Mickey Bailey had collaborated on a memoir of their lives, I would like to think that they would have produced a narrative very similar to my own.

Since the Bailey Papers have been so important to this biography, a few words should be said about the writing to be found there. What might immediately strike, and perhaps shock, the reader about Ken Bailey's letters is his often crude and erratic spelling, which may have been due to the mild dyslexia from which he suffered. He could write plain

Author's Note and Acknowledgments

for plane, picknick for picnic, roop for rope, prophet for profit, coffey for coffee, male for mail, stoor for store, made for maid, seaders for ceders, Cypress for Cyprus, Surly for Shirley, dinamight for dynamite, died for dyed, cheleshays for clichés. He preferred typing because his handwriting could be difficult to follow, but he was a poor typist whose uncooperative fingers could produce strange, unpredictable arrangements of letters that are only decipherable from the context. On occasion he approached letter writing the way he might have engaged in a long rambling conversation with a close friend with whom he was entirely at ease—that is, with false starts, digressions, and long blocks of words with multiple and unrelated subjects. As thoughts came quickly to mind, he would often abandon traditional punctuation, simply typing dashes where a more conscientious writer would have carefully constructed clauses and phrases, punctuated with appropriate comas, periods, colons or semicolons. He knew this about himself and often prefaced his letters with apologies and a caution to his readers to be prepared for the worst. Yet for all these incidental distractions, his letters were obviously the work of a clear, forceful mind, one easily recognizable from his books, DVDs, and cassettes. Moreover, as Bailey moved from using typewriters to computers in the 1980s, his writing became appreciably better as he made use of spell- and grammar-check. I have therefore decided to spare the reader Bailey's more dubious ventures into creative spelling and punctuation and even rare lapses in diction by correcting such errors as he surely would have himself if he had wanted to sacrifice the time necessary to make the effort.

Although I have focused on Ken Bailey's letters, Mickey Bailey's letters make up at least half of all the letters in the three boxes of the Bailey Papers labeled family correspondence, and they are crucial to providing key background information and insights into Ken's life and thought. Mickey, unlike her husband, was a fine speller and could generally be counted on to write grammatical sentences, yet she too, from time to time, resorted to strings of phrases or clauses connected by dashes, for she, like Ken, approached letter writing as if it were a one-sided conversation in which the usual rules of writing could be suspended in order not to interfere with the rapid flow of thought. In terms of content, the two differed mainly in that Ken was analytical where she was descriptive.

Other correspondents who also appear in the Bailey Papers include Ken Bailey's parents, children, and extended family. Ken Bailey's father, Ewing W. Bailey, was known to be a somewhat distant man, but in his correspondence, he could be effusive in his descriptions of places and accounts of events, and the professional discourses he engaged in with his son denote a relationship of mutual admiration and respect. Reading Annette Bailey's account of her early life provided the greatest surprise and delight in my reading of the Bailey Papers. With a gift for narrative writing and a dry British wit, it is unfortunate that she did not write more. Sara Bailey, in contrast to her parents, always wrote letters that employed accurate spelling, grammar, and style. In later life the phrases she used in some of the letters she wrote her father were eloquent, moving expressions of the love and gratitude she felt for her parents. She was the ideal and certainly necessary secretary-editor that Bailey needed to make his books the clear, incisive expositions that they are. David Bailey's letters defy easy description except to say that they could often be poetic, humorous, and playful departures from convention. While Sara added beauty and order to the family, David brought an exuberant *joie de vivre*, which enlivened all their lives and, at family gatherings, must at times have elicited broad smiles and peals of laughter. To be consistent, I have corrected the occasional misspellings or grammatical errors in the writings of the Bailey family members who are quoted in this text.

    I visited Mickey Bailey twice in the summer of 2022 at her apartment at Shenango on the Green, a Presbyterian retirement home in New Wilmington, Pennsylvania, where she was in an independent living arrangement. The first time I met her was early in July 2022 when I was on my way to New Haven to begin my study of the Bailey Papers. In my enthusiasm for the subject, I inadvertently overstayed my welcome, so taxing this dear ninety-three-year-old woman that I left her slumped and dozing in her chair. Naturally, I resolved to be more sensitive and courteous on future occasions. Over the course of my reading of the Bailey Papers in the subsequent month, I soon concluded that a substantial number of the letters were missing. When I returned to Mickey's apartment in early August, I was prepared to ask her if she were holding on to any of the family correspondence. At the beginning of our conversation and before I had a chance to raise the subject, she produced two bound volumes of family letters that she had deliberately withheld from the collection at Yale. She offered no explanation or excuse, but after reading them in subsequent weeks I concluded that she must have kept them close by for entirely sentimental reasons as they provided a tangible link to her past and to a much beloved husband, who had died six years before. Later, after discussing the matter with Sara, another possibility emerged: Mickey initially held on to them to keep a promise to Sara not to disclose information about her daughter's health issues as they had developed over the years. Perhaps Mickey later changed her mind because she came to realize that the letters were crucial to writing a full biography of her husband, which she knew he had wanted. Consistent with this interpretation is that she insisted that, when I was finished with the letters, they should be given to Sara, not Yale Divinity School. She wanted Sara to make the final decision about their disposition. Ironically, if this is the case, Mickey's unease about these letters was entirely misplaced because, being mostly from the 1950s and sixties, they include little about Sara.

The third time I visited Mickey in New Wilmington was on October 1, 2022. By this time, I had read all of the Bailey correspondence and had written first drafts of several chapters. I called her the day before to say that I would be driving in from New Haven and arriving at about 2:00 p.m. to see her. When I appeared about an hour late due to traffic and heavy rain along the way, I found Mickey slouched in her chair, awake but drowsy. Remembering my previous resolution, I pressed on cautiously, reading aloud to her sections of my initial draft of chapter two that concerned her early life for which I needed her input because the material in the Bailey Papers on this subject was either nonexistent or at best sketchy. She affirmed a number of my conjectures and corrected several of my missteps. As we worked through the material, she became increasingly alert and engaged. She was especially intrigued by quotations from her brothers Dale and Floyd—included in this early draft but not the final version—which she had entirely forgotten, probably not having looked at them for seventy years. Later we moved onto the subject of Jonas Salk and her participation in the development of the polio vaccine, and toward the end of our conversation she was showing faint but unmistakable hints of enjoying our time together. Finally, I asked her about a letter that Ken had written in the last years of his missionary career about a box that he said contained family "treasures," one of which was a mummified hawk. It was on this occasion that she told me the story of how Annette Bailey had acquired the hawk in the 1920s, and then, with a soft chuckle and twinkle in her eye, she looked at me and asked, "Do you wanna see it?" Moving slowly with the aid of a walker, she led me to a closet in her study, messy with the memorabilia and precious vestiges of a rich, full life. When I opened the closet, she directed me to take down the box from the top shelf. I saw three boxes there and retrieved the largest one that was clearly labeled "treasures." But she said, "No, not that one. It's in the shoe box." On opening this other box, I saw a small brown object about eight inches long and two and a half inches in circumference that had black sparking eyes and a small hooked beak. To my utter amazement, I found myself holding an artifact that had been sealed in the tomb of Pharaoh Tutankhamen over thirty-four hundred years ago.

Before my research was complete, I visited Mickey several more times, usually to ask a question about some obscure point or seek her opinion about something I had written. Always interested and helpful, she never made me feel as though I were intruding or imposing. In her last years, she suffered from kidney failure and congestive heart failure. Sadly, she passed away on January 4, 2023, just ten days shy of her ninety-fourth birthday. Her memorial service was held February 4, and her ashes were laid in the same plot as her husband's at Fair Oaks Cemetery in New Wilmington. Plain-spoken and unassuming, it might have been easy to underestimate her. Yet, this stouthearted midwestern woman participated in the development of the Salk vaccine, taught literacy in traditional villages in Upper Egypt, lived fearlessly in war-torn Beirut, and throughout it all remained steadfastly devoted to her husband and children. In an earlier generation, she might have lived in a sod house and helped to tame the rolling prairies.

I want to express my gratitude to a number of other individuals who helped me with this project. Those interviewed or consulted for this book include Bruce Bailey, Leslie McGarvey Bailey, William D. Crooks, David Dawson, Baki Sadaka Girgis, Jean Isteero, Darren Kennedy, Nada Malik, Sara Bailey Makari, William McKnight, Mary Nebelsick, Anne Zaki, and Emile Zaki. I am indebted to them as their insights about the life and work of Kenneth Bailey invariably kept my research moving in the right direction. Mariana Katkout, a professional translator living in Cairo, Egypt, gave invaluable assistance to ensure the accuracy of my spelling and translations of Arabic words and phrases. There were also four readers who generously gave of their time to peruse and comment on my manuscript, each contributing a different perspective to the project. My brother James Parker provided a number of helpful comments on the writing of the prologue and first four chapters. George Sabra, who read chapters 8–13, was my expert on Lebanon and NEST, having lived through the difficult years of the Lebanese Civil War and written a history of NEST—an institution key in Bailey's life and one that Sabra has served for a number of years as president. David Dawson, Bailey's very good friend during the last two decades of his life, was not only

Author's Note and Acknowledgments

knowledgeable about Bailey's life and career but also about mission and recent Presbyterian history. In carefully reading the entire manuscript, he was able to correct, affirm, or supplement my account in always helpful and sometimes subtle ways. Finally, Sara Bailey Makari, whose personal knowledge of her father is now unsurpassed, read an early draft of the manuscript and then graciously agreed to read the final version as well. With a copyeditor's thoroughness and care, she smoothed out occasional infelicities of expression and offered thoughtful insights throughout. Though I benefited from the four readers' observations and comments, naturally any errors of fact or judgment remain my own responsibility.

Select Bibliography

This is a select bibliography in that, for example, it does not include every article that Bailey ever wrote or every review of each of his books. Rather, it only includes those that are specifically cited in the biography.

The primary documents listed below are the main sources for the biography, and the abbreviations given to them here are used throughout the footnotes. These are followed by Bailey's books and articles, which appear in alphabetical order. Ignore the opening articles "A," "An," and "The."

Bailey stated on his website and other places that he had written over 150 articles. I located 176 among the Bailey Papers. However, only 124 had full citations, while most of the remaining 52 articles were either unpublished or the publications where they appeared have not yet been located or confirmed. Readers interested in Bailey's articles will find them in the Bailey Papers, boxes 41, 42, 43, 45, 53 and 64.

PRIMARY SOURCES—ARCHIVAL MATERIAL

Bailey Papers—Kenneth E. Bailey Papers, Yale Divinity School Library, cataloged as RG 274. This collection consists of eighty-four boxes of material that was in Bailey's study when he died. It includes family and professional correspondence as well as articles, biblical commentaries, and Bibles that Bailey collected in the Middle East over a period of several decades. Much of this biography is based on the family correspondence contained in boxes 27, 28, and 29, which is further subdivided into numbered files. The archivists at the Yale Divinity School may soon reorder these materials by date. Future researchers will still be able to find the letters I have noted by ignoring my references to file numbers and searching boxes 27–29 by date order.

FoMENTS Records—the Foundation for Middle Eastern New Testament Studies (or FoMENTS) maintained the minutes of its meetings and various files on its work. Most of these are with the Bailey Papers. Many of them, however, were until recently also held by David Dawson, and it is his collection that I consulted. They are now part of the collection of the Presbyterian Historical Society in Philadelphia.

Ewing M. Bailey Papers—these are Ewing Bailey's personnel records from the Presbyterian Church, which are now held by the Presbyterian Historical Society in Philadelphia. They include application forms and letters from the mission field. It is not an extensive file, but it contains information about his military service and academic background that is helpful.

Kenneth and Mickey Bailey Papers—these are the Baileys' personnel records from the Presbyterian Church, which are now held by the Presbyterian Historical Society in Philadelphia. They include application forms and letters from the mission field.

Minutes of the American Mission in Egypt from 1885 to 1966—this is held by the Presbyterian Historical Society in Philadelphia.

Black Volume—this is a bound volume of Bailey family letters, which were mostly written by Ken and Mickey Bailey. They are in reverse date order and have handwritten pagination, with pages from 1 to 599. They begin in 1955 and continue through 1970. However, the first 113 pages are out of date order, and the first two letters are from 1972. This is currently in the possession of the Bailey family but will soon be given to the Yale Divinity School library. However, access will be restricted for some time.

White Volume—this is also a bound volume of Bailey family letters that are mostly by Ken and Mickey Bailey. There are also some letters by Ken Bailey on behalf of the Pre-Seminary program in Assiut. The date order is generally arbitrary, and there is no pagination. The bulk of the letters are from 1955 to 1965, but at the back of the book there are 41 pages from 1944 to 1954. The volume has 286 pages. This is currently in the possession of the Bailey family but will soon be given to the Yale Divinity School library. However, access will be restricted for some time.

Ewing Bailey Papers, Volume 1—Ewing gave this volume a handwritten title: "Family letters written by Ewing Bailey to his family, 1926–1930." It has handwritten pagination, with 239 pages. Inserted at the front is a five-page handwritten essay by Annette Bailey, "A Memorable Christmas Day." This is currently in the possession of the Bailey family but will soon be given to the Yale Divinity School library.

Ewing Bailey Papers, Volume 2—Ewing titled this "Occasional letters of Ewing Bailey sent to friends, retired missionaries & former short termers, 1945–1960." The letters are poorly bound, and most are no longer attached to the binding. There is no pagination, and the total number of pages is 163. It also includes a twenty-three-page pamphlet, *Survey of the Work of the American Mission in Egypt, January 1956*. This is currently in the possession of the Bailey family but will soon be given to the Yale Divinity School library.

Miscellaneous Bailey Family Documents—Ken and Mickey Bailey kept a number of personal files in a file cabinet in their apartment at Shenago on the Green. When I interviewed Mickey several times in 2022, she occasionally found a file for me on a subject that we were discussing. I now have ten files of various family documents. These include copies of a deed of land issued in 1786, family photographs, and some of Ewing Bailey's photographs taken in Egypt and Ethiopia. There are also a mission photo album from 1905 and several of Ken's record books. These are currently in the possession of the Bailey Family but will soon be given to the Yale Divinity School library.

PRIMARY SOURCES—BAILEY'S BOOKS AND ARTICLES

Bailey, Kenneth E. *The Cross & the Prodigal: Luke 15 through the Eyes of Middle Eastern Peasants*. Revised and expanded. Downers Grove, IL: InterVarsity, 2005.

———. *The Cross and the Prodigal: The 15th Chapter of Luke Seen through the Eyes of Middle Eastern Peasants*. St. Louis, MO: Concordia, 1973.

———. *Cross-Cultural Mission*. Pittsburgh: Pittsburgh Theological Seminary, 1984. This is a recording in three cassettes of Bailey's 1984 McClure Lecture: "A Tale of Three Cities," which was also published under this title in 1989. See below.

Select Bibliography

———. "C. S. Lewis, Thomas More and Bitter Conflict." *The Presbyterian Outlook* 185, no. 16 (2003) 9, 16.

———. THE DOCTRINE OF GOD *for Village People (A Series of Twenty Plays on the Doctrine of God Using Village Characters)*, bound typescript, May 1961. A copy of the thesis is in the Pittsburgh Theological Seminary library.

———. *Finding the Lost: Cultural Keys to Luke 15*. St. Louis: Concordia, 1992.

———. *God Is . . . Dialogues on the Nature of God for Young People*. Monroeville, PA: Youth Club Program, 1976.

———. *God Is . . . Dialogues on the Nature of God*. Rev. ed. Toronto, ON: FFM, 2005.

———. *The Good Shepherd: A Thousand-Year Journey from Psalm 23 to the New Testament*. Downers Grove, IL: IVP Academic, 2014

———. "Informal Controlled Oral Tradition and the Synoptic Gospel." *Asia Journal of Theology* 5 (1991) 34–54. Later published in *Themelios* 20 (1995) 4–11.

———. *Jacob & the Prodigal: How Jesus Retold Israel's Story*. Downers Grove, Illinois: IVP Academic, 2003.

———. *Jesus through Middle Eastern Eyes: Cultural Studies in the Gospels*. Downers Grove, IL: IVP Academic, 2008.

———. "Kenneth Bailey's Inaugural Lecture at the Opening of CMEC." Edited by Michael Parker. *Cairo Journal of Theology* 7 (2020) 41–48. http://journal.etsc.org.

———. "Metaphors Matter: The Confessions and a Gang of Four." *The Presbyterian Outlook* 184, no. 22 (2002) 5, 7, 9.

———. *Open Hearts in Bethlehem: A Christmas Drama*. Drover Grove, IL: InterVarsity, 2005. (This includes the DVD, *Open Hearts in Bethlehem*. Folk songs: words, music and performance by David Bailey. Choir Anthem: words by Daniel Thambyrajah Niles; music by Lois Hopkins; performed by The Westminster College Chamber Choir under the direction of Robin Lind and accompanied by Ashley Rexrode.)

———. *Paul through Mediterranean Eyes: Cultural Studies in I Corinthians*. Downers Grove, IL: IVP Academic, 2011

———. *Poet & Peasant: A Literary-Cultural Approach to the Parables in Luke*. Grand Rapids, MI: Eerdmans, 1976.

———. *Poet & Peasant and through Peasant Eyes: A Literary-Cultural Approach to the Parables in Luke*. Grand Rapids, MI: Eerdmans, 1983.

———. "Psalm 23 and Luke 15: A Vision Expanded." *Irish Biblical Studies* 12 (1990) 54–71.

———. "Recovering the Poetic Structure of 1 Corinthians i 17-ii 2: A Study in Text and Commentary." *Novum Testamentum* 17, no. 4 (1975) 265–96.

———. "Rejoinder to 'Mission in the Context of the Struggle for Justice: In Search of a Theological Perspective on Development,' by Paul Löffler." *Theological Review of the Near East School of Theology* 2, no. 2 (1979) 21–25.

———. "Review of Robert Gagnon, *The Bible and Homosexual Practice* (Nashville: Abingdon, 2001)." *The Presbyterian Outlook* 183, no. 37 (2001) 23.

———. "The Structure of 1 Corinthians and Paul's Theological Method with Special Reference to 4:17." *Novum Testamentum* 25, no. 2 (1983) 152–81.

———. "A Tale of Elephants and the Mouse: Presbyterians, 10-A and the World Church." Presbyterians for Renewal, published on website July 14, 2011. Currently published online by The Fellowship Community. http://fellowship.community/how-does-the-world-church-view-10a/.

———. *A Tale of Three Cities.* Pasadena, CA: Presbyterian Center for Mission Studies, 1989. (This is Bailey's McClure Lectures on Cross-Cultural mission, given in 1984. See too Bailey Papers, box 42, folder 2.)

———. *Through Peasant Eyes: More Lucan Parables, Their Culture and Style.* Grand Rapids, MI: Eerdmans, 1980.

———. *When the Wind Is Right* (one-act play). Downers Grove, IL: Contemporary Drama Service, 1976.

———. "Worsh-o-tainment: A Needed Neologism?" *The Presbyterian Outlook* 185, no. 3 (2003) 10–11.

SECONDARY SOURCES

Adams, James E. *Preus of Missouri and the Great Lutheran Civil War.* New York: Harper & Row, 1977.

Anderson, Terry A. *Den of Lions.* New York: Crown, 1993.

Armstrong, M. A. "English, Scottish, and Irish Backgrounds of American Presbyterians, 1689–1729." *Journal of the Presbyterian Historical Society* 34 (1956) 3–18.

Ayrout, Henry Habib. *The Fellaheen.* Cairo: Schindler, 1962.

Barentsen, Jack. Review of *Paul through Mediterranean Eyes*, by Kenneth E. Bailey. *Review of Biblical Literature* 15 (2013) 364–67.

Barth, Markus. "Justification: From Text to Sermon on Galatians 2:11–21." *Interpretation: A Journal of Bible and Theology* 22, no. 2 (1968) 147–57.

Batten, Alicia J. Review of *Paul through Mediterranean Eyes*, by Kenneth E. Bailey. *Toronto Journal of Theology* 32, no. 1 (2016) 155–56.

Bauckham, Richard H. *Jesus and the Eyewitnesses: The Gospels as Eyewitness Testimony.* 2nd ed. Grand Rapids, MI: Eerdmans, 2017.

Berry, Bill, ed. *Into All the World.* Pasadena, CA: Berry, 2002.

"The Book Awards: The Best Books of 2011." *Christianity Today,* January 2012, 44.

Book of Confessions: Study Edition. Louisville, KY: Geneva, 1999.

Bowman, John David. Review of *Jesus through Middle Eastern Eyes*, by Kenneth E. Bailey. *Brethren Life & Thought* 54, nos. 1–2 (2009) 93–94.

Brown, G. Thompson. *Presbyterians in World Mission.* Rev. ed. Decatur, GA: Columbia Theological Seminary Press, 1995.

Brug, John F. Review of *Finding the Lost: Cultural Keys to Luke 15*, by Kenneth E. Bailey. *Wisconsin Lutheran Quarterly* 91, no. 4 (1994) 315–16.

Bultmann, Rudolf. *The History of the Synoptic Tradition.* Translated by J. Marsh. Oxford, Blackwell, 1963.

———. *Jesus and the Word.* 1921. Reprint, New York: Scribner's, 1958.

Burge, Gary M. "Kenneth E. Bailey: An Ambassador Serving the Middle East and the West," *International Bulletin of Mission Research* 41, no. 2 (2017) 152–59.

———. Review of *Through Peasant Eyes: More Lucan Parables, Their Culture and Style*, by Kenneth E. Bailey. *Journal of Biblical Literature* 102, no. 2 (1983) 341–42.

Canon, Lou. *President Reagan: The Role of a Lifetime.* New York: Public Affairs, 1991.

Carruthers, Jeanne. "Holy Week Drama in Jerusalem." *Presbyterian Life* 17, no. 6 (1964) 16–17.

Chapman, Colin. *Whose Promised Land? The Continuing Crisis over Israel and Palestine.* 1983. Fully Revised and Updated. New York: Lion, 2015.

Select Bibliography

Church and Homosexuality. Louisville, KY: Office of the General Assembly, 1978. https://www.pcusa.org/site_media/media/uploads/_resolutions/church-and-homosexuality.pdf.

Coggins, Wade T. "What's Behind the Idea of a Missionary Moratorium?" *Christianity Today,* November 22, 1974, 7–9.

Constitution of the Presbyterian Church (U.S.A.) Part II, Book of Order. Louisville, KY: The Office of the General Assembly, 2004.

Crossan, John Dominic. Review of *Poet & Peasant,* by Kenneth E. Bailey. *Journal of Biblical Literature* 96, no. 4 (1977) 606–8.

Cuthbertson, Kenneth L. *The Last Presbyterian? Remembering the Faith of My Forebears.* Eugene, OR: Resource, 2013.

Danker, Frederick W. Review of *The Cross and the Prodigal. Concordia Theological Monthly* 44 (1973) 312.

Davenport, F. Garvin. *Monmouth College: The First Hundred Years, 1853–1953.* Cedar Rapids, IA: Torch, 1953.

Dibelius, Martin. *From Tradition to Gospel.* Translated by B. L. Woolf. London: Nicholson and Watson, 1934.

Docherty, Susan E. Review of *Paul through Mediterranean Eyes,* by Kenneth E. Bailey. *Irish Theological Quarterly* 77, no. 3 (2012) 314–15.

Dodd, C. H. *The Parables of the Kingdom.* London: Nisbet, 1935.

Doran, Michael. *Ike's Gamble: America's Rise to Dominance in the Middle East.* New York: Free Press, 2016.

Drury, Cliford M. "Presbyterian Beginnings in New England and the Middle Colonies," *Presbyterian Historical Society* 34 (1956) 19–35.

Dunn, James D. G. *Christianity in the Making: Jesus Remembered.* Grand Rapids: Eerdmans, 2003.

———. "Kenneth Bailey's Theology of Oral Tradition: Critiquing Theodore J. Weeden's Critique." *Journal for the Study of the Historical Jesus* 1, no. 1 (2009) 44–62. (See Dunn's letter to Bailey on this subject, October 24, 2001, Bailey Papers, box 43, folder 1.)

Engfehr, Lois, and Glen Thomas, eds. *Proclaim His Salvation: Concordia Seminary—75 Years on the Clayton.* St. Louis, MO: Concordia Seminary, 2001.

Fisk, Robert. *Pity the Nation: Lebanon at War.* 3rd ed. Oxford: Oxford University Press, 2001.

Foster, Robert B. Review of *Paul through Mediterranean Eyes,* by Kenneth E. Bailey. *Theological Studies* 73, no. 3 (2012) 732.

Frankfort, Henri. *The Birth of Civilization in the Near East.* Bloomington, IN: Indiana University Press, 1951.

Friedman, Thomas L. *From Beirut to Jerusalem, Expanded Edition with a New Preface and Afterword.* New York: Picador, 2012.

———. "Lebanese Reopen Beiruts [sic] Airport," *New York Times,* September 30, 1983, A8.

———. *The World Is Flat.* New York: Picador, 2007.

Gagnon, Robert A. *The Bible and Homosexual Practice: Texts and Hermeneutics.* Nashville: Abingdon, 2001.

Gendy, Sherif. Review of *The Good Shepherd: A Thousand-Year Journey from Psalm 23 to the New Testament,* by Kenneth E. Bailey. *The Westminster Theological Journal* 77, no. 2 (2015) 400–402.

Select Bibliography

Gerhardsson, Gerger. *Memory and Manuscript: Oral Tradition and Written Transmission in Rabbinic Judaism and Early Christianity*, Copenhagen, Den.: Ejnar Munksgaard, 1961.

———. *Tradition and Transmission in Early Christianity*. Lund, Swed.: Gleerup, 1964.

Gilliland, Thomas Matthew, Jr. *Truth and Love: The United Presbyterian Church of North America: A Fifty-Year Retrospective.* United States of America: United Presbyterian Conservancy of North America, 2008.

Gill, Malcolm J. Review of *Paul through Mediterranean Eyes*, by Kenneth E. Bailey. *Themelios* 37, no. 1 (2012) 60–61.

Grangaard, Blake R. Review of *Jacob & the Prodigal*, by Kenneth E. Bailey. *Interpretation* 59, no. 2 (2005) 218, 220.

Greidmanius, Tjardus, dir. and scrip. "The Shot Felt 'Round the World." Produced by Steeltown Entertainment Project in association with WQED Pittsburgh and University of Pittsburgh, copyright 2010 Steeltown Entertainment Project &1905 Productions, LLC.

Hagner, Donald. "New Aids for Biblical Scholarship." *The Reformed Journal* 28, no. 2 (1978) 28–29.

Halliwell, Martin, *American Culture in the 1950s*. Edinburgh, Scot.: Edinburgh University Press, 2007.

Hedrick, Joan D. *Harriet Beecher Stowe: A Life*. New York: Oxford University Press, 1994.

Hogg, Rena. *A Master-Builder on the Nile: Being a Record of the Life and Aims of John Hogg, D.D., Christian Missionary*. New York: Fleming Revel, 1914.

Hollenbach, Paul. Review of *Finding the Lost: Cultural Keys to Luke 15*, by Kenneth E. Bailey. *The Catholic Biblical Quarterly* 55, no. 4 (1993) 793–94.

Holm, Randy. Review of *Jacob & the Prodigal*, by Kenneth E. Bailey. Διδασκαλια [Didaskalia, "Teaching" or "Instruction"] 15, no. 1 (2003) 74–76.

Hultgren, Arland J. Review of *Through Peasant Eyes. More Lucan Parable, Their Culture and Style*, by Kenneth E. Bailey. *Word & World* 2, no. 4 (1982) 401–2.

Hunter, Archibald M. "The Interpreter and the Parables: The Centrality of the Kingdom." *Interpretation* 14 (1960) 70–84.

———. *Interpreting the Parables*. Philadelphia: Westminster, 1960.

Jamison, Wallace N. *The United Presbyterian Story: A Centennial Study: 1858–1958*. Pittsburgh, PA: Geneva, 1958.

Jeremias, Joachim. *The Parables of Jesus*, Rev. ed. London: SCM, 1963.

Jewett, Paul K. *MAN as Male and Female: A Study in Sexual Relationships from a Theological Point of View*. Grand Rapids, MI: Eerdmans, 1975.

Johnson, Luke Timothy. Review of *Through Peasant Eyes: More Lucan Parables, Their Culture and Style*, by Kenneth E. Bailey. *Interpretation* 37, no. 1 (1983) 102–3.

Jones, Catherine. Review of *Paul through Mediterranean Eyes*, by Kenneth E. Bailey. *Studies in Religion* 41, no. 4 (2012) 618–19.

Jülicher, Adolf. *Die Gleichnisreden Jesu*. 2 vols. Tübingen: Mohr [Siebeck], 1888, 1899.

Kelsey, Hugh Alexander. *The United Presbyterian Directory: A Half-Century Survey 1903–1958*. Pittsburgh, PA: Pickwick, 1958.

Kiehl, Erich H. Review of *Finding the Lost: Cultural Keys to Luke 15*, by Kenneth E. Bailey. *Concordia Journal* 18, no. 4 (1992) 420.

Kim, Charles, prod. *Blessed Be Egypt My People*. New York: Vimeo, 2016. https://vimeo.com/1251611601.

Select Bibliography

Krause, Mark S. Review of *Jacob & the Prodigal*, by Kenneth E. Bailey. *Journal of the Evangelical Theological Society* 47, no. 3 (2004) 526–28.

LaHurd, Carol Schersten. Review of *Jesus through Middle Eastern Eyes*, by Kenneth E. Bailey. *The Catholic Biblical Quarterly* 73, no. 3 (2011) 605–7.

Lee-Barnewall, Michelle. Review of *Paul through Mediterranean Eyes*, by Kenneth E. Bailey. *Journal of the Evangelical Theological Society* 55, no. 3 (2012) 622–24.

Le Gry, Alan. Review of *The Good Shepherd: A Thousand-Year Journey from Psalm 23 to the New Testament*, by Kenneth E. Bailey. *Journal for the Study of the New Testament* 37, no. 5 (2015) 11–12.

Leith, John H. "On Choosing a Seminary Professor," *The Presbyterian Outlook* 177, no. 8, (1995) 6–7, and 11.

Le Strange, Guy. *Palestine under the Moslems: A Description of Syrian and the Holy Land from A.D. 650 to 1500*. New York: Houghton, Mifflin, 1890.

Lewis, C. S. *The Weight of Glory*. New York: HarperSanFrancisco, 1980.

Löffler, Paul. "Mission in the Context of the Struggle for Justice." *Theological Review of the Near East School of Theology* 2, no. 2 (1979) 13–20.

Longfield, Bradley J. *Presbyterians and American Culture: A History*. Louisville, KY: Westminster John Knox, 2013.

Lorimer, Jack. *The Presbyterian Experience in Egypt: 1950–2000*. Denver, CO: Outskirts, 2007.

Lund, Nils Wilhelm. *Chiasmus in the New Testament*. Chapel Hill, NC: University of North Carolina Press, 1942.

Marius, Richard. *Thomas More: A Biography*. New York: Vintage, 1985.

Marsden, George M. *Reforming Fundamentalism: Fuller Seminary and the New Evangelicalism*. Grand Rapids, MI: Eerdmans, 1987.

———. *The Twilight of the American Enlightenment: The 1950s and the Crisis of Liberal Belief*. New York: Basic, 2014.

Marshall, Howard I. *The Gospel Luke: A Commentary on the Greek Text*. Exeter, UK: Paternoster, 1978, 1979. Also published as *The Gospel of Luke: The New International Greek Commentary*. Grand Rapids, MI: Eerdmans, 1978.

Martin, Ralph P. *New Testament Foundations: A Guide for Christian Students*. Vol. 1, *The 4 Gospels*. Grand Rapids, MI: Eerdmans, 1975.

McAllister, J. Gray. *Edward O. Guerrant: Apostle to the Southern Highlanders*. Richmond, VA: Richmond, 1950.

McDougal, Dennis. "What the World Got Wrong about Rodney King." *Los Angeles Times*, March 3, 2021. https://www.latimes.com/opinion/story/2021-23-03/rodney-king-beating-30-anniversary.

McEleney, Neil J. Review of *Poet & Peasant*, by Kenneth E. Bailey. *Theological Studies* 38, no. 3 (1977) 565–67.

Metzer, Bruce M., and Michael D. Coogan, eds. *Oxford Companion to the Bible*. New York: Oxford University Press, 1993.

Minutes of the General Assembly of The United Presbyterian Church in the United States of America. Part II: Annual Reports of the Major Program Agencies. Philadelphia: Office of the General Assembly, August 1960.

Minutes of the Seventy-Fourth General Assembly of the United Presbyterian Church of North America. Pittsburgh: United Presbyterian Board of Publications and Bible School Work, 1932.

Select Bibliography

Mohler, Albert. "The Year's Best Books for Preachers—2006." *Preaching Magazine*, 2006. https://www.preaching.com/book-reviews/the-years-best-books-for-preachers-2006/.

Moxnes, Halvor. Review of *Jacob & the Prodigal*, by Kenneth E. Bailey. *Scottish Journal of Theology* 58, no. 3 (2005) 354–56.

Moynihan, Martin, trans. and ed. *Letters: C. S. Lewis, Don Givanni Calabria: A Study in Friendship*. London: Collins, 1989.

Mueller, Don A. *Eyes upon the Cross: A Cycle of Plays for Lent*. Boston: Baker Plays, 1962.

Nagel, Curtis F., prod. *Clippers at War*. A film by Pan America World Airways System, 1945. Available as a DVD, and online at https://www.youtube.com/watch?v=0TzpFX2BPPI.

NEST. "The Bailey Chapel—Dedication Service Nov 24, 2021." *YouTube*, November 29, 2021. https://www.youtube.com/watch?v=sF62cBJWXvQ.

———. "Near East School of Theology—Memorial Service Kenneth E. Bailey, October 9, 2016." YouTube, November 2, 2016. https://www.youtube.com/watch?v=ogI5Mh6lBnA.

Neusner, Jacob. *Writing with Scripture: The Authority and Uses of the Hebrew Bible in the Torah of Formative Judaism*. Minneapolis, MN: Fortress, 1989.

Newbigin, Lesslie. *The Gospel in a Pluralist Society*. Grand Rapids, MI: Eerdmans, 1989.

———. *The Open Secret*. Grand Rapids: Eerdmans, 1978.

Oshinsky, David M. *Polio: An American Story*. Oxford: Oxford: University Press, 2005.

"Pan Am at War." *Time Magazine*, May 18, 1942, 73–74.

Parker, Michael. "Kenneth Bailey: A Scholar with a New Way of Looking at the New Testament." *The Presbyterian Outlook*, October 28, 2016. https://pres-outlook.org/2016/10/kenneth-bailey-scholar-new-way-looking-new-testament/.

———. *The Kingdom of Character: The Student Volunteer Movement for Foreign Missions, 1886–1926*. Pasadena, CA: William Carey Library, 2008.

Partee, Charles. *The Story of Don McClure, Adventure in Africa: From Khartoum to Addis Ababa in Five Decades*. Lanham: University Press of America, 2000.

Partrick, Theodore Hall. *Traditional Egyptian Christianity: A History of the Coptic Orthodox Church*. Greensboro, NC: Fisher Park, 1996.

Perkins, Pheme. Review of *Through Peasant Eyes: More Lucan Parables, Their Culture and Style*, by Kenneth E. Bailey. *The Catholic Biblical Quarterly* 44, no. 1 (1982) 139–40.

Piper, John F., Jr. *Robert E. Speer: Prophet of the American Church*. Louisville, KY: Geneva, 2000.

Reed, David A. Review of *Jacob & the Prodigal*, by Kenneth E. Bailey. *Review of Biblical Literature* 6 (2004) 408–11.

Riesenfeld, Harald. "The Gospel Tradition and Its Beginning." In *The Gospel Tradition*, 1–29. Philadelphia: Fortress, 1970.

Rogers, Jack. *The Bible, and Homosexuality: Explode the Myths, Heal the Church*. Revised and expanded. Louisville, KY: Westminster John Knox, 2009.

Sabra, George F. *Truth and Service: A History of the Near East School of Theology*. Beirut, Leb.: Libraire Antoine, 2009.

Safris, Lynn Milligan, ed. and comp. *Milligan Stew: A Collection of Memories*. Privately published, 1990. (A copy can be found among the Bailey Papers.)

Select Bibliography

Sanneh, Lamin. "Christian Missions and the Western Guilt Complex." *The Christian Century* 104, no. 11 (1987) 330–34.

———. *Translating the Message: The Missionary Impact on Culture.* Maryknoll, NY: Orbis, 2008.

Sargent, Andrew. Review of *The Good Shepherd: A Thousand-Year Journey from Psalm 23 to the New Testament*, by Kenneth E. Bailey. *Criswell Theological Review* 13, no. 1 (2015) 142–44.

Schmidt, Karl Luidwig. *Der Rahmen der Geschichte Jesu* ("The Framework of the Story of Jesus"). Berlin: Trowizsch, 1919.

Seventy-Fifth General Assembly of the United Presbyterian Church of North America. Pittsburgh, PA: United Presbyterian Board of Publication and Bible School Work, 1933.

Sharkey, Heather J. *American Evangelicals in Egypt: Missionary Encounters in an Age of Empire.* Princeton: Princeton University Press, 2008.

Shellnutt, Kate. "Died: Kenneth Bailey, the Scholar Who Made Jesus Middle Eastern Again." *Christianity Today*, May 25, 2016. https://www.christianitytoday.com/news/2016/may/middle-east-expert-kenneth-e-bailey-dies.html.

Smillie, Gene R. Review of *Jesus through Middle Eastern Eyes*, by Kenneth E. Bailey. *Journal of the Evangelical Theological Society* 52, no. 2 (2009) 375–78

Smith, John Coventry. *From Colonialism to World Community: The Church's Pilgrimage.* Philadelphia: Geneva, 1982.

Smylie, James H. *A Brief History of the Presbyterians.* Louisville, KY: Geneva, 1996.

Snyder, Graydon F. Review of *Jesus through Middle Eastern Eyes*, by Kenneth E. Bailey. *Currents in Theology and Mission* 37, no. 1 (2010) 60–61.

"Statement and Recommendations." In *The Church and Homosexuality*, 57–62. Louisville, KY: Office of the General Assembly, 1978. https://www.pcusa.org/site_media/media/uploads/_resolutions/church-and-homosexuality.pdf.

Storie, Deborah. Review of *Jesus through Middle Eastern Eyes*, by Kenneth E. Bailey. *Pacifica* 22, no. 1 (2009) 96–109.

Sunquist, Scott W., and Caroline N. Becker, eds. *A History of Presbyterian Missions: 1944–2007.* Louisville, KY: Geneva, 2008.

Tatu, Silviu. Review of *The Good Shepherd: A Thousand-Year Journey from Psalm 23 to the New Testament*, by Kenneth E. Bailey. *Themelios* 40, no. 2 (2015) 268–69.

Taylor, Nicholas H. Review of *Paul through Mediterranean Eyes*, by Kenneth E. Bailey. *Journal for the Study of the New Testament* 34, no. 5 (2011) 90.

Tennyson, Alfred Lord. *Alfred Tennyson: The Major Works.* Edited by Adams Roberts. Oxford: Oxford University Press, 2000.

———. *Idylls of the King.* New York: Penguin,1983.

Thurston, Burton B. Review of *Poet & Peasant*, by Kenneth E. Bailey. *Encounter* 38, no. 4 (1977) 392–93.

Timmer, John. Review of *Through Peasant Eyes: More Lucan Parables, Their Culture and Style*, by Kenneth E. Bailey. *Calvin Theological Journal* 16, no. 1 (1981) 80–81.

Trinity Church Mercer. "Dr. Kenneth E. Bailey Memorial Service." *YouTube*, June 6, 2016. https://www.youtube.com/watch?v=oeR9Lfp2hpA.

Turner, Geoffrey. Review of *Jesus through Middle Eastern Eyes*, by Kenneth E. Bailey. *Heythrop Journal* 53, no. (2012) 310–12.

———. Review of *Paul through Mediterranean Eyes*, by Kenneth E. Bailey. *Heythrop Journal* 54, no. 1 (2013) 130–31.

Select Bibliography

Vaz, Mark Cotta, and John H. Hill. *Pan Am at War: How the Airline Secretly Helped America Fight World War II*. New York: Skyhorse, 2019.

Virtue, David W. *A Vision of Hope: The Story of Samuel Habib, One of the Arab World's Greatest Contemporary Christian Leaders and His Plan for Peace in the Strife-Torn Middle East Where the Cross and Crescent Meet and Where the Bible, Koran, and Torah Vie for Center Stage*. Eugene, OR: Wipf & Stock, 1996.

Volk, Miroslav. *The End of Memory: Remembering Rightly in a Violent World*. Grand Rapids: Eerdmans, 2006.

Wahba, Tharwat. *The Practice of Mission in Egypt: A Historical Study of the Integration between the American Mission and the Evangelical Church of Egypt, 1854–1970*. Carlisle: UK: Langham Monographs, 2016.

Walls, Andrew F. *The Missionary Movement in Christian History: Studies in the Transmission of Faith*. New York: Orbis, 1996.

Walther, James Arthur, ed. *Ever a Frontier: The Bicentennial History of the Pittsburgh Theological Seminary*. Grand Rapids, MI: Eerdmans, 1994.

Weaver, Dorothy Jean. Review of *The Good Shepherd: A Thousand-Year Journey from Psalm 23 to the New Testament*, by Kenneth E. Bailey. *Interpretation* 71, no. 1 (2017) 103.

Weeden, Theodore J., Sr. "Kenneth Bailey's Theory of Oral Tradition Contested by the Evidence." *Journal for the Study of the Historical Jesus* 7, no. 1 (2009) 3–43. (Bailey Papers, box 45, folder 2; see too box 43, folder 1, and James Dunn's letter is included.)

Weir, Ben, and Carol Weir, with Dennis Benson. *Hostage Bound, Hostage Free*. Thorndike, ME: Thorndike, 1987.

Westfall, Cynthia Long. Review of *Jesus through Middle Eastern Eyes*, by Kenneth E. Bailey. *Priscilla Papers* 24, no. 1 (2010) 30.

Wiesel, Elie. *Night*. Translated by Marion Wiesel. New York: Hill & Wang, 2006. This was first published in Yiddish in 1956 and translated into English in 1960.

Willis, John T. Review of *The Good Shepherd: A Thousand-Year Journey from Psalm 23 to the New Testament*, by Kenneth E. Bailey. *The Catholic Biblical Quarterly* 79, no. 3 (2017) 515–16.

Wright, N. T. *Jesus and the Victory of God: Christian Origins and the Question of God*. Vol. 2. Minneapolis: Fortress, 1996.

———. *The Resurrection of the Son of God*. London: Society for the Promotion of Christian Knowledge, 2003.

Zuck, Roy B. Review of *Jesus through Middle Eastern Eyes*, by Kenneth E. Bailey. *Bibliotheca Sacra* 167, no. 668 (2010) 498–99.

Zwemer, Samuel M. *Islam, A Challenge to Faith*. New York: Student Volunteer Movement for Foreign Missions, 1907.

Index

Abu Hennis, 293
Aesop's Fables, 178
Aharonian, Hovhanness, 131, 139, 170, 193
Al-'Assal, Abu al-Mufaddal ib, 159
Al-Assal, Hibat Allah ibn, 306
Al-Azhar University, 19
Al-Bana, Hasan,18
Al-Haram al-Sharif, 261
Allison, Dale E., 341
Al-Miskin, Matta, 306, 334
Al-Muquddassia, 271
Al-Nur, Menes Abd, 84, 86, 100
Amendment 10-A, Presbyterian *Book of Order*, 328, 329
American Board of Commissioners for Foreign Missions, (American Board), 128
American Cemetery, Cairo, 242
American Christian Literature Society for Moslems (ACLSM), 20
American Community Church in Beirut, 209
American Community School (Beirut), 169, 222
American Hospital of Tanta, Egypt, 75
American Mission, Egypt,12, 18, 20, 27, 31, 53, 61, 120
American University in Cairo (AUC), 12, 18, 51, 60, 65, 203
American University of Beirut (AUB), 126, 131, 133, 203, 221, 222

Amos, 87, 100–101, 130
Aquinas Thomas, 336
Arafat, Yasser, 211
Arburhnot, Charles, 140
Aristotle, 178
Arthur Meriweather Inc., 163
Assemblies of God, 161
Assiut College, 11,12, 27, 31, 88, 89, 95, 101, 111, 113
Assiut Hospital, 16, 53, 54, 57, 58, 60, 65, 90
Assiut University, 94, 95, 117
Associate Presbyterian Church (APC or Seceders), 9, 45
Associate Reformed Church (ARC, or Covenanters), 9, 11, 36
Association meetings, 20, 21, 53, 54, 56, 61, 62, 72, 76, 88, 98, 102, 103, 114
Association, formally known as the Egyptian Association of the Missionaries of the UPCNA, 20
Assiut College, 339
Athanasius, 336
Augustine of Hippo, 177
Awlad al-'Assal, 159
Ayia Napa Conference Center, 205, 209
Ayrout, Henry Habib, *The Fellaheen*, 147

Bach cantata, counterpoints, 320
Bahnan, Fuad, 211, 212
Bailey Family Genealogy, 24–25

Index

Bailey Papers, 163, 176
Bailey, Alexander, 7, 8
Bailey, Annette née Meader, 12–17, 20–23, 27–28, 30–33, 62, 75, 77, 202, 269, 303, 309
Bailey, Austin Smiley, 8, 9, 10
Bailey, Bruce and Barbara, 312
Bailey, Cameron, 313, 315, 339
Bailey, Carrie née Paton, 8, 10
Bailey, David Mark, 121, 124, 155, 161, 165, 169, 173, 189, 193, 199, 205, 208, 211, 213, 215, 216, 222, 223, 224, 230, 232, 233, 235, 237, 239, 240, 243, 244, 257, 258, 262, 268, 270, 271, 275, 279, 304, 309–10, 311, 312, 313, 314
Bailey, Ethel Jean "Mickey" née Milligan—her youth, college years, and work with Jonas Salk, 38–45
Bailey, Ewing McCready, 8, 10–13, 17–23, 26–31, 62, 68, 75, 77, 160, 315
Bailey, Frank, 332
Bailey, James Bruce, 23, 27, 28, 29, 30, 31, 32, 34, 35, 138, 304
Bailey, Jane née Brown, 7, 8
Bailey, John, 8
Bailey, John and Susan, 332, 339
Bailey, Kelcey Tess, 267, 313, 315
Bailey, Kenneth E., books, plays, articles, lectures, and sermons:
"Biblical Foundation for Mission," 197
"Christian Leader as a Father," 3
CMEC, Inaugural lecture, 293–96
Cross & the Prodigal, 300–301, 302
Cross and the Prodigal, 82, 109, 143, 146–51, 157, 196, 264, 266
Cross-Cultural Mission: A Tale of Three Cities, 225
"C.S. Lewis, Thomas More and Bitter Conflict," 287
DOCTRINE OF GOD for Village People, 80–82, 84, 100, 101, 164, 299
"Father and the Son Who is Not a Son," 82, 85

Finding the Lost (movie), 115, 259, 261, 264–67, 269, 280, 288,
Finding the Lost: Cultural Keys to Luke 15, 70
God Is . . . Dialogues on the Nature of God, 299
God Is . . . Dialogues on the Nature of God for Young People, 164, 176, 209
God is Love, 300
Good Shepherd, 243, 264, 275, 327, 333, 338
"Informal Controlled Oral Tradition and the Synoptic Gospels," 253–56
Jacob & the Prodigal, 264, 277, 281, 287–91
"Jesus as Theologian: A Compendium of his Theology," 267
Jesus Interprets His Own Cross, 228
Jesus through Middle Eastern Eyes, 103, 158, 228, 302, 305–9, 324, 325
"Judgement with Justice," 37–38
"Leadership in the New Testament," 2
"Major Concepts in the Qur'an and the Arabic Bible," 154
"Metaphors Matter: The Confession and a Gang of Four," 284–85
Open Hearts in Bethlehem, 281, 292, 298–99
Poet & Peasant, 159, 176–87, 192, 196, 249, 264, 267, 308
Paul through Mediterranean Eyes, 302, 316–23, 324, 325, 342, see too First Corinthians
"Reflections of Forty Years of Life and Service in the Middle East," 272–73
"Rejoinder," 203–4
"Reprocessing Anger into Grace," 331–32
"Resurrection," 156–57
Roar of the Lion: A Study in the Prophecy of Amos the Shepherd, 87, 100–101, 130

Index

"Saint Augustine and Plato: A Discussion of the Influence of Plato on the Thought of Saint Augustine" (college thesis), 38
"Singer of Malakal," 195–96
Study of some Lucan Parables in the Light of Oriental Life and Poetic Style (Dissertation), 145
"Tale of Elephants and the Mouse: Presbyterians, 10-A, and the World Church," 329–30
Tale of Three Cities, 226–27
Through Peasant Eyes, 109, 157, 159, 175, 188, 191, 192, 201, 205–7, 209, 222, 267, 272, 309
Two Sons Have I Not, 110, 150 272
"Vision is Born," 159
When the Wind is Right, 162–63
"Who is a 'World Christian'?" 201
"Women in the New Testament," 199
"Words of Faith," 2
"Worsh-o-tainment: A Needed Neologism," 287
Bailey, Leslie née McGarvey, 243, 257, 258, 262, 268, 270, 275, 279, 311, 313
Bailey, Margaret née Gailey, 8
Bailey, Sara Jan, 83, 91, 124, 125, 155, 161, 165, 166, 169, 173, 188, 189, 190, 193, 194, 199, 202, 208, 213, 214, 215, 216, 224, 228, 229, 230, 231, 232, 233, 237, 238, 239, 240, 246, 248, 252, 253, 257, 258, 268, 269, 271, 281, 282, 283, 293, 302–3; see too Makari, Sara Bailey
Bailey's Hollow, 155, 163
Banks, Jill, 269
Barensten, Jack, 322
Barth, Karl, 120, 336
Barth, Markus, 120, 176
Batten, Alicia J., 322–23
Battle of the Hotels, 168
Bauckham, Richard, *Jesus and the Eyewitnesses: The Gospels as Eyewitness Testimony*, 256
Bean, Gordon, 283
Begin, Menachem, 198, 213, 247

Beirut College for Women (BCW), 132, 135–36
Beirut International Airport, 151, 166, 217, 302
Beit el-Salam, 57
Bible and Homosexual Practice, Robert Gagnon, 284
Bible Society in Egypt, 268
Bible Society, 158, 161
Bir Shaytoun, Bailey's trip in the Eastern Desert, Egypt, 103–5
Birth of Civilization in the Near East, Henri Frankfort, 92, 94
Bishop, Eric F.F., 334
Black Forest Academy, 213, 216, 217
Black Monday, massacre at the Dome of the Rock, 261
Black, Don, 56
Black, Matthew, 153
Blessed Be Egypt My People, 339
Board of Foreign Missions, UPC, 21, 47
Board of Pensions, Presbyterian, 238, 282
Bolling, Landrum, 230, 244, 249
Boman, John David, 307, 308
Book of Confessions (PCUSA), 284–85
Book of Jubilees, 289
Book of Order, Presbyterian Church, 328
Brown, John, Bishop of Cyprus and the Gulf, Anglican, 253, 260
Browne, Dale, 306
Browning, Robert, "Rabbi Ben Ezra," 5
Brug, John F., 267
Bultman, Rudolf, 138, 253
Bunyan, John, *The Pilgrim's Progress*, 177
Burge, Gary M., 38, 206–7, 301–2, 340

Calabria, Don Giovanni, 287
Calvin Worship Symposium, Calvin College, 339
Calvin, John, 9, 177, 336
Cambridge University, 218, 225, 269
Camp David Accords, 198, 201, 247
Canon Theologian of the Diocese of Pittsburgh, Bailey as, 281
Canon Theologian of the Episcopal Diocese of Cyprus and the Gulf, Bailey as, 253

365

Index

CARE (Cooperative for Assistance and Relief Everywhere), 74
Carey, George, Archbishop of Canterbury, 2, 4, 269
Carmichael, Kenn, 88, 90, 99
Carter, Howard, 16, 17
Center for Middle Eastern Christianity, see CMEC
CEOSS (Coptic Evangelical Organization for Social Services), 68, 84, 86, 87, 89, 90
Chapman, Colin, *Whose Promised Land?* 219
Chiasm (or chiasmus), chiasmic, 182–84, 236, 318, 323
Chiasmus in the New Testament, Niles Wilhelm Lund, 183
Christmas in Egypt, Bailey's observations, 102
Chrysostom, John, 304, 336
Church Mission Society (CMS), 252
Church of Beirut, 128
Civil War, Lebanon, 208
CMEC (Center of Middle Eastern Christianity), 293–96, 324, 325, 326, 339
COEMAR (Commission on Ecumenical Mission and Relations), 79, 86, 98, 99, 140, 142, 172
Commando (Palestinian fighters), 163
Committee for New Testament Studies, 283
Community Church, Beirut, 154
Concordia Press, 146, 157, 160, 175, 188, 192, 193, 260, 263
Concordia Seminary, 139, 142, 144, 146, 157, 160
Confession of 1967, 123
Conrad, Joseph, *Lord Jim*, 195
Coptic Evangelical Organization for Social Services, see CEOSS
Coptic Orthodox Christians, 11
Coptic Orthodox leaders, 11
Coptic Orthodox priests, 71
Coptic Renaissance (13th century), 159
Corniche Beirut, 151
Council of Chalcedon, 294

"Cowboys," Bailey's donors in California, 239
Crooks, Bill and Karen, 332
Crooks, William "Bill," 340
Crossan, John Dominic, 185–86, 206, 255
Cumberland Lodge, 1, 4, 269, 272
Cyprus, historical background, 259–260

Dagher, Ibrahim, 139
Daigle, Tim and Elizabeth, 332
Dante Alighieri, *Divine Comedy*, 187
Dar el-Thaqafa, 99, 130, 146, 324
Davies, John and Nancy, Christmas with the Baileys in 1964, 113
Dawson, Dave and Joani, 332
Dawson, David, 323, 333, 339, 340
Dawson, Don, 297
Deir Abu Hinnis, 58, 73, 75. 76, 77
Deir el-Barsha, 67, 68, 73, 74, 76, 77, 87, 88, 96, 107, 296
Die Gleichnisreden Jesu, Adolf Jülicher, 178
Diocese of Jerusalem of the Episcopal Church, 132
Dodd, C.H., 178, 179, 254
Don McClure Memorial Lectures on Mission and Evangelism, Pittsburgh Theological Seminary, See McClure Lectures
Doyle, Steve, 258
Druze, 165
Dunn, D.G., 255
Dye, Marjorie, 58
Dyslexia, 34, 221

Eastminster Presbyterian Church in Wichita, Kansas, 293
Eastwood, John and Shirley, 35
Ebert, Doug, 279
Ecce Homo, 230, 242, 245, 256, 261
Eerdmans, see William B. Eerdmans Publishing Company
Egyptian Association of the Missionaries of the UPCNA, see Association
Eisenhower, Dwight, 59
Elder, Earl E., 17, 20

Index

Elizabeth II, 2,3
Emerson, Ralph Waldo, 282
Ephrem the Syrian, 336
Episcopal Church, 329
Episcopal Diocese of Cyprus and the Gulf, 272
Episcopal Diocese of Pittsburgh
Eskimos, 205
ETSC, 57, 65, 88, 92, 110, 237, 293, 315–16, 324, 325, 339
Evangelical Church in Egypt, 20, 68, 105, 105
Evangelical Lutheran Church in America, 329
Evangelical Lutheran Church in Jordan, 132
Evangelical Theological Seminary in Cairo (ETSC), 57, 65, 88, 92, 110, 237, 293, 315–16, 324, 325, 339
Evangelium in Evangelio, 146, 265, 290
Eyes upon the Cross: A Cycle of Plays for Lent, Don A. Mueller, 99, 107

Fair Oaks Cemetery, 341
Farrell, Hunter, 305
Father, God, 265–66
Fellaheen, 147
Fellowship of Middle East Evangelical Churches, 341
Fellowship of Presbyterians, 330–333
Finney, Davida, 58, 65f, 66, 68
First Corinthians, 153–54, 223, 236, 241, 248, 314; see too Bailey, Kenneth E., *Paul through Mediterranean Eyes*
First Intifada, 241, 245–47
Flannelgraph, 55
Fletcher, Vernon, 161, 218, 193, 195, 196, 197, 209
FoMENTS (Foundation for Middle Eastern New Testament Studies), 283, 284, 292, 302, 304, 323, 324, 325, 326
Form criticism, 178, 192, 207, 254, 256, 337

Foundation for Middle Eastern New Testament Studies, see FoMENTS
Frankfort, Henri, 92, 94, 97
Fraternal workers, 129
Friedman, Thomas L., *From Beirut to Jerusalem*, 208; *The World Is Flat*, 319
From Colonialism to World Community, John Coventry Smith, 226
Fuller Theological Seminary, 169, 170, 199

Gagnon, Robert, 330, 284
Galilee area, Lebanon, 140–41
Gastroenterology Department, Hadassah Medical Center, 252
Gendy, Atef, 293, 324, 325, 340
Gendy, Sherif, 336–37
Genesis Rabbah, 289
Georgia United Methodist Group, 249
Gerhardsson, Gerger, 254
Gibson, Bob, 160
Gibson, Dick, 251
Gibson, Mel, *The Passion of the Christ*, 335
Gill, Malcolm J., 322
Girgis, Baki Sadaka, 296
Global Mission Unit, PCUSA, 251–52
God as Father, 265–66
"God Box," 170
Goulder, M.D., 184
Grace, Girgis, 95, 112,116, 117, 118, 119
Grangaard, Blake R., 290
Great Temple of Ramses II, Abu Simbel, 32
Greek Catholic Seminary, Beit Sahour, Israel-Palestine, 256, 261
Grier, James H.
Grove City College, 202, 208, 213, 228, 232, 234, 237, 243, 306
Grove Manor, 339
Guerrant, Edward Ownings, 26

Habib, Samuel, 65, 66, 71, 72, 84, 85, 87, 89, 196
Hadassah Medical Center, 252

Index

Haflat samar, 254
Haboush, Stephen A., 334
Haigazian College, 132, 135
Haines, 188
Hanna, Ed, 210
Hathaway, Alden Moinet, Bishop of Pittsburgh, 281
Helsinki, Finland, 272
Hilgendorf, Denell, 194, 316
Hilgendorf, Dennis, 139
Hilgendorf, Dennis and Ellen, 189
Hilgendorf, Eric, 315–16
Hilgendorf family, 134, 168
Hill, Elizabeth, 110
Hogg, John, 37
Holm, Randy, 290
Hollenbach, Paul, 267
Holliday, William, 176
Holloway, Richard "Dick," 4
Home Mission High School, Frenchburg, Kentucky, 26
Homosexuality, issue in PCUSA, 284, 327–33
Hopkins, Joe, 190
Hopkins, Paul, 215, 219
Humphrey, Hubert, 144
Hunter, Archibald M., 177
Hussein, Taha, 19

Ibis, 12, 57, 71, 73, 75
Ibn al-Salibi, 334
Ibn al-Tayyib, 306, 324, 325, 334
Ibrahim, Badie, 95, 117, 118, 119
Institute for Middle Eastern New Testament Studies, 158–59
Integration, 88, 102
Intifada, 241, 245–47
Ireland, Mary Louise, 332
Israeli Defense Forces (IDF), 210, 245
Israeli-Palestinian conflict, 246–48
Isteero, Albert, 122, 175

Jabbours, 252
Jeremias, Joachim, 174, 178, 179, 265
Jerusalem Center of the Study of Early Christianity, 261
Jerusalem Document (in Luke), 184, 185

Jesus as "metaphorical theologian," 264–67, 288
Jesus, the Bible, and Homosexuality, Jack Rogers, 330
Jewett, Paul K., *MAN as Male and Female*, 199
Jones, Catherine, 322
Josephus, *Antiquities of the Jews*, 289
Jülicher, Adolf, 178, 180

Kassab, Joseph, 341, 342
Kataluma (inn or guestroom), 141, 299
Kennedy, Darren, 324, 325
Kennedy, John F., 89, 101
Kenneth E. Bailey Chapel, NEST, 341
Kent State University, 232, 233, 238, 240
Kepha, Moshe bar, *Commentary on Luke*, 324
Kerr, Malcolm, 221
Kerygma Bible Series, 341
Kidnapping, Beirut, 222, 223
Kiely, Ray H., 217, 221m 223
Knesset, 194
Krause, Mark S., 291
Krikorian, M.P., 334

Labor Party, Israel, 247
LaHurd, Carol Schersten, 307–8
Lake Mohonk Conference, 226
Lambeth Palace, 1, 2
Lamsa, George M., 334
Law 38, 54
Law 40, 53
Law 583, 54
Le Grys, Alan, 337
League of Nations, 165
Lebanese Bible Institute, 136, 137
Lebanon, Civil War, 164, 165
Lee-Barnewall, Michelle, 322
Leitch, Addison H. (or Ad), 80
Les Misérables, 269, 273
Lewis, C.S., 275, 287
Likud Party, Israel, 247
Linnemann, Eta, 179
Literacy program or campaign, Egypt, 65, 66, 68, 71, 74, 84
Löffler, Paul, "Mission in the Context of the Struggle for Justice," 203–4

Index

London School of Tropical Medicine, 252
Lorimer, Jack, 53, 72, 76, 84, 85, 89, 99, 196
Lorimer, Kathy, 242
Louisville Presbyterian Theological Seminary, 106
Lund, Nils Wilhelm, 183
Luther, Martin, 117, 336
Lutheran Church-Missouri synod, 139, 140, 144

Makari, Emmanuel, 315–16
Makari, Sara Bailey, 306, 311, 315, 316, 332, 333, 339, 340, 341
Makari, Victor, 302, 303; 305, 311, 315, 325, 326, 339, 340, 341
Man in the Gray Flannel Suit, Sloan Wilson, movie and novel, 270–271
Mansur, Kamil, 20
Marines, 231 killed in Beirut in 1983, 218
Maronite Christians, Lebanon,165
McClanahan, Paul, 88
McClure Lectures, 219, 223, 225
McCormick Theological Seminary, 219, 225, 249
McKnight, Bill, 283
McKnight, Bill and Carole, 332
Metzger, Bruce and Michael D. Coogan, *Oxford Companion to the Bible*, 235
Middle East Christian Outreach (MECO), 227
Middle East Christian Outreach in Larnaca, Cyprus, recording studio, 250–251
Middle Eastern Biblical Studies, 324
Mikhail, Wageeh, 326
Milligan, Bertha, 85, 86
Milligan, Bruce, 39, 40, 83, 144, 153
Milligan, Bruce and Pat, 144, 215
Milligan, Dale, 39, 40, 49, 53, 83, 110, 123, 124, 137, 141, 162, 163, 164, 168, 169, 170, 171, 188, 1978, 221, 275, 276

Milligan, Dale and Doris, 49, 110, 137, 168
Milligan, Floyd and Marg, 190, 199
Milligan, Leslie, 85, 86
Milligan, Mary, 223
Milligan, Pat, 332
Milton, John, *Paradise Lost*, 187
Mishrisky, Labib, 110
Mission as cultural imperialism, 262–63
Missionary Kids (MKs), 170, 235
Moghabghab, Faddoul, 334
Monmouth College, 10, 11, 34, 36, 38, 41
More, Thomas, 287
"Morte d'Arthur," Alfred Lord Tennyson, 297–98
Moxnes, Havor, 290
Mueller, Don A., *Eyes upon the Cross: A Cycle of Plays for Lent*, 99, 107
Multinational Force (MNF), 211, 218
Munich massacre, 145
Mus'ad, Elder, 81
Muslim Brotherhood (Al-Ikhwan al-Muslimum), the Brothers, 18, 19

Nahda, 11
Nasser, Gamal Abdel, 59, 115, 132, 134
Nasserite Party, 157
National Council of Churches of Christ, 66
National Evangelical Church of Beirut (NECB), 128
National Evangelical Synod of Syria and Lebanon (NESSL) see the Synod
National Pact of 1943, Lebanon, 165
Near East Council of Churches (NECC), 122, 127
Near East School of Theology, see NEST
Neguib, Muhammad, 59
Neshannock Presbyterian Church, 283
NESSL, 341, see too Synod
NEST (Near East School of Theology), 122, 124, 126, 130–31, 132, 135, 137, 139, 151, 154, 158, 162, 163, 164, 167, 168, 169, 170, 171, 172, 193, 194, 203, 204, 209, 212, 213, 214, 215, 217, 218, 221, 222, 223, 224,229, 234, 275, 334, 341

Index

Neusner, Jacob, 289
New Wilmington Missionary Conference, 33, 123, 144, 161, 297
New Wilmington Mission Conference, 338
Newbigin, Lesslie, 49, 72, 273–74, 278
Nicene Creed, 336
Niles, D.T, "On a Day," 298
Nixon, Richard
Nolin, Ken, 99
Nostra Aetat, 109, 111–13
Not by Chance, 279–80
Novum Testamentum, 158, 223
NTSC (National Television System Committee) system, 251

Obergefell v. Hodges, Supreme Court case, 328
October War (1973), 156
Operation Peace for Galilee, 210
Origen of Alexandria, 177, 180
Oslo Accords, 247
Ottoman Empire, 164
Owen, Charles Archibald, 11
Oxford University, 218, 225, 268

PAL (Phase Alternating Line) system, 251
Palestine Liberation Army (PLA), 208
Palestine Liberation Organization (PLO), 165, 210, 211, 212, 213, 214
Palm Beach Hotel in Larnaca, Cyprus, 302
Pan American Airways, 33, 133
Parables of Jesus, Jeremias, Joachim, 174, 178
Parables of the Kingdom, C.H. Dodd, 178
Paracelsus Clinic in Switzerland, 282
Partnership (in mission), 226
Passion of the Christ, 335
PCUSA headquarters, Louisville, Kentucky, 251
Persian Gulf War (1990–91), 261
Phalangists, a Christian party in Lebanon, 163
Philip, Prince, Duke of Edinburgh, 2, 3
Philo of Alexandria, 289

Pittsburgh Theological Seminary, 36, 45, 80, 110, 115, 120, 136, 143, 175, 187, 237, 299, 324, 341
Pittsburgh-Xenia Theological Seminary, 43, 45–46, 57, 75, 79, 70
Plays or theater in Egypt, Bailey's description, 107–8
PLO (Palestine Liberation Organization) 165, 210, 211, 212, 213, 214, 247
Polio, 43–45, 48
Pope, Alexander, 186
Presbyterian Board of Foreign Missions, 128
Presbyterian Church, background and various branches, 9
Presbyterian Church headquarters, New York, the "God Box," 120. 122. 123, 170
Presbyterian Church in the USA (PCUSA), 79, 221, 227, 229, 234, 327
Presbyterian theological education (seminaries), Bailey's comments, 276
Presbyterians United for Biblical Concerns, 124
Presbyterians United for Biblical Confession, 123, 124
Pre-seminary course or program, Egypt, 88, 89, 92, 93, 111, 117
Pre-seminary Newsletter, Egypt, 93
Pressly Memorial Institute (PMI), 111
Princeton Theological Seminary, 19, 144, 228, 239
Problems in the Education of Teachers for Egypt with Special Reference to the American Mission (dissertation), Ewing McCready Brailey, 27
Program Agency (Presbyterian mission organization), 140, 157, 169, 170, 171, 175, 210, 215, 216, 219, 220, 221, 224, 227, 238, 239

Qaldas, Adib, 68, 69, 293
Quaestiones Evangeliorum, Augustine of Hippo, 177

Index

"Rabbi Ben Ezra," Robert Browning, 5
Radio Voice of the Gospel, 88, 95, 124
Rahbany, Abraham Mitri, 334
Reagan, Ronald, 213, 239
Redaction criticism, 192, 207, 337
Reed, David A., 290
Reed, Glen, 56, 60, 75
Rhee, Syngman, 171
Riesenfeld Harald, 254
Rizqallah, Ghobrial (Gabriel), 106
Rogers, Jack, *Jesus, the Bible, and Homosexuality*, 330
Rommel, Erwin, 31, 32
Roy, Martha, 196
Rural Church Service Team, 71, 72

Sa'id, Ibrahim, 306, 334
Sabra, George, 341
Sadat, Anwar, 194, 198
Sahyouni, Salim, 219
Salk, Jonas, 43–44, 47–48
Sanneh, Lamin, "Christian Missions and the Western Guilt Complex," 263
Sappho, 259
Sargent, Andrew, 337
Saudia Arabia, 172, 196, 197, 209
Scharlemann, Martin, 139, 146
"Scholar Who Made Jesus Middle Eastern Again," Gary M. Burge, 340
School of Oriental Studies (SOS), 17–18, 51, 52, 55, 56, 60, 63
Schutz American School, 30, 31, 50, 103, 175
Second Vatican Council, 109, 111–13, 119
Seman, Wanis, 209, 217
Shakespeare, William, 186, 195
Sharm El Sheikh, 242
Sharon Regional Medical Center, 338
Shenango on the Green, 338, 339
Shenango Presbytery, 283, 306, 339
Shite, Shi 'a, 165
Shot Felt 'Round the World, 332
Sidi Bishr camp, 30, 31, 57, 71, 90, 102, 103
Sisters of Zion, 230
Sitz im Leben, 178

Six-Day War, Israel, 132, 134, 135, 246
Smalley, William, 161
Smillie, Gene R., 308
Smith, C.W. F., 174, 178–79
Smith, John Coventry, 172, 226
Snyder, Graydon F., 307
Southern Baptists, 137
Special Committee on a Brief Contemporary Statement of Faith, 123
Speer, Robert E., 172
St. Catharine's Monastery, 296
St. George's College, 261
Stelling family, 134, 168
Stelling, John, 139
Storie, Deborah, 308–9
Stransky, Thomas, 249, 252, 257, 258
Student Volunteer Movement for Foreign Missions (SVM), 11
Sudan, Bailey's 1978 trip, 194–96
Suez Canal, 12, 18, 59, 61
Sundberg, Rodney, 112, 118, 120
Sunni, 157, 165
Swanson, Mark, 237
Synod (National Evangelical Synod of Syria and Lebanon) (NESSL), 127, 128, 129, 139, 142, 210, 215, 219, 227, 341, 342
Syond meetings in Egypt, Bailey's description, 105

Tantur Ecumenical Institute for Theological Research, 228, 229, 230, 234, 235, 237, 241, 242, 244, 245, 248, 249, 251, 252, 253, 256, 261, 271
Tatu, Silviu, 337
Taylor, Nicholas, 323
Temple Mount, 261
Tennyson, Alfred Lord, 17, 26, 297–98
Theater or plays in Egypt, Bailey's description, 107–8
Theological Review of the Near East School of Theology, 168, 196, 201
THESIS cassettes, 161, 162
Thompson, William, 334
Thurston, Burton B., 183
Tillich, Paul, 138

Index

Travel Narrative (in Luke), 184, 185
Trench, R.C., 146
Trimmer, John, 206
Trinity Episcopal Cathedral in Pittsburgh, 281
Troodos, Cyprus (mission campgrounds), 213, 302
Turner, Geoffrey, 307, 322
Tutankhamun, 16
Tutu, Desmond, Archbishop of South Africa, 3–4
Tyndale, William, 287

"Ulysses," Alfred Lord Tennyson, 26
Union of the Armenian Evangelical Churches in the Near East, 132
United Church of Christ, 329
United Presbyterian Church in the USA (UPCUSA), 79, 128
United Presbyterian Church of North America (UPCNA or UPC), 9, 11, 12, 18, 30, 123
University Christian Center, Beirut, 132
University of Notre Dame, Indiana, 228, 229

Via, Dan O., 179
Videos recordings, transferring Bailey's cassettes to DVDs, 292–93
Volf, Miroslav, *The End of Memory*, 311, 321

Walls, Andrew, 289
Walther, James A., 340
Warren Lectures, University of Dubuque Theological Seminary, 267
Weir, Ann, 242, 316
Weir, Ben, 122, 133, 210, 224
Western Seminary, 79
Westfall, Cynthia Long, 207
Westminster College, 8, 190, 228, 339

Westminster Confession of Faith, 9, 123, 284
Westminster John Knox Press, 298
Wiesel, Elie, *Night*, 321
William B. Eerdmans Publishing Company, 159, 176, 192, 193, 197, 202, 205
Willis, John, 336
Wilson, Sloan, *Man in the Gray Flannel Suit*, 270–271
Windsor Great Park, 1, 269
Women's Concerns of the Middle East Council of Churches, 200
Women's General Missionary Society (WGMS) of the UPC, 26
Woodland Cemetery, 202
World Literacy and Christian Literature Committee of the National Council of Churches of Christ in the United States, 66
World Mission Initiative (WMI), 324
World Mission, Presbyterian mission organization, 305
World War I, 10, 15, 165
World War II, 31
Worldwide Anglican Communion, 1, 4
Worldwide Ministry Division of the Presbyterian Church, 283
Wrede, William, 255
Wright, N.T., *Jesus and the Victory of God*, 241, 255, 288

Xenia Presbytery, 8
Xenia Theological Seminary, 19, 45

Yom Kippur War (1973), 156
Youth Club Program, 164, 188

Zaki, Anne, 339
Zaki, Emile, 96, 113, 296, 339
Zuck, Roy B., 307
Zwemer, Samuel, 11, 19, 20

www.ingramcontent.com/pod-product-compliance
Lightning Source LLC
Chambersburg PA
CBHW060550230426
43670CB00011B/1762